FIGHTING FOR THE DREAM

為夢而戰

FIGHTING FOR THE DREAM

VOICES OF CHINESE AMERICAN VETERANS

FROM WORLD WAR II TO AFGHANISTAN

VICTORIA MOY

Chinese Historical Society
of Southern California

Published by Chinese Historical Society of Southern California,
Los Angeles, California
www.fightingforthedream.com

Second printing October 2015

Cover design: Marija Vilotijevic
Author photo: Michele LoBosco

A short section of the introduction had appeared, in slightly different form, in *The Huffington Post*.

Library of Congress Cataloging-in-Publication Data

Moy, Victoria, 1981-
Fighting for the dream : voices of Chinese American veterans from World War II to Afghanistan / Victoria Moy.
    pages cm
Includes bibliographical references and index.
ISBN 978-0-930377-05-2 (pbk. : alk. paper)
1. Chinese American veterans--Biography. 2. Chinese American veterans--History. 3. United States--Armed Forces--Chinese Americans. 4. Chinese Americans--Biography. I. Chinese Historical Society of Southern California. II. Title. III. Title: Voices of Chinese American veterans from World War II to Afghanistan.

E184.C5M694 2014
355.0092'3951073--dc23

2014036577

Dedicated to America;
for both younger and older generations,
so we may know each other better.

CONTENTS

ACKNOWLEDGMENTS

Thank you to the veterans and their families in this book who so generously shared their stories.

I would like to thank Eugene Moy of the Chinese Historical Society of Southern California (CHSSC) for his wisdom and community involvement, and for his support in getting this published. Thanks to editors Tylar Pendgraft and Forest Sebastian, Will Tham for design help, Johnny Chan, Simon Chhuor, Gilbert Hom, John Jung, Fenton Fong, Rick Eng, Marian Chew, and Gordon Hom for pushing this book along. Thank you Mark Johnson for the final editing and type design.

Special thanks to this project's biggest supporters Dr. Wing Mar and Joyce Mar, Dr. James Bok Wong and Betty KC Yeow, The Sauvage-Mar Family, Jeff and Louise Mar and family, The Mar Chun Family-Craig, Gayle, Sarah, Jesse, Anne, Reid, and Emery; Major Kurt Lee, Eugene Moy and Susan Sing, Virginia Chow, David J. Louie, and Ken Moy.

Greatest appreciation to veterans/friends Will Chan for saying "you can't do this alone, we need a team!" and putting together an amazing website, Wilem Wong for miraculously getting things to come together, Jerry Miki for your generous wisdom, Pakee Fang, the first veteran to share his story for this book, and Jerry Chan for spreading the word.

For your constant support and always being there, thank you Uncle Harold and Aunt Yvonne. For the lovely summers and housing me in Maryland, thank you Ed, Evelyn, Chris, and Ben. Thanks to my dearest friends Tony Powell for years of emotional support and meticulous proofreading and Allison Cheung. For inspiring ideas and for feeding me, I thank my parents.

Gratitude to the American Legion Kimlau Post, and to the late Christina Lim, Sheldon Lim, and Mack Pong for organizing Chinese American Flying Tigers reunions and preserving history that'd otherwise be lost. To the late Kathleen Vach for the transcriptions.

Much appreciation to our backers Michael Lindgren, Jennings Wong, Judy Sue-Fang Kuan, Bayer Jack-Wah Lee, Rajiv Menjoge, Mo Pan, See-wan Szeto, Darren Louie, Thomas Doherty, Matthew Seto, Edward J. Davis, Edward and Evelyn Seto who have generously contributed to making this book happen.

Thanks to my teachers and mentors Susan Shapiro, Gerald Jonas, Sharon Mesmer, and John Reed.

INTRODUCTION

Surrounded by an abundance of Cantonese-style roast meats and lomein, as well as the standard American Thanksgiving fare of turkey and cranberry sauce, I stare up at a wall lined with portraits of Chinese men in military uniforms and squadron hats. The room is decorated with award plaques, photos of soldiers, and the American flag. While Grandpa shoots the breeze with other Chinese grandpas who wear fedoras and speak Dick Tracy style (like the black-and-white Hollywood movies—in old timer's slang and accents), Grandma chats gaily with the other wives in sing-song Toishanese (a dialect of Cantonese). Within that one room, there's a men's language, and a women's language; an "English world" and "Chinese world." I don't get why grandpas speak English and grandmas speak Chinese, why there's a linguistic divide along gender lines in my grandparents' generation. This is my life growing up in New York's Chinatown in the 1980s.

The Thanksgiving and Christmas parties my grandparents took me to were at the American Legion on Canal Street, which Chinese American vets set up in Chinatown after World War II.

I was fascinated with my Chinese grandpa being super American—in his speech, his mannerisms, and dress. In his retirement years, we watched *Gilligan's Island*, *Bonanza*, and *The A-Team* together. He sang "As Time Goes By," about how a kiss is just a kiss and a sigh is just a sigh, while my often unhappy grandmother, excluded from our English-speaking camraderie, worked at her sewing machine nearby. I had no idea how my grandparents, absolutely opposite in personalities, came together. I imagined my grandpa had always been the loving romantic I knew, and that my grandma had been once, too, but hardened with age.

When I was 8, I interviewed Grandpa for a school project on Ellis Island and immigration. He looked straight ahead, avoiding my eyes, as he answered my questions.

"I was born in 1920. I had a mother and grandmother. I never met my father. He was in America working on railroads to make money to send home. We stopped hearing from him one day, don't know what happened. We needed money, so my mother and grandmother sold our land to buy fake papers for me to come to the U.S."

I learned that China was plagued with famine and crumbling government infrastructure, that many families in Toishan (a prefecture of Canton) pegged their hopes on little boys to support families, since only sons of Chinese who were already U.S. citizens were allowed to enter the U.S. The Chinese Exclusion Acts, and other laws in force until 1965, severely limited Chinese immigration into the United States, but exceptions were made for the sons of Chinese men already here. Since my Grandpa's real father was out of touch, the family bought fraudulent documents on the black market that identified someone else as his

Tommy Moy a.k.a. PFC Kwong D. Hom

father.

"I came to America by ship in 1933 when I was 13 years old," Grandpa told me. "When I got to New York, the man who was my paper father* tried to swindle me and leave me at Ellis Island. I called the Moy Family Association. They rescued me. Then I went to Rhode Island, where my cousins owned a laundry. I worked there and went to high school. I was the only Chinese. When I graduated, World War II broke out and I joined the Army."

When I asked him, "What was the happiest moment of your life?" I thought he'd tell some romantic story about how he met my grandma. Instead, he said, "My happiest days? It was with the boys, in the Army. That's when I first felt like a real American. I was an airplane mechanic for the Flying Tigers. There were over 1,000 of us, Chinese Americans, with the 14th Air Force. We traveled through the Himalayas, India, and Africa, to China."

Grandpa sang me army songs, and taught me to march like a soldier. His pride in being American was intense. I wondered if I would ever feel the same way.

Every Veterans Day, hundreds of Chinese American veterans from the American Legion Lieutenant B.L. Kimlau Post march in their colorful, decorated uniforms down Mott Street. In my twenties, years after my grandfather had died, I worked as a reporter for a small downtown radio station. I covered the Veterans Day parade in Chinatown. I began interviewing Chinese American vets who had served in one or another of America's wars, from World War II to the most recent conflicts, in Iraq and Afghanistan. Across generations a common thread emerged in their stories, one my Grandpa would have appreciated; for many of these Chinese American vets, military experience was the main channel to enter, or advance within, mainstream American society.

* Paper father means "father on paper" or father according to legal papers.

Some World War II veterans I spoke with were able to bring wives over immediately after the war through the Chinese Alien Wives of American Citizens Act and the War Brides Act. Others, like my grandfather, had to wait years.

When I was "old enough to understand," my grandmother told me that she'd never forgiven her family for giving her away so young, at 16, in an arranged marriage. (Not the *Casablanca* romance I imagined my grandparents had.) After the wedding in Toishan, Grandpa returned to New York alone, worked in restaurants and sent earnings back. It took 12 years before my grandmother and her first-born son, my father, could gain entry to the United States. Dad was 12 when he first met his father.

After raising a son without a husband in China for over a decade, my grandmother has lived in the United States for more than 50 years. For 40 of those years she worked in garment factories. But without an easy command of English, she was never able to enter the "American space" to which my grandfather's military service gained him full admittance. Her anger at the cruelties of life haunted me as a child. It still does.

My family's history isn't unique; it was a pattern and landscape for much of the Chinatown community. Story after story, it became apparent how arbitrary it is that some ethnicities, races, and family members are allowed into America to be "real Americans" while others are not.

At the Veterans Day parade, I met Pakee Fang, who was just 24, a year younger than me, and returning from Iraq. Hung Szeto, 40, who had a baby daughter and wife, was about to leave for Iraq in a week to be an infantryman. They said they were very proud to serve.

In Confucian Chinese tradition, the martial is frowned upon. Distinction is made between the cultivated literary gentleman and the petty man who fights. Emperors of the early Sung Dynasty strove to define their rule based on civil and literary values and culture (wen) above martial power (wu), although both are seen as yin-yang components, each affecting the other. "Good iron is not used for nails; good men do not become soldiers" is a common Chinese adage. Even the characters of my grandfather's Cantonse name, 國安 (Quok On) translate to *nation* and *peace*, or peace for the nation. His name was common among boys then, given that they were born in a time when their country was ravaged by war. Hopes for the nation were placed on individuals in their names. When so much of Chinese culture is anti-military, I wondered why Chinese American men and women from my neighborhood volunteered to go to war. It wasn't something I ever thought about doing.

At the parade, some young and old veterans clumped together for a picture. "We're four generations of Chinese American veterans here! If you're a writer you should write a book on us!" they said.

Not a bad idea. So I started by asking them to tell what their lives were like before, during, and after the military. More interesting to me than battles and fighting is the way lives are transformed: how, why, and when nationality imprints itself onto one's identity. Being American was something my grandpa talked about with intense pride. This is something I saw throughout my community.

Interviewing scores of Chinese Americans across generations gave me a unique look at America in the last 100 years. Although these are the stories of a small, specific group of Americans, they tell the story of America itself—in both the nation's moments of glory and its moments of dark injustice. It didn't take more than a few interviews with vets of different generations to learn just how much U.S. policies—especially policies on immigration—shape societies and communities, and deeply affect families and lives personally.

It took four generations in America before my entire nuclear family could live on one continent, where my parents could watch their children grow under their own care. Pain suffered by previous generations takes a long time to heal. The realization that it's history and not fate—the result of politics and prejudice that can be overcome—makes it somewhat easier to bear.

The stories I have compiled here are histories of Chinese Americans, told in their own words, through the lens of a definitive American experience—serving in the U.S. military during times of war. In many instances, these stories document the most frightening experiences and reversals that can happen in a lifetime—from facing death, losing loved ones, losing everything one knows, to having to make one's way in a completely foreign world from the bottom up and having to learn to be at home in a foreign place. In reading these personal experiences together can we begin to frame the history—revealing both its unique and familiar strands, and its breadth and diversity—that is the Chinese American experience.

These are stories about the American dream, about Chinatowns, about youth, life, old age, how America was, and how it is still evolving. Each chapter in this book begins with a summary of what was happening in general in U.S. history and its effects on Chinese American communities during the particular war under discussion. The background gives context to the oral biographies. I did not verify the details in these men's and women's stories. The point of my book is to document first-person accounts of how the participants see and remember.

Personal stories illustrate the full impact of history on the individual life. For me, this personification is more important than an overgeneralized, interpretive narrative of a particular group in America.

In lieu of America's great immigration debate, we should listen and learn about what really happens in order to truly appreciate how immigrants and their descendants have contributed and are contributing to America. Policies shape families. Policies shape lives. Policies shape people. And here are the stories of people who have helped shape America.

PART I: WORLD WAR II

Chinese Americans in Service

At the beginning of World War II, 77,504 Chinese were recorded to have lived in the U.S. and as many as 25% (approximately 20,000) served in the armed forces.[1] Because of the unbalanced pre-war gender ratio, this amounted to one-third of all Chinese American males between ages 15 and 60. Sixty-one percent of those who served, like Elsie Seetoo, Mack Pong, and Al Chinn, were born in America. The other 39% were born in a foreign country.

In New York City alone, 40% of all Chinese Americans between the ages of 18 and 36 enlisted or were drafted—the highest ratio among any national grouping in the country—compared to only 11.5% of the general U.S. population having served in the armed forces. Peter Woo, Lester Fong, and Richard Y. Chin are representatives of the 40% of Chinese American New Yorkers who joined the war effort.

Unlike African Americans and Japanese Americans, Chinese Americans who joined were for the most part assigned to integrated units. Al Chinn, Genson Lum, Lester Fong and Dr. Wing Mar were all either the only Chinese or one of few in their units. Many Chinese Americans in integrated units were given lowly tasks like mess attendants, waiters for captains and admirals. Some Chinese GIs saw combat in Europe or the Pacific. About 25% were assigned to the Army Air Corps, which included segregated all-Chinese units.[2]

Of the scant Chinese female population, many joined the armed forces in either the WAC (Women's Army Corps) or WAVES (Women Accepted for Volunteer Emergency Services).[3]

The All-Chinese Units

As early as November 1942, the idea to create all-Chinese groups began with Lieutenant Sing Y. Yee of 859th Signal Service Company in Springfield, Illinois. The plan was to recruit Chinese Americans to support the efforts of General Claire Chennault of the Flying Tigers (American pilots who went to China to defend against invasion by Japanese forces) in the China-Burma-India Theater.[4] Richard Y. Chin talks about the bustling excitement when recruitment was happening in New York.

There were ten all-Chinese American units.

The historical report of the 987th Signal Company, an all-Chinese American outfit of the regular army, activated in June 1943 at Camp Crowder, Missouri, explains the rationale behind the formation of these segregated units: "All personnel were Chinese-speaking American soldiers of Chinese parentage. It was understood that the unit was organized expressly for duty in China, one of its functions being to further liaison relationships between American and Chinese troops in that theater."[5] Wayne H. Wong and Richard Goon were both in this all-Chinese American 987th Signal Company.

The other nine all-Chinese American units[6] which were part of the 14th Air Service Group that took shape in 1944 in Venice, Florida, included:

407th Air Service Squadron
555th Air Service Squadron
1077th Quartermaster Company
1157th Signal Company
1544th & 1545th Ordinance Companies
2121st & 2122nd Trucking Companies
14th Air Service Group Headquarters' Squadron

About 10% of all Chinese Americans in the military were part of the 14th Air Service Group.[7]

Within just the 407th Air Service Squadron (which Peter Woo, Kay Wong Chin, Earl Jung, Sam Jue, Mack Pong, Richard Y. Chin were in) 45% of the men—like Mack Pong—were from California, 17%—like Peter Woo, Earl Jung, and Richard Y. Chin—were from New York City, and the rest were from 26 other states. The diversity in age ranged from some being barely in their teens, and who lied about their age to join, to a few in their fifties. There were many paper sons. Some spoke very little English. Others spoke very little Chinese. 57% of the men were born in China, 43% were born in the U.S., and 23% attended colleges in the U.S. or China.

Within the 407th Squadron, 40 men were named Wong. Three had the same first name of Henry. To avoid confusion, the officers affixed the last two digits from their serial numbers to their names. They became Henry Wong 13, Henry Wong 30, Henry Wong 36.[8]

Chinatowns were Bachelor Societies

From the 1880s to the 1940s, Chinatowns were bachelor societies. The discriminatory Chinese Exclusion Acts, beginning in 1882, were a series of increasingly restrictive laws that severely reduced Chinese immigration. At different times, these laws prohibited Chinese women and laborers, and only permitted Chinese who were merchants, students, diplomats, or sons of citizens. These laws rode on and reinforced a wave of anti-Chinese sentiment, resulting in many Chinese returning to China and the shrinking and disappearance of many Chinatowns. It was in this environment and these difficult times that some of our early veterans were born.

To circumvent the Exclusion laws, many Chinese immigrated as paper sons using fraudulent papers claiming "son of citizen" status. The San Francisco earthquake of 1906 destroyed City Hall and all birth records, allowing thousands of Chinese to claim they were citizens who over time claimed the fathering of sons, opening new slots for more paper sons.[9]

New Changes

Joining the U.S. military afforded Chinese Americans new opportunities like the GI Bill and citizenship. Partly as a reward to Chinese American veterans for their service, and with Chinese American veteran protests via the VFW, the government repealed the Exclusion Acts and allowed veterans to bring wives to the U.S. via the War Brides Act and Fiancées Act.[10] Wayne H. Wong, Kay Wong Chin, and Tom Lew talk about meeting and finding their wives, and taking advantage of their new right to bring their wives over.

World War II was a watershed moment for minorities including Chinese Americans. Defense jobs opened up, freeing Chinese Americans from being confined predominantly to working in laundries, restaurants, and grocery stores.[11]

Thirty percent of Chinese men in New York found employment in defense-related industries such as a navy shipyard in Brooklyn and airplane factories in Long Island. In 1943, 15% of the shipyard workforce in the San Francisco Bay Area was Chinese. Many defense-related companies continued to hire Chinese after the war. The experience helped dispel many prejudices and integrated minorities into the U.S. labor market.[12] Kay Wong Chin and Tom Lew talk about how they stayed in government jobs even after the war because those were work places that hired and didn't discriminate.

Families

With passage of the Chinese Alien Wives of American Citizens Act, the War Brides Act, and Alien Fiancées and Fiancés Act, Chinese American veterans could send for their wives and children.[13]

Between 1945 and 1950, 7,449 Chinese women immigrated to the U.S., representing 80% of all Chinese arrivals. The gender ratio between Chinese males and females went from 18.9 to one in 1900 to a near normal 1.8 to one in 1950. Chinese American communities transitioned from bachelor to family-based societies.[14]

Through a decade of formative struggles in the 1940s, the World War II generation achieved citizenship for themselves and their family members, transformed Chinatowns, and helped to establish the integrated landscape we know today.

CHAPTER ONE

Genson Lum 林子貴 (1922–2008)
U.S. Navy

Genson Lum called himself the "Yellow-Faced Jackie Robinson" because he was a machinist's mate instead of a steward or cook, the jobs most common for minorities at the time. He arrived in Sacramento in 1937 as a paper son and was a houseboy in San Francisco before settling in New York after the War, learning the trade and making a living in TV repair. He was one of few Chinese Americans in the Chinese Training Program at the U.S. Naval Training Center in Miami, Florida, which trained 1,000 Chinese navy men in 1945 in a lend-lease program. He passed away in 2008.

When I joined the Navy I was the only one to get a technical rating—it means I got a trade. I didn't have to go through basic training. At that time, all the Chinese, Filipino, and Negro boys could only be stewards and cooks. I'm lucky. This young navy officer—he was young—he didn't know about such a thing as segregation. He wrote a letter for me that carried weight. I became a 3rd class machinist in the Navy, and that's how I accidentally broke the color line.

It was not until 1952 that President Truman became the first one to finally integrate the Navy and the whole Armed Forces. He was nicknamed "Give 'em hell Harry" and had the big guts to fire MacArthur and order the drop of the first bomb.

Legally, on paper, on record, I was born in Glen Island, Mississippi in 1922. In the old days, many Chinese people came to America with [fake] citizen papers. See, every Chinese, when they went back to China, even if they stayed there just one year, would report they got two sons, no daughters. Even if they got no sons, they sold those papers to others to come to America as citizens' sons. The paper was worth a lot of money. I came to America as a native-born because in the next village there was a family—the Chiu family—whose papers said they were Lums. Mr. Jo Bo Lum was my paper father. They were a father and mother with six kids born in Mississippi. In 1929, it was the Depression—the mother and family and sick kid went back to China. All the Chinese people went back to China when it was depression time. The second boy died in the village in China. So in 1937, when conditions were better, the mother sold that piece of paper to my family. I took over as number two son of the family. That's how I came to America as a native-born. I came with my paper brother, Tom.

I didn't have to come through Angel Island. When the family came over,

we took the Northern Pacific Route. We went up in Seattle. Because we were citizens, we didn't have to be impounded in immigration. But we still had to stay in immigration for four days to get that paper from San Francisco to transfer up to Seattle. That was it.

I had a grand uncle in Sacramento, Chinatown. He had a store, and I was to stay there for about four or five months, until I knew how to say "yes" and "no," then I went to work. The school principal recommended me to a private family for a schoolboy job. That's how I made my living. I did house chores, did some shopping, got room and board, all on about $8 a month. That was my luckiest break. Dinner then cost 15¢ for a bowl of rice and a bowl of soup.

Originally when I came over I was supposed to follow my brother-in-law to New York. He went back to China and married my sister. But I waited for him in San Francisco. He was supposed to come a year later, but he didn't come. I was 15 years old, so I stayed out there and worked as a houseboy. I worked for four different families. I knew them through my paper route. They got to like me. One of them, Mr. Lily, he was the nicest one. He's the one who treated me like I was his own son. They didn't treat me like a houseboy. I even ate with them. He had no children. He was an Irishman. He took me on vacation to his hometown in Portland, Oregon. He was a personnel manager for a department store in San Francisco, O'Conner Moffat—now it's Macy's. It was one square block in downtown San Francisco near Union Square. I grew up there with four years of school in English—two years in high school, two years in grammar school. Mrs. Lily was a hosiery buyer for one of the fanciest ladies' shops.

I wound up with them. When Mr. Lily died, my wife and I brought her over for a 10-day visit in New York. After that I lost track of her. She went up to Alaska to live with her younger sister.

See, when Pearl Harbor was bombed, everyone went to work in the ship-yards and did all kinds of defense work. Even the Chinese ladies went to work in the shipyards. So I went to apply for defense work—I was still in high school. They asked me what I majored in in high school. I said one term machine shop, one term auto shop. So he got me down for machinist's helper.

Even with all the work in the San Francisco Bay area, they didn't place me … They sent me down to Naval Air Station North Island in San Diego. So I took the Greyhound bus, went down to San Diego, lived in a Quonset hut near the dock for housing for the defense work. It had no doors—both ends were open … like a hot dog. So I took the ferry over to North Island to work to be the machinist's helper. Six months later, I got my army draft card notice, because I was 19 years old. At that time, the army draft was 18 to 38. The machine shop was run by a navy engineer officer. We made the 50-caliber belting machine. We put the bullets into the belt for the navy fighters. The navy officer got to like me because I was the only one who didn't smoke. I'm the last one to stay and clean up at quitting time. So when I got the army draft card notice, I showed it to the navy officer, and he said, "Lum, screw the army." He wrote me a big letter of introduction to the navy recruiting station, telling them to give me a small technical rating, which means I had a trade. I was a second-class machinist's mate, assigned to Point Loma navy base.

So I worked in the machine shop. Put on a uniform. They gave me a third-class machinist's pay in the navy. I didn't have to go to basic training in San Diego. I never learned how to swim! I reported to the Point Loma Naval Base, which is on the north end of the San Diego harbor. It's the home base for a dozen PCs, which stands for patrol crafts that patrol the southern California coast in case the Japanese submarines land some spies. That's what the Navy base was for. I was in the Navy for eight months; I made second class petty officer. I got the certificate for promotion also. After that, four months later, we got the sea draft, and … we went off to sea. I went to San Francisco and picked up the AKA [Auxiliary Cargo Attack]. Our job was to pick up marines and soldiers in Hawaii after they finished jungle training and to take them to the invasion. We went to Fiji island, New Caledonia, New Guinea, Saipan, North and South Guam, Marshall Island, Subic Bay, and Laiti. After Laiti, my luck changed. The next stop would have been Okinawa.* There were kamikazes. But I got transferred back to Miami, which was my life-saver.

At that time the ship's captain summoned me up to his wardroom. He said "Lum, are you a Chinaman?" I said, "Yes sir!" "I've got an order from the Navy Department to get you out of here." So he told me to see the yeoman and I got my transfer order. I didn't know where I was going. I thought they were going to send me to China at that time. So from Subic Bay, I caught a navy ship to Pittsburg and I got back to Pearl Harbor. From Pearl Harbor they gave me another sea order and transferred me back to San Francisco. At the transfer station, they gave me another sea order transfer with a railway ticket to Miami.

When I got down to Miami, I finally found out I'd been sent to a Chinese Navy training program. I was the only Chinese with a technical rating. See, China did not have a navy during the early part of the war with the Chiang Kai-shek government—the Japanese pushed them all the way to Chungking. It was all Japanese occupation. The Chinese training program prepared China to have a navy after the war. They sent about 1,000 Chinese personnel. They took a bus to Calcutta, took a train to Bombay, then the U.S. Navy sent troop transport and picked them up to go to Australian waters, [through] the South Pacific, to San Pedro Harbor. Then to Miami by train. It took about 10 days.

Most of them, the Chinese personnel, were college-educated fellows, not just any Tom, Dick, and Harry. We used all four of the hotels on the Miami side as living quarters, and the city dock warehouse as a training center classroom. When we finished the training, we gave China eight little ships under a

---

* The battle of Okinawa was one of the bloodiest battles between the U.S. and Japan during World War II. The dropping of the atomic bomb on Hiroshima and Nagasaki occurred just weeks after the fighting in Okinawa ended.

Some of U.S.S. Decker's crew, Miami, Florida.Foreign Naval Training Center, 1945.

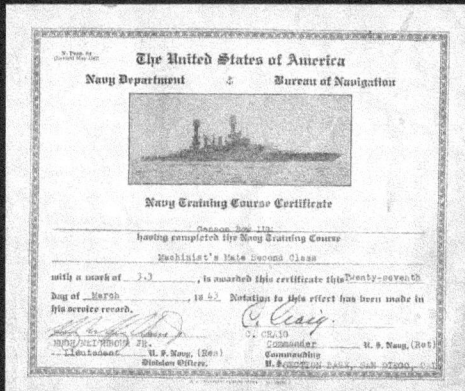

Genson visits his family in China

Genson visits Mr. and Mrs. Lily

Genson with Chinese Navy members

During furlough, with paper mother at the fanciest hotel in the Pearl River Delta

With Seminole Indians in Biscayne, Florida

中央海軍訓練團第四五期輪機官兵合攝於一〇五〇登陸艦兀罗三

Genson, bottom right, with Chinese Navy at Tsingtao Chinese Navy Training Center

lend-lease deal. We also lent-leased to England. (We had to protect them in order to use their land for training our own people.) We gave the Chinese a D.E.—destroyer escort. A smaller destroyer built for convoy duty. That was the ship we went to China on.

They gave me a book—kind of like a yearbook—when we finished training in Miami. The Chinese Navy yearbook. This is probably the only book like this in this country, because it was given to me by the Chinese navy's commanding officer. It happened that his last name is my last name. He called me "didi"—little brother. Small world. *Tong Chu* [name of book] translated literally to "together in a ship." It's the Chinese equivalent of "lucky bag."* The term implies a mutual responsibility aboard ship for one another's interest and property. This book is a record of the American personnel and the Chinese navy men that were involved. And there was no discrimination. Because I did my work nobody bothered me.

This [Chinese navy training] program was almost a year long. They came over early '45 and from this book it tells all the different kinds of training—there was a fast course in English first. There were schoolmarms in Miami who teach them English so we don't need to translate in training. They know a certain amount of English already with their college education. Then they go through all kinds of different physical training on ship.

Sometimes the locals invited us home for dinner. Every weekend we got parades in Biscayne Park in the waterfront, the main portion of the Miami side. There were a couple of Chinese families I always visited when I was down there. There were two Chinese restaurants there where we ate all the time.

We took eight ships when we finished in Miami down to the Guantanamo Navy Base for open sea training for one month. Then, on the way back to China under Chiang Kai-shek's order, we made seven stops, three days each, to visit the Chinese communities. And each place, like Havana and Mexico, gave us the biggest welcome parties. The Chinese immigrants and people, ahead of time, raised money and made donations to welcome the Chinese Navy. In Mexico, the three days the Chinese Navy visited [the Chinese immigrants] was one of the proudest, brightest days in their history. Because all the Chinese immigrants living in Mexico were living under horrible Mexican rules. They were not allowed to do any government work or civil service work. And if you had a business, like a grocery store, if you had three employees, one had to be Mexican. We went into the part in Acapulco, now famous as a resort.

With ten busloads [of Chinese sailors], we went up to Mexico City to join

---

* A Lucky Bag is the term for the United States Naval Academy yearbook dedicated to the graduating classes. A traditional Lucky Bag has a collection of photos taken around the academy and photographs of each graduating officer along with a single paragraph describing the individual written by a friend. While no one knows for sure, it is speculated that it is named after the "lucky bag" that contains the possessions of sailors who lost items at sea. Each year every midshipman and graduating officer receive a Lucky Bag and is archived by both the U.S. Naval Academy and the USNA Alumni Association.

the Mexican Independence Day parade—Cinco de Mayo.

From Miami we went to Panama, and put the eight ships through the Panama Canal. We made stops in Havana, Panama City, Acapulco, San Pedro, the harbor in Los Angeles, then Hawaii, Yokohoma, and Shanghai. They sent me to a Chinese navy training center in Tsingtao for another year. I've still got pictures of that. Tsingtao is a beautiful city, beautiful harbor. A lot of people think Tsingtao beer is a Chinese beer, but it's not. Tsingtao beer is originally a German beer made by a German brewery. Because the Germans occupied Tsingtao after the Opium War.

Mr. Lum,* the official, burned the opium that the British grew in India and pushed into China. There's a statue of him in Chatham Square now. The man with the queue. When Lum burned the opium, that started the Opium War. Eight European countries sided with the British against the Chinese. After China lost the war, everybody got a piece of China. In Shanghai we got the international settlement. And Tsingtao went to Germany. And Port Arthur went to Japan. That's how the Tsingtao beer came about. The Germans built up the city Tsingtao and started the brewery. People drink the beer and say, "It tastes like the German Heineken." It does. The original brewery was built by the Germans.

During World War II time, on one of the invasion trips to—actually it was Marshall Island—after we secured the island, we got a recreation party. Then we picked up coconuts and drank coconut juice or played baseball. We also had beer. I drank a whole case of beer because there was no drinking water to drink. I just about passed out. My shipmate had to carry me back to the ship.

Let me tell you a story about the Marshall Island group. A lot of people don't know—let me tell you a story about it. The Marshall Island group is about 350 miles southwest of the Hawaiian Islands. They're made up of four little islands called Kuagenlin (where I went, and the first island taken back from the Japanese), Majero, Enevita, Bikini. Each little island, they've got a lagoon inside. A ring—little atoll that surrounds it. Bikini Atoll became very famous because after the war we used Bikini Atoll to test the hydrogen bomb. After that bomb was set off, the whole island became bare … bikini! The ladies' swim suit was named after bikini island, because it was all bare! Interesting huh? That's a little Americana that an old Chinaman knows.

When the Chinese Communists started coming down in '47, the U.S. Navy got me out and back to San Francisco for my discharge. At that time, I got the GI Bill. I could use it for four years for school—any kind of school—even dancing school. So I took up a TV electronics course. At that time, San Francisco did not have something like a TV school. Only Chicago and New York did. So

---

* Lum is the Cantonese version of the name Lin. Lin Zexu was appointed as governor of Canton in 1839 by the Qing emperor to reduce and eliminate the English opium trade in China.

I came to New York for TV trade school, and learned how to fix a TV set, and found a wife in New York also. It's a small world. When I married my wife, I had no grocery bill. My father-in-law owned the biggest grocery store in Chinatown. In the old days, they even sold groceries wholesale to all the restaurants in Philly and New Haven and Boston. And my wife got a family of eight—four brothers are medical doctors. When I'm sick, I get special care. So I don't need a doctor. I've got the biggest horseshoe up my ass.

* * *

I finished TV school and worked on TV repairs starting in '48. For years I worked two jobs—five days a week for the Jews and Italian merchants in Brooklyn as an inside TV shop mechanic. Then, after work on weekends, I had my own private TV customers, even some of the mafia on Mulberry Street, and all the Chinese family associations, restaurants, and hand laundries all over the city. I did that on weekends, so for 40 years I worked two jobs, 60 hours a week, minimum. I just about have more TV repair experience—on the old sets, not the new ones—than anybody else alive.

When I go out Sunday morning and people say I should go to church for Sunday service, I say, "No, I give people Sunday service with TV repair."

Now when I look at a modern-day TV set, I feel like Rip Van Winkle. That's what I feel like—obsolete, out of date. Because with all of these modern-day electronics, I just can't keep up.

* * *

I was lucky I did not come to New York right away. If I had followed my brother-in-law, and if I hadn't worked as a houseboy in California with the American folks who treated me like their own son, I would've been making my living as a restaurant waiter or cook. Or hand laundryman. I never would have had the chance to learn English or a trade.

When I had my 30-day furlough* in Tsingtao, I took my paper mother to Canton. I put her up in the biggest hotel in the city.

My wife's a real New Yorker. She was born and raised on Chinatown's Pell Street. But in those days, New York's Chinatown was only Pell and Doyer Street. When my wife was a little kid, if they walked up to Mott Street, Italian kids would chase them back. Pell and Doyer in those days.

Back then there were gang wars and tongs. One tong on Pell Street, one tong on Doyer Street. The biggest tong was on Mott and Canal Street. Tongs in those days were like fraternities. Everyone had to join one. If you owned a laundry and someone opened another on the same block, you'd go to the tong

---

* vacation for people in armed forces

to settle it. Otherwise you got a tong fight. That's why people joined tongs: for protection.

On Chinese New Year you give the tong a red envelope full of money. They demanded it. If you didn't, they'd come to restaurant and scare your customers away. Right now, there's no more tongs, but I think in Queens there are gangs.

CHAPTER TWO

Peter Woo 伍覺良 (1919–   )
U.S. Army Air Force

Peter Woo was 91 when I first interviewed him. He did intelligence for the U.S. with the Flying Tigers and talks about how he started his own business, becoming one of the U.S.'s largest shrimp exporters, partly with the help of influential friends. He became an important community leader in New York's Chinatown and in international politics, and was instrumental in establishing the American Legion Kimlau Post.

Both my social security card and my American passport say I was born in 1917 instead of 1919. And actually I don't know whether I was really born in 1919, or maybe 1920. This is because I was born in a village in China. At that time we didn't have birth certificates. All I know is that my parents adopted my older sister about 10 years before I was born. She's still alive and in New York now.

After starting school, at five years old, it was only three months before my teachers said I was too smart for first grade (we didn't have kindergarten then, just first grade) and jumped me up to fourth. The reason for this was that before I started, my sister had taught me mathematics and Chinese writing, amongst other things. After finishing fourth grade, I continued my education there for two more years, and then went to school in the city. There was someone I knew from my village who attended what they call Taishan Normal School. I had heard that when you graduated, you could become a teacher. To get accepted into the Normal School you had to be at least 16 years old and pass a test. A guy from the village who had also attended the school was head of the student association and had a lot of influence. He advised my mother to lie about my age. How old they said I was, I don't remember, but they did finally get me in.

When I graduated from the Normal School I went down to the village and taught at two schools, to get experience. Everybody called me a "baby teacher." Even later, when I got to the United States, a lot of my students were in the army with me, some of them older than I was.

Although it's hard to believe and hard to explain, when I graduated from the famous Taishan Normal School, I was the youngest graduate, at about 12 years old.

I had an uncle who came to school here in the United States, whom my father supported. My uncle was with the Ford Company, supposedly an engineer. After, he went back to China and was a high official in Nanking with the government, which, at that time, was the Kuomintang. My father told him that I, 12 at the time, would follow him to Nanking.

My father was in the United States, my mother still in the village. My father was a Chinese merchant, who did business at 26 Pell Street at the Chinese herb store. Being the only son, my mother of course wouldn't let me go. But my father insisted.

Alone, I went from the village to Hong Kong. And then in Shanghai nobody arranged to pick me up. My uncle didn't arrange anything, seeing himself as a big shot who didn't have the time, being a high official in the Chinese government. It was either that or maybe because he was young at that time, too. Maybe he had a girlfriend. Either way, he didn't care about me, so I arrived in Nanking on my own.

From there I started high school in order to learn Mandarin. At that time, University of Central Government was the most famous, so I put in my name and took the admissions test. Either I was lucky or smart, I don't know, but they accepted me into the selective Central College, which belonged to the government.

Once I got there, I figured out that my uncle didn't want me around him much. When I told him I wanted to go to Central College, he said, "No, I am going to bring you to the village. You have to attend the American school, the Zhong Wah Catholic College that belongs to the United States. Eventually you're going to the USA and I want you to learn more English." That's what he told me. You know, at that time, I couldn't say anything, because he was supposed to be the one to give me the money. He didn't want to give me the amount of money it would cost to go to Central University. At the Catholic College, he wouldn't have to pay as much, especially since he knew the principal there. So we took the train from Nanking (the trip takes about an hour and half), and then a car into the mountains, to the big university.

I still remember when he brought me in. The American principal greeted him and asked me what my name was. At that time I didn't have an American name, so I told him my name in Chinese, and he recognized it. He even knew which words for which phonetic sound my name was. He knew Chinese really well, spoke Mandarin 100% better than I, or any ordinary Cantonese could. I was surprised that he was a white American and spoke so well.

I got into the school and stayed for a year and a half, at which time I applied to school in New York, at NYU, and because I had attended the American College, they accepted me. That was in 1936.

My father had asked me to attend school in the United States. At the time, the economy of United States was just like now, worse than now. When I arrived, I looked at my father, and his business (which wasn't doing very well) and asked him, "Why don't you let me run the business? That way, I can make my own money before I go to college, or become a doctor."

* * *

Some Chinese who were already in the United States asked me to be their partner in opening a seafood store. After they made the smooth talk—"I know so many people," and "don't worry, you'll make money"—I went back to talk to my father. I was so young. My father asked me, "Are you sure that you know them well? Are you sure you could trust them?" I said, "Yes." He responded, "How do you know about doing business? You don't know anything. And you're going to start and do business?" You know what I told him? I said, "Daddy, if you could do business so well, I think I can do it 100% better than you can!" Even now, I still feel sorry from my heart for saying that, but I was young and didn't know what I was doing. After that comment my father told everybody, his friends and so forth, and those people came around and laughed at me. After that, I needed startup money.

Back then, the Chinese had something where each person contributed $30 or $100 a week, and whoever needed money would agree to pay $1 interest or something like that, and then you'd get a whole bunch of money. So my father pays and puts in my name, and I got about $3,000. At that time, $3,000 is more than $30,000 here now, because when we rent a store over there, it's only $100 a month at that time.

With my $3,000 we bought a small truck. There were three partners. One said he had owned a restaurant for a long time. He said, "I know everybody running the restaurants. You can sell them shrimp, you can sell them fish, and you can sell them lobster." The other partners, Mr. Ching and Mr. Yuen, I didn't know as well. At that time, they must've been 40 or older, but I was only a baby! They tried to cheat me. I was the foolish one who put in all the money, and they were partners with me. [They didn't put money in.] So that's how I got started.

At that time, New York had not more than 10,000 Chinese, with maybe about 50 Chinese restaurants. My father was here for a long time and did business in Chinatown and there were not too many Chinese. Almost everybody knew him.

My math is very good, you know. And I figured that if I could do 500 pounds of shrimp each day, I could make money, or at least cut even. I'd hire a truck guy to drive a truck for $20 a week. I thought I'd figured out everything. My father brought me to every restaurant and told them, "My son is going to be doing a shrimp and fish business. Please help him."

At that time, no Chinese ever sold shrimp or lobster at all—that was done by the Italians. I was the first one to compete with them. "Of course, if this is your son, I will give him my orders." I was so happy and convinced that I was going to make it.

I will always remember that on the day we opened up we only got orders for 145 pounds. I expected more than 500 pounds. You know why? Because when you call up those bosses in the restaurants, they say, "Gee, I don't know whether if you supply me today, you'll still be in business the next day, and whether you'll be able to send me my delivery or not. After all, you're new. Wait until you run the business a little longer before I give you my order!" Everyone told us that.

My goodness, after that I had to go to whatever restaurant myself, to try to get the orders. It was hard. I'd get up at 5:00 in the morning and go down with my partner to the market to buy things. We had no credit at all then. And I made the deliveries myself, too! I needed a license to drive, so I paid $5 to a guy who took my test and got me one. After six months, my insurance company didn't want to accept me anymore—so you can imagine what my driving's like. All those troubles. I couldn't even think of it. Anyhow, in the afternoon, I made deliveries. When I finished with the deliveries, I visited all the restaurants around New York—Brooklyn, Bronx, Queens, New York's five boroughs. And after I came back I called every one of our restaurants to see if they need orders delivered the next day or not. The restaurants asked me to call at night time, at 8:00 or 9:00, so I'd make calls till around 10:00. That was a long and very tough day. But after about two years, from 145 pounds a day, I could sell over 1,000 pounds a day.

To cut it short, within another two years, we [were selling] 10,000 pounds of shrimp every day. Every day!

After I came back from the army, my partners took my business away. That's why I feel so guilty, because I wouldn't listen to my father. At that time, when they inducted me into the army, I told my partners, "Okay, I'll leave everything here as it is, and you'll operate the business. Good? When I come back, we're going to do this together. If you have profit put it on the side for me." Both of them said, "No, either you have to sell your share to us, or you let us run it." They couldn't give you any commitment at all, and I was so mad at that time.

[The army] inducted me, no matter what excuse I tried to use, whatever I tried to tell them, "I have a business, I cannot go to the army," and so forth. They even came in and arrested me to get me in. So I left and [the partners] only gave me $2,000 or so.

I was mad because I was stupid. When they forced me into the army, I should have thought, "What is money? I may die." When you are young you think differently. I should have known that if I did make it home alive I could create my own business, since I was so powerful and every customer knew me, everybody was my friend.

After my partners took over the business they made a lot of money. I thought that they'd give me some when I got back, but after 3½ years in the army, when I returned and went to see them, they told me, "We're going to give, no, loan you $5,000 or $10,000. You go back to China and get married." I told them no, that I didn't want it. I wanted my business back, but they wouldn't give to me. They rejected me.

So after, I get somebody else and I start to do my own business. They still thought I'd given up at that time. And when I started, at the beginning, they still tried to fight with me. But I was so lucky, because I had friends with me, who treated me so good. It used to be that the fish market, the dock, was controlled by powerful people. They controlled the market and without them you could not do anything.

There was one person, Joe Socks, who controlled the seaport. When I came back from the army, and I was trying to start my own business, I saw Joe and told him my story. He said, "Okay, Peter. Tomorrow, if they come down, I'll tell all the wholesalers that whenever I have shrimp coming in, if they sell to Peter Woo for a dollar a pound, they got to sell it to them for a dollar and a quarter." Nobody dared to sell fish to [the old business partners] for a dollar. After, they tried to fight with me, because I know all the customers and so forth, and if I bought the shrimp for a dollar, and their cost was a dollar and a quarter, I could sell it for a dollar ten and make 10¢ a pound, which was a lot of money at the time. Of course they couldn't compete and lost all of their business. I also had the biggest wholesalers, who were good friends of mine. Whatever was in short supply, they'd sell to me first, and not to them. That's how I forced them to give up their business. They had to close. And that's when I started to sell 10,000 pounds a day.

* * *

I joined the U.S. Army in 1943. First I had military training in Camp Robinson, Arkansas for maybe three months. Then they transferred me to Texas, at Camp Fannin, to teach all the Chinese who did not understand English, for about two months. Next they transferred me to Patterson Field, Ohio, the 14th Air Force Unit.

At the beginning, I didn't even know why they sent me to join the Chinese in the 14th Air Force. Then somebody from the U.S. Army Air Force Headquarters asked me if I wanted to do what they called "secret service." Like, what they called intelligence service when they shipped us overseas, to the Far East.

Because I know how to write Chinese, and speak Cantonese, and also Mandarin, they needed somebody like me on the other side. I asked them, "Why did you think to use me, to transfer me over here?" And he told me they looked at my record, and saw that I went to a college that belongs to the U.S. Catholic College in China. So they understood that I must have known Mandarin, and could also be put together with all the overseas Chinese [who are Cantonese].

After I had a long talk with them, my only request was not to do hard training or jobs like KP. Do you know what KP is? It's kitchen patrol, where you clean up floors and do hard work in the kitchen. I didn't plan to do that.

They made me promise that, no matter what, I'm supposed to keep all the secrecy between—I don't even know who. I don't know who the orders came from, actually.

I never mentioned anything to your grandfather [Kwong D. Hom a.k.a. Tommy Moy], who was so close to me. Most people were assigned to a trucking company, mechanic department, master supplier or something like that. But they put me in Administration. I'd just go in there, and I could go out and walk around or go anyplace—nobody bothered me. The guys in the 407 Service Group always looked at me and laughed, saying, "You don't have to do KP job. You don't do anything, and I don't know what you're doing here!" They didn't know that I was assigned all the secret translations.

* * *

I'll tell you a story. When I was being shipped to India, from Norfolk, Virginia, there were over 100 what they call Liberty ships. Because at that time, ever since the Pearl Harbor bombing, the U.S. Navy wasn't too strong, since the Japanese destroyed it. So when we were shipped overseas (the Japanese and Germans were allied), we had no big U.S. Navy Air Force to escort and protect us. Although there were 100-something Liberty ships altogether, they only had small speedboats with [explosives], in case Germany's submarines came in.

On the way [to India], we had been threatened two or three times. The captain of the ship announced that everybody carry a gun, put their helmet on, and sit down, because the enemy's submarine was nearby. They knew it. And they even told us! They announced that, since the submarine is here, we're going to shut down all the lights. There are three compartments in the ship. We lock the iron door and everything in the third part, and we're in the middle. So the captain tells us, "If the enemy shoots us from the submarine, if they hit us in the middle, God Bless you. If they hit the first part from the ship in the head, then we're still safe." And now everybody is so scared, because it's the first time we're going to, you know, war. Everybody sits and plays cards.

After that, we heard a lot of explosions from the sea. Everybody was so scared. But, luckily, we made it to Africa. Northern Africa, Oran. When we landed over there, people were so poor. Even with money, when you went outside in the city, which was supposed to be a big city, you had no food to buy, nothing at all. You'd go to the U.S. PX* but you wouldn't have anything to buy. All you could buy, maybe, if you were lucky, was a cup of coffee from the U.S. Army.

We were stationed in Oran for a couple of days only. Then we took another big ship, the Queen Elizabeth Line, I still remember, a big commercial business ship. The 407th Squadron was only about 200-something people. But when we got into the ship, there must have been over 10,000 people. Some of them were British. It was so crowded that some of us slept on dining room tables. Some people slept on the table, some people under the table. We had to go along near the coast because we were afraid that Germany had a lot of submarines. We went near Egypt and all the places which the Germans didn't occupy yet. And then the Red Sea. It was so hot, the ship, because they had no air conditioning. The food was ruined.

When we finally landed in India we got into training. From the dirty Ocean, we went up near China's coast, from India to China. We stayed in a town called Kanchuki. We saw lots of the Chinese Army from China training in India. We also saw some fire in the airfield. We flew from there to China over to the Himalaya Mountains.

[The Allies] flew suppliers to Burma from India. Sometimes they called me in if the Chinese Army had any trouble. Sometimes a bunch of them went into the Indian movie theater to see movies. They didn't pay. So when they complained to the Americans, the Americans asked me to explain to the Chinese Army Headquarters to control those Army men and not start trouble.

---

* In the U.S. Armed Forces, BX is a common name for a type of retail store operating on United States military installations worldwide. Originally akin to trading posts, they now resemble department stores or strip malls. Known as the Base Exchange (BX) on Air Force bases, they are also referred to as a Post Exchange (PX) on Army posts.

City of Ankiang, China, 21 January to 10 April 1945. Photos from Richard Y. Wong.

* * *

When [the Allies] flew into Burma it was all mountains. They only had one place to land. Then the U.S. airplane arrived and unloaded supplies: ammunition, food, and medical supplies.

The Chinese Army over there was supposed to fight to try to stop the Japanese and occupy whatever area they occupied. The Japanese were on the higher parts of the mountains. They had two machine guns up there facing down. Anybody beneath got killed. But the Chinese Army, they were commanded: Up! Fight! Fight! Fight! After trying so many times and losing so many soldiers, the Chinese wanted to go up and take over the machine guns.

So the Chinese Army Headquarters let the Americans know. They asked the Americans to send in the Air Force to bomb the thing. And I had to go with them to be the interpreter.

The Chinese tried to occupy the top of the mountain in order to fight and advance, but they couldn't get up. The soldiers kept going upward, but the Japanese with the machine guns were shooting downward from up there. But once the Americans killed the soldiers with the two machine guns, the Chinese soldiers were able to run up to the top. They had so many people that the Japanese had to run away in defeat.

Sometimes the Chinese Army doesn't even treat their soldiers like they're human. The captain could shoot or hit them. I saw it with my own eyes. I was telling those captains not to do it. They did it anyhow.

The next thing I remember, we landed in the airport of Kunming. Because at that time we didn't have radar [that was any] good. After we landed there, we were lucky they had two runways. The Japanese were flying over and following us, and when we landed, they started to bomb. Luckily there was another runway.

* * *

In Japanese-occupied Hankou, they had a lot of Chinese Armies sent in, but their ammunition wasn't that good. Their training wasn't that good. And although the U.S. Air Force kept coming in to bomb the Japanese, the Japanese Army had a lot of good training. The Chinese, they didn't. Some of them had never even sat in an airplane, you know, because they were drafted from the villages and so forth.

So when the U.S. were in the skies, the Chinese didn't know that it was the U.S. Army. And up there the U.S. Army wouldn't know that below them were the Chinese and not the Japanese, because between the Chinese and the Japanese lines, it's only about two miles.

Once the U.S. started bombing, the Japanese knew to run away and hide themselves under trees. But the Chinese Army—because of their training—they didn't understand. Instead they'd all run out and look up and ask, "What's in sky?" Of course the pilots up there thought they were bombing the Japanese Army—they fired down, bombed them, used machine guns. They killed a lot of [Chinese people].

The Headquarters of the Chinese Government found out. They put in an urgent request that the Americans explain to them, "Why do they shoot their own allies?"

At our airport, they brought in two top military army men and Chinese Army generals, and also two Air Force headmen. When they met together—at that time it was a real confidential thing—I was called in to meet them. I'm only a small guy, nothing. The Chinese have on their side about two or three Oxford graduates with doctoral degrees. I remember one of them from the USA was from Columbia University. You know, their English sounds better than mine. But yet, when we sit down with the American side, and they do their interpreting and everything like that, sometimes I tell them, "Well, you understand. You don't need me." But they say no, I have to talk to them, translate whatever they say. And I have to translate to the Americans before they answer.

So, to make it short, myself and the Americans and two Chinese together worked up a plan to send to the Chinese government. They ordered me to translate it into Chinese within 24 hours to send to the Headquarters. They came in and sat with me to create a plan for the U.S. Headquarters to approve. The decision was, from here on, the U.S. airplanes will fire three shots. When they fire three shots the Chinese should know that it's an American airplane. The Chinese have to go outside onto the field and hold up a sign with an arrow pointed toward the Japanese enemy. And besides that, if it's one mile away, they put down a "1." If it's two miles, they put down "2." So when the U.S. Air Force is up there, they will know the Japanese are only a mile away or two miles away. And they'll start to go down and bomb the hell off them. So that's what I did. I had to write up the plan in 24 hours. After that, we operated pretty smoothly.

* * *

Most of the 407th Squadron was Chinese-born. When you were put into the 407 group, according to what they say, it meant you were of the highest education in the USA for the Army or Air Force. Most of them either had college or higher education, because their IQ was so good, the whole unit.

The 407 had a lot of smart people, real smart people, like William Hoy. His English was very good, perfect. He was the editor for *Gung Ho*—the weekly newsletter of the 14th Air Force. I was the Chinese editor of the Chinese section of the newsletter. Even the biggest magazines here in New York, they included *Gung Ho* in their magazines. Everybody in the USA knew it at that time, not just the military.

I wrote about the army life, leaving, and all these other things. And I wrote that some in the army were lonely and had nothing to do, and wished that a girl outside would write in order to give them courage. And later on, it kept me so busy, you know why? Some girl from Hawaii College, a Chinese girl, [started writing letters] to them, and not just one—a few of them. Some of these men didn't know much Chinese, but [the girls] wrote in Chinese, so I had to write for the men to answer them. Funny thing. Later on, I was in Hawaii with a guy who I wrote for, and we visited the girl who he wrote to many times. When they met I was with him. But when they talked about those letters, inside my heart, I was laughing at the guy. They went out and the girl didn't like him!

* * *

I put up this American Legion [building in New York]. At the beginning, nobody could run the American Legion because there were tongs in New York. They try to force you to do this, they try to do that, nobody dared to do anything. But even the guys running the American Legion that was originally across the street [before they built the new one]—they were gambling there, playing cards or dominoes, they made lots of money. Before I joined in, they must have made thousands of dollars, but the money disappeared. They were fighting each other. There was a guy who was a lawyer—they put him in as commander of the American Legion. They swore him in, but after three months, he had to run away and never come back again. That was complicated. Because at that time, 60-something years ago, there were hoodlums, and they were all fighting each other. Plus, those guys who came out of the army, they fight with the Japanese, they fight with Germans—they don't care. So about six years after American Legion was opened up, they called me in. Everybody said, "You have to come in, only you can run it." Because they had seen that when I was in the 407, even with the captain—even with the hoodlums—nobody dared to get me in trouble.

I remember when we went overseas in the ship, there was this crazy guy from New York. Because the first sergeant raised hell with him on the ship, he took his gun and … tried to shoot [the sergeant]! Everybody ran away. Everybody was afraid of him. Finally the lieutenant came in and said, "Peter, only you can stop him, please go and help." I'm going to the guy—crazy, I was so young!—saying, "Hey, Herbert, come on, give me the gun." He looked at me, and I don't know why, but I said, "Are you crazy? If you don't like him, we'll go to China and kill him. Don't do it here! You're going to be in jail for the rest of your life." He listened to me and gave me the gun. Just like that.

So it's funny—maybe I'm lucky. When they had so much trouble in the American Legion, and they asked me to please join in, I joined. I was the first American Legion guy who had never been in the Executive Committee, and never been a vice commander, to be a commander.

So I get elected at the American Legion. I remember the first meeting; in the meetings, they always fight. If it's the Chin family or the On Leung organization or the Hop Sing Organization … Either they're trying to do the gambling thing or trying to control the power. Everybody's fighting each other.

So the first meeting I was a commander, one of the toughest guys, called Mr. Gee—everybody knew him—he raises hell and jumps up. I say, "Shut up, sit down there. Otherwise I'll tell the sergeant to bring you out, and you cannot belong to the American Legion anymore." It's funny, nobody dared to do that, but when I tell him, he sits down quiet. And from there on, the toughest guy, and everybody else, listened to me without going against me … just like that.

When I started to investigate the [Legion's] accounting for the six years since they'd opened, they only had $4,000 in the bank. But we had four different bank books. The people from before funneled money into their personal accounts. "Unbelievable," I said. Because I was in business, and even in college or in high school, my mathematics was very good, I set up a system. I called back all the money, including the $4,000.

The bank account was going to belong to the American Legion. In two years, the American legion bank had over $70,000. At that time $70,000 was a lot.

The guys in the Legion were talking all these years about trying to own a building for the American Legion. I went to a real estate broker and actually tried to buy this building for myself. I think it was $280,000 or something like that. I go in and give him $10,000 deposit. Now I have the opportunity to get the building across the street from the original American Legion.

In the meeting I told [our members] I was going to buy this building for myself, and that I'd paid the deposit already. I asked for a meeting to see if the guys wanted to buy it: "We have $70,000 already and we could afford to do it." And I said, in order to make sure I'm being fair—everybody's afraid that maybe I'm doing this to make the money and so forth—I set up a committee of 12 people to talk to the broker, to see how much the building really cost. After they talked, they came back and said, "We'll leave everything to you to do the whole thing." So that's the end. We moved [the Legion] from there and I took care of everything. I even promised the bank that I would put up my personal guarantee if the American Legion Kimlau Post defaulted on payment in order to secure the loan. Fortunately the Legion was able to make the payments, and from there on, that's how I got all the respect from them.

* * *

You know, all my life, I've been very lucky, very fortunate to have a lot of friends with me. I think the reason that they all like me is because, first of all, I never expect anything from them. And I'm always honest with everybody. If I can do something to help, I'm willing to do it. If I can't do it, I'll tell you, "No, I cannot do it."

I've helped so many people, in Immigration, with the Fire Department, Building Department … you name it. I can't remember how many of them there are.

There was a guy who worked for me in the Democratic Club at the time. He was a seaman. He got arrested and on bail, ran away. Again, they arrested him and put him in jail, in immigration. The next morning, he was going to be deported back to China. His wife came to me and cried and asked me to help him.

Because I was the leader of the Chinatown Democratic Club, a very powerful club at the time, I had a lot of connections with the state and federal. I belonged to the National Democratic Committee and was the Chinese Division Chairman. That's why I knew lots of congressmen. I had the nerve to call Washington, D.C., the congressman for Chinatown, at 4:00 in the afternoon. When I called him, he was still at the meeting in congress. I told his office to connect me at the meeting, and finally I got to him. I told him "I've got somebody here they arrested and will deport tomorrow morning. I want you to hold him there and get him out."

He said, "Peter, right now it's 4:30. I'm still at the meeting. How can I do it?" I said, "Look, please talk to the Chairman of Immigration now. He's the only one who could make a call to New York now and ask them to hold it."

And immediately the chairman called New York and nobody was there. The commissioner's already off, and the deputy commissioner's off. He got back to me and told me nobody's there and hung up. So I called him again and asked him to tell the immigration commissioner to call up the police department, and ask them to send somebody to the jail and [stop the deport order] until further notice. He finally did that. And to cut it short, I got the seaman off. I got him the green card. I got him citizenship too. I paid the money, all the money. I never asked them for a penny. So that's why I have the power that I get.

Not just that. When there were raids, when they went into every restaurant, arrested all the cooks without any green cards and so forth—everyone was very annoyed, very scared. All the Chinese and the Chinese Benevolent Association had a meeting—about getting each organization to donate money to hire lawyers. But those people were just concerned about making money for themselves. So people said, "Why don't you send a representative to meet Mr. Peter Woo?" So when they came in to meet me, I made one call. Everything quieted down.

* * *

Most of the American-born Chinese at the time didn't care about who Chiang Kai-shek was, to tell you the truth. Usually the American-borns, especially the ones born in California, only knew about the USA. Other things, they wouldn't know. Chiang Kai-shek, I don't think he was too good.

Chiang Kai-shek was more a dictator. He called himself democratic—you've got to be that way in order to get the U.S., the stupid politicians, to think he is so-and-so.

You know, the National American Legion, at that time—this was 60 years

Peter Woo with Robert F. Kennedy and Mayor Robert Wagner

ago—put up a resolution against Communists, to the UN. I was the one who sent the resolution in to the National American Convention. I was the guy behind the scenes to do it. At the time, all the Chinese here were against the Communists. But I am happy and proud that China is doing so well today. When the War was just over, the American Legion was the most powerful organization in the USA. Two-thirds of the U.S. Congress and senators belonged to the American Legion. The U.S. sends the national commander of the American Legion overseas to meet all the heads of the military and government. That's the system.

After the war, Taiwan was very dependent on me. Chiang Kai-shek's son wanted me to meet him. He sent their overseas commissioner, who's supposed to be in charge of the whole world's overseas Chinese, to make an appointment with me. At the beginning, I said no. But the guy kept crying to me to do him a favor. So I made the arrangement with him, 11:00 in the morning. He sent a car to pick me up at the hotel. I go there, the commissioner by my side, and they have the nerve—the two guards stand there and search me! I was so embarrassed, because I belonged to the American Legion National Distinguished Chairman committee. And I'm the National Democratic Committee of the Chinese Division Chairman. And I'm also a leader of Chinatown Democratic Club and a State Committee Chairman. In the USA, when I went in to see Kennedy, or Johnson, they'd hold [hug] me like that—I could go in anytime. It got me mad that they searched me, even when the commissioner was with me.

We go one flight up, another guy searched me again. [Chiang Kai-shek's son is] on the third floor. I'm there at 11:00. I stay there from 11:00 until 12:30. When he finally gets in I raised hell with him. I said, "From here on, don't even ask me to do anything. Don't even ask me to meet you." He says he doesn't know what's going on. I said, "Look, when I'm in the United States, if I go in to see the President, I walk in and he holds me like that." I said, "You made me so mad today, so embarrassed. I didn't want to come. Your commissioner asked me to come. He was with me and they have to search me before I see you. Who the hell are you?" Nobody even dares to do it that way. That's a real story.

I was going to Washington, D.C., back and forth. I was so close with them. When Kennedy was the President—and his brother Bob Kennedy, later on, was a New York senator, he and I were so close. When he was the head of the Department of Justice, I could call him directly on his telephone.

Kennedy was nice to the Chinese, especially nice to me. When he was senator later on, his brother passed away. He won the U.S. senate from New York, and I was with him. I was the first one to draw in, at that time, a quarter-million persons in Chinatown for the parade for him. That's why he respects me so much. When he was in the Department of Justice—and whenever he sent any men to New York, he always told them to meet me … and ask if I needed anything, and so forth. When John Kennedy was running for President, I took about ten people to Washington D.C. to meet him. See, at that time, the American Legion was very powerful. His father was an ambassador from the USA to the British. Very powerful in politics and in the nation. When he started to run—I'm talking about John Kennedy—his father went in to see a very influential man in New Jersey, who was a very, very good friend of mine. When he came to New York, it happened that Carmine Desapio, another very influential person, was a very good friend of mine. Because I belonged to the Democratic Party. Abe Beame, when he got elected as mayor of New York, the next day he called me down to his office. He said, "Peter, what do you want?" I was kidding around with him. I said, "Abe, I like your job but you already got it, and I don't want to fight with you, you know?" He was laughing. Then I said, "If you give me a commissioner job, it won't pay me enough." I was the biggest shrimp seller, so we're laughing at each other. And then later on I said, "If you ask me … I want to recommend a Chinese to be a commissioner." So that's how this woman, I don't remember her name, I made her deputy commissioner. She didn't even know that I was the one who recommended her. I'm that type. I don't want to get credit or anything like that.

When I was young, after I got discharged from the army, I played mahjong and smoked three packs of cigarettes a day. I wasn't married yet. One of the stars from China, a very famous actress—I won't mention her name—I was kidding around and said, "I like you, you know … If you're with me, I'll do anything for you." She said, "I like you a lot. But you smoke. I don't like that." So I said, "Well, if I cut off smoking, could you give me everything?" She said, "Yes, I'll give you anything." I said, "Are you sure, you mean it?" She said yes. She was world famous at that time. I said, "All right." From that day on, I never smoked another cigarette, not even one. That's me.

CHAPTER THREE

Kay Wong Chin 陳其操 (1923–2010)
U.S. Army Air Force

Kay Wong Chin immigrated to Manchester, New Hampshire, at the age of 15, and served as a medical and surgical technician in an all-Chinese American unit, the 407th Air Service Squadron of the 14th Air Force (known as the Flying Tigers) in World War II. Most of his duty during World War II was with the P-51 fighter unit in Laohokou, China, a small front-line air base. He wonders whatever happened to a nurse he threw into a plane to save her life as enemies approached. He explains why he refused a promotion, feeling insecure about his language abilities. After retiring, he spent his years in Fort Walton Beach, Florida. He passed away in November 2010.

I came to the United States in 1939 from Hong Kong. When I was 15 I arrived in Manchester, New Hampshire. They put me in first grade. You know how little a first grader is? They had all the little desks in there—I couldn't put even my knee in there. Finally they got a chair from outside the hallway so I could sit. I knew very little English at that time. At recess, the teacher came to me, gave me one-to-one instruction, and said—I remember very distinctly what she asked me. She held a pencil and said, "Kay, this is a pencil." She said, "Repeat. Pencil." And I didn't say a word because I didn't understand what she wanted me to do. *(Laughs)* That's how I started. After four years, I got very little basic English, and then the Army got me.

When I first arrived in Manchester from China I was the only Chinese in school. There were no Blacks there in those days. In that area, there were not many Chinese. The Principal was real nice to me, and he said, "You know, really there's not much I can do for you but if you want me to, I'll ask the Draft Board for a postponement. Maybe they'll let you stay in high school." I said, "Please." *(Laughs)* So the Principal sent a letter to the Draft Board. He explained the situation. He said, "This guy has been here for not very long, really his English is not very good for him to get in the service." So they gave me six months' postponement. So I just walked into high school, hardly learned anything, and my mind was not even there. But I stayed there just about six months and then the Army got me.

I got a letter from the President of the United States. It said, "Greetings. You're drafted now." So I joined the Army. After a short training in Springfield, Illinois, we went to Wright Patterson Field for technical training. Originally, I

Resting at Dog Hill in Kay's home village, 1945

wanted to be an airplane mechanic. But then a doctor in the formation one day pointed his finger at me and he said, "I want you." I said, "Why, Doc?" He said, "Well, you come with me. You'll be my assistant." He said, "You're going to get some training." I got approximately six months of technical training as a medical technician and after we finished training, we went overseas.

We went to Africa, India, and flew over the Hump to Kunming, China. After Kunming we went to Hsian to Laohokou to Chihkiang. While we were in Chihkiang the war ended and we went to Shanghai. We re-enlisted there and I transferred to Beijing where I met my wife. We got married and we came back to the United States in 1947. Two of my kids were born in Springfield, Massachusetts where I was stationed when I came back from overseas. From there I went to the Azores islands. We spent 3½ years there.

After my tour of the Azores, they sent me to Eglin Air Force Base, Florida, in 1952. I was really fortunate. That's the place where I worked with the people who really enjoyed working with me and I got promoted pretty quickly.

From tech sergeant I was promoted to master sergeant. Later, in 1958, the Air Force established a new rank of senior master sergeant. (Senior master sergeant is the most difficult enlisted promotion to obtain.) Until you pass a test you cannot get promoted. Only maybe 10% in the Air Force at that point passed the test. I was one of them and got promoted. I put that senior master sergeant stripe on in 1958. I was an aeromedical superintendent and the most senior enlisted man in that career field at that point. I worked for a commander who really liked me. He got transferred to Japan and became a general and asked for me. So I was lucky again! I went to Japan and with his backing I got a really tough job. I was in charge of Professional Services, in charge of all medical personnel assigned to the hospital. There were several hundred people under me at that point, including the Japanese nurses. I found out the Japanese are not like the Chinese—I did have problems with Japanese nurses. I mean they really almost hated me to the point where, you know, when I walked in there and gave them orders, they tried to hide.

What year was this?

1960 to '64.

Were there a lot of hard feelings still between Chinese and Japanese?

Well, no, that was during the Korean War period. Let's see—I was lucky, I didn't have to go to Korea because I was in charge of the place [Base hospital in Japan].

Did you feel like you ever had problems working with Japanese people because they invaded China and you had—

Because I'm Chinese, yeah. It was more difficult for me than the Caucasian previously at the same job, you know. With him, they obeyed the orders and moved on. When I got there, you know, they were different. But I made them work anyhow. So the Japanese are funny. They don't like Chinese and they look down on the Koreans—all these neighboring people. They think they were top of the world at that time. But then, I'm not there as someone from China, as such. I was from the U.S. Air Force. So they had to take my orders. They had no choice. The people I had there, the Japanese doctors, flight surgeons, came to us for training. We trained them, their doctors.

When you came to America, when you were 15, did you already have family members here? Did you have family members who were already in Manchester?

Oh, yeah. I had a brother over here. He was working in a restaurant. You know, most of the Chinese during the early days, in the '40s and '50s, they all worked in restaurants or laundries. Really, when I finished the war activities, I wanted to come home, get out of the service and go to school, but then I got married. So therefore I had to look for a job, and I couldn't find a job when I came home. So I had to re-enlist and stay in the Army, and then within a year got transferred to the Air Force.

Who was the first person in your family to come to the United States?

My grandfather. I think he operated a laundry, and then he got, you know, the other people and later on, one by one, he got down to me.

Do you know when your grandfather came?

Oh, if I got here in 1939, it must have been in the 1910s. You know how the Chinese work. If you had a son back home, at a certain age, they send him over to help. I was attending school in Hong Kong but they had no good jobs in Hong Kong, and it was really hard to make a good living. So then we [decided to] chance it—come over here, and maybe we can do better. So I wasn't planning to get into the Army in the first place, but then World War II started and you had no choice when they drafted you. My brother said, "I was planning for you to go to MIT, get a degree in Mechanical Engineering, you know." But then after I got married I couldn't do all that.

I came to the United States by the ship Queen Mary from Hong Kong, all by myself at the age of 15. We landed in Vancouver. And I had to take a train. They put one of those nametags, a note on my shirt, and the conductor was supposed to see where I get off. I transferred to Boston from Montreal. There were people who'd see that note and they'd grab my hand and move me. Immigration got me and put me on the little island, Ellis Island. The period of waiting was almost a month. They interview you; they make a decision if you stay or send you back home.

Why did you have to come by yourself?

Because there was no one available and it was the only way to do it. My father wanted me to come over here, so they thought the best way to handle it was the way other people had done it before. In the old days, when you're 15 they say you're old enough to do anything. So you can cope, you can take care of yourself. So that's it.

Can you tell the whole story of how your family got here?

Well, naturally from my grandfather. I don't understand how they did it. I was too young even to question the thing, you know. And they never talked about it.

How did you feel when you were in the Flying Tigers and came back to your home-town, Hoiping [開平]?

Well, during the war, people didn't really notice. I mean the people were so poor after the war, 1945. When I went back there, the only ones who welcomed me were my own family. They were really happy to see me. I only spent a short time there, you know, a little visit. And then I went back to Shanghai. I must have been about 22 or 23.

I really had a rough time in the Army because my English was not up to snuff. I had to work twice as hard as everybody else to get promoted. I had to show them that I could do better. That's one thing I learned. And I did, and that's how I got promoted.

The first job I was at Laohokou. I was the only medical technician assigned to that outpost, a fighters' squadron outpost. One doctor gave me a lot of train-ing, and he had to depend on me and I had to depend on him. If he wasn't there, I had to know how to take care of the patients. Because I had more knowledge than any of the other technicians, even those with higher rank than I was, in the hospital, people immediately noticed. Someone said, "How come you're lower rank than the other people and they don't have half your knowledge?" It was because the doctor gave me the training, one-on-one.

What were some of the things that he trained you to do?

An example, we took care of a Chinese soldier. He happened to pick up a Japanese bomb with his hand and the thing went off. And all his fingers and all his skin on his hand were all gone. So the doctor looked at it and said, "There's nothing we can do. We're going to amputate his hand and make a stump out of it." And we worked several hours to amputate. You take all the bone off, tie off all the bleeders, and pull the skin together and sew it together. And I followed his procedure and knew how to suture him up and tie the bleeder off, you see? That's how you really learn. If you don't work one-to-one with him, you don't get that kind of training. And afterwards, you have the knowledge. When there's a similar case you know what to do. When somebody gets sick and comes to you and there's no doctor around, he depends on you.

I'll tell you a very interesting story—I mentioned Laohokou. Laohokou is the fighter unit. The Japanese are on one side of a river. The Chinese soldiers on the other side of the river tried to hold off the Japanese across the river. We, the American fighter squadron, were in back of the Chinese Army a few miles away flying above, helping the Chinese get the Japanese off their river. That was our mission. And one day we couldn't hold them. The Japanese overran us, and we had to evacuate out of there.

I gave the men two hours' notice. "Each of you pack your gear and run out of here. We'll have a plane out there waiting for you. I want you to pack everything you've got. Within two hours we get out of here!" There were Chinese nurses I had hired to help me with the patients, who were up in the ward. So we started getting out of there and I'm thinking about a Chinese nurse. I said, "What will happen to her? The Japanese are going to catch her. They're going to kill her."

So I went higher up and talked to my doctor and said, "What should I do? The nurse works for us." And I got orders. He said, "You can take her with you." So I told the nurse, "You can come with me if you want to. The airplane is out there. I got orders. I can take you in the airplane and get you out of here."

She was happy at first. She said, "I'll go home and get my stuff." So she went home. In 30 minutes she came back with a little bag made of cloth—a tied knot around some clothing, I guess, and she came toward me. She was crying and she didn't say anything, just stood there crying. I said, "Come on, let's go." She wouldn't move. And I said, "What's wrong?" She said, "I've got a mother and my sister here, and if you take me, what's going to happen to my mother and my sister?" I said, "I got orders only to take you. I cannot take your sister and your mother." I said "You have to make that decision yourself. If you want to stay behind, nothing I can do. But if you want to come with me, you're going to have to leave your sister and mother behind."

Boy, this was a real rough thing. And she cried and followed me to the airplane. We had a C-47 there waiting for me to get on. All the people were

Kay and Mary wedding photo, 1947. Army base, Beijing, China.

already on board waiting to take off. We had orders to get out of there as soon as possible. Here I am with a B4 bag, with all my gear. The plane engine is revving up, ready to go, and here the nurse behind me is crying. She doesn't want to get onboard. And I didn't know what to do. So finally one of the guys up there saw me, he said, "Forget what she says. Grab her and throw her up here. We'll give you a hand. We'll pull her in here and let's take off. We can't wait that long." So that's exactly what I did. I threw her up; the other guys they grabbed her and threw her in the airplane while she was crying and we took off. And we landed on another base. I went to the hospital there and talked to the people in charge and got her a job. That's the last time I saw that nurse. And then after the war I came home. I kept on thinking, "Whatever happened to that nurse?"

I often wonder what happened to that place [Laohokou]. I tried to get back there many times, but there's no tourism in that little town. There's no hotel there. The people told me, "We can take you over there except there are no accommodations for you." I never went back there.

How did you meet your wife?

Well, that's another long story. Remember I said we went back to my village? I went to Guangzhou. That's where the Americans had the base and had airplanes in and out of Guangzhou. So I met one of my good friends in the village. I said, "Yeah. They're going to transfer me to Beijing." He said, "You know, you don't speak Mandarin. I know people up there." He gave me a name and address in Beijing, and when I went out there I looked for that individual and that individual happened to be Mary's good friend. When I talked to those people in

Rescue alert duty at Myrtle Beach, SC, 1965

Cantonese, they didn't quite understand me, so they got Mary involved. *(Laughs)* Mary speaks both Mandarin and Cantonese, you see. I took her out. And then, of course, again in Beijing, we had to evacuate out of there in '47 because the Communists were moving in—the U.S. was friends with the Nationalists, you know. So we were told, "We understand you people have girlfriends." He said, "Either you drop them or you marry them because you're going to have to get back to the States in a hurry." So they gave me a short notice and instead of dropping her I got married.

We have three children. My son Kenneth was in the Air Force. My older daughter is Jane, who is a retired Air Force major, spent 20 years in the Air Force. And my younger daughter who's in the Boston area, is a human resources manager.

After I retired I was a little bored, and in the military when you get out you're entitled to the GI Bill. So I said, "Well, let's go to school." At that time I was about 52, I think. I was the oldest in the class, sitting there with 19 and 20-year-old children. And the professor picked on me all the time. I took a course in Psychology and the subject that day was *(laughs)* older people, you know. The teacher asked, "Mr. Chin, what do you think about that?" *(Laughs)*

My hobbies are fishing and tennis. I really enjoyed fishing while I was on active duty. After work, a group of us would go out and have lots of fun. But I didn't realize when you retire, all your neighbors have to go work and you've got nobody to go fishing with you. I mean, you're all by yourself with no fun left. So gradually I said, "Well, I just have to do something." I went to school and trained as a draftsman. I am qualified in all phases of drafting. I worked for an RCA contractor on the Air Force base.

What kind of things did I do? For instance, they're able to find a Russian tank and they bring it to the base and try to figure out how everything in the tank works—the guns and everything else. Then they want to modify a particular piece of equipment and there's where I come in. The engineer goes in there and looks at it and says, "Well, you know, this is too small an area" or "The location of the gun isn't exactly right. We want to make changes in there." So they have me there and tell me, "We want to do this, do this, do this." And then I have to draft all these changes, all these measurements, and make a blueprint out of it, and then they can send it to the shop. It's really interesting. I like that kind of job and I did this for eight years.

Kay Wong Chin at work

So when did your English get better?

Well, I really don't speak much better. I constantly miss the S. I know with plural you're going to put the S in there, but I miss them. And this is not right. And that's one of the reasons I did not get commissioned to be an Officer.

One of the commanders I worked for liked me a lot and said, "I'll put you in for direct commission." I said, "No, sir." He says, "How come? You out-perform all the other people I know. You should be an officer." But I said, "I do not have the basic English skills to become an officer—because you have to be able to speak and write properly, and I do not have that capability." And he always told me, "You're okay." I said, "No, I will not take a job that I cannot perform." So I turned him down. If I'd said yes, I would have been at least a first lieutenant and I probably would've retired at least a major or a lieutenant colonel, but because of my English background I didn't want to take that responsibility. So I did very well on my job, every job I performed in the Air Force, and that's why they gave me all kinds of commendations.

Some people with college degrees worked for me. Sometimes it was pretty difficult. Like, you know, being enlisted people in the service, you perform some labor work, like cleaning up. And one day one of the college guys who worked for me cleaning up said, "My hand doesn't fit the broom." I said, "You're wrong. You learn to do it one way or the other, whether it fits or doesn't fit." You know, that kind of thing, you see?

My oldest daughter, who was in the Air Force for 20 years, went to the University of South Carolina, in Columbia, South Carolina. She majored in biology. At that point I was planning for her to have a career as a medical doctor. And I said, "Well, you go ahead and go to medical school." And she said, "Dad, I'm tired of school." I said, "What are you going to do?" She said, "Well, I'm going to find a job." She applied to a medical technology school in southern California. They had a waiting list of about 10 months. She decided that was too long. So, behind my back, she went to see the Air Force recruiter. She thought she could get away with it, but then I'm in charge of the section that sees everyone who applies! Her name had been submitted to me as one of the people coming to get a physical. So I was really upset. I really didn't want her to join the service.

Why didn't you want her to join the service?

Well, after I had my training in the Air Force, I thought she could do better. Being a female, she would get married instead of joining the service, you know. It's just not for females. That was the old days, way back. But anyhow, finally she convinced me. She said, "Dad, what do you want me to do?" She said, "I'm tired of waiting, and I need to find a job." She said, "At least with the Air Force, I'll have a job and you don't have to support me anymore." So finally I let her get in.

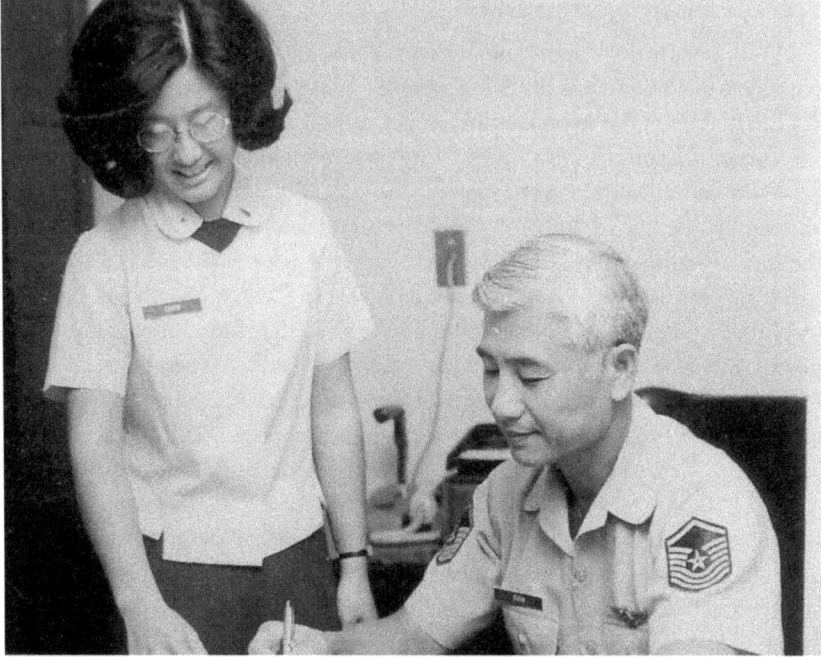

Military reenlistment oath being officially administered by Kay's daughter,
Lt. Jane Chin, at Hanscom Field, Bedford, Massachusetts, 1972

Can you show the picture where your daughter is re-enlisting you? Where she's swearing you in?

My daughter had not been in the service for very long, about two years [at the time of my re-enlistment]. She was a first lieutenant. This was my last re-enlistment. I requested that she be the officer who re-enlisted me so she flew from San Antonio, Texas to Hanscom Field AFB, Massachusetts, to swear me in. As an enlisted man, you serve either 4, 6, or 10 years. You sign a contract. Then you swear in and sign the paper for that length of time you're going to be in the service. So they put this picture in the *Air Force Times. (Laughs)*

CHAPTER FOUR

Dr. Wing Mar 馬榮賢 (1924–   )
U.S. Army

Dr. Wing Mar was raised in Stockton, California, and was sent to Okinawa in World War II. He describes being gunless with a seasick, yelping monkey on his shoulder as he walked onto the deserted beachhead of Okinawa, and sharing a foxhole with a Navajo Code Talker. He used his GI Bill to attend college and then went on to medical school. He practiced medicine in the Torrance/South Bay area beginning in 1956, and was one of the founders of the California Association of Long Term Care Medicine. He was recognized with the highest honor by the Los Angeles Metropolitan YMCA with the Golden Book Award for his dedication to the Torrance/South Bay YMCA. He later became involved with the CHSSC (Chinese Historical Society of Southern California), and edited the first of a book series called Portraits of Pride. For this, the Torrance Arts Commission awarded him the literary award for excellence in 2012. He has been in retirement since 2002.

I was about six months old when we landed in Seattle. How we got to Stockton and got settled is beyond me. Without the help of the Mar family clan, I do not think we would have left China.

I was born in a village called Toisan [台山], Guangdong, in 1924, and came as a son of a paper son. I arrived in Stockton, California (where my father was waiting) after my voyage with my mother and brother. Because of our father's false papers, we never discussed our immigration status, even privately, among ourselves. This was so my brother and I need not lie if asked about it. But later in 1958 I participated in the Confessions Program to be properly naturalized as a U.S. citizen.

Father worked for the Chinese casino owned and operated by the Mars. Mother worked in the strawberry fields and in the packing shed of the fruit orchards, and later at the canneries. My parents and an uncle-chef started a restaurant after accumulating enough capital. The Depression hit Stockton hard and unfortunately we went bankrupt. Within weeks my parents started another restaurant with much cheaper fare that attracted farm workers. From there my enterprising father hired many of those farm workers and contracted large farms to help with the harvest. Because of World War II, many farmhands were already called to service, making a shortage in the fields. Unfortunately, father had

Wing Mar, 6th from right, front row. 3rd grade, Lafayette School , 1932.

cancer and died in 1942. My brother and I completed the contracts my dad had secured; and then I was called to duty in the Army.

Not long after our entry into the United States, Mom planted a vegetable garden probably similar to the one she had in China. She must have thought it through and had a commercial goal in mind. The key to the success of our family enterprise depended on us renting the "Yellow House" with proper zoning. She could now do farming of Chinese vegetables and even raise chickens. Stockton in the 1920s was mostly rural. The Yellow House for us was a stroke of luck and the result of the good eye for a good deal. Dad had an 8-foot fence built surrounding the backyard for raising chickens and security. Without realizing it, the vegetable garden was our family's first business venture. The reputation of Mom's fresh vegetables was such that my father had no trouble selling them to Stockton Chinatown's two Chinese grocery stores. Dad might have even marketed to the two eateries—On Lock Sam and Canton Low restaurants.

There were many canneries and packing sheds in the Stockton area and there was seasonal work for the women in town. Being a cannery worker was the one job Mom kept as her occupation throughout her life.

The Prohibition period (1920–1933) caused a shortage of alcohol here in the U.S. We read in newspapers and saw newsreels about the breakdown of local and federal laws with increasing criminal mob activities. American industrialists were importing whiskey from other countries and that was legal. After 13 years, the Prohibition law was repealed because of all the unintended consequences. However during that time the making of Chinese rice wine (bok dill) which was used as a "confinement diet" for new Chinese mothers, was presumably exempt.

Some families, including my parents, started distilling the alcohol in our kitchens. There was a Chinese man who spoke perfect English and Cantonese whom we called "Yun Bak". He brought over a copper still and taught Mom how to mix the rice-wine mash for fermentation in wooden barrels. In San Francisco, Dad found a store that would buy whatever excess brew we distilled, and this was good news. When we had several 5-gallon bottles of rice wine ready to go, Dad would drive us to a store in San Francisco Chinatown where the proprietors were always happy to buy the rice wine.

When Dad completed all his business dealings and we were on our way home, he would stop at a Big Boy to buy us all barbeque beef sandwiches and root beers in the city of Tracy. That was a must-do (and a big treat for me) of the routine business trip. In reflection, those years might have been the happiest for Dad. I remember his singing of Chinese folk songs while driving home as if he did not have a worry in the world.

Mom told us to talk to him as she was doing so he would stay awake while driving. There was no air conditioning in cars those days and it was not comfortable in the summer heat. I remember how much I enjoyed the stop in Tracy for the soft drinks with ice. How happy we were on those family trips to San Francisco, enjoying the food in Chinatown, shopping, enjoying the Chinese opera, eating shellfish at Fisherman's Wharf. Everything seemed to be going pretty well while we lived in that Yellow House.

* * *

I was 17 years old when Pearl Harbor was bombed on December 7, 1941—a graduating senior at Stockton High School and, to my surprise, I won the Bausch and Lomb Class Science Award. The nominating teacher recognized my curiosity and my interest in life science. That surprising validation on commencement night at the Stockton City Auditorium in January 1942 sent a powerful tingling jolt to me from head to toe. I wish I could have had a chance to tell the science teacher how her vote of confidence in this mixed-up high school student was life-affirming.

I now recall that the Japanese students in my class were not at graduation, as they were all sent away to internment camps.

A year later, on December 6, 1942, I enlisted in the reserve in the Army Specialized Training Program (ASTP) for pre-medical students. This program was cancelled after I joined, due to heavy losses of our troops by German forces in Europe, and there was a need for infantry soldiers and not pre-medical students. I was ordered to report to Fort Benning, Georgia, for basic training. There, I spent Christmas and got the flu in that cold winter of 1943. After basic training, which included forced marches of several miles, target practices, and survival skills, I was sent to Camp Livingston in Louisiana to join the 86th Infantry Division. I was with new troops being further trained before shipping out to Europe. (The division was nicknamed Black Hawk after an Upper Midwest Native American tribe that fought U.S. troops during the Indian Wars. Evidently the 86th had some empathy for the brave but defeated insurgent warriors to take their name.) I was psychologically and physically prepared for life as a soldier with an unclear future.

Before the Black Hawk 86th Division was deployed to Europe I was abruptly transferred to the 10th Army Corps in Fort Sam Houston. This new corps was being formed with the Marines and Navy into a group to invade Okinawa with the code name "Operation Iceberg." I did not understand the reason for my rapid re-assignment and was not enlightened by anyone, and I dared not ask because of the tight security about military secrets.

I was specifically assigned to the 711th Tank Battalion-headquarters as a member of the intelligence section. I had the position of a clerk. Having taken a typing class in school, I was a pretty good typist. I had also typed the menus for the family restaurant. The typing thing might have been the key to my transfer to a battalion headquarters where they could use someone with clerical skills and the ability to speak some Chinese. (In those days, not many males knew how to type.) My task was to learn Mandarin while doing the clerical work for the intelligence section. In Hawaii I was asked by someone if I would join the counter intelligence unit being formed in the Corps. I agreed to the proposal but nothing more happened except I was told to continue to learn Mandarin on my own since we were invading Formosa, now called Taiwan [Operation Iceberg], in a few months.

During the closing days of Operation Iceberg I was told by an observant buddy that there was another Chinese American soldier who was a cook in the close-by 7th Infantry Division. I did visit him; I think he might have been a paper son, for he did not divulge much about himself as to his immigration status and appeared older than registered. That was my last encounter with him and I concluded there were just two of us who were Chinese Americans in our invading army. There were many Chinese draftees who were paper sons in the Army, but not assigned to Operation Iceberg.

I later read officially that there were Nisei soldiers in the 10th Army Corps Intelligence Division interrogating prisoners, preparing millions of propaganda leaflets to be dropped from the air to persuade the civilians to go to the hills and away from the scene of combat. The Nisei officers were also to gather information from captured documents such as maps and enemy deployment for the planned assault of Japan. I conclude now that it might have been an unspoken policy to send Chinese American draftees and recruits to Europe or the China-Burma-India Theatre because of the possibility of us being mistaken as Japanese soldiers in the heat of battle. I probably just fell through the cracks and inadvertently got assigned to the wrong theater of war. My conjecture at the time is that this was a unique snafu. The deployment of Chinese American soldiers was a sensitive subject for me and I did not talk about it much at the time.

To continue with my story, the 10th Army Corps, including my tank battalion, celebrated Christmas 1944 in Hawaii. We then sailed to the Island of Leyte in the Philippines, which had been recaptured a few months earlier by General Douglas MacArthur and his Pacific Army Command, including the 7th Division. We spent January, February and March of 1945 to prepare for the assault on Formosa [Taiwan].

When I found out that the real target was Okinawa instead of the Island

Wing Mar, circa 1943

of Formosa, I realized I was learning the wrong language. Rather than learning Mandarin I should have been learning Japanese. This sudden change of strategy by the War Department was a ploy to confuse the enemy so they would use their stretched and declining resources to defend Taiwan while we would be attacking Okinawa as planned. So the order for me to learn Mandarin was part of the ploy to outwit Japan's military intelligence. But the Japanese military was wise to our strategic plans. Tokyo Rose [Japanese radio propaganda] already knew of our plans and she announced over radio that their troops were waiting for us in Okinawa and she reminded us not to forget to bring our own coffins.

The troops were finally told the truth only when we were out at sea in the midst of a typhoon as we were sailing to the real target—Okinawa. All the troops and the sailors were oriented as to the reason for the coming assault of Okinawa and the importance of victory. This information was delivered to us in each ship of the Armada from the broadcasting system of the Navy—and then on to the Japan mainland. I was relieved somewhat because Formosa had steep rocky cliffs which posed a big danger for our tanks while Okinawa had beaches without steep cliffs where we could land and occupy more easily and safely. The 10th Army Corps with the Marines and Navy landed on a beach in Okinawa on April 1, 1945, Easter Sunday, without any resistance from the Japanese, for the Japanese strategy was to fight from caves and extensive tunnel fortifications in rough terrain further back up the hills. I could not be happier, for I was seasick the whole time on this small flat-bottom ship called an LSM [Landing Ship

Medium]. I was so terribly seasick in the middle of the typhoon that I would rather face the enemy than be on that ship any longer! This small ship had the capacity for at least four tanks and other armored vehicles, which unloaded off the LSM to the beach, while the Jeep I was in was the last to leave.

The sailor who was the baker of the ship gave me two cans of turkey if I would take the seasick monkey that was the ship's mascot off the boat. Everyone loved the sailor because he made us cookies. He was the sailor who played the saxophone by my bedside to soothe me while I was vomiting because of the typhoon's 20–30 foot waves. I was touched as we disembarked because he looked like he had been crying for our safety as we were going to battle soon. I agreed to take the sick monkey and must have looked pretty strange riding in the back of the Jeep with a sick monkey sitting on top of my left shoulder. I stuffed the two cans of turkey stew inside my field jacket with my M1 rifle on my lap. I was going to the beach in grand style by myself with a driver.

Now, 68 years later and reading the declassified official Army report of the Battle of Okinawa, I wonder if I should be the one weeping for the sailors and marines instead. The report stated that even after we, the Army, already landed, kamikaze pilots still continued to torpedo cargo ships such as the LSM that transported me to the beach head. The defending strategy of the Japanese Air Force was to destroy the cargo-supplies needed by our troops by attacking transport ships. Reports describe enemy aircraft firing anti-aircraft projectiles, hitting the well-deck of an LSM, wounding nine Marines and two "Bluejacket" sailors. I must have luckily disembarked a bit earlier from that LSM.

So now I wonder what happened to my sailor friend who gave me two cans of turkey stew and his monkey as I rode off the ship. I hope he made it home to Chicago safely. We should have wept for the sailors rather than vice versa.

But I could not believe what happened next in my landing off the ship. The driver of the Jeep drove into a large shell hole in the coral reef and the front end was stuck with the engine pointed downward. The beach had been bombed heavily for a time by the Navy to neutralize enemy resistance and to blow up underwater mines. Those bombs accounted for these large shell holes. After a couple of unsuccessful tries by our tank commander to pull the Jeep off the hole with his tank he yelled that his tank is worth a quarter of a million dollars while a Jeep was just a few hundred. He then figured the risk and stopped trying to yank us out and left us to fend for ourselves.

I waded quickly to shore for I could see behind me large ships were coming in and would crush the Jeep. I panicked because I couldn't swim, and left my gun, duffle bag, and the cans of turkey in the jeep. But I did keep the monkey who was yelping loudly on my shoulder. After getting on shore I noticed that there was an amphibious tractor left running by some engineer group which landed earlier and had abandoned it for the night. There was no enemy group at the beach. The engine was warm and running so the monkey and I crawled in and dried up and spent the night watching the 1,400 naval ships off the coast being attacked by the Japanese planes in the balmy evening sky. Occasionally I would hear a booming noise when a kamikaze pilot struck a ship. Also, our battle ships were making their own noise shooting at the caves where large guns were rolled out on railroad tracks to fire at the battleships. After a few rounds they would retreat back into the caves, protected with closed steel doors.

At the deserted beach I was hoping to see one of our airplanes in the sky. But with fear and surprise I saw a Japanese Zero plane with the red sun symbol circling above me so as to make a suicide strike to a ship. It was eerie, for the beach appeared abandoned, and it seemed like the plane just ignored me. It may be that the Japanese pilot was looking for a more valuable target to dive into and die for, for his emperor, other than this comic scene of a single soldier with his yelping monkey and no gun.

Next morning, I heard voices coming to the beach looking for me. Our tank crew came across some non-combatant civilians whom they wanted me to interview. Also they found a suicide torpedo rocket with a seat but no engine, which was meant for a suicide bomber. I deemed that our higher-up intelligence would have categorized this senseless torpedo already, and they would have figured out how to destroy this suicide armament. It was one more item to photograph and categorize for intelligence data.

The interview I had with the civilian family was unsuccessful as to gathering much useful intelligence information, but I managed to ask the civilians if they needed food and water by writing it in my limited knowledge of a few Chinese characters which native older Okinawans knew, and with gestures which they seemed to understand. We then sent these civilians to the Military Police for triage and placement.

For the next few months, my official duty was to record our victories for our battalion as we gained control of the island. A large number of enemy soldiers were killed. Unbelievably, our tank battalion lost only one man due to a non-battle recreational drowning during Operation Iceberg. Our unit, 711th Tank Battalion, was defensively placed to guard the flank and go behind the 713th Flame Throwing Tank Battalion. The 713th was the right unit to pursue the enemy in their fortifications using the mechanized flame-throwing guns installed in Hawaii by special machinists contracted for this job.

These flames went much further than the standard flame-throwing guns, making them more efficient and effective. The 711th Battalion of tanks were not mechanized, but had only standardized equipment and were placed behind the 713th as a defensive unit whose job was to protect any attack from the side or back. The infantry and the scouts added further protection to all the tanks. This strategy resulted in the reported killing of 4,788 Japanese soldiers by the 713th Flame Throwing Tank Battalion and the loss of 8 dead and 111 wounded of the 713th Tankers. The Japanese soldiers were petrified of the napalm flames and were surrendering in significant numbers for the first time since the beginning of the war with Japan.

I had already given the monkey I brought ashore to a friendly sailor heading back to the Philippines. There were no longer any typhoons; besides, the monkey's chattering was a problem. He was giving away my position to snipers in the two days he was with me. I finally got a replacement carbine for my M1 rifle lost at sea which I thought was an unfair exchange of gun power. The M1 is a much more powerful gun.

When the headquarters staff, including me, patrolled our camping area, I threw a few grenades into caves around our camp, or into the ubiquitous sugar cane fields where an enemy soldier could hide, but I doubt I killed anyone. As it was, we could not bury the corpses left behind by the advancing 7th Infantry Division. The stench was terrible, with flies covering our food in a few seconds as we went through the chow line. Finally it became a priority to bury the dead in a timely schedule. Digging graves was a dangerous task, exposing the group to enemy fire, but later on it became safer.

A tragic story of the danger of exposure to enemy fire is the death of General Buckner, our commanding officer. He was hoping to create some goodwill and persuade more enemy soldiers and civilians to surrender. But due to the Japanese military propaganda of American atrocities, the families were jumping to their deaths from the cliff tops to the ocean in anticipation of the coming defeat. The general was officiating in the marriage of a prisoner-of-war pilot to a Japanese nurse in open view. Unfortunately, Japanese artillery shelled the wedding site and killed General Buckner. I do not know what happened to the couple.

For diversion and recreation I was asked to publish a newsletter, which I was glad to do. The talented men who tended the tanks were distilling alcohol from the sugar cane in the nearby fields through the metal stills they had fabricated. There were plenty of grateful customers. One smart-aleck suggested we make fake Japanese flags from our bed sheets using my calligraphy for deceptive authenticity to sell as battle souvenirs to sailors and pilots, but that seemed too deceitful. Besides, we needed our sheets. Most men were making jewelry with attractive seashells found at the coral reefs for their wives and girlfriends back home. One of our men fell at the treacherous coral reefs and drowned while exploring for his perfect seashell. The irony is that he was the only fatality in our battalion during the whole campaign.

All through the five months of battle the Japanese were bombing our positions with large guns sliding on railroad tracks, from caves protected by steel doors. At the same time, their caves and defensive positions were bombarded by our battleships, with our big guns not far from shore. I was getting used to the fireworks on display, with the loud noises each night. But we still needed our foxholes because we were indiscriminately shelled at night. In the earlier phase of the campaign, when the fighting was intense, I was asked to share with a fellow soldier the use of my foxhole.

The Native American Scout who asked me did not have time to dig his own foxhole that day and asked if he could share with me that night. Navajo Code

Talkers had the job of protecting and leading tanks, and they were completely exposed when doing so. They used their native language to keep communications among themselves secret. People inside the tanks couldn't see everything; they were limited by having only periscopes to see their surroundings, and there were blind spots. They may not have been able to see suicide bombers strapped with explosives before it was too late. So they relied on the Navajo Code Talkers to navigate the terrain. It was probably the worst job. I wonder about the adequacy of having scouts leading the tank columns without regular and adequate infantry coordination while they advanced into enemy territory. They were put in a particularly dangerous position.

The Native American scout came back from the worst day they had. He said to me, "Can I stay with you in the foxhole? Because I didn't have time to dig a hole." He was a big man. Luckily, we both fit. At night, they're bombing and bombing, and I'm still able to fall asleep. Maybe it's because I'm used to Chinese firecrackers. But he was trembling throughout the night, because of how scared he was from his experience that day. And he had to get up and do it again and again. But I heard he survived. Nobody died.

At night, all the tanks are in a circle. We have wires around, so when anyone trips on it, flares will shoot up and we can see who they were. If they didn't have right password, we would shoot them.

World War II finally ended on August 25, 1945, after the U.S. dropped the atom bomb on two Japanese cities. I was shocked and felt a sense of guilt and shame after hearing over the radio of President Truman's decision to use the two atom bombs and incinerate two cities so we did not have to invade the main island of Japan. It seemed like there was a disproportionate use of massive force. Also by then I knew that we were already winning in Operation Iceberg. I was recording the increasing number of Japanese soldiers surrendering, so I was questioning with my buddies the need for the atom bombs from that perspective. That was my first instinctive response without any rationalization. The soldiers I talked to agreed. Then upon reflection I appreciated the fact that I could have been killed if we had to execute Operation Downfall [invasion of the main island of Japan], if the A-bombs were not dropped. However I am now opposed to war as a way to settle disputes and support those who work for peace.

The Okinawa campaign was the largest battle in the Pacific. Ultimately, 200,000-plus American soldiers, sailors, airmen, marines and 1,400 American ships were involved in the battle. Our estimate of Japanese defensive forces was 120,000 under General Ushijima. Their units were of seasoned soldiers from their campaigns in Manchuria and other parts of China. The Japanese Air Force was estimated to have 10,000 airplanes, of which 2,000 were committed to defend Okinawa and were used by young kamikaze pilots trained to dive like human torpedoes toward ships in battle.

During the first few weeks of Operation Iceberg, Japanese suicide bombers were destroying our ships off the shore of the landing area and I remember recording the high number of casualties of our sailors from the kamikaze suicide dives. In contrast, American foot soldiers in Okinawa had flame-throwing tanks traveling along their sides in destroying enemy fortifications and caves. So our foot soldiers were protected and our casualties were lower than expected in our Army and Marine units. The Japanese soldiers in Okinawa were no match for our forces with the latest mechanized heavy armament, new technology, and high morale. As the war progressed, we were destroying the enemy air power with our superior air force, so our ships were a lot safer and Navy casualties leveled off.

After the last battle of World War II was over, I was waiting for deployment to Korea. I was promised a promotion to staff sergeant. My decision as to whether to stay in the army for the promotion was made for me when I was hospitalized for a non-serious leg injury in a minor non-battle accident, and a skin condition. The war had ended and already I was conveniently sent home on a hospital ship, U.S. Hope, to San Francisco's Presidio on November 15, 1945, for later discharge!

With the benefits of the GI Bill, I was able to enroll in school to continue my studies toward a medical degree with my BA at Berkeley and then my MD at Stritch School of Medicine at Loyola University in Chicago. I met my wife Joyce at Berkeley and she has been my partner for more than 65 years. Though there were barriers to being admitted to medical school, out-of-state schools were less restrictive. There was an unofficial policy that UC San Francisco Medical School, the closest and least expensive school, only took two or three Asian students per year. Stanford had never taken a Chinese student except from China. USC was the same, and classes were only admitting about 70 students per year at each school.

We always felt that our community of Torrance was supportive and we have found ways to integrate ourselves here. Our three children attended public schools here. They are all married and we have six grandchildren and one great grandchild.

CHAPTER FIVE

Al Chinn (1923–   )
U.S. Army and U.S. Air Force

Al Chinn, of Portland, Oregon, was drafted to serve in World War II at the age of 19, and did not leave the military until the age of 50, after also serving in the Korean War and the Vietnam War. He did a total of 7 years of active duty in the Army and 22 years of active duty in the Air Force. He shares wartime anecdotes and talks about dangerous missions carrying supplies on a truck on the Burma Road, being sent on a mission into North Korea, and flying on reconnaissance missions in Vietnam.

I travel around the country with this bag. When I first got into Kunming, China, this is what I wore on my shirt, and also I've got this Flying Tiger here. Later on with the military, with the Air Force, I was in the 5th Air Force and the Pacific command. This is my flying wings here, and this is a United States of America emblem. These are all the awards I won here. This is a Chinese tape [ribbon] I got here. I got this in Beijing, and I was with the air command crew flying 3-star generals of the U.S. Air Force. This one, I was flying in the military, flying stars, and this one is a command crew patch here. These are all the awards. I've got more medals than that, but that's all I put on there. This is my flight bag.

Stationed with the 521st Military Intelligence Service. Unit
was moving from South Korea up north to North Korea

What goes inside a flight bag?

What's inside the flight bag? I carry all my flying stuff. I've got an oxygen mask, medical supplies, my clothes, toilet articles, and stuff like that.

Where were you born and what was your family like?

I was born December 19, 1923 in Hubbard, Oregon, a little town. My father, I don't know too much about him because he came from the old country and he passed away when I was really small. My mother, I believe, was born in California somewhere. I don't know too much about her. My parents were farmers.

I was drafted in the United States Army in 1943. After basic training, I was sent to CBI: China, Burma, and India. I arrive in Bombay, India, by boat and later on I go to Calcutta. In Calcutta they have a big army supply depot there, and my company, the 2122 QM Truck Company, whips to the depot and draws out about thirty-five 2½-ton trucks for our convoy with a 1-ton trailer tied behind. We put the bow and the tarp on and we load the truck with eight 55-gallon drums of gasoline and four 55-gallon drums in the trailer. Some of our trucks have 50-caliber guns mounted on top of the cab.

We get all ready for convoy and we draw two cases of rations. One is K-ration. It has dried biscuits and crackers in there. The C-ration is canned powder, eggs, sausage, beans, and stuff like that. In addition to what we draw for the ration, we also have five gallons of water for each truck. That is for drinking water and water to brush your teeth.

Each one of us has a pack of morphine. In case we get shot or in case we get wounded or get hurt, we use that morphine to inject near the wound to ease the pain until we can see a doctor. There was no medical people, no ambulance, and no communication at all during the trip over the Burma Road.

The Burma Road is about 750 miles long before we reach the Flying Tigers in Kunming. It takes us many days to drive 750 miles because the road is very, very dangerous. It's all handmade road. We're going up and down the mountain to pass over the Himalayan mountains, up one side and down the other. It's extremely dangerous. If one of our people should miss the road or miss the curve, he will go down in one of the canyons there and the canyons are very deep, so there's nobody to go down there to rescue him. We can't get down there at all, so he'd be gone for sure, because with all that gasoline on board and all that weight, he's done, he's finished. We can only drive around 40, 50 miles a day because we're trying to avoid the Japanese Zeros along the way to Burma Road.

What are Japanese Zeros?

Japanese fighter planes. The Japanese snipers along the road. The convoy ahead of ours had been wiped off, so we passed them up. So the army engineer used a bulldozer and pushed him over the cliff. We don't know what happened to the people because they were all blown up. They had gasoline we think. We were very careful. We could only drive daylight hours.

2122 MC Truck Company, Calcutta India.
Al Chinn with pet monkey on his shoulder.

At sundown, we have to pull aside and hide. We can't leave the truck. We all sleep at the back of the truck on top of the gasoline drums. We can't go outside at night because there might be some Japanese sniper along the mountain there, trying to shoot us down. We're told if anybody moves around outside, we're supposed to shoot them and kill them because they don't belong. We don't want nobody around our convoy truck because of all the gasoline there.

What was your job?

My job was motor sergeant in charge of the rear end of the convoy. We had three officers in the convoy: Captain Beacher; our executive officer was Lieutenant Miller, first lieutenant; and the transportation officer was a second lieutenant. He was supposed to be in the back of the convoy with me but he got scared and he stayed at the front of the convoy. Myself and three other mechanics brought up the rear end of the convoy. The front end don't know what's going on around the back end, the back end don't know what's going on at the front end because we don't have any kind of communication, none at all. It was very rough and we took several days to get into Kunming. My company, 2122 QM Truck Company, provided real close support to our Flying Tigers at Kunming, China.

Was your company an all-Chinese group?

No. Our officers are Americans [Caucasians] and the rest of us are Chinese [Americans].

How many people were in there?

They were at least two of us, anyway, because two to each truck. Some of our

Kunming, China, 1944. Guarding the runway with a .55-caliber machine gun

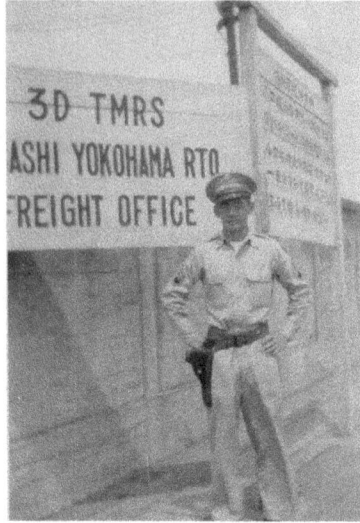

Yokohama, Japan, 1950. During the occupation, worked with the Provost Court.

trucks were mounted with subbers, 50-caliber machine guns. When we got into Kunming, China, we kept at each end of the runway with a 50-caliber machine gun. We lived in pup tents at the end of the runway. We were supposed to guard each end of the runway to keep the Japanese from bombing the runway. If they did that, the Flying Tigers could not take off or land. We provided strict support down there, watching the Flying Tigers.

The Flying Tigers would take care of the air, and the ground troops like us took care of the ground, so when the Japanese flew low, trying to come in to bomb the runway, we would shoot them down at both ends of the runway. But if they went up high, the Flying Tigers would shoot them down from the air.

So I think we did a terrific job there keeping them away. I'm sure that's what caused them to surrender. When they surrendered, I was near Hostel Ten in Kunming and it was about 9:30 at night. The fireworks broke loose and I thought the Japanese had invaded us. I got real scared, so I looked for a place to hide in the rear end of the truck.

Later on I found out that Japan had surrendered and our troops were excited and very happy, so they fired away their machine guns, big guns, and there was gunfire all over the place. I found out that the Japanese surrendered, so that was a big relief for me. I stayed with the Flying Tigers until after the war. After the war, I was reassigned to the Philippines for a little while. After the Philippines, I went to Shanghai and I stayed there. Then, they reassigned me to Nanking. It's Nanjing now. I was training the Chinese Army engineers and troops on how to operate road-building equipment—bulldozers, graders and stuff like that. I stayed in China until 1947, then I went home to Oregon.

After I went home, I was shipped out. I ended up being in South Korea in

1947 for one year. Then I went to Japan in 1950. I was a sergeant at that time in the Army. I was working with the Occupation Provost Court.

What was your job there?

I was administrative at that time when Japan had no authority to try foreign nationals. [When] our civilian sailors would go into port in Yokohama and get drunk, when they missed the ship we'd send them to Tokyo.

Me and two MPs would go into Tokyo in the Big Eight, the jail there, pick them up and bring them back to the ship. We called it the "Big Eight" because the prison was run by the 8th Army in Japan. I would take the prisoner and two MPs who escorted me there. I would then go up and talk to the captain of the ship to see if they could take that prisoner back to the United States. Well, I had to ask him [the prisoner] for a fine. So the ship captain would pay the fine, I'd turn [the prisoner] loose, and then take the money back to the courthouse.

In 1951, I went back to Korea. In 1952, I worked from the south and I was in intelligence again, Military Intelligence Detachment, MISD. I worked from the south up to North Korea. We were surrounded up there in North Korea by the Chinese communists and also the North Korean communists. They waited for us up there, and they didn't have too many people, hardly any machinery or weapons to go further down south to fight us. So they waited till we got up there. General MacArthur had sent one battalion of Marines up there. He didn't think we'd need too many people, so I was with the 8th Army 10th Corps, MISD, Military Intelligence Detachment. All I did was deal with prisoners.

What did you do with the prisoners?

Try to interrogate them with an interpreter. We got a South Korean interpreter with us, so I would ask the interpreter to ask them certain questions.

What kind of questions were they?

What they eat, where they live, where they're from and why are they fighting. They said they've got no reason to fight, but the government ordered them to fight, but they don't have any weapons. We found out that there was one gun per five soldiers. If one got shot down, the next one could take over the rifle and shoot. One rifle for five soldiers. One follows the others.

Anyway, they had us surrounded up there. It was 3:00 in the morning before we even got out. We were cut off from water and food. Our airplanes from Japan or South Korea flew in there and dropped some water and some rations for us. We were all surrounded there. We couldn't get back because the airports and seaports were rigged with mines.

The Navy ship was out at sea. They couldn't come into port to evacuate us because they might hit one of those mines that blow the ship up—they know that. So anyway, we're really desperate to get out. The Army had called in a group of fishing boats from South Korea and Japan to go rescue us, but we couldn't take the equipment out of North Korea. We had lots of tanks and a lot of ammunition, a lot of guns, big guns up there and a lot of motorized vehicles, and we can't move them. We can't take them south and we can't go any further north because we're right at the Manchurian border. Anyway, we decided to run all that equipment in a big giant pile and our bombers in there dropped bombs and destroyed all that stuff before we left.

So after we destroyed all that stuff, the fishing boats moved in because they were so light, they wouldn't hit the mine. So we all jammed into the fishing boats, in a fishing hold where they kept the catch, and we headed down to Pusan, South Korea. The military didn't have any quarters for us down there at all. They put us up in these South Korean cheap hotels. We had to sleep on the floor. They were infested with bugs and large rats. I couldn't sleep at night. I stayed awake. We carried our own blankets. We didn't have any mattresses, no pillow, and no nothing. Each of the military guys at that time carried a backpack with what we called a horseshoe blanket roll, so we had to live on that.

In 1952, I decided to get out of the Army after nine years of active duty. I got discharged out of the Army for approximately six months. I couldn't find a good job on the outside so I decided I should re-enlist in the Air Force. At that time I already had credit for nine years that counted toward my retirement. So I went to the Air Force in 1952 and I did some training on aircraft down at West Palm Beach, Florida. And then I decided that I'd like to go flying as a crew member, a load master.

I started flying around 1953. I flew in the United States here for a while. Then I was later on transferred overseas to Japan.

What kind of airplanes did you fly?

I first started up with a Globemaster C-124 hauling cargo over to the islands Kwajalein, Guam, and Hawaii. I did that for a long time and then I got transferred again back to Japan about 1960, somewhere along there.

Then I was assigned to a military reconnaissance, flying a C-130 turbo jet-type airplane, doing reconnaissance over North Vietnam in 1963. I would leave my wife and sons at Yokota Air Base, Japan, where I was stationed and I took off three weeks after every month. We would go to Bangkok, Thailand.

We stayed there. We had two ground crews and two air crews flying over there. We got up in the morning at around five, went out to the airport. We would have breakfast there, pick up a TV dinner. Then we'd go up for a 10-hour mission without coming down, flying around a circle in North Vietnam. Then we'd come back down after 10 full hours, not one minute after and not one minute before, exactly 10 hours. We had a lot of high-tech radios and stuff on board that airplane.

When you were flying 10 hours a day, what was it for?

Reconnaissance. Looking down on North Vietnam and seeing what they're doing. What we were doing was we flew up there around a circle. We'd have no marking on our airplane. All the windows were covered up so they couldn't identify us. They'd think maybe we belong up there.

One day, it did happen. Three Russian MiGs bumped us, one on the tail, one on the left wing, one on the right wing, and they flew really close to look us over. I don't know why they didn't order us to land. We were trained, in case they ordered us to land, to refuse them. If we're going to refuse them then they may fire a warning shot. At that time, we go in what we call Condition One. If we go in at Condition One, then I would stand back at the rear door and get ready to bail out. But if they should fire a warning shot, then I would be the first one to bail out.

We had about 6 or 8 high technicians onboard on that airplane. I would order them to follow me if we bail out. By the way, we carried two parachutes, one on the front, one on the rear. One we called a "one-man dinghy."

You have a one-man life raft in case we land in an ocean somewhere. If we bail out at that high altitude, the air is thin there, so in our main suit we carry a little oxygen bottle there. We'd have to freefall for maybe 10,000 feet or so before we put the oxygen bottle into use because it didn't carry that much oxygen. The air is really thin. If you use that oxygen up, you're going to be dead, so you don't use the oxygen until you get further down.

Another time I was up there, it was about noontime and I had just heated up a TV dinner for lunch for the commander, for the captain of the ship. I handed him the TV dinner while he was sitting in the cockpit there, eating on his lap. All of a sudden, he threw it on the cockpit floor and I was on a headset. We had to stay on a headset all during the flight to monitor and see what's going on. He threw it on the floor and I heard that the ground people—the ground intelligence people who were watching us every minute of the day while we're up there—they sent us a warning. They said, "Abort the mission, abort the mission, abort the mission now."

Apparently, the North Vietnamese had aimed a missile at us, and they could shoot us out at 50,000 feet. So the captain put the C-130 out on full throttle and we flew up a little higher and went back to Thailand. We didn't complete the mission that day. So the second crew took off the next day. We had quite a few incidents there. We don't carry any water when we bail out. We don't carry any food when we bail out. We rely on the ground people with a helicopter to monitor us and they will pick us up if we go down in the water or inland.

If we landed inland … normally, we'd get rid of the parachute before we got into the water, otherwise you'd drown. Then we'd inflate the one-man life raft to survive on. If we landed inland, we'd try to use these fake Elgin watches. We carried about six of them.

Fake watches?

Elgin watches, wristwatches. They were fake, cheap ones. We used that for bargaining food with the local people in the village until we get picked up. If they decided they didn't want the watch, we also carried little gold bars. People like gold bars there, so we carried little gold bars to try to bargain with them for food. The only things we carried were signal flares, to let the helicopter people looking for us know we were there. We'd fire up the signal flare, so we let them know where we landed.

Is this during the Vietnam War or before?

Before.

Before the Vietnam War? This was not considered during war yet?

We only carried a pistol and lighting flare. We didn't carry any rations—no water, no nothing. We relied on the rescue people to go pick us up.

Anyway, due to the sensitivity of that type of mission, we could only do it for one year because it was very dangerous. The Air Force figured that one year is enough. They would have another crew take over. When I got down, I went to Japan. I was assigned to a DC-6. We called it a C-118, four-engine prop, propeller-type aircraft. I was hauling supply and troops into South Vietnam. It was still really dangerous there. Our propeller airplane had to land like a jet and take off like a jet. The North Vietnamese people were trying to shoot the planes down when we were most vulnerable with small arms. Every time we landed, we had to take a pencil to check underneath the wings and see if there were any bullet holes in the airplane.

That was in 1963. That airplane was not designed to fly and land like a jet, but we had to do it. When we hit the runway, when we went in, we'd stay up pretty high and make a dive for the runway just to get away from the North, the bad people. When we took off, we'd sit on the runway and the pilot would put that plane at full throttle and have the brakes locked, then turn the brakes loose and we would climb like a jet.

One time I went over there, I was gassing the airplane on the wing and our helicopters were dropping the chemical Agent Orange. They dropped that stuff down to kill the vegetation on the on the ground so the North Vietnamese couldn't hide. I did that until 1963. I came back to the United States and started flying a smaller-type airplane. I was at Andrews Air Force Base and I started flying over Europe—Germany, France, Italy and stuff like that. That was better flying at the time. We had a lot of Embassy people and offices there, in Germany, Italy, France, places like that. I made Embassy runs, taking VIP people over their land. I made five trips overseas.

By this time, what year was it and how old were you?

I was drafted when I was 19. After all this, I was about 50 when I got out. I had 9 years active duty in the Army, 22 years active duty in the Air Force.

After 1963, somehow I went back overseas, back to Japan again, and then I stayed on flying status from 1953 to 1974. I went back to Japan and I left Japan in 1974 and got out, retired.

When did you get married?

1955, December.

Were you overseas?

I was here in the States and I was in the Air Force.

Do you want to share how you met your wife?

How I met her? On a blind date. Some of my military friends knew her. She was working for the state hospital in Washington. At that time, I was living in the McChord AFB barracks. One day, they invited me to go out there to meet her. One thing after another—here we are.

I ended up with 31 years of active duty with the U.S. Air Force and the Army. The major reason why I went back in is because I had 9 years in the Army and they told me I could retire and I could get credit for 9 years, so I was going to count for 20 years. For 20 years, they gave us 50% of your base pay, and if I went 30 years, I'd have 75%. I was shooting for 75%.

So I did a lot of work, three wars, and after I got out, I worked at the Portland Airport in security, checking baggage and stuff like that. I worked out there for about 9 years, off and on. Also my brother had a funeral escort business in Portland. So in between, by that time, I'd ride motorcycles, escort funerals in Portland. Yeah, I ride Harley Davidsons. I was close to 70, I think, at that time.

How old are you today?

Today? 88.

Lucky.

I got a disability from the VA, my hearing loss. When I was flying a C-130, a reconnaissance-type airplane, it made a lot of noise. I monitored engines' start and I monitor engines' shutdown with the powerful ground power turbine unit running right through my ear.

I could not wear ear protection because I had to listen to the cockpit. I had to tell the pilot up there the ground clearance. I had to check all that basic stuff like the hydraulic and pressures and all that stuff before, and I had to remember to give that to the pilot. If he said the pressure reading was this and that, I had to remember that. So when he went through the checklist really fast, when it came to my turn, I had to answer really quick and then I had to count the number of blades on the prop of a certain engine before the engineer put the mixture in.

Most of my life was involved in airplanes. I took a lot of training in West Palm Beach, Florida. Each type of airplane—I flew in six different types of airplane—each type I had to go to learn about it. Learn about just a little bit.

Your parents were farmers. Who are the earliest people in your family to come to America? Parents, grandparents?

I don't remember my father because he died when I was really young, but I understand that my mother was from California or somewhere. I don't know her history. I don't know none of her family. I don't know none of my father's family. The way I understood him, he jumped ship from China.

Around what time, what year, do you think?

That was before I was born. That's probably in the 1800s or something. I don't know much about him because he passed away when I was really young. He had an accident.

Did you have siblings? Who did you grow up with? Who raised you?

Myself. I started working when I was a young kid. I was about 8 years old; I was working at the farm, picking hops, picking berries, and stuff like that, making a few bucks. My mother worked a little bit too. My mother worked in a farm, picking hops and stuff like that.

How many brothers and sisters do you have?

I have two brothers and five sisters. They were all born here.

Did your siblings go into the military?

Yes. I had two brothers. [All] three of us went in the military. My two sons were both in the Air Force. My number two son is a Portland police officer, and my number one son, he works in a Diebold electronic firm in Oregon. My brother Willy was in the Army.

Mrs. Chinn: Bing [another brother] was in the Air Force.

In your family, did you speak Chinese or pretty much just all English?

I speak some. When I was in China, I learned a little bit of Mandarin, so I can understand Mandarin better than I can speak it, but I can speak some southern dialect, Cantonese. My mother used to speak a lot.

And in the Military, being Chinese, were you always one of the few?

I left the Chinese unit, the Flying Tigers, and went into the Air Force. I was the only Chinese around.

And did they treat you just like any—

Yeah. They treated me like everybody else. I was a crew member and had no problem at all. I didn't see any Orientals in there. When the war was over, they went back to laundries and restaurants. I didn't have a restaurant or laundry to go to so I went back in, and I don't remember seeing any Chinese other than myself. I was in with the white people all the way through.

Anything about being Chinese American or anything like that?

Mrs. Chinn: Oh, one thing: You know, where we're from there weren't that many Chinese. I mean there were a lot, but it was not like San Francisco or anything. One of the reasons that he wasn't discriminated against is he does not look Asian. If you see a picture of him in his early days, he really looks Caucasian. People even nowadays think he's got the Philippine extraction or something. In those days I think it made a little difference.

When you were growing up was there any discrimination? Was there any difference for Chinese Americans before the wars or after?

No, that's about it. You know, that's my life story. All of it spent—a lot of time was spent overseas. I had five overseas tours in a row, always involved in either the Flying Tigers, the Korean War, or the Vietnam War. I was at the wrong place at the wrong time. Every time they had a war they'd send Chinn over.

I remember mostly everything that I did in the Flying Tigers because that is stuck in my mind, I can't get it out. Every time a Flying Tiger comes around, I remember everything I did with The Flying Tigers.

Did you see yourself as more of a Chinese person or an American person, or equally both?

Well, both. I had worked with a lot of Chinese people [when I was in China with the Flying Tigers]. I think they're great. They're friendly and they're very nice, generous people. They're always smiling when they talk to you. I get along with them real good.

And the other Chinese Americans—When you first went to training were you surprised to see so many other Chinese Americans?

No, not at all. No problem I can think of. Sometimes they called me Spanish, or Russian—not Russian but Mexican. Some of them think I'm Mexican.

Mrs. Chinn: Where did you have basic training?

I had basic training in 1943 at Camp Barkeley, Abilene, Texas. Thirteen weeks.

Mrs. Chinn: You can tell her about Rosalie Clark, the nurse.

Oh. When I was in the military hospital [Harmon General Hospital] in Longview, Texas, in 1943 … after basic training I caught blood poison somehow out there in the desert, and anyway I was supposed to ship over to North Africa.

I had ended up in the hospital and my captain came up in the hospital and asked the nurse if I was ready to go, and the nurse told him, "No, he's still taking medication." So the captain says, "Well, we're going to North Africa with the infantry and we're going to have to leave him behind." So they left me at the hospital.

While I was in the hospital, I'll tell you how bad they needed troops in the Army. I was in the hospital barracks at about 9:30 at night. All of the lights had to go out. This soldier had a bunk right next to mine and every night he would bring a glass of water and put it by the nightstand. It didn't bother me at that

China, 1944. Drove a 2½ ton "wrecker" as the last vehicle in a 30-plus convoy

time. I thought maybe he needs a drink before he goes to bed. So one night it caught my eyes, I happen to be looking over and he was digging into his left eye, standing there with the lights out, and I can see, but he's real close. So he was digging in his left eye and he pulled out a marble ... a glass eye. He put it in a glass of water. So I said, "Golly, what are they doing? A guy with one eye was drafted. His number came up." They call these people 4-Fs, so they will never go overseas, they will never carry a rifle. They will do local work around a hospital or wherever.

Another time I went to the hospital for a final checkup, and before I left there I walked into the hospital ward and this other soldier was brought into the military hospital on a stretcher. He looked awfully sick and awfully pale. They put him in a military hospital bed, and he was a soldier, and he was drafted. So they needed people real bad that time. The drafting ...

What year was this?

That was in 1943, in Longview, Texas.

Mrs. Chinn: [The man with the glass eye] was Chinese.

So I give credit to his nurse. At that time the nurse seemed like she liked me for some reason because I played tricks with her. I was in the hospital bed. I knew when she came on duty. I'd let my leg hang along the side of the bed there and she'd come cover me up, push my leg back in there, so somehow we got acquainted. She saved my life. She told the captain that I wasn't ready to go to Africa, North Africa. So I stayed in the hospital until after they left. So this nurse got acquainted with me, and we were not supposed to fraternize with officers. She was an officer, a lieutenant. So every night when she got off of work, when I was in the barracks, I would walk her back to the barracks there, and we took a few pictures together. She's a little bit older than I am.

Mrs. Chinn: She was Caucasian. Tell Victoria about the guy that spoke Chinese.

Oh, there was another guy when I was in the hospital. This guy was from Texas and when I was in the hospital they put him in what they call Section 8. He don't want to speak English, he don't want to eat, and he's Chinese. So they asked me to go and talk to him. He was locked up because he didn't answer their questions and he refused to eat and he refused everything they told him to do. So they locked him up, they thought he was Section 8, he was crazy. So anyway, I went there and talked to him and he spoke very few words to me. He told me that he had a laundry in New York and he didn't want anything to do with the military. He was drafted.

Did he say it in Chinese or English?

He told me in Chinese. So anyway, I tried to translate to the doctor what he said. So one day about a week later they decided to discharge him. They gave him an honorable discharge because he wasn't qualified for the military because he couldn't speak English. But he could speak English. They gave him a train ticket and they gave me a Jeep and wanted me to take him out to the train station and make sure he got on the right train to go back to New York. When I got out there he said, "I'm okay, I'm okay." He says, "I'm all right." So he's as happy as the dickens. He spoke English—he spoke English better than I do. So he told me he's going back to his business—laundry, because his wife was running the laundry while they took him. So he shocked me. When I took him out there he said, "You go back to the base. I'm okay, I'm okay." So anyway, that's my life: 31 years of active duty, three wars.

Mrs. Chinn: Did you tell her about Korea? When you were in Korea? And it was so cold that—

Yeah, that I stayed in a foxhole there.

Sorry, a foxhole?

When I first got north, they didn't have any place for us to stay, so this other GI from Hawaii and I shared a foxhole there, way up in Hamhung. We didn't have any barracks there, so we stayed in the foxhole and watched for the Chinese and watched for the North Koreans coming down from the Manchuria border. So he'd take a nap and I'd be alert. We had a poncho over our head in the foxhole and it was pretty deep, about 5 to 6 feet low and side by side. So we had a poncho and when it rained and was cold and miserable we could only stand up, we couldn't sit down. We even aimed the rifle out, so if we see anybody coming across at night, we're supposed to shoot him. We don't know who they are.

Mrs. Chinn: What did you use for heat? How did you keep warm?

We wore a lot of clothes. They got military boots.

Mrs. Chinn: You told me you had a barrel.

Oh, when we were in the barracks we had to burn gasoline in the tent stove mixed with oil because we didn't have any kind of fuel. So we put motor oil mixed up with gasoline, and that was in the barracks. When we first started going north to Korea, it was so cold there, and miserable cold where we would keep our clothes on three weeks out of a whole month without taking no shower, no nothing. We were always on the move. Continuously on the move. All walking, foxholes, and stuff like that.

Mrs. Chinn: Tell Victoria about when you had to take the two spies back to Korea, and you couldn't tell the difference between the good Korean and the—

Oh, I have another story. When I was with the military intelligence there in South Korea, my commander sent me a letter that said, "You can't turn nothing down." Once your commander tells you to do something you have to do it. I didn't want to go.

I was picked to take the Jeep, go down to Seoul, and pick up three South Korean spies. I got a strip map to go down to Seoul to pick these guys up. They don't have any street names or nothing. I only got a strip map to go find these people.

Seoul was evacuated because the U.S. was going to bomb the capital of Korea, and so the U.S. evacuated everybody out of there immediately. So these three spies were hiding in one of the buildings there and I was supposed to pick them up and take them up to North Korea. They were supposed to go up there and gather information for our Army use. So anyway I found them.

It's real dark and spooky. I honk the horn and so they come out. I have my rifle ready on the left side. I don't know whether it's going to be South Koreans, or North Koreans playing games. So I have my rifle on my left side of the Jeep there, and I just let them know that I have a rifle there so in case they play any tricks then I was going to shoot it out with them.

Again, we don't have any radios and no communications. So, lo and behold, I load the three Koreans and start heading up north. I'm supposed to drop them off someplace up there, they didn't tell me exactly where. The further north I get … it … looks so isolated, it's open and there's no road. I have to go through the field. So I get real shaky. It's getting dark and my Jeep is held down with sand bags in the back in case I hit a mine. And so finally I get real, real scared as we get real close.

So I tell them get out, and if they didn't get out I was going to shoot them because I don't know for sure if they're South Korean. They're supposed to be South Korean. They're supposed to go up North and bring back information for our Army use, and so they come back as prisoners. They bring back information. They're marked on their body so they can identify themselves that they belong to South Korea and they're working for American Army. I was shaking. If I should blow a tire, or my Jeep went dead or something like that, I would be stuck out in the middle like a sitting duck. They would shoot me.

You didn't have to hand them over physically to anyone? You didn't have to bring them to the doorstep of something, or—

No.

You just had to put them in the general area?

No. No communication at all. They just told me to go north as far as I could, not exactly where to drop them off. I wouldn't know anyway, but I was already in the North.

So those guys were just supposed to find their own way somehow afterwards?

Uh-huh. So I get really shaky and nervous because they can take a pop shot at me anytime they want to because there are North Koreans hiding in there. So anyway, I drop them off and I head back and I keep praying. I say, "What happens if I have a flat tire or the engine breaks down?" I would be stuck out there by myself.

I couldn't call, no walkie-talkie, no communication to contact my people, so finally, lo and behold, I made it back to the South. When I got back to the South my unit started moving up North, so I had to go back up North again. These three South Koreans were supposed to go there and mix up with a North Korean and bring back information—see what they're doing, how many troops they've got there, where they're located, where they're training, how many guns they have, and so on and so forth. They're supposed to bring that information back to the U.S. Army to use.

What year was this?

That was in 1951. Anyway, it wasn't any fun with all them…. All three wars were very tight on me…. She [Mrs. Chinn] saw the letter I got at home. I was ordered to go. You can never say no to an officer when they order you to do something. You are a GI—you're government issue. So you can't say anything. When they tell you to do something, whether it's life or death, you have to go, no doubt about it. If you don't, they lock you up in the brig.

Mrs. Chinn: He was invited by General Marshall to go to a dance, and he doesn't dance. He didn't want to go. Tell Victoria, you know, the invitation you got from the General, when you were in China.

Oh, yeah. When I was in Nanjing, China, five star General Marshall was in charge of the Chinese command, and that's when I was over there training the Chinese Army engineer troop how to operate heavy equipment, road building equipment, bulldozer graters and stuff like that.

But General Marshall for some reason had invited me out to his house for a luncheon. I was shocked. I was a staff sergeant there at that time, and I got a letter from General Marshall, five star general, inviting a staff sergeant to his house for dinner.

I told my boss, the sergeant in charge of me, that I didn't really want to go because I'm a staff sergeant and he's a five-star general, so the sergeant told me, "I'll whip your butt if you don't go." He said when a general invites you like that, and there's hundreds and thousands of troops out there, and they pick you, you've got to go.

So they gave me a Jeep and I drove to the General's house there and he had a party, a kind of buffet party. He'd invited several military guys there and each GI had a Chinese girl escort. The minute after I shook hands with Mrs. Marshall at the door, and General Marshall, the aide took me inside and they assigned me a Chinese girl for my escort. So anyway, yeah, General Marshall, I got his invitation.

My wife's aunt was in Nanjing and was a warrant officer in the U.S. Army, and didn't get invited, and here … I'm just a general GI, and for some reason or another, I was invited. I was the only one out of my company that was invited. I got the invitation card at home.

Mrs. Chinn: The invitation is just a little mimeograph thing but it has his autograph on it.

Okay, do you want to show us the dog tags?

Oh, the dog tag? At that time in 1943 we didn't have any ID card, none whatsoever. If we went on a pass or something, it was just a written note by the NCO or the sergeant or something like that. You had to carry a dog tag. Nowadays they have ID cards with pictures, but at that time they didn't. Oh, I might as well tell you about the pay then. In 1943 all recruits were getting $50 a month, and if you had a family at home to take care of, you had to make out a form, so some money came out of your $50 paycheck.

If you made a form you had to buy a $10,000 life insurance in case you couldn't make it home. So more money comes out of that paycheck. We got paid cash every month. So I had a form and also had a $10,000 life insurance for my mother, and my final pay came out to $27.50 a month at that time. All recruits were getting $50 a month.

Was that a lot of money at that time?

Well, you could buy a hamburger for 15¢ and a bottle of pop for a nickel then.

So that's a lot of money.

When I first come out of flight school there, after 150 hours check-out they would issue me a wing. If I flew 7 years straight through I would get the star—15 years straight through, then I'd get the wreath of the star. That made me a chief air crew member.

Al and actress Jane Russell on a
USO tour during holidays

Actress Jane Mansfield, a bit player
on the same tour as Jane Russell

* * *

This is my VA card. I met with Jane Russell while I was in Japan.

How did you meet Jane Russell?

I was in Japan. I was flying then and she and Bob Hope and all of them people went over there on a USO type of show. So I have to fly them over to Okinawa and all the other little island places around Japan, and she was on my airplane. One time she wasn't feeling good and I took her in the compartment and I gave her an oxygen mask and I said, "How do you feel?" and she said, "Not so good." So what had happened was we got these portable oxygen bottles. I didn't turn the valve on. I forgot to turn the valve on. So later on I didn't tell her—I go monkey around there and I turn the valve on and I say, "How do you feel now?" and she said, "Okay." but I had the valve closed.

Mrs. Chinn: You almost killed her.

Al Chinn: So that's how I met her. *(Laughs)*

CHAPTER SIX

Earl Jung (1924–   )
U.S. Army Air Force

Earl Jung grew up in an era that discriminated against multicultural families. He was born in St. Louis, Missouri, and moved to Chinatown in Manhattan, New York, at the age of five. During the War, he was part of the Chinese American unit 407th Air Service Squadron of The 14th Air Service Group. His career was in education. He received a degree in fine arts from Hunter College (he entered its first co-ed class) and attended Teachers College at Columbia University. He was a principal at Bushwick Outreach Center and is known as an innovator in art and education. Though he never taught art, he has a collection of work from his painting career stretching from 1959 to 2005. (This chapter was written with the help of Gloria Jung.)

I was born in St. Louis, Missouri, in May 1924. My father was Chinese, a doctor from China who spoke Taishanese and no English. My mother's background was shrouded in secrecy since she was part black (unacceptable in those times), Indian, Scottish, and Spanish. Her maiden name was Bennett. My father came to New York presumably looking for more Chinese and a better life. He was very involved with a Chinese association on Mott Street. He was also a very well-respected man, but not a family man. I was younger than five when I was sent to live with my father in New York. It was an all-male Chinatown. I lived with Chinese men, and was alone a lot. The association fed me. Looking back, I see how difficult it was not speaking English and not looking Chinese.

Family Portrait, 1944

Top row (left to right):
Jung, Sun (uncle)
Jung, Hen Yee (Earl)
Bennett, Lucille (mother)
Lum, Mei Gok (sister)
Jung, Fon Ton (brother)
Yee, Jimmy (brother-in-law)

Bottom row (left to right):
Jung, Gokmun (brother)
Tlach, Gum Goke (sister)
Shewchuk, Hon Su (niece)
Jung, Hen Sou (brother)
Jung, Bat Sun (father)

Young Earl Army portrait   Earl at his 75th birthday celebration

Life was very male-oriented until a year later, when my mother and older sister came. That was good for me, because now it wasn't only men, and there was another child. When mom came, she held the family together with my father's brother (Zee Sook). We had a full Chinese brother from our father's first wife in China, two sisters from my mother, and three brothers from the same father and mother—six children altogether.

As a teenager, I wanted to become a lawyer but my father said people don't trust Chinese lawyers, so I couldn't be a Chinese lawyer. I wanted to learn a lot. There was lots of cultural tension and obstacles. Lower Manhattan then was Chinatown and Little Italy. There was a lot of strife between Chinatown and Little Italy. My cultural strife was that I wasn't accepted by either group. I befriended a half-Chinese friend and married a half-Chinese woman when I got out of service. It was a fairly short-lived marriage. We have a daughter, Camille. I am [now] married to Gloria Jung, and we have a daughter Maria. I was 64 when Maria was born, possibly making her the youngest of her generation.

When I was inducted into the U.S. Army, I was placed with a diverse group of young men. Then my name was called out, and because it was a Chinese one, I was removed and placed in an all-Chinese unit. At first, I was disappointed that I had lost my chance to be in a diverse group. I thought finally I was not going to feel ostracized by the Chinese, or be pigeonholed as a non-Chinese or a white person. But in the long run, once I was accepted, I developed lifelong friends and it was all good.

We traveled to CBI: China-Burma-India. There was an incident. One day at noontime, everyone was in their tents and I was cleaning my rifle and I didn't realize it was loaded. There wasn't much light. I accidentally shot it and the bullet went straight through a number of tents. The bullet went right over my friend Tommy Moy's head. If he didn't lie down at the moment and was sitting up sewing as he usually was, he would have died. I didn't hurt or kill him. I felt like the luckiest man in the world.

I was very patriotic and felt strongly about bringing Hitler down. After the military, I used the GI Bill to study art, and studied great painters of the abstract expressionist schools. Because I'm Chinese American, I was on the outskirts of the art community, and they didn't believe Chinese could paint. I felt I was overlooked. Now that East and West are meeting in a much more compatible way I believe my art might get the recognition I deserve.

I loved the 407, being in the military, and going to reunions, even though it's been hard to travel these days.

I felt strongly about going to college. I received my degree for Fine Arts from Hunter College on the GI Bill, and entered its first co-ed class. I then attended Teachers College at Columbia University. I have a collection of work from my painting career stretching from 1959 to 2005. One of the 407 members, Gene Wong, has one of my works in his home.

In my career as an educator, I created a program called Peer Group Leadership. I also taught math, and was a principal at Bushwick Outreach Center, where I was asked to supervise teens who were previously incarcerated. I took my standard poodle to class and played classical music for them. I created the Peer Group program and it was through this program that I met my current wife, who was also a teacher.

Note: At the time this was written, Earl's memory had been altered due to a stroke. It was fortunate that he had told these stories very often to his wife, so that she was able to recount them for him.

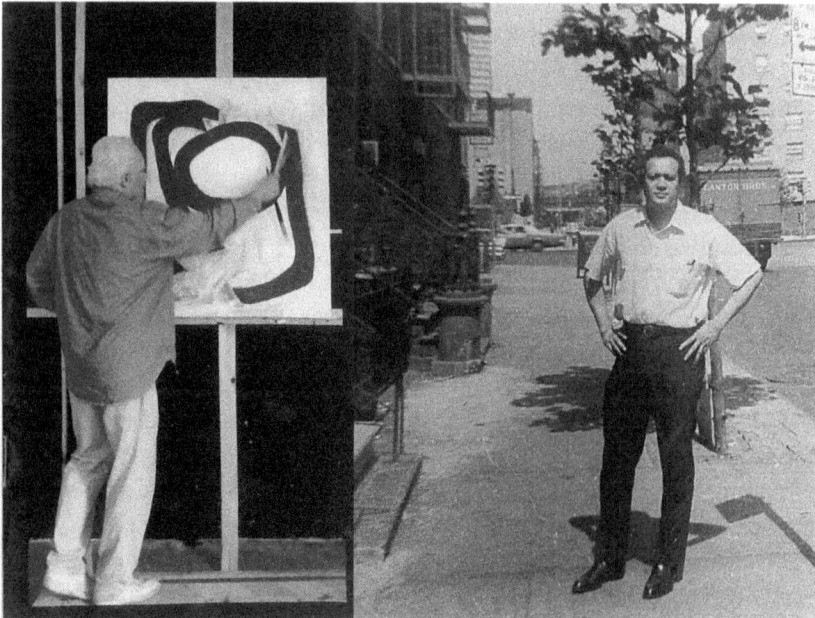

Earl painting in his
studio in his late 70s

Earl outside his first
NYC studio in the 1960s

CHAPTER SEVEN

Tom Wah Sun Lew 劉華新 (1917–   )
U.S. Army

Tommy Lew was born in Oakland, California and sent back to China to get a Chinese education. With turmoil in China, including having a brother kidnapped by bandits, he was sent back to the United States at the age of 17, and he describes "being born again," sitting in a first grade class, learning a new language and new customs. After the War, he worked at the Alameda Naval Air Station until retirement. He talks about post–World War II legislation to push for further civil rights for Chinese Americans. He was commander of the VFW East Bay Chinatown Post 3956 in Oakland in 1986 and 1991.

I was born in the United States, in Oakland in 1917. I have four brothers and six sisters, eleven of us altogether. I'm the youngest of the sons; I'm number nine, and there are two girls younger than I am.

My father was a part-owner of a fruit-packing cannery in Oakland. That was the biggest Chinese-owned business in the Bay Area at that particular time. It packed whatever fruit was in season. Whether it's for Del Monte, or whatever company, you fill the order, then you put their label on it. A lot of business came from England. Most of these cans were actually shipped to England. As far as I know we were the only Chinese-owned cannery around. I think we might have had some Caucasian partners—but it was mostly Chinese-owned.

When I was five, my parents brought me back to China. The idea of the older generation was you got to bring your kids back to get some Chinese education, otherwise they're going to become foreigners. That's a no-no. If you're Chinese, you've got to remain Chinese—you've got to get some Chinese culture. That was the thinking of my parents' generation. We always intended to be back, naturally, the U.S. is our home. You just wanted to get enough Chinese culture and then we would come back to live in the United States.

I guess my father was the first one from my family to come to the U.S. Then my family went back to China in 1922. I was really too young to realize what the political situation was. You know, you don't pay any attention to that kind of stuff when you are five or six years old.

We lived in Guangzhou. Most of the time, actually, we lived in Gung Yit, a little city. We built a two-story house there. I think we rented out the downstairs part of it to somebody else, and we lived upstairs. We were never hungry. We were fairly well-off.

My parents continued their business in the U.S. while we were in China. My oldest brother (Joe) had a family of his own established in the U.S. He took over the business end of affairs. And then I think the cannery later closed and reestablished in Antioch, a farming community; it's where all the fruits and vegetables are grown, closer to the source of supply for the canning business than Oakland.

China was in turmoil in the '20s. Did anything happen to you or your family then?

Yes. As a matter of fact, my brother Bill was kidnapped by bandits while he was in boarding school in China, and we had to pay a good ransom to get him back. You had to be fairly well-to-do to send your kids to boarding school, so that they could go to school and go to the dormitory. He was held maybe six months. They raided the boarding school, took the kids ... during some kind of festival. My brother George also went to that school at the time but he had gone home for the festival break.

The bandits were able to kidnap people from school, and the government, the police, apparently didn't have the ability to rescue the people that were kidnapped.

When I came back (to the U.S.) I was 17 and sent to Newman (a California farming community). My brother George was in charge (living in Oakland) at the time. I guess he wanted to get me out of the way and he sent me to—There are some Chinese folks from my general area in China, they have a restaurant (in Newman). I guess there must have been about a half a dozen or so people working in the restaurant, the owner and then the others. We lived there. We worked there, and then they have in the back of the restaurant a little house, and it had rooms people lived in. And they're kind of a place to send new arrivals to from our village area to go to (elementary) school there (to learn English, especially) and then work at the restaurant.

When I was 17, it was time to get out and earn my own living. I didn't have anybody to support me. I didn't have any parents anymore. I had to come back here and earn my own living, you know? I had my brother George here, and then I stayed with him and then that's about it. He was not well off. He was just working as a janitor, and he rented a kind of—a rooming house kind of place. And then we just struggled along.

The cannery business that my family had went bankrupt in the Depression. It sustained my family from the turn of the century up to the Depression. It was run by my two brothers (Joe and Wah Chuck), and they were the sons of the first mother.

My parents were dead years before I came to the United States. That's what I was told. I was too young to understand. My father died of heat stroke. He was building a new house or was supervising construction of a new house in China and he died of heat stroke. My mother, as far as I can remember, died of breast cancer in China. As far as I can remember I came back to the U.S. by myself.

Sgt. Wah Lew, China, 1944

I was natural-born. I had a birth certificate, so I didn't have any problem in that regard. Although they did keep me in Angel Island overnight to process. I guess that was the practice. They throw you in and lock you up, until they're ready to process your papers. I was kept either one or two nights. It took about 18 days at that time to journey from China to the U.S.

I didn't know one word of English when I came back. I had to start all over. It was like … being born again, like coming to a brand new world where I don't even know the language, where I don't even know the customs.

I was 17 and I was in the class with the first graders. In Newman they didn't have the special classes like they had in San Francisco or Oakland for foreign students. In Newman, in a small town, you don't know anything. *(Laughs)* You go with the kids to the first grade.

Well, the War broke out in 1941. I was drafted into the Army in March 1941. That was a few months before the war started, but they already started the Selective Service. I was 24 years old, and I got drafted right away. I spent almost six years in the Army. I didn't have a chance to finish high school before they drafted me. I earned my high school credentials after I came back from the service actually.

If they didn't draft you, what do you think you would have wanted to do next, in your life?

Probably, I'd go wash the dishes in one of the restaurants. Maybe I'd learn enough English and get a better job and then do something else.

I worked in Alaska during the summer vacation time. This was before World War II happened, in approximately 1935–36. That was the salmon cannery season—in the summer, you see.

I also worked for families as a houseboy, live-in. I'd do their chores and so on and go to school and then I'd come home and do whatever they needed done around the house. Yeah, for a Caucasian family. Oh, they were nice, you know? They treated me okay with the work and things I had to take care of, whatever housework there was to be done. A lot of people in the area hired Chinese school kids in my similar situation. They're live-in help, you know? I got a bunk in the basement, and lived in there.

I know that some people said they were eager to join the Army because they wanted revenge on Japan for invading China. Did you have any of those feelings?

Well, of course there's there's that kind of feeling. We all hated Japan for invading China, and they also invaded the United States. They bombed Pearl Harbor, remember? So they were a common enemy to both China and the United States.

Were you ever in combat?

No. I never shot at Japanese in my life.

Where were you when the Pearl Harbor bombing happened?

I was already in the service. I was in the kitchen having breakfast and someone told me that the Japanese attacked Pearl Harbor. I said, "What's Pearl Harbor?" I didn't know where or what Pearl Harbor was. Anyway, I found out soon enough!

So when they drafted you, did they put you immediately in the Chinese American outfit, or in some other one first?

No, I was in Camp Roberts, a mostly Caucasian outfit in California. But then most Chinese, at the time, instead of doing other duties, were mostly in the kitchen, as cooks, you know? That was the thinking of the Caucasians—Chinese are good cooks. As far as I'm concerned, it was okay. It was a good duty. A cook, you work one day and then you get a day off. You work every other day.

If you were a minority you were either an orderly or you were a cook. The people in the better jobs or higher positions always seemed to be the White man.

Camp Roberts was a basic training center. Normally people come in for basic training in 13 weeks and they ship out to someplace else. I ended up remaining there as part of the permanent cavalries there, that's what they called it.

Tom Lew in military uniform with four of his
brothers, circa 1942.

Then a new training center opened up in Arkansas. Part of the cavalry, the
permanent force in Camp Roberts, was transferred over to Arkansas to run the
new camp that opened in Springfield, Illinois. They were putting this group together that eventually became the 14th Air Service Group of the 14th Air Force
(The Flying Tigers). The Chinese Americans, some of them were sent there,
and some of them volunteered to be part of it. General Claire Chennault headed
the Flying Tigers, the American Volunteer Group [AVG, that was training the
Chinese Air Force in China] and he wanted a group of Americans that could
also speak Chinese. So he made a call for Americans who could speak Chinese,
which were of course Chinese Americans. I was part of the group that answered
that call. General Wittemyer was the commander of the American forces in
China at that time, and called for it, and our outfit was formed.

In Arkansas, were Blacks and Whites segregated?

Generally speaking, yeah. It was very much segregated in Arkansas, in the
Deep South. In Camp Robinson I was, of course, in the outfit with the Whites.
But there were no Blacks in our outfit. There was a black outfit in Camp Rob-
inson that was separate from us. They were all Blacks.

And Chinese people were generally considered white?

Yes.

When it came time to transfer to the Chinese American unit, did you do it just because you wanted to see what that was like, or was there some special incentive?

I think I liked the idea of going with these units to serve in China rather than the possibility of shipping over to Europe, you know? In the Army, you could be sent anyplace. This way, when I volunteered to be with this group, I had a good chance I would be going to China instead of the other way around.

I had a sister and some distant relatives in China. But I didn't get to see them. They were in a different part of China. I was in Kunming and the Chungking area. My sister lived in Guangdong Province. I was a supply sergeant in the Headquarters Squadron in the 14th Air Service Group. My job was to take care of all the soldiers' needs: their clothing, shoes, their guns, ammunition, whatever supply a soldier needs, it's my job to furnish it to them.

Was it unusual or special for you to be with so many other Chinese American men?

I felt good. I was in a mixed outfit, all races, before I transferred in there, but I was comfortable.

I remember riding in a convoy, driving into Japanese-held territory. We actually crossed the line ... we were on the way into a camp in Cheng Yi. We were actually getting ready to go in, and there were MPs there outside and we were going to go into the camp, but an air raid was taking place and they wanted to disperse everybody. So we kept on going, away from the station, and then we realized we'd gone too far and then came back. If we had kept on going another few more miles we would have ended up with the Japanese army.

Pretty much the rest of the time was mostly peaceful. The Japanese were pretty much driven off in the air and didn't come in anymore. You know, after the Flying Tigers drove them out of the air, there were no easy pickings anymore. Before the Flying Tigers got in there, they came in just for the hell of it sometimes, dropped a bomb or two, and killed a lot of people. And then after the Flying Tigers moved into the area there was no more of that kind of activity. They didn't want to pick a fight.

In Hunan Province they cooked with lots and lots of peppers. We had some China cooks to do the kitchen work. They do what they're supposed to for the Americans. But when they finish for the Americans, they cook for themselves and that's ... when things get hot. *(Laughs)* When they cook their own stuff the peppers are just so strong. It's strong enough to drive me out of the kitchen!

For the outfit that consists of Chinese Americans, they would cook whatever to our own tastes. The Chinese American Mess Sergeant would trade our potatoes with a Caucasian outfit for their rice, so we'd get more rice.

I used to run across Chou Enlai from time to time. Chou Enlai was part of the leadership that was in collaboration with the Allied powers. Chou Enlai later became premier of China.

Well, the happy time for me while I was in the military was when I went over to Peking and met up with my wife, and then we got married and had a family. You know, it was part of the process of my life. I stayed in a 1-year exten-sion after I was eligible to come back—to be discharged.

I met my wife when I was stationed in Peking, and there was this guy, John Wong, he's from Peking. As a matter of fact, he was going to school in the United States when he got drafted. He was in our outfit, and he introduced me to look up some of his old friends in Peking. So this friend introduced me to my wife eventually. And she was a nurse in this hospital, and this doctor I was introduced to ended up getting us, my wife and me, together. That's how things worked out. Yes, she's considered a War Bride.

She worked in the other base hospital as a registered nurse for four years. She spoke English well. She was born in Qinhuangdao (秦皇島, the Eastern end of the Great Wall, in the Bohai Sea), and was raised in Beijing, was from a prominent Beijing family. She went to Peking Union Medical College, which is a Rockefeller-granted college. So it was required for all the students there to speak English. That's why she was fluent in English. And she also spoke Mandarin. But when she came to the United States she had to learn Cantonese, because all the relatives spoke Cantonese. In fact all the Chinese in America then were all Cantonese. There were really very few Mandarin-speaking Chi-nese, if any at all. Although her family is Cantonese, they just didn't speak a lot of Cantonese at home as she was growing up (because they lived in Northern China).

After the war, when I was still in China, I went back to the village to find my older sister Jenny. My father had taken his wife and younger children back to China in March 1922 and then died that autumn. My mother died a couple of years later and my older sister Jenny took care of raising me. I returned to the U.S. in the early '30s, but Jenny stayed in China, married, and was widowed during the war, with two kids. Nobody knew where she was. So I went look-ing for her, and I was able to find her. I took her to the American Counsel in Guangzhou and got some help from them, and eventually she got passage back into the States. The American Counsel gave them financial assistance and loans to eventually get passage in the troopships and come back to this country. There wasn't much of any kind of commercial transportation right after the war, you know? So people with connections in the military got their family transported in troopships to come back.

Because she was also an American citizen and born here, she was entitled to the help from the American Counsel. That's what the American Counsel is supposed to do, help their own citizens in a foreign country. At that time, there wasn't flying, you traveled by ship in those days.

My sister's younger son Warren didn't come back, though. He stayed in Hong Kong, but came to the U.S. later. You had to be born before a certain date to be eligible to come back, and I think he missed the date by a day or two and had to wait a long time before he could come. He had family in Hong Kong that he stayed with until he was reunited with his mother and sister later. He actually

On the 14th Air Force Reunion China Tour in 2010. At the Flying Tigers Exhibit at the Overseas Chinese Museum in Jiangmen, China, Tom points to a wartime picture of himself.

had a private bill sponsored in Congress. That's how he got over. That was not in a public law but by a bill forwarded through a local congressman. I was kind of the project champion. Being a veteran, we have access sometimes to some legal advice on how to go about and how to get things done. Well, I had come back from the war and joined the VFW. Yes, I was active—pretty active for a while.

I was VFW commander of that Chinatown post in Oakland in 1986 and 1991. The post, Eastbay Chinatown Post 3956, was founded in 1959. I think I joined in the 1960s. The VFW was in existence since back to the Spanish-American War.

And was the VFW in some way partially responsible for the repeal of the Exclusion Acts?

As a matter of fact, it was. It was a member of our post who initiated that (David Wong), and he got the Congressman George P. Miller pushing it. And this fellow [Wong] actually had a self-interest in it. He wanted to get his mother over here from the old country, and that was the way he went about it, and it got through and it benefited everybody. We got the legislation eventually passed to allow the GIs to bring their families over from China. David's vision was to further civil rights for Chinese Americans and Chinese American veterans in terms of immigration law and fair treatment in the community.

VFW is a veterans organization. It represents veterans and makes sure benefits like VA Hospital benefits and GI Bill benefits are not lost.

After the war, I went back to Oakland in September 1946. My first son Morgan was born in the States at Permanente Hospital in Oakland.

When I went to look for houses, there were certain areas where Chinese weren't really allowed to buy. It wasn't a hard and fast rule, but it was well known, and it was discrimination. But there were no laws against discrimination then.

There was a house for sale on Huntington Street that said "Open House," and we wanted to go in and take a look. And the real estate agent said, "I can't show it to you." The realtors were the gatekeepers. The realtor wouldn't show us the house, but the owner of the house did. We ended up buying that house.

We wanted to live in a better neighborhood, you know? Just like anybody else, we happened to like the neighborhood. You don't necessarily want to live there in Chinatown. You want to live in a residential area. This was, like, 1954 or 1955 when Morgan was 6 or 7 years old, entering second grade.

What job did you take when you came back after the Army?

Well, the only job that didn't discriminate against us was a government job. My first job was in the naval supply and I later turned over to Alameda Naval Air Station. This was a civil service job. The business world outside of Chinatown wasn't really open to us at that time. We pretty much had to work for the government to have a decent job. Civil Service does not discriminate. Most of the people in our situation went to work for the government.

I retired when I was 56 or 57. With Civil Service you get credit for military time, too. So I think I got 25 or 28 years or something like that. I forgot.

I consider myself just as much Chinese as American. Being a Flying Tigers veteran has been a big part of my life. I spent almost six years in the military. That's a pretty big chunk of anybody's life. Many of my friends are also veterans. I go to the majority of Flying Tiger reunions. My Mahjong group friends are also mostly veterans, whether they're Tigers or not, they're all in the VFW, Veterans of Foreign Wars. So it's a very close-knit group. And I play Mahjong quite a bit; it's a big part of my life.

The Chinese government on this trip [The Chinese American Flying Tigers Veterans and Friends' China VIP Trip in Guangzhou] has been honoring you as VIPs with these very fancy dinners and a lot of media attention. Was this how China reacted throughout or just more so recently?

I don't remember being paid much attention before, so I guess that's more of a recent realization of the service that we have done for the country, that they thought enough of us to [celebrate us this way]. I don't remember if the American government paid attention to us like this.

CHAPTER EIGHT

Mack Pong 余啓迪 (1920–   )
U.S. Army Air Force

Mack Pong, 93, has organized Chinese American Flying Tigers reunions in different cities around the country for more than 50 years, taking the crucial role of keeping friendships and the history of Chinese American veterans in World War II alive. Friends with everyone he meets, he can remember the name and face of every veteran who served in the all-Chinese 407th Air Service Squadron of the 14th Air Force, especially since he was the Army mail carrier. He lives in San Francisco. Excerpts come from our conversation in 2008, in a joint interview with Daniel Huang, who wrote a thesis on Chinese American vets in World War II.

I grew up in Fort Worth, Texas. I was born there in 1920. I believe we were the only [Chinese] family that had kids. We were four boys, my father, and mother. But my father passed away in 1933. He was only 39 years old. He had appendicitis. In those days it was fatal, but now it's cured very easily.

That was in 1933, and my widowed mother was trying to take care of us as best she could during the Depression. My mother did all kinds of chores that she could get. She took in laundry and did shirts and so forth. Everything was by hand at home. We did it from the house, and an old store.

In those times cities were small. We got a whole house. But I think the one we lived in did not have hot water. Of course the summers were harsh, up to 100°, so it wasn't needed. But whenever we needed water we had to boil it in big pots.

My maternal grandparents lived in San Francisco. In 1935 they suggested that my mother come out to San Francisco and take a look. I think at that time my uncle was getting married, and my mother wanted to attend the wedding ceremonies. She came out with my younger brother, but then they decided that they would stay there. The rest of us, the three, we boarded the train from Texas and went to San Francisco.

The Chinese families in Fort Worth, we were—well, it shouldn't have been—they were very clannish. The Yees stick with the Yees; the Mas with the Mas; the Ngs with the Ngs. Because, in those days, immigrants from China, they couldn't go outside of their clan. It was the Depression and there was not enough work, so you had to stick to your own clan's restaurants and laundries and small mom-and-pop groceries.

Mack Pong with Squadron flag at Chihkiang

The Chinese-owned restaurants in Forth Worth were all American cuisine. There was no Chinese food at that time. That's why we grew up with American food and we longed for American food. There wasn't a Chinatown in Forth Worth. If there was, it might consist of a couple of living quarters.

No, there wasn't discrimination against the Chinese-owned businesses. Well, there may have been isolated incidents, but we didn't have enough people to be discriminated against. If they want a target, they want to target a big audience, they don't want to target just a few. Because they wouldn't get any publicity out of it. I mean, that's my opinion. But then we encountered some discrimination, but we would just let it go into one ear and out the other.

One family, the Ma clan, had a regular restaurant uptown. During lunchtime, they catered to the office crowd so it was jam-tied, and toward the evening, they had evening patrons, families. My family, the Yee clan—they had the restaurant that was further down, and we catered to bachelors, pensioners and people making a little less money. Our restaurant was all-American. A regular menu with roast turkey, roast beef, and meat loaf, fish, chicken—the whole variety. No Chinese. They might throw in some chop suey or chow mein and noodles, that's all.

Each clan was only about 20 people. Restricted [Chinese] immigration was in effect. They could not bring their wives over. Even the Mas and Ngs, they made money, but they couldn't do it. I think Mr. Ng, toward the later years—say around '36 or '37—they may have gotten around to it by—I don't know by which method. They were related somehow [to somebody with influence] or—Well, I was a young kid; I didn't understand those arrangements then.

My mother was able to come because she was an original, see? Her family had two boys and one girl. In those days you had to register with Immigration who was born in China. My maternal grandfather, he put down—He made a boy out of her, see. Instead of registering her as a girl, they registered her as a boy when she immigrated. I don't know how that worked. It was kind of an intricate setup.

Before you immigrate—I don't know whether you heard of it—they ask you a lot of trick questions. Whether this was located north or this was located south, how many windows their house had.

Ninety percent of the immigrants were paper sons. My grandfather came earlier, but my mother had to wait a couple of years. I don't know what the arrangement was at that time. They never explained it to me.

There were quite a few Chinese before us in Fort Worth. There were a lot of them here in the 1900s, 1915. A lot of them worked on the railroads in the 1800s. We were following them.

My parents came to Fort Worth because the Yees (my clan) had a restaurant in the Colony in Fort Worth. In those days you could not be selective, you had to go where you could. *(Laughs)* Wong, K. Scott, who wrote this book, *Americans First*, he even asked me, he says, "Why did you go to Texas?" He didn't understand that too. I said, "You had to go there." The other clans would not take you in, unless you were so special, you could do hard work and this and that. That's my explanation on it.

I lived in Fort Worth until I was 15, until 1935. What was growing up there like? Well, we were students that went to school, came home, and then we had home chores hereabout. Nothing spectacular, just a regular childhood. We sold newspapers and magazines, any work that you could get. I was the only Chinese in my school. My classmates and I spoke to each other and got along. There's always a bully, even in those days. But they didn't bother me. There were no black kids. They were segregated. Texas is a southern state.

The Chinese were integrated with Whites in Texas. But in some parts of Mississippi they considered the Chinese as more inclined to be in the Black schools. There were quite a few Chinese in Mississippi, in the towns where the Mississippi River flows through—they call it the Mississippi Delta—and they ran groceries that catered to the Blacks. If the town was small enough, they had to cater to the Whites, everybody had to come to them.

The Chinese kids who were raised down there, they have quite a Southern accent. There's Charlie See Lum Jr., Fred Cole; they were from the Arkansas side of Memphis. You know Memphis is Tri-State—Mississippi, Arkansas and Tennessee—right in that corner there. They all spoke with a Southern accent. Some of the fellows *(laughs)* from the West Coast, they were kind of surprised.

You talked about isolated acts of discrimination. What were some of those?

Well, we couldn't fight it because we were alone. You had to take it. Because we were in business, we had to make a living. Oh, there's another thing I want to bring up: In those days people were lucky to get something to eat. There was no work. Yet there was very, very little crime. Not like good times like these, and then there's crime.

We slept with our doors open, even in the poor district. So that's why I complain. In those days we never had any trouble. Yet now you have all kinds of trouble. We had no unemployment insurance, we had no welfare, and we had no food distribution. We were on our own, sink or swim. But of course food was cheap, 8¢ a dozen eggs. But you've got to have 8¢. Pork chops, 10¢ a pound or sometimes two pounds for 15¢, you've got to have 15¢. Bread, four loaves for a nickel; and it was fresh, piping hot from the oven.

We made the best to survive. As Tom Brokaw said, we were the greatest generation. *(Laughs)*

My father was more or less a partner of the restaurant he worked at. They had to pitch in and put out the initial money to open up. I worked at the restaurant after school if they needed me.

There was no dating because we had no money then. Dating, you've got to have a few cents, a nickel anyway.

We'd lived in Texas for so long, when we moved to San Francisco we found it strange. Chinatown was very crowded. We had the whole house [in Texas], whereas when you come to Chinatown you're lucky to get two rooms. So it's the difference from a big place to small.

When we came out to San Francisco, my maternal grandfather and grandmother [already living there] remained for another year, or year and a half. Then they went back to China for good. That was around 1937. In those days they had land in China in the village, and that was their home. They did not consider America their home.

My mother, she said that this is the best country in the world. She said, "Don't let anybody kid you, despite the Depression and everything." She said, "in China you may have had a better time, but—" Well, she had a little vision. She said, "This is not going to develop. You'd be winding up as a peasant." A lot of people did send their kids back to China. But my mother was against that. She said that in this country, if you were a ditch digger you would be better than the ruling class in China. *(Laughs)*

My grandparents went back to their village, Toisan. All Chinese [in America] at that time were from the Pearl River Delta. In those days [families in China] had to depend upon their [husbands and sons to immigrate to] America to send them money back to China, remittances. Otherwise, they'd starve to death.

But now of course everything has changed. You've got [Chinese] people [in America] from the North, South, West, and from all over China. In those days the immigrants from Northern China, like Shanghai and Beijing, were all of the professional class—professors, doctors, scientists, and commercial people. They did not have to go through the paper son business because if you were accepted as a merchant or scholar, then you could come in.

Daniel Huang: What was your outlook on life? Did you feel you didn't have a chance to do as much because you were Chinese or because of your economic status?

We just went along with it. We couldn't fight it. Even when I was about to graduate from San Francisco, the high school counselor told me "You know your chances are limited." "Yes, I do. I do know, I understand." So they even tried to discourage you from going to school. Not all of them, but some. Well, I made up my own mind. I didn't listen to them all the time. But we had no jobs. We had to work in restaurants and laundries and grocery stores. And gambling houses too. Don't forget that the Chinese were running big gambling houses. We had college graduates who were working in restaurants. They couldn't get a job. So we were trapped. We couldn't get out of Chinatown. But from World War II on, everything opened up because they had to hire us because there was nobody left. But even as far as 1950 and '50-something, there still was discrimination. But in the 60s it got better; and the 70s, if you were willing to work, you got it.

When Japan invaded China, they had this slogan: "The greater Asian hemisphere," or "the Greater East Asia co-prosperity sphere." Their reason was Japan had no natural resources, none whatsoever. So they had to go into China to get the resources to run their factories. Even some history teachers in high school, they promoted that—that Japan was absolutely right in invading China. We couldn't say anything about it, though. We just listened. We judged for ourselves. They said that Japan was a very advanced country without resources, and that's the reason why they'd go in. But had they gone in peacefully, I think they could have made a go of it, instead of fighting.

In school, the Whites were predominant. The Chinese in those days, they had big families—five or six kids. So they always populated the schools. In our class, I would say at least 150 out of 1,000 students. Blacks were very few in San Francisco. They were mostly over in Oakland and Berkeley because they were porters and they worked on the dining car on the trains, and Oakland was the end of the line. San Francisco's on water. So their trains stopped in Oakland, and we ferried across.

Daniel Huang: After the war broke out in Asia, what was the feeling among the Chinese people in your community?

Well, some wanted to fight the Japanese. Some were apathetic: they didn't care one way or the other. There were a lot of them who thought that the Japanese were Asians, so leave them alone. I was a young kid. At 16, I didn't know enough to have feelings. I was drafted in '43; I was not a volunteer. I waited until they got me. At that time I was working at the post office.

I started working in the post office in 1942. Before then I was working in restaurants. In '42 I was 22. Those post office jobs in those days were hard to get because it was the Depression, and many people who worked in the post office were college graduates. I was working in Vallejo, which is about 30 miles from San Francisco, and then they put out an examination. We had to take an examination in those days, rough too. I think that I took it in '41 and within a couple of months they hired me. So I was tickled to death to get a job like that. Then I lasted until 1943 in April. Then I got drafted.

In a video I saw, it said the post office originally thought you were white, from your last name?

No. That incident was in San Francisco. See, in Vallejo we were smaller in number, so we got along great. As a matter of fact they all liked that we come in. But in San Francisco, those days the postmaster was under politics, the politician selected him. He knew nothing about the post office. There was a McCarthy there. He did not want Chinese despite the fact that we took the test and passed. He just shoved the results of the test into a corner or a wastebasket. So you've got that incident. That was after the war too, about '45. There was a Gum H. Hall who passed the test and he came in. He was Chinese, see. The postmaster thought he was white. So we had the last laugh there. Once he got in, they couldn't disqualify him. That was the incident. A lot of people get a kick out of it—that when Gum Hall came in, the postmaster didn't know whether to jump off the Golden Gate Bridge. He was quite embarrassed.

I was 23 when I got drafted, but I don't know why they waited so long. Most people got drafted at 18, upon graduation from high school. There was a little luck [when I was drafted]. There was an all-Chinese group being formed. It was an opportune time that they threw me in there. That's why I already knew everybody else. We went to Springfield, Illinois. That was kind of a staging area to get us together. From there, they broke out and formed an Air Service Squadron, our group. That consisted of about two service squadrons, then they had signal companies, they had quartermaster companies, they had ordinance. All those units constitute an air service group.

They gave out orders where to go, but we were lucky. We trained at Patterson Field, and then we got through the training. In 1944 we first went to Oran in Algeria to await a ship that was going to take us to India. We were bound for China, but it was not open at that time. So we went to Oran and waited for a ship to take us to Bombay. Oran at that time was a shifting point for Italy too. Some of the fellows said we were going to Italy. I said, "No, no. We're going to Asia." But, regardless of where we were headed, we knew [we'd be in] the Chinese company. But of course if things got bad, then we could have gone over there to Europe. I mean, that's my interpretation.

We felt no discrimination [in the U.S. military]. Except—I forgot ... Or maybe in Patterson Field. I don't know what was going on, but there was a point where some of the black soldiers in another unit saw what was happening and said to us, "You want us to help? We can help you." So something must have gone wrong, but with so many people I didn't hear what was going on. So that was only one. They wanted to help us because they were a minority and—

Daniel Huang: If you're asking about the incident with the black soldiers, Mr. Goon told me that some Chinese American soldiers from the 407th Squadron met some white women, and they started getting together, and dating and going out to parties. It was completely innocent, nothing bad. But some of the white soldiers took offense, and I think they threatened the men from the 407th so the black soldiers offered to help out the Chinese soldiers.

I didn't know that episode. Maybe that was at Patterson Field.

We went to India first. We stayed about six or seven months at Dinjan and then we were taken into China. We went in at Kunming in Yunnan Province in '44, because all the other western provinces were in the hands of the Japanese. So we were restricted to a few provinces in western China: Yunnan, Guizhou, Sichuan—basically those three. But they border a little bit on the Eastern side some of the adjacent provinces, such as Hunan, Jiangxi, Shaanxi, Hubei—those places. They border those principal States.

Daniel Huang: As a member of the 14th Air Service Group, what were your duties there?

They made me the mailman of the 407th because I had that postal experience. I wish they had sent me somewhere else where I could think of another specialty, but I never fought with them.

In our company, in our location, we didn't get out and fraternize or anything like that because we had to work all day long. And those places were small places, small cities. Sometimes we had an opportunity to go out and go to a restaurant. We used trucks. Once we got into China, we used trucks to transport us to the other bases. We changed bases from time to time. Then we got into some of these roadside restaurants on the way in to have dinner. Technically we're supposed to eat our rations, but we got approved to eat at the roadside restaurants. We had a fellow by the name of William Hoy—I guess you heard of him. He was a journalist [Chinese American]. He spoke Mandarin and Cantonese and English, so he was—He did all the ordering—in Mandarin of course—but they turned out to be very good meals. Some of the fellows said, "Oh this is not too hygienic." William Hoy told the restaurants, "be sure that you cook it well done, so if there's any bacteria it's gone." As a matter of fact, I would say those meals were more delicious than some of the fancy restaurants.

There was some talk about how there was tension between China-born and American-born Chinese Americans?

Well, I think they give too much attention to that. As far as I'm concerned I take in anybody. I get along with both sides. The people who come to the reunion, they're China-born and American-born. Like Earl Jung is American-born. Paul Tom came here early, but like Jim W. Chin and Hong J. Wong, they came over as immigrants from China. I get along with all of them. I don't make any difference. Our parents told us to get along with people.

Were your brothers also drafted?

I'm the oldest brother. The second brother, he was a member of the Head-quarters of the 14th Air Force. So he went over with us—not at the same time, but a different time. Then the other one, he was in the Air Force, as a navigator. The youngest brother, Lee, he did not get drafted until the tail-end of the war. He only spent less than a year. He was over in the Philippines.

He could have gotten out of it because there is a law that you cannot draft all the boys together from a family. One can stay home. But he turned that down. He went anyway. He said if he didn't go, he would not have had the opportunity on the GI Bill to go to college. So he made the right move.

There were some—well, we made the distinction—they were mostly China-born. They were afraid of getting killed. So they went into farming. They were exempt because they were growing food for the armed services. So they did not have to serve, but they didn't get any GI Bill or benefits.

Do you think that most of the Chinese people who enlisted or who were drafted were safer than, say, a white American because they weren't often given front line duties? Like being a cook or something?

That's one of the reasons, a very valid reason. But some wanted to come over and see China, because they were born there and they felt that's the territory they wanted to see.

Daniel Huang: In China the idea of a frontline was kind of the confusion, be-cause it was dangerous everywhere you went. You could get bombed any-where. … We didn't have the complete air superiority we had in Europe. In Europe we could stop the Germans from bombing us because we had far more planes and far more war materiel, but in China you could get attacked anywhere, basically.

We were more or less neglected. We were there solely as an occupying force to keep the Japanese there instead of the Japanese going to the front. Because that way you could keep some of the troops away from the fighting—I mean, kind of a stalling action. But we had plenty to do. We had to service the air-planes, we had to supply armaments and food, and we did the repairs. So we had plenty to do.

Each service squadron broke out into small satellite units to go to the fara-way places and more or less functioned as a team there, which I didn't get to. Like some went to Xian, some went to Yenxi. But we … staffed about six or seven bases. I, being the mailman, just stayed behind. But I did get to see the other bases.

Did you mingle with the locals?

They didn't come around, or they wouldn't let them come around. Except on days off you go into town, but to some very few towns, they're small towns.

There were a lot of Chinese who had been to the United States, but they went back to China and got caught in the war. They couldn't come back. A lot of them followed the American troops into the western provinces, and they ran little restaurant businesses and so forth. One was Chin Wing Dep. Wing lived in an apartment in San Francisco. I remember him. He was a rent collector then, back in '36 or '37. Then he went back to China, so we looked at him. I said, "Are you Chin Wing Dep?" "Yeah." "Yeah I know, I know."

It was strange going to China for the first time because we'd never been there before. Most of them spoke Mandarin because we were in Mandarin territory. We were not in Guangdong because that was in the hands of the Japanese already. But after the war we came back through Shanghai and we did see some Cantonese speak Chinese there.

Coming home, we got a trip around the world. We left through Shanghai on a ship. We crossed the Atlantic; we went into the Mediterranean Sea, down the Suez Canal, the Indian Ocean. We flew into China, and then came back from Shanghai to Seattle, Fort Walton, and then we dispersed there.

As a Chinese you didn't have any strong sentiments or position against the Japanese?

No, I didn't. No, because they fought in China, but they did not fight against us, against the Chinese Americans. As a matter of fact, in Shanghai I noticed the Chinese—they said if you behaved yourself the Japanese never bothered them. So *(laughs)* no bitterness, no.

In our travels, we traveled from Bombay, India to Calcutta by train. We saw a lot of the country. Then from Bombay up to Dinjan in the province of Assam, we had to take a train to Tistamugat. Then we had to change to Brahmaputra River steamer. Then we went to Pondu, we had to change to a narrow gauged railroad to get up to Dinjan. Oh, that was the toughest part of the trip. They did not have cranes except at Calcutta. When we got off the train at Tistamugat, we had to move everything hand by hand. As a unit, newly formed unit, we had to stop in Calcutta at a depot called Kanchrapara; that was the supply depot. They gave us all the equipment that we asked for, needed, clothing and even kitchenware. They gave us a stove. See, we had the supply depot there at Kanchrapara, which is a little suburb of Calcutta. We had to take all that stuff up by hand, heavy load. If anybody survived that, you're good.

We carried heavy equipment like ones for repairing airplanes and gasoline drums. Well, we had our own cooks. You got stoves. No refrigerators, of course. Then we had generators. We had a lot of excavating equipment.

What did you think about some of the places you saw?

Oh, Assam, they had been having civil war for the last 60 or 70 years. They're isolated from India, way in the corner up there that borders China. It's a very rich province with a lot of resources, but those tea plantations stand out. They made the best tea there. I think some of them were Chinese-owned. I got a taste of that Darjeeling Indian tea. It's very good. As a matter of fact, I take it over the Chinese tea. It's supposed to quench your thirst. And a nice strong taste. One of the 555, Harry G. Lee, married one of the daughters of those tea plantation owners. She only passed away about a couple years ago. They are down in southern California. He had a ranch that grows avocados and lemons. Made out very good.

We also had a doctor. He fell in love with one of the daughters from the tea plantations. So he married her. We had advised him. I said, "You're 20 or some-odd years her senior. You better not." He wouldn't take our advice. She dumped him like a hot potato. You know that's not going to work out. I heard he was a doctor in Chinatown here. His specialty was venereal disease. In those days, high society took it as an embarrassment. He had to make house calls.

* * *

On the trip back from Shanghai, we stopped in Yokohama. We couldn't get off. We stopped in Honolulu. We couldn't get off. We went to Seattle to await trains back to our destination. The Chinese community in Seattle gave us a great welcome when we came back. They gave us a nice time.

After the war, well, I went back to work. I was nearly 25. Most of the fellows, the younger ones—they took advantage of their GI Bill, went to school. In our family, it was decided the two oldest ones would work and support the family. The two youngest ones were going to college. One studied engineering; one studied [pharmacology]. My brother went to work for the Naval Air Station in Alameda. I kept my post office job.

Did you start a family right after the war?

No. Well, I'll tell you everything. In Vallejo, I had girlfriends, but it didn't come out right. I am glad they told me. I worked in the post office at that time. It was a very poor-paying job. One of them even told me, "You don't make enough money for me." Thank you. *(Laughs)*

Well, that's the truth. Then the other one, well, I wasn't proposing marriage or anything like that because she'd been married three times. The other one, I think she was married two or three, too. We lost contact.

In those days, if a Chinese woman married two or three times, was that considered—

Not right. Unless they were flirtatious or they worked as bar girls or something like that, yeah, because they meet people all the time.

I waited until 1948. The end of 1948 was the deadline that you could bring a wife over from China [with the War Brides Act], which I took advantage of. I was in Vallejo. We were in a rooming house with Old Fong. He was in the same boat as I was. He said, "Let's go back to China and take advantage of this bill." I thought it over. He said, "By golly, we should." We married in China. You could bring a wife over very easily then.

We marry today, tomorrow, we're on an airplane coming back. But you had to go into the American consulate, have the marriage there. So we had the papers. Then they gave us the visa to bring a wife over. That was very easy. Now, I understand, it takes months to do that. Years. They ask you for so many papers it's not funny.

In our time we made very little money. It was rough. We had to use an airplane. It was me and the wife. It was a 726. That was nearly $1,500. That was a lot of money in those days. We had to take the ship because we had to save the money for the airplane. The ship took about 18 days, which we could have stayed in China and visited for 18 days. It was a pocketbook issue. The ship was, I think, a General Gordon or something. It was an ex-troopship. Then we were down in the dormitory, third class. The first class was good. We didn't have money for that. Nobody had any money. So then we returned to civilian life.

How did you meet your wife?

My uncle, my mother's brother, was in China. He found one. We told him, I said, "Some poor girl that would appreciate going." We turned out right. *(Laughs)* We've been married 60 years. Something was definitely right there.

You went back to California?

Yes, I went back to my job and transferred to San Francisco in 1948. In those days, the post office wouldn't accept transferees. Then somehow they had to loosen up a little bit and I transferred to San Francisco in 1948. So when my wife came over, we lived in hotels, small apartments, until about '49 or '50. Then we bought a house, a flat, two stories. My brother's in one; I am in the other one. We've lived in the same house ever since.

Was she able to adjust to American life pretty quickly?

Oh, she had to. Well, she didn't speak that much [English]. Conversation only, she did. She went to school for a few hours a day, just to learn a little English. So, as the years go along, you adapt. Some who won't adapt, they speak Chinese all the time. You can't do that. Even when they work together, they speak Chinese. How are they going to learn English once the boss goes away? You got to speak in English and learn.

Was there a community of a lot of Chinese women who came over?

In San Francisco, yes. In San Francisco, New York, Los Angeles, Boston.

Chinese were treated much better after the war?

Oh, yeah! But not perfectly. Discrimination will go on for another hundred years. But it's minor, it's isolated, in our case. In a lot of other cases, no. Well, I like to needle people. Even though I was working in the post office, I wanted to see how they felt. I saw an ad for a U.S. Rubber Company, United States Royal.

Mack Pong with wife Mary and grandchildren, 2008

They made tires. I went there. He said, "You know what I mean." I told him, "I know precisely what you mean." I just left.

It meant he's not hiring even though they had advertised for employment. Then another time it was the Police Department. They were very kind, you see. They liked their own group. I just went down there just to needle them. They see me going to the testing office. They gave me a dirty look. I figured from that that they didn't want me. There are a lot of Chinese policemen now. I even tell them we're in the mainstream. We've got thieves, we've got panhandlers, we've got hijackers, we've got everything. We've got lawyers, we've got doctors, we've got farmers, we've got truck drivers. We can fit in anywhere.

How many kids do you have?

Four kids and four grandchildren. I have three boys and one girl. The girl was the oldest and then followed by three boys. One's a doctor here in China-town [in New York], at the clinic. Then another one is a doctor in the Kaiser Group in South San Francisco. My daughter works for the UC Hospital. Not in the hospital but some kind of administration with the pharmacy. Then another son is in Denver with the Morrison-Knudsen Company. He's an engineer. One is in Denver, one is in New York, then one in San Francisco. One is Burlingame, which is only 20 miles down the road.

Your children are all very successful. Did you ever put pressure on them or did they just naturally—

No, no. That was not my philosophy. As long as they make a living. If they're going to wind up with something less than desired, well, then I am going to speak up. But they all wound up pretty good.

Daniel Huang: Would you say that the opportunity they had to get an education was an opportunity they wouldn't have had before the war, do you think?

Well, they could go to college. But whether they're going to find a job or not is the question. It's not the educational process. You could go to any school. I mean, of course, if you go to private school, you got to have a little money. The state schools, it was very cheap in those days.

Why was mainstream society more open to Chinese people after the war?

Well, I imagine they found that we were good workers and they started hiring. Once they see that you're good—That's why I tell people to make a good impression. So it's going to be good for the next generation or those following you.

Now they prefer to have Chinese, in many instances. But I don't know whether they want to give them the big jobs or not. Oh, you talked about discrimination. I think Dr. Wen Ho Lee was highly discriminated [against]. They've got no proof on him whatsoever. The FBI's mentality is that all Chinese are guilty until proven innocent. That's the way they look at you. But yet, they want to recruit Chinese.

CHAPTER NINE

Sam Yuen Jue 周沃全 (1910–2011)
U.S. Army Air Force

Sam Jue, at the age of 91, with his wife and daughter, talked about some of the struggles of living in Rolling Fork, Mississippi, a city that lagged behind most parts of the country when it came to civil rights for minorities. He talks about his family's grocery business, how the Black and Chinese communities depended on each other, and how he met his wife. He passed away in 2011, survived by wife, children, and grandchild.

When I was 16 I came over to this country [from Guangdong, China] and I came to Mississippi. There was some racist trouble. I couldn't go to public school then. So I had to hire a person to teach me English.

My daddy was operating a grocery store here already. I had a sister who lived in China and a brother who came over later. Both have passed away. I am the oldest.

My uncle came over here first. Then he brought my dad to come over. Then we came over. I came in 1936. But I don't know what year my daddy came over here. I was 16. I hired someone to teach me from ABCD up. The teacher was Caucasian.

Mississippi used to be very hard, you know, with racial problems, and—

Mrs. Jue: They segregated: Blacks, Blacks; Whites, Whites.

We would overcome it. But since the war, I went to the service and came back—everything's changed. We're the same as the other people.

Mrs. Jue: They let them go to school and vote and everything else.

How many Chinese were in Mississippi?

There were four families, four stores in the town Rolling Fork. The creek runs through there. That was what they named the town. The creek was built during the Civil War for the Southern people to get supplies there.

The four families were little families. All grocery stores. We had to work from 8 a.m. to 10 p.m. every day. Saturday I had to work till two in the morning. And Sunday I had to work a half-day. We had to work real hard to overcome all the problems.

Racial problems? How were Chinese and Blacks treated?

We don't look at that like the White people look at that. We look at Blacks—human beings. You know what, they are all uneducated, lowered, and they are friendly to us, to Chinese. That's why we can stay in business.

Whites—they are higher education. They are better at everything. But I can't say they are better people, you know, they're just human beings like everybody else. But they have problems to fight, like getting over their hardships like we do. They treat us better than they treat black people.

Sam's Daughter: We didn't exactly belong to either one. So we were just sort of there.

Most are good people. But they have a law: They say, in school, one family against you, you can't go. That means you don't have no chance.

What was it like growing up in China?

Well, I [was a] little more fortunate than some of them. I went to school. But we were 8 years old before we started school. We started from 8:00 to 6:00 at dark, every day, six days a week.

What did your father do in China before coming over?

Farming, I guess. I didn't know him then. He went to Nicaragua, Central America, before America.

Sam's Daughter: The Chinese immigrated to Nicaragua? A lot of them?

Yeah. Mm-hm.

Sam's Daughter: They have a business there? A store?

It was easier to go there than the United States.

Sam's Daughter: Probably an immigration thing where they had the quotas. It was probably easier for them to come through Central America. I had cousins who came in through Canada.

Sam's Daughter: Your dad, what did he do in Nicaragua?

I guess work. Just come and work. He was a laborer. I wouldn't know what for. My mom stayed in China.

How many years of education did you get with the person you hired?

I took a couple years. The lady who taught me died. She was pretty old. She was a lawyer's wife. Everybody liked Chinese. But the law—they have some kind of unjust law.

I worked in the grocery store for a few years and then I got drafted to the army. I was 23.

Were you a paper son?

Yeah. I am a paper son.

Two Chinese right close to draft [drafted at about the same time] went to Camp Shelby in Mississippi. One week later, they call us two to give us the order, to say you all need to ship out.

We didn't know where to go. They said follow the direction. So they got us train tickets and an order. That envelope said Springfield, Missouri. So we stayed a little while in St. Louis, and finally we got to Springfield. And we hired a taxi cab. All over town, looking for the place—the military. The cabbie kept saying, "This town don't have no military." He finally thought about it and said, "We got an army hospital here, treating wounded soldiers. So I'll take you there to see if they can help you." So we finally go there, and they kept on saying, "We understand. We know what your problem is." He laughed. He said, "We know what your problem is," and points to the other side at a whole bunch of people. He says, "They're going to Springfield, too. But in Massachusetts, not Missouri! They come here too."

Sam's Daughter: Was it Illinois or Massachusetts?

We [were supposed to] go to Illinois. They [were supposed to] go to Massachusetts. But we all ended up in Missouri.

Was it a misprint? Did they write it incorrectly?

Sam's Daughter: Yes. They wrote it incorrectly, and a whole bunch of them ended up in Missouri.

Then they called back to Camp Shelby. About a week later, we found out where we had to go. And we went to Springfield. We found a bunch of all young Chinese. We didn't know what was going on. Finally, about a week or two later, they separated us from Engineering, Signal Corps, and all them kind of people.

That's what the 407 and the bunch of people meeting today [at this Flying Tigers Reunion] are. I was in 407. We called ourselves Engineer Squadron, but my job was to fix the tail assembly in the flap of airplane. And do all the painting.

When you first started service, what was that like? Were you the only Chinese among the—

We were separated. Black people were in a different [section]. I was with the Whites then. You know the famous Japanese [442nd Regimental Combat Team] from Hawaii, training down there. They made a picture show out of it *[Go for Broke]*. When I went down there, I thought they were Chinese. I asked them, "You're Chinese? Where you all come from?" They looked at us, you know, we're all Chinese, and said, "We are Japanese Americans." They were at Camp Shelby. We only stayed in Camp Shelby about one week.

How did people treat you while you were there?

Well, it's all right in the camp. It's just the law. You know, most people are generally nice, most people like us, but there's bound to be somebody who don't like—

Sam's Daughter: Where did you go next?

Then I went to Springfield, Illinois. Then finally they interviewed each person and separated us into different groups. Over there, we had the 407 and 1157 Signal Corps. Then after we took 13 weeks basic training we, the 407, were sent to Dayton, Ohio for school and training. We were requested by General Chennault of the Flying Tigers.

We were about halfway trained; they wanted us to go over. Our commander said, "No, we can't send our boys there with half training." But they say, "You have to come." Our commander said, "I can't do that. I retire. I quit." They needed someone else to take over. We really half-trained when we went over there. They said, "We need you bad."

We went to Newport News, Virginia. We went on those little bitty—what do they call those—Liberty ships. Took some 20-something days to cross the Atlantic. At nighttime, they get all together—300-something ships. Like a big city. In the daytime, they're separated. They try to dodge the submarines.

Did you like being in the Army?

Right now, I like it. We went around the world. We'd go to the Mediterranean, go to Suez Canal, Red Sea, Indian Ocean, go to India, and fly over the Hump to China. We come back to Seattle. We made one line around the world.

I enjoyed all the places I got to go, but I'll tell you the truth, I was scared. I was scared that the submarines would sink the boat. I don't mind on land, but I was scared in the water.

Then when we fixed to leave India to go to China, the commander said, "That's the most beautiful trip you can take, the most dangerous trip you can take." He said, "If something happens to your plane, everybody for themselves," when we went over the Hump. We went over China and we got bombed. I don't know how they knew we were there. Then we separated into several small groups, sent along to help with Chinese defense. I was in one of the small groups.

I felt more American than Chinese. My mother was still in China, in the mainland. They had to hide sometimes. When the Japanese came, they hid, go to the mountains and hide. But she survived it. She went to Hong Kong after the war.

Sam's Daughter: When the other soldiers found out they were going to China, didn't you say they thought they were going home, or close to home?

Yeah, I thought I would reenlist, for six more months, to change my unit and get to go back home, but I was already in the boat, they said "You're too late." I had to come back to the U.S. I got back to Mississippi and married.

Sam's Daughter: How long between the time you came out of service till you married Mama?

Mrs. Jue: He came out of service in '45.

I was discharged after Christmas.

Sam's Daughter: They married in August '46.

I was 26 years old when I got back home.

Can you tell that story about how you met?

My friend introduced us—

Mrs. Jue: His friend told him about me. And he told my daddy about him.

So I went over there to see her. We met each other.

Sam's Daughter: Did you go to her house to meet her?

Yeah.

Sam's Daughter: That was typical back then, introductions.

By six months, let's see. I went to Memphis, Tennessee, all the time to see her.

Sam's Daughter: She lived close to Memphis, Tennessee.

How long was it to travel from Mississippi to Arkansas?

Mrs. Jue: 200 miles.

Takes about four hours by car. Sometimes we liked to ride bus or train. The train stop was near our store.

What did you do for fun when you dated?

I helped her do a little housework sometimes. *(Laughs)* They don't have no running water! I had to go pump water for her.

Mrs. Jue: We didn't have running water, not in our town.

Then you got married and moved to Mississippi.

Mrs. Jue: That's where we've been ever since.

And I worked at a grocery store, what my dad did. And I raised my children.

Sam's Daughter: He and his cousins inherited the grocery store from their fathers.

Then all the family partnership left. I took it over by myself.

Did you sell American groceries or Chinese groceries?

American groceries, and a hardware store. You had to sell a little bit of everything in the country. Medicine, everything else.

How many children?

Sam's Daughter: I have two older brothers. There were several Chinese that grew up within 30 or 40 miles of us. There were lots of Chinese back then. Daddy and his friends used to play mahjong, at least once a week, sometimes twice a week.

There were four or five families 40 miles away, one 20 miles away. We'd get together.

Sam's Daughter: In the neighboring town, there were seven families. In our town of Rolling Fork, which had a population of 1,200, there were two or three in our town. Greenville had lots of Chinese. My generation, when they grew up, moved to bigger cities, like Houston and California. And there are still a few of us left in Mississippi.

Every Sunday we get together. One week, it's my house, the next week it's someone else's house.

CHAPTER TEN

Richard Y.W. Chin 陳英和 (1924–2011)
U.S. Army Air Force

Richard Y.W. Chin of New York City, talks about his experience at Ellis Island, his arranged marriage, and the excitement of the formation of the all-Chinese units which would be sent off to the CBI theater. He was highly involved with the American Legion Kimlau Post and, for many years, with Mack Pong, organized reunions for Chinese American World War II veterans.

My name is Ying W. Chin. I came to this country with a son who was a citizen, on the ship the President Taft. We docked in Seattle, Washington, and were sent to a room with a lot of cages.

I was saying, "We're not jailbirds!" They said, "Chinese immigrants go to that room for waiting for questioning." When it was time for the immigration officer to interview me, every time he asked me a question, I cried out, "Wahhhh!"

I don't know whether I was playing or real scared, afraid of the White man. That was the first time I saw a white man in front of me. I was 9 years old. Every time he asked me a question, asked me how old I am, what I am, what is my name, I hollered out and yelled. Then he gave up questioning me.

The interpreter sent me back to the immigration room where they kept us all. They didn't want us to run out in the city. The immigration man said, "Okay, okay." He passed me.

After World War II, immigration came to look for me to ask me to join, to be naturalized. This is my naturalized paper. [Shows his naturalization papers.]

After the immigration man passed me to come into the United States, my so-called father, my paper father, took me from Seattle to Boston to New York by train to meet my father in Brooklyn. He had a laundry there and that was the first time I met my father. I never met my father even when I was born. My mother got pregnant and he came to Canada. From Canada, he smuggled into the United States, and then I don't know how he got to New York. Most of the people who came from our village were in Manhattan.

What was he like? How old was your father then?

He's about 30, 45 or something like that. My father took care of [the man who brought me here]. From what I heard, the paper father charged my father $100 a year. So I'm 9 years old—that's $900 plus travel or something like that. He charged my father $1,000 for bringing me over. It was worth it. That's how it works.

I stayed with my father for a long time. On Sunday his worker, my village cousin, took me to a church: First Chinese Presbyterian Church on 31st Street between First and Second Avenue. My cousin took me every Sunday from Brooklyn to Chinatown by subway up to 34th Street and we walked down to 31st Street. I went to the church until the time I joined the Army in 1942 or 1943.

* * *

In 1936, my father brought me back to China and I got a match—how do you call it?

Arranged marriage?

Yes, arranged match marriage for me to marry a lady in 1938. I was 14. At that time, all the Chinese got married by 14 because [parents] want their sons to come to the United States. They make them [boys] marry and leave them [their wives] at home. The United States didn't let any women come with their Chinese husbands. There was, at that time, that law.

June or May I got married. I didn't like it. The church minister had told me, "Don't get married," because he knew the future suffering of the young man at that time.

My father went back with me [to China] and he died in 1937 and my mother forced me to marry. So I married this lady; I left her home, the poor girl. She was about the same age. She stayed home [in China] and I was over here and that was suffering man and wife. That's wrong. When they see young people they tell them, Don't get married too early.

I came back from China to the U.S. in January 1939. We had a World's Fair in Queens. I was working at the World's Fair as a waiter until the fair closed. That was a good job. It was very, very crowded with all kinds of people.

What kind of food did they have at the restaurant you worked at?

This guy, he's from Seattle, Washington. He's a white guy. He uses Hawaiian hula dancers and he used Chinese food for his restaurant. He used Chinese waiters and Chinese cooks. And Japanese, one or two. And I think it was three Filipinos working with us as waiters in the restaurant.

I came back here. I was doing all kinds of work, pressing shirts in a shirt pressing company.

Roosevelt's second lieutenant Sing Wai Yee came up to New York to recruit American Chinese to go to China to join the American Air Force serving in China. They wanted the Chinese Americans who can speak Chinese to interpret for the white people. Anyway, we got 100 young men in New York to volunteer together to join. Then we got sent to a Manhattan induction center to ask them to let us join the Army. I was 17 then.

The induction man said, "We want your mother or father to give us the okay to induct you." I told them my father died, my mother's still in China. She can't come over here. He says, "Okay." He signed me up; I got accepted. Then later they sent me a letter to go to camp in New Jersey.

The government sent me a letter to report to Fort Dix. So all of us—100 of us reported to Fort Dix. We were processing. We were in line to take shots for prevention to go to China. We took about five or six shots; prevention for all kinds of things.

A hundred of you went? All from Chinatown?

We lived in Chinatown, New Jersey, Manhattan, Queens, Bronx, Brooklyn, all over this area. We all came, to our knowledge, at Roosevelt's request. At that time, we were all mad at the Japanese invading China. They were invading Manchuria first, Korea first and the Japanese were using the Korean young men for their Army to invade China through Manchuria and then from Manchuria down to Peking onto Shanghai onto Nanking, then all the way slowly down to Canton, even down to our village in 1937–38.

Everybody was so angry over here. Even in Chinatown, Mott Street, they had a parade from Canal to Chatham Square. They used a big flag, a big street-wide flag. Nine young ladies pulled the flag and walked down from Canal Street to Chatham Square. The flag was for receiving money. People threw money down from their windows to the street to the flag to collect the money for Chiang Kai-shek's army.

So we were all getting mad at the Japanese. We were all willing to go to China to join the U.S. Army, the Air Force.

You told me once that when you were still in China you were standing on a roof and you saw a Japanese bomber in a plane and he looked you in the eye, smiled, and waved, before flying off into the distance and dropping a bomb in a nearby city.

I went back to China with my father in 1936. I went to school in Canton City, Pui Ying High School. The Japanese in 1936 had invaded Canton already. Then I said I'd better go back to the village, maybe it's safer over there. I went back to the village. [It has] a river going out to the Pacific Ocean. There are two big mountains over there and between, the river. So the Japanese had an airplane that was on the ship.

Airplanes lifted up from the aircraft carrier and flew up to Taishan, Daosan, and over our building. I was on top of the building, running on top of our building. I know that the Japanese are invading us already. So the guy was in the airplane and he looked back at me and I looked at him and we looked at each other's eyes. Then a few minutes later, he flew over and bombed, that's 5,000 tons. After he finished bombing, he went back down to the two mountains in between the river. So I said I think I'd better go.

You told me you were real young, 13 years old.

He waved at me and he looked at me and I looked at him and he flew away.

Did you also say he smiled?

I think so. I don't know, I don't remember. They were invading [China] like kids playing. My wife and my mother came out to Hong Kong with me. In Hong Kong, we took an Empress liner.

Anyway, I came back to the laundry where my father [used to work]. The guy said my father had sold the laundry to him. I didn't know about that. My father didn't tell me that. Then I stayed in the laundry for a couple of weeks or so, and then I moved to 31st street, the Chinese Presbyterian Church. They have a dorm there on the third floor. There's four or five guys living in there.

Do they speak English or Chinese?

Chinese. They accommodated the working people for service. Usually in the morning they had service and between 2:00 and 3:00 at night. The church was big. In the basement, we had a kitchen so we cooked foods and ate at night time.

From there I went working in Chinese laundries where we would press shirts. They had four or five companies like that. So we would go over there, I worked from one place to another. They would pay you 3¢ a shirt.

* * *

When the Japanese bombed Honolulu I said, "You'll be sorry." Right after that, Roosevelt ordered and contracted a lot of machine places, to make airplane parts, guns, machinery. There's a machine shop at Bendix Aviation. That machine shop I was in was making parts for the airplane meters. I worked there for a couple of years.

After I finished working and training in the machine shop, I went to the small companies. They were prejudiced. I went to ask for a job. They said, "No job." But then a white guy with the same training followed after me, and they accepted him. I waited outside for him and said, "Hey, how come you ask for the same job and you got it, and I don't get it?" Then I figured I bet they're prejudiced there. They don't hire Blacks or Chinese. Later on I found a job advertised in the New York Times. It was President Roosevelt's doing. He ordered the big companies to hire minorities, Black, Chinese, even Japanese, whatever. I went for that.

So I went to the Brooklyn Navy Yard, that's a government company. I went there to look for a job and they hired me the next day. I said, "Hey, that's good." Under Roosevelt's order they hired minorities. They hired me so I went to work for about two months. The Brooklyn Navy Yard was also doing the same thing, machine shop work. I was working on the 5-inch anti-aircraft guns on either the Missouri or the big war ships. There were two war ships being built at that time in the Brooklyn Navy Yard.

Roosevelt sent an army lieutenant from Washington D.C. to come up to New York to recruit as many as he could, Chinese from all over New York's five boroughs. Most of them were laundry men and restaurant owners.

We all got there in Fort Dix and we were all processed there. A couple of months later we got sent to Springfield, Illinois. From there the army separated us wherever they wanted us to go. I volunteered for the Air Force for a machine shop; they sent me to Columbus, Ohio. Now by that time they must have gotten 1,000 American Chinese boys already. I volunteered for the Air Force and they have another unit, Signal Corps 987 at Camp Crowder.

So these two groups there are going like crazy now, accepting American Chinese, however many they can get. They went to army camps to ask the Chinese whether we wanted to go serve in China through the Air Force or the 987th. They got a couple hundred in Camp Crowder, the 987th Signal Corps. Ours was the 407th.

After, we were training in Patterson Field, Ohio. A couple months later we went, a whole 200 of us—they put us on the train to Newport News, Virginia to get on a ship. There were about 25 troop ships waiting for us, some ships and submarines.

I happened to learn how to Morse code: "dit dit dit dit dit dah dit," that kind of stuff. I went to the front of our ship and I saw a sub chaser blinking lights: "dit dit dit dit dit dah dit," or something like that, and I happened to know how to receive that. I received a sentence. It said, "Enemy submarines ahead." So I went back inside to the bottom of the ship. You know what those guys were doing?

What?

They were playing mahjong. I said, "Italian submarines in bottom of the ocean," and those guys don't ever care. They just played mahjong. [When] night-time came, our sub chaser dumped the explosive down in the ocean [toward the enemy submarine]. Boom boom. The ocean waved, it hit our armament, our ship. Boom boom, boom boom, and like that. I said, "Hey, it's coming, its bombing." They don't care, they're playing mahjong. They're training their nerve not to care.

We sailed zigzag from Atlantic Ocean to Oran, North Africa. We stationed there for a couple months. All of a sudden our company leader, our captain, got an order to get on this one ship. We were all supposed to be going on this ship but some other company went on that ship. By the time the ship got to around Sicily, a German submarine bombed it. The ship got bombed. How do we know this? An American swam to the North Africa shore and he came back to Oran and he reported that the ship was bombed. We were supposed to be in that ship. We would have been dead before we got to our destination.

From Oran we took the Suez Canal to the Red Sea to the Indian Ocean and then to Bombay. From Bombay we took the open-top train with no windows. It was hot like crazy. We took the train cross-country. We stopped at Calcutta, about 30 miles away from Calcutta. We stationed there and we were waiting to fly over the hump, the Himalaya Mountains, to Kunming. What is that road going up to Kunming, on the Himalaya Mountain?

The Burma Road.

They built a road from here, Assam Valley, go up and up-up-up to the mountain and then come down. That's a lot of driving. Some truck tried to back up and it dropped down off the cliff. That happened many times.

Then, from Kunming, we went to different city airports. We were stationed in China for two or three years, some in the southern part. The 987th Signal Company was somewhere around Kunming and the western part of southern China. I was stationed in Guiyang for a little while and then went up to Chungking. This airport was 30 miles [from] Chungking and we were stationed there for a little while. My last assignment was for Chungking. They were waiting for assignment to Hubei, Enshi.

So what kind of activities happened when you were stationed?

The pilot takes the airplanes to bomb or to fight with the Japanese airplanes—they call it dogfight—up there in the air fighting each other. A B-29 at that time, four engines, supposed to be big, went to bomb Japan. Our pilots came back to our airport and their plane dipped. I said, "Why are you doing that? How come you come back to the airport and you dipped your airplane?" He says, "Nervous." He says, "Things I shouldn't do, I did it, so I nearly got killed". That's the way you learn.

CHAPTER ELEVEN

Richard Goon 阮福志 (1924–   )
U.S. Army

From Fall River, Massachusetts, Richard Goon joined the 987th Signal Corps Company, an all-Chinese unit. His father served in World War I. He, his uncles and brothers served in World War II, making them a military family. After the war, Richard became a lawyer, a restaurant owner, and then in retirement an actor, starring in an Italian "Karate Kid" movie.

I'm 89 years old now. I've been elected as commander of the local CBI Veterans Association in my region. They elected me because I'm the youngest and everyone else is over 90! We're less than 20 members now. Women outnumber the men. There are more widows. The club is called Gold Coast Basha and it's for veterans who were in the CBI [China-Burma-India] Theater. Ten years ago, we were 100 members from all of Florida and we met in Orlando for reunions. But they disbanded three years ago. But our local chapter meets now if we have even just four or five people. Every month we go to a different restaurant for lunch. We don't do dinners anymore because it's dangerous for us to drive at night. They give us a room, we set up a flag. We pledge allegiance, sing songs. Most of our members are white pilots from the Flying Tigers.

The first person in my family to come to the U.S. was my grandfather's younger brother. He came in 1903 to work in a restaurant and save money. There wasn't much work available except in restaurants. After a year or two, he went back to China to bring my grandfather over. After a while, my grandfather brought my father to the U.S.

My father came to the U.S. when he was only 13 years old. When he was of age, he joined the U.S. Army in World War I. He was shipped to France as a private first class in the Army, with the Artillery Unit. He was involved in the war in Germany somewhere. Later on they transferred him to Military Police and he guarded German soldiers. He served I think for about two years, was discharged, and came back to America. Then he went back to China and married my mother in 1918 or 1919, and brought her to the U.S. He had no problems bringing her over because he was a U.S. veteran. My brother was born, and then I was born in 1924 in the U.S.

Then in 1926 when I was two years old my mother took my brother and me back to China for the purpose of learning Chinese. She didn't like very much living in the U.S. because she could not speak English, and my mother couldn't

Training at Camp Crowder, Missouri. Richard Goon third from left.

write or read. So it was very difficult for her to live in the U.S. I went to elementary school and junior high school in China. I came back to the U.S., to Fall River, Massachusetts, when I was 14 years old, in 1938. By that time, in 1938, the Japanese had already invaded China. They took over Manchuria, Nanking, and Shanghai and were coming down toward Hong Kong. My father knew that and thought we should get out before the Japanese occupied the whole country. So we left in 1938 to come to the U.S. and I went to school and learned English and continued my education.

My father had a restaurant, and we lived in Fall River, Massachusetts. In 1942, I was 18 years old and joined the Army. I had basic training in Camp Hood, Texas. I was in the Artillery Tank Unit, Tank Destroyer Unit for three months, as a gunner. The guns make so much noise that it can impair people's hearing. Well, that didn't happen to me because I wasn't there that long. I heard that they were organizing all-Chinese [American] units to go to China to serve with the 14th Air Service Group. So I asked for a transfer and got transferred to a Chinese [American] unit at Camp Crowder in Missouri. I went to Signal Corps School, and learned how to be a cryptographer, which is a code man, we did secret codes.

When I transferred into the Chinese American unit, that was the first time I saw so many Chinese people in America! They were all Chinese. In our unit alone [the 987th Signal Company, 14th Air Force], there were over 100. The 987th unit was the only one with all Chinese members, including officers. Other units, like the 407th, had Chinese members but Caucasian officers. With all the Chinese [American] units together, there were over 2,000. Most of us came from Toisan [台山] and we spoke the same dialect and had a lot of things in common. We got along fine together, we trained together, and because of that, even after the war we continued our friendship and had reunions together. That's why we have reunions every year, to meet old buddies and have a good time.

Richard Goon at center. Outpost in Comu.
7 miles behind front line.

After training in Missouri, we were shipped over to China. We took Liberty ships that stopped in Australia to refuel and then to Calcutta, India. From Calcutta we went to Assam, India and flew over the Hump, the Himalaya Mountains, to go to Kunming, China. And my whole unit was all broken up in teams, about six members each, to go to units stationed on the border between China and Indochina—which is now called Vietnam, but before it was called French Indochina. I was stationed near the Indochina border. And, besides my regular duty in the Army, I was asked to do some buying for the mess hall—that's where they served dinner. My main duties were buying all—At that time you used firewood for cooking, and used charcoal for heating. So I had to buy all the wood and charcoal, all that I could lay my hands on.

The Chinese Army furnished a cook to cook for us and sentries to guard us, for our unit. But the American GIs, the Caucasians, didn't care for Chinese food that much. Some of our people in the compound, in our unit, were Caucasian, like the veterinarian doctor, and a sergeant helping the Chinese Army maintain mules for transportation. All those trails, motor vehicles couldn't go on them, so they used mules for transportation. We also trained the Chinese Army to fight. We tried to modernize the Chinese Army. We had to give all kinds of modern weapons to the Chinese Army because they didn't have good weapons.

When the infantry officers trained the Chinese soldiers, of course we needed an interpreter to translate instructions. We had a Chinese interpreter, but his English was very limited, and couldn't get the message over. So the officer in charge asked me if I could help, and I did. And so I helped train the Chinese Army to use all kinds of modern weapons, especially machine guns. At that time the Chinese Army mainly had only rifles, not machine guns. So we trained them to use the 30-caliber and the 50-caliber machine guns, and we also trained them to use the bazooka, which was new even for our Army.

987th Signal Corps special maneuver in Missouri, 1943

While I was training the Chinese unit, I had a chance to meet all high-ranking officers including the Commanding General of the Chinese Army. I got to be very friendly with him, because I translated for him and our officers.

The place where we lived was very run down. We lived in a vacant Chinese temple, and an officer asked me to do something to make the living conditions better—which I did. Of course, we had to spend some money. At that time, the exchange rate in China was one dollar to 300 Chinese yen. We got a lot of money because of the Lend-Lease program. The Lend-Lease program was where the U.S. lent or gave the Chinese Army all the weapons they needed. In return they gave us some Chinese money to take care of ourselves in the unit, in the Army. So we used that money to improve our living conditions.

The Signal Corps work I did was always behind the line, about 7 miles behind the actual front. So we didn't really engage in the fighting. In Haiphong, Vietnam, the Japanese controlled the airport. So that was our target and we were training the Chinese soldiers to invade them. We found out that we were going to attack a Japanese position in September, and we were all trained and ready to go, but in August the atomic bomb dropped, and the war ended. So we were lucky because the war ended before we had to go.

When Pearl Harbor happened, I was in Fall River. I was only about 17 years old. I heard on the radio that the Japanese attacked and a lot of American sailors died. We were surprised and angry that someone attacked us, and many, many people enlisted in the Army to fight.

I was one of four people in my unit to receive a Bronze Star medal for meritorious service. No officers got awards. The other three who got medals were Joe Yung, Kai S. Chan, and Wayne Wong. Many people in the Army griped when they were given assignments. But I did a lot of extra jobs like buying, translating, interpreting, remodeling the living quarters, and I was glad to do it.

After the war, I went back to finish high school. It took me a year to finish, and then I went to college. The first college I went to was Washington

Richard Goon, left, and Yin A. Yee, right.
14th ASG, 987th Signal Company at Comu.

and Jefferson College in Pennsylvania. After one year I had transferred to the University of Miami in Coral Gables, Florida. I transferred because the first school was an all-boys school in Pennsylvania. I didn't really care for it because I wanted to meet some girls. So I transferred to Miami, which was co-ed, and the climate was different too. I cannot stand the cold weather up in Pennsylvania. In Miami, the weather is very similar to the weather in China, where I spent time as a boy. So Miami weather agreed with me.

I majored in English and then went to law school. At the time not very many people could afford a college education. Because I was in the Army I was entitled to GI Bill rights. And that's how I could afford to go to college. After four years it ran out. Then I had to pay for law school on my own. My father helped me with the tuition and living expenses.

I was learning mostly civil law, and so the cases I handled were usually contracts, wills and accident cases. After I graduated I went into partnership with two schoolmates. I handled civil cases and the two other partners handled criminal cases. When we first went into practice, we had just graduated and I didn't have much experience. We were young. It was very hard to make a living. One partner couldn't do it and went to the FBI. Then I quit the law practice. Because I couldn't get into the FBI or any kind of government service, I went into the restaurant business; that's my family business. My sisters and my brother, they all have restaurants. And the third guy in our law office kept with law and later became a judge. He's the judge who tried the Ted Bundy case—Ted Bundy, the serial killer—and sentenced him to die.

After I quit law I went to Hollywood, Florida, to work for my sister for a

while, and then opened my own restaurant in Deerfield Beach, Florida. I opened the restaurant when I was 45 years old and had it for 20 years, until I was 65, when I retired. We served Chinese food. I did pretty good.

After I retired, I got involved in the movie business. I got started with *Miami Vice*, the TV series. Then I got a lucky break and did a series of Italian movies called *The Boy in the Golden Kimono*. It's a very nice film and I enjoyed it very much. It's an Italian "Karate Kid" and I was the Mr. Miyagi.

I met my wife in Miami after I left college. She's from Massachusetts too. And I'm from Massachusetts. So we kept on talking and then went on a date, and then we fell in love and got married. She's of French descent. We were married for 54 years and then she passed away. We have three children, three sons. And then of course we always wanted a daughter, we didn't have her, so we were lucky to have a granddaughter.

My family is really a military family. My father was in World War I. He served in France. My brother Tom and I joined the Army together in World War II. We were in the same unit throughout the war. My uncle Freddie served in World War II, too.

My brother Thomas died about five or six years ago. He came to the reunions with me. He liked to meet old friends, the old buddies, to talk about old times. He enjoyed that. My sister owned a restaurant, and then become a banker. She was very successful. I think she has 13 bank branches, each doing very well.

I submitted two anecdotes to the Library of Congress and was interviewed on Voice of America. It was broadcast right from Guangzhou!

CHAPTER TWELVE

Lester Fong 鄺榮耀 (1917–   )
U.S. Navy

Lester Fong's clothing factories in New York's Chinatown produced uniforms for the U.S. military in the Second World War. Later he was drafted into the Navy and stationed in Guam, where he witnessed kamikazes. Post-war, he worked in real estate and served as Commander of the American Legion Kimlau Post. He was 93 at the time of this interview.

When I first came to the U.S. I don't believe I liked it too much, because all the Chinese were either doing laundries or restaurants. That's not a job I liked. At the time I liked doing sportswear very much. First I worked for Arrow Shirt Company and got experience there. After that, a few of us friends started a sewing factory on East Broadway in Chinatown doing army military clothing until I got drafted to the Navy. I lived with my brother until 1943 when I was drafted into the Navy in World War II. I was a U.S. Navy petty officer 3rd class. Then I sold my factory over to my partner.

I was born in 1917, in Canton [Guangdong], China. I immigrated in December 1939 because China was in a war with Japan, and that's why my father wanted me to come to the U.S. and live with my brothers in New York. My father was in San Francisco and my grandfather was in Hawaii. I came by ship through the Pacific. It took me 29 days. The ship was what they called Lao Meen Ho—I don't remember the English name.

My father was in San Francisco; my grandfather had taken him there. By [the time I was born], my father had already gone back to China after being in San Francisco. I grew up with my father and mother. My grandfather was in Hawaii. He was the first one in my family to come to the U.S. At that time, when he came to the U.S., they had sailboats in Macau. See, my grandfather was a locksmith, an iron man. They tried to draft people to come to the U.S. but you had to pay a certain amount of money for the food before you could get into the boat. And my grandfather liked the idea of coming to the U.S., but didn't have any money.

A person said to him, "Well, you have a big blanket, you know? In Hawaii, it's warm. You don't need that in Hawaii. Why don't you pawn it? And then you can get the money and pay me and you can go to Hawaii." See, that's how he pawned it and got the money to go to the ship. I don't remember how much, but whatever it was, when he pawned it, it was enough for him to go to Hawaii.

When he was in Hawaii, he didn't find any job he could do. But he saw the farmers, and their cows. The farmers weren't able to handle the cows the way they do in China. And my grandfather suggested to the people, "Well, I can help you—to make these cows listen to you." Because he was an ironman. He knew what to do. And he helped these farmers pierce the cows' noses, and made rings for them. Then the farmers could handle the cows. When the cows get a tickle in the nose in there, they listen. That's how he made his money there. Then he opened a hardware store in Hawaii. After a few years, he made some money. He got a lot of people over to help him take care of the business, and went back from China, and a lot of people (cousins in the village) went to Hawaii. That's the very big story about my family. And he has four sons. He was 36 when he went to Hawaii.

When I first came to the United States, my brother wanted me to go to work instead of school because of my age. I had to make a living. And I looked at this laundry work and all this, and I don't like it. Restaurants—I don't like it.

I went to school for a very short time but did not finish high school. When I was going to school, it was very tough, because there weren't too many Chinese here. There were no special classes for foreigners. Even when I joined the Navy, I didn't speak English well and didn't understand well. But during that time, I learned a lot.

Then I wanted to try to do sewing, to be a fashion designer. At that time the Arrow Shirt Company opened a sewing factory. Then I signed up and learned how to sew using a sewing machine. My friends and I opened a sewing factory on East Broadway. That time, we did government work, like military uniforms. After, when they drafted me, I had to go to the service, then I let my factory— my friends operate it.

I entered the military service; I took a train to Rhode Island. At that time it was very tough work. A lot of training. After training nearly half a year, they sent me to Florida for more training, and then to Norfolk, Virginia, to do amphibious training, and I picked up a ship from there and went to the Pacific.

I was assigned to the LST (Landing Ship, Tank) in the Pacific. I was in a LST. I think I remember the number was 760. I was a boat's mate. I had to drive the LST which takes soldiers or tanks onto land, to fight. We were on Guam Island, in the Pacific. At that time, everybody was so scared. We were so young. I was 21.

I handled the landing and transported personnel and hardware. Yes, of course I was scared. The most memorable, scary part was the Japanese suicide planes. When they came, we were all so scared. We didn't know which ship they were going to go into, who'd get hit, you know? Every day you'd see it. They'd find some ship to hit. We lost lots of LSTs there, in the Pacific. I don't know how many we lost. We were lucky if we got back. And in a short time, Americans made Landing Ship Medium (Rocket), LSM(R), with machine guns on the side to shoot them. After that, we won the war.

They didn't use the LST ships anymore after that. After the war, the U.S. sold a lot of them to China. They junked a lot of them between New York and New Jersey harbor.

I was the only Chinese in my unit. They didn't have any Chinese units yet. At that time English was very hard for me to speak. My English was not that good. When they drafted me—actually, they looked at whether you wanted to go to the Army or Navy. They suggested 'why don't you go to the Navy?' so I said "I'll go to the Navy."

So how did they train you if you didn't speak English well and you were the only Chinese person?

Well, I had to go follow them, with what the rest of the unit did together. That's how.

That's so scary—

It is.

I did overseas duty close to eight months. After I got back to Norfolk, Virginia, I waited for discharge. I took a weekend off to come celebrate the opening of the American Legion [in Chinatown]. In the beginning we didn't have too many members: 150 or something like that.

When the American Legion [in Chinatown, New York] began to organize with Willy Hong Art there, we were on Worth Street. In 1945, the time the Legion [in New York's Chinatown] was organized, I was in Virginia and came to New York on a weekend pass, and I came back to join my friends who organized this legion here. When they had the Grand Opening, they had members from the Air Force, the Army, but they had no Navy. I was the only Navy boy.

I knew a bunch of older people from Chinatown, like some of these older men from On Leung. People my brother's age. And a lot of them were drafted, and came in and joined. We celebrated the Grand Opening with a parade.

I became post commander for the American Legion [Kimlau Post]. Before that, I was color guard and volunteered to do all the parades. Then after that, they made me Chinese secretary, then treasurer for quite a long time. I was the one to find this building with Joseph Chu.

After we bought this building they elected me as commander. All floors in the building were used for the legion. There were six stories. Third floor for games. Fourth floor, commander's office. Fifth floor was a pool table. Sixth floor was for kung fu exercise. At that time, we had about 800 or 900 members. We were open every day, 24 hours.

* * *

How did I start a company? At that time, it was not easy to get employees. Not many Chinese women in the U.S. here. I had to train them how to sew before they could work for me. In 1952, I opened on Mulberry Street here. In a year or two, a lot of Chinese women didn't have regular work and didn't make regular money. I got more employees and did two factories. I did fashion sportswear for women. I did business 1952 to 1976.

Then I went to business school at Pace University, and learned real estate and made sales on houses. More [Chinese] people immigrated here and began to buy houses for living. Then I stopped the sewing factory and did real estate, around '78 till 1984, when I retired. After I retired I saw people doing tai chi in the park, then I began to learn. Then my friend, a Catholic father who's Chinese who knows I can speak English, said [to go to] the UFT [United Federation of Teachers]. So I went to the UFT and taught tai chi exercise. People liked it, classes got bigger I taught tai chi at the UFT for 20 years. They gave me a big citation/award. I said, if you give it to me, I will retire. I taught two women, two teachers to take my place. Today I am enjoying my time with my family and my brand new great-granddaughter!

CHAPTER THIRTEEN

Elsie Seetoo 陳貞潔 (1918–　　)
Chinese Red Cross Med Relief Corps (1942–44)
U.S. Army Nurse Corps (1944–46)

Elsie Seetoo was born Elsie Chin in Stockton, California. When the Depression set in, she and her family moved to China in a time of intermittent political unrest. She talks about her "long walk" of about 700 miles to join the Chinese Red Cross Medical Relief Corps in Guiyang, and then the U.S. Army Nurse Corps. After the war, she attended the Women's College of the University of North Carolina for her bachelor's degree. She became a translator, technical publication writer-editor, translated *The Barefoot Doctor's Manual*, and raised her family in Washington, D.C.

I was born in Stockton, California in September 1918, just before the Armistice to end World War I was declared, which was on November 11, 1918.

My mother came over to the United States in 1917. She didn't have to stay at Angel Island long, because my father had several Chinese ministers whom he knew, and they vouched for him. As of 1910, there were these restrictions on the Chinese moving around the place. I didn't know that until later. My father couldn't leave Stockton without special permission. If he wanted to go to Fresno or someplace, he had to get a statement from a well-respected minister—that he's a person in good-standing, and not a gangster or something like that. Chinese ministers were very well respected.

And some years before that, my father had expected to go back to China to finalize marriage plans for my oldest brother. This was around 1911, I guess. But then it turned out that before it could take place, this oldest brother died of an epidemic. To make matters worse, our ancestral village was burned to the ground, because there were problems with neighboring villages fighting over irrigation rights, I was told. So my father had to change gear. At the time, he was a cook for a very wealthy family in Stockton, for whom he had worked for over 20 years. But the only way to bring my mother over to the United States was to have his status changed. So he left Mrs. Jackson, the woman who employed him, and started a Chinese import-export store for Chinese groceries with a friend. And that made him a Chinese merchant. So, being a merchant, he could bring his family over. That was how he applied and brought my mother and brother over to the United States.

My father had come over as a laborer in the 1880s, at the time of the building of the transcontinental railroad, although I don't think he worked on the railroad, as such. According to what my brother told me, he was chopping wood around the Oakland–San Francisco area. He might have been made a camp cook or something like that. He was a young man, only 20 years old. Before he came to the United States, at the age of 18, he was sent to Xinhui [新會], a town not too far from our ancestral village, to learn how to be a cook. Cooks were apprentices, and they might line up with a store to do the cooking. At night when the store closed for the day, everybody would bring out their boards and sawhorses, and sleep on them in the store overnight. In South China, people just sleep on boards with a little mat on top. Because, the climate is such—you know, who wants to sleep on sheets and get all sweated up, when it's so humid? I think some of those practices still persisted until the time that we went to China in 1931.

My ancestral village, called Shanzui [山咀], was located in Xinhui district. The custom then was that the Chinese men would come over to the United States and work for so many years, save some money, and then return to China to get married. Or, they were already married, but then saved money, and went back to maybe build a house. And the laborers were only allowed to stay one year in China, and then they had to come back [to the U.S.]. Otherwise, they'd lose their privilege of being over here. That was what I was told.

I had one older brother who was 9 years older than I and he was born in China. My younger sister, almost two years younger than I, was born in Stockton.

My father had a Chinese grocers' import-export business that carried dried mushrooms, dried shrimp, preserved plums and salted fish. The store was the only place that had a refrigerator, and it was usually stacked full of beer. We didn't have a refrigerator in the house. The store's icebox was literally an ice-box. The iceman would come with the block of ice carried by tongs to put it in the icebox. My father also had a little vegetable patch back at the house where he grew things like Chinese parsley. I remember the bananas in the store, the boxes of tea—the old time boxes that had these ancient Chinese figures imprinted on them—somebody with a gown and long beard, or bare-headed, on a cliff looking over to the distance. I used to think that maybe that was what China looked like. There were also the imported almond cookies.

I went to public school. My father took me to kindergarten and I didn't know a word of English. Because, having grown up in an all Chinese-speaking family—well, even then, I didn't speak that much Chinese. My parents were busy working. My mother in those early days learned how to use a sewing machine and worked for a Chinese dry goods store that also sold garments. Later on she would do mending for Chinese men who didn't have families here. They might need a sleeve shortened, or their pants shortened. She was kept pretty

Mama, Stella, Elsie, Papa, and Harry in Stockton, California, circa 1922

busy that way.

Stockton had a small Chinatown. It was one block, or a block and a half. Right next to it was the Japantown, and on the other side was a Filipino congregation. There was a Chinese Mission, which later became the Chinese Christian Church. They rented a space below to what was the Chinese Benevolent Association building. The top floor was used for Chinese school. The ground floor had three storefronts. The mission took one storefront. It was about two blocks from where my father's store was.

Chinese school was divided into two big classrooms. We went in the evenings from 5 to 9 p.m. Behind this building was a basketball court. I remember convincing the Chinese teacher to put up a punching ball pole out there because I liked to play punching ball during recess. And that was Chinese school, and we went for maybe three or four years. I did well—supposedly did well in Chinese—because much of the time was tracing over Chinese characters, or practice writing them with brush and ink.

During the day I had a good time in public school. Maybe the first year was a little rough because I didn't know English. I didn't know what this Japanese boy did, but the teacher said something to him. He pointed at me, and said I did it. But I did not know how to rebut him. So I had to sit in the corner as a dunce. Back in the old days, that's what they did if you were bad. Stockton at that time had a very large Japanese community. I think the Japanese American community was larger than the Chinese one.

In those days, we'd get promoted every half-year. It's not that you complete first grade and then go on to second. You go from low first to high first, and low second to high second. I was in fourth grade when I got promoted to low fifth. So I skipped high fourth. Then I was the only Chinese girl in the class. And

Wilbur Choy was the only Chinese boy in my class. He later became a pastor in Stockton.

So that was how it was until I finished seventh grade. And I had just started the eighth grade when it was time to move to China. Of course, in the intervening years, there were Camp Fire Girls.

There were quite a few Chinese families in Stockton. Some girls, a few years older than I, had what they called a "Triangle Club." I was told I was too young to join. But there was Mrs. Ogden, an American lady who started a Campfire Girl group for us at the Chinese Mission. She had an automobile and came every Saturday to take us to the Camp Fire House. We would have a short meeting, then do crafts. So that was an outlet for me.

One time, I must have been about 9 years old when Princess Der Ling came to town to speak to an American woman's group in Stockton. She was a princess—one of the ladies-in-waiting to the last Empress Dowager of China during the Ching Dynasty. (I think recently there was a book, or somebody wrote another book about her again.) But this woman's group was talking about, "Well, it would be nice to have some Chinese girls come to help serve tea after the talk." That was how our Camp Fire group got involved, and we were told to go in our little Chinese frocks. All I had was just a Chinese top, and wore it with my Camp Fire Girl pleated skirt to help serve tea and almond cookies. We went, and all that I remember was, she was a princess. You know, at my age back then one would have read all these fairytales about princesses. Then some of the older girls in the group said, "Well, let's ask the princess for lunch tomorrow." She accepted and we had a lunch of noodles at one of the Chinese restaurants in Chinatown. We told her about our being Camp Fire Girls and what we did. I had a Camp Fire Girl handbook with me. Nobody offered to show theirs to her, but I did. Then she wrote in my autograph book, "What a charming girl you are!" In English. I liked that. She was married to an American. And that was about all I knew at the time. When I got home, I wanted to tell my mother all about it. But I couldn't find the words in Chinese to tell her. I didn't know that much in Chinese. My Chinese was just limited to, you know, everyday words like, I'm getting up, I don't want to eat this or that. But I couldn't tell her about how she was a nobleman's daughter—that she was a princess to the Empress Dowager.

When we were little girls we used to get a lot of these little red envelopes on the first days of the Chinese New Year. Back in those old days, there were more single men among our Xinhui clan folk living in Stockton without their families. So they'd come to the store during Chinese New Year and my sister and I would greet them with "Gung Hay Fat Choy," meaning "wishing you to prosper," and receive these little red envelopes containing a quarter. I was a bad girl, since I was supposed to turn all the money back to my mother. But I wouldn't give her all the money. I would save a couple of quarters—usually they came in quarters—to buy myself Valentine cards to give to my teacher. *(Laughs)*

And at Christmas time, my father would say, "Now, let's give your teacher a box of tea." We didn't think she would like tea. We wanted to go to the *(laughs)* dime store to buy something else. But you know, that was a child's mentality then. We just thought that that was too "Chinesey." We didn't want that. Of course, in later years that's just what I did. You know, after I left Women's College [now University of North Carolina at Greensboro] I would send a couple of my professors tea, and kept up a correspondence with them for a few years, until they passed on.

I was 12½ years old when my family went to China. In 1931, the Depression had set in. My father had lost a lot of his savings in the stock market. We lived in a house that my father had to pay rent for every month. Maybe business wasn't very good anymore. The clan folks, you know, people from our same village, had opened another store across the street to kind of compete with him. My father was a little straight-laced, and perhaps incurred the ill will of some of the clan folks. See, some of them may have gone back to China for one year, then come back and say they have a son born in China. If it's a daughter, they still say it's a son. That's how we always hear about paper sons, but no paper daughters. Sometimes they need someone to vouch for their statements, but my father might have refused to do it. But my brother came over to the United States as a merchant's son.

In 1931, when we had been in China for several months, my father showed us a volume of Chinese genealogy. But it was all based on the male line, you know, the girls weren't counted. The women noted as spouses weren't even given a name—only the surname [their maiden name]. But it was interesting to look at because I could trace all these distantly related folks. It gave me a chance to know who was who.

Yes, this was life in the countryside. And while I was there I was kind of unhappy. I'd wonder, "Am I going to become a country bumpkin like that?" Sometimes some of these old ladies would come by and say to my mother, "Oh, in a few years she will ready to be matched with somebody!" Such is the attitude of some of these village women. But I knew my father wouldn't do anything like that—and I had enough of a rebel in me. But then, when you're that young, and you're still depending on your parents, what can you do to stop such gossip? So you just kind of half-go with such gossip and laugh about it. Of course at that time one of the important things was to get my brother married! Because, he had lady friends in the U.S. before we left for China.

We didn't think it was time for those things [marriage] to happen anyway. Our brother was still in high school. But that was one of the reasons I think my mother wanted to go back to China. She kept bugging my father. (It took three years.) But I know my brother had other lady friends (not necessarily specific girlfriends). I remember visiting—he knew how to drive. He would borrow a clansman's car and take us for a ride and stop over to see them. He was a good brother in some ways. And one of them knew how to play the

piano. Then he thought it might be a good idea for me to learn, to take lessons. So he approached my father about it—for 50 cents a lesson. And my father agreed. So I started taking piano lessons. But my father wouldn't buy a piano. He said I could practice on the wheezy old organ that he had salvaged from his early, early days—long before my mother joined him—when he went out with a group, somewhat like the Salvation Army, on street corners to sing hymns and proclaim the Word, to try to get converts. And somebody would play that wheezy old organ. I think that was part of the Chinese mission. After that was discontinued, my father got that wheezy old organ, and later took it to China too. But I said, "Well, I can't practice on that!" So then my brother got the key to the Chinese mission, which was just a block and a half away from our house. I practiced on the mission's piano.

We figured from my birth certificate how old my father was. He was born in 1863. He told us that he came to the United States when he was 20 years old. Then we added 20 years, so it was 1883 when he came. My mother spoke mostly Chinese. But my father managed to get by. Frequently, in the old days, the Chinese would ask him to go with them to court, or to see the doctor, or something like that. He had worked for Mrs. Jackson for over 20 years. Hers was a well-to-do American family. He had to know some English. Even though it might not be exactly grammatical, he managed all right. He also had several pastor friends, Chinese pastors. There was a Rev. Chan, who had an American wife. So when my sister and I were born, he asked Rev. Chan's wife to give us our names. She gave me the name of Elsie. And when my sister was born she said, "Let's call her Stella."

* * *

In China you can go outside the town limits in Xinhui and see what are called "ghost lights." The Chinese have the practice, three years after their dead are buried, to dig up the coffin and collect the bones, and put them in an urn. With the bones, there's all that phosphorous flickering around. So, you know, they call it guihuo [鬼火] or "ghost fires."

They put the bones in an earthenware crock and re-bury it, three years after the body had been buried and was supposed to have decomposed sufficiently for the bones to be collected. And should they uncover the coffin and the body hadn't decomposed properly, that meant the burial ground was not auspicious.

I don't know if they still do it. But that was the custom back in the old days that I remember, in Xinhui. I don't know what they do now, and because of the population problem, cremation is very popular. Supposedly, my parents' bones have been recovered and cremated. We were depending on my niece, who was still in China back in the 1970s. We were told that my parents' tombs had to be dug up, and moved elsewhere to make way for a road.

On our return to China, my father had built a few houses, three in a row. We lived in the third one. And the first two were rented out. We had a gate outside the small compound.

[The Chinese] think that when you come back from the United States you should have money. Considering the exchange rate and all that, my father did have some savings that allowed him to build these houses. But they were, by everyday standards, modest. When I went back there to look, in 2002, they had been torn down, now just a mass of bricks. When the Communists took over, they took over all property and nobody owned property anymore. The land belonged to the state.

Anyway, my parents wanted to get my brother married after we got to China. There were all these go-betweens coming with pieces of red paper—with inscriptions on them, with young ladies' birthdates, zodiac signs etc. I don't know how you're supposed to match them and see if they're auspicious. These matchmakers were all coming like that, and kept on coming. My brother wouldn't have anything to do with it. So finally the pastor at the local Lutheran church that my father found on our arrival in China came up with an idea. He asked one of his congregants, a local dentist, "Don't you have a goddaughter who's going to school out there in Canton?" "Oh, yeah, she's marriageable age all right, already 19. Her father had come back from Cuba with some money and sent her out to Canton to go to school." So I don't know how they maneuvered my brother to go out to Canton to meet my future sister-in-law. But that was it. And I don't think there was much dating going on. They were married in October. And we had just arrived in China in April.

My new sister-in-law was very well-trained. She knew how to sew, knit and embroider. Of course, I had taken some sewing lessons back in Stockton. That was part of the public school program. In Domestic Science, we also learned how to cook—make applesauce—and how to wait on tables. It was kind of fun. But then my sister-in-law who's good at this also taught me how to make a Chinese cheongsam, and how to put the collar in right. I was the envy of some of my schoolmates later on, when I persuaded my father to let me go to the same school in Canton.

The following year I started in seventh grade or the first year of junior high at the Pooi To [培道] Girls High School in Canton. I lived in the dormitories with 90% of the students. A few were from overseas—several from the United States, a couple from Australia, and several from Canada.

I remember by tenth grade, my father said that he didn't have any more money for me to continue. As a result, I went to the local school in Xinhui, a normal school for elementary school teachers, for one semester as a day student. After that, I didn't want to stay there anymore, and came up with another plan.

I wanted to attend a Catholic girl's high school in Canton as a day student. I had kept up a correspondence with a former schoolmate whose parents had thought it was too expensive for her to attend the earlier girls high school where she had been living in the dormitories with me. Now she said to me, "Why don't you come and join me at this Catholic girls school?" Her mother who also knew me approved and thought I could live with them and attend school together with my friend as day students. I attended this Catholic School for one semester. It was a breeze and I played some hooky that semester. Going there required some tuition. But, as a day student, it wasn't so much. The school was fairly new, trying to get off the ground.

That summer my brother came back from the United States. He had gone back to Stockton for college and completed his bachelor's at the University of the Pacific. He had attended St John's University in Shanghai where he had spent quite a bit of my father's money, and didn't get anywhere. So my father said he had to buckle down. He had had a good time in Shanghai, playing baseball and frequenting nightclubs. Oh, my brother, was he a ladies' man! *(Laughs)* And even when I was going to school in junior high back in Canton, he'd come to see us—sometimes on weekends—and some classmate, on seeing him, would say, "Gee, your brother is good-looking."

I was about 17 when he came back that summer. I had been having all kinds of big ideas. I wanted to go to up to Nanjing [南京] because one of my friends had gone there to study at Ginling College's high school. So I told my mother that my sister and I wanted to go. My mother said, "Well, let's wait until your brother comes back." See, we really didn't have any money to go. So after he came back, supposedly to help us with tuition, his solution was for us to go back to Pooi To in Canton.

And that was the year that I had a boyfriend and spent a lot of time supposedly dating. You know, we couldn't go out from the school grounds except for one day a month if we were boarders. I would only see the boyfriend on Sundays at BYPU [Baptist Young People's Union] meetings. It was a gathering, usually at a missionary or Sunday school teacher's house. We were supposed to meet weekly and discuss topics in special quarterlies. And then after that, because the boys had more freedom than the girls, the boyfriend would walk me back to school. Otherwise, the girls couldn't go out at all except once a month. The only way to play hooky was to go to BYPU or Sunday School to see the boys. And then you got to be walked home, or walked back to the school campus, that's about all. So it was very, very—I don't know how you put it—you know, very naive. None of the stuff you see young people doing nowadays. *(Laughs)*

That year, some schoolmates got typhoid and a couple of girls died from it. We'd go to the funerals. We'd buy flowers and go to funerals. Back in those days, the bodies didn't get embalmed. So the burial had to take place within a day or two. Otherwise the body would begin to decompose and didn't look very good.

My sister also came down with typhoid and was sent to the nearby Baptist hospital. Since it cost a lot of money, and my brother was paying for it, it was hard on his salary after a couple of weeks. He had come back from the U.S. and was now teaching science at a boy's high school. He managed to get my sister back to Xinhui, an overnight trip by boat, to where my parents lived. She was cared for at the town's small hospital where our parents could keep an eye on her. Later on when I began nurse's training I discovered that with typhoid, getting better was really about good nursing care. We had typhoid patients in the hospital and they got well mostly because of good nursing—good care, and good isolation techniques. And making sure the patients take their liquid nourishment.

The Japanese invasion of China began in earnest in 1937 with the bombing of the eastern seaboard. I was 19 and still had one more year to go to finish high school. When Canton was bombed, that was a shock. It was unsafe. The school moved to the countryside. All the wealthy people moved to Hong Kong.

The Japanese bombed places like railway stations. There used to be a military school in Canton and that was probably one of the targets. My high school moved upstream to this town called Gaoyao [高要] and it was right on the banks of the Xi Jiang [西江]. We were there for one semester. A student body of 500 plus had shrunk to 50 students. The students who didn't go flocked to True Light [真光] Middle School which had moved to Hong Kong to study there temporarily. So the following semester Pooi To also moved to Hong Kong. Many of the students who had weathered it at True Light came back, even though we were just housed in what was meant to be a storefront. The classroom was a storefront. Upstairs was our dorm. So that was where I finished my high school. Some of the big Chinese universities had moved inland. Zhongshan [中山] University moved up to northern Guangdong. Qinghua [清華] and Jiaotong [交通]—these famous universities moved inland to Kunming. They became the Joint Universities of the Southwest [西南聯大].

The bombings were frequent. It was just not safe in a place like Canton.

Outside Red Cross Dormitory, 1942

They didn't bother with some of these little hick towns, you know, like Xinhui and Jiangmen [江門]. They were taken over by the local puppets. And if they didn't have any strategic value, the Japanese didn't bother. See, back in the old days, the overseas Chinese had built this Xinning Tiehlu [新宁鐵路]—the railroad, that started from Beijie [北街] all the way into Taishan [台山]. It passed through Jiangmen and Xinhui, Gungyi [公益], all the way to Taishan. Because it was the overseas Chinese [華僑] who needed this railroad to go back and forth. The Japanese just picked up the railroad and used the scrap iron for whatever purposes needed. They just demolished the railroad. So there was no more Xinning Tiehlu.

* * *

After graduating from high school, nursing was my only option at that time. What was I going to do? I might have gone back to the country, the village, and taught school. But I didn't relish that. So I entered the Queen Mary Hospital in Hong Kong to begin my training to become a registered nurse [RN]. We were called "probationer nurses." From the very beginning, we'd get $40 Hong Kong dollars, of which we paid about $18–20 for our meals. The other $20 was our spending money. With that, I could be self-sufficient. And if I was frugal I might have $5 to give my sister, who was still in school. After one year you got promoted, and your salary increased to $45. The year after that, $50.

We did night duty too, when we'd get a little more responsibility. And when it was quiet, and the interns had their medical books lying around, we could pick them up and read what we want. After about a year or so, we'd get to write the night report and use new terms we'd picked up. So, by the time we were in our third year, we were considered pretty senior. The most senior ones among us,

ELSIE CHIN   ANC N-745463

In homemade khakis when commissioned   See the charcoal trucks lined up in a row
in the U.S. Army Nurse Corps

after passing their qualifying exams, receive their RN certificate and get to wear different hats. In the 5-year program, that's when the graduate nurses go into the maternity program and learn to deliver babies. But I did not get that far. I ended with just the 3-year nursing program.

I was just finishing my final exams at the time when Pearl Harbor and Hong Kong were attacked on the morning of December 8, 1941. Japan had started this massive attack throughout Eastern Asia: Indonesia, the Philippines, Southeast Asia, and China, as well as British-held Singapore. The hospital was taking in casualties from the constant bombing and shelling going on. Because of the Japanese blockade, bombing and shelling, no food supplies were coming in and it was just a matter of time till Hong Kong would fall. Hong Kong surrendered after two weeks. The Japanese had to bomb the place to make it surrender. There was a food problem. It was cold. I was told later there were corpses left out on the street. People were hungry.

When we knew that the Japanese were taking over the hospital, we started moving out. The patients who were able to go home had all been sent home. And those who couldn't leave were set up in temporary facilities in the "Great Hall" of the University of Hong Kong—its auditorium.

What was I going to do now? I knew I did not want to stay in Hong Kong under the Japanese. Nursing was my only option at the time, so I thought about going inland to join the Chinese Red Cross Medical Relief Corps. I had heard about it earlier from a patient, Agnes Smedley, an American writer, who had written about her experiences in China. But first I had to get out after the Japanese occupation was more or less complete, and transportation by boat to Macau, a neutral Portuguese colony, was resumed. My brother, who was an immigration officer, no longer had a job and was going to take his family of four back to Xinhui where food shortages were less of a problem. And I was going with him; also three of my nursing friends who did not have any place to go after the hospital disbanded. They wanted to contact their relatives inside unoccupied China.

Xinhui had been taken over by the Japanese and held together by local collaborators. For the local Chinese, they were more or less left alone if you minded your own business and not try to raise objections. I think that's how my parents were weathering it, even though there were times my mother was hauled in to answer for something to do with grain collection. There were times when food was short. Remember the local dentist I had mentioned earlier, the one who was a behind-the-scenes matchmaker for my brother? He had a son who collaborated with the Japanese, and after the war was over, the local populace really tore him up.

Well, once back in Xinhui, my parents were happy to see me, but I told my mother I wanted to go inland to Guiyang [貴陽] with my friends to join the Chinese Red Cross Medical Relief Corps. I had heard about the group's work. My mother said, "No, you shouldn't go. Why be so thick-skinned? You don't even have a contract or an invitation to a job." But I said, "I know I'll find a job. Nurses are needed." And she said, "What makes you think so?" I finally said, "Well, I have my three friends here. And if we stay you're going to have a food problem because you'll have to feed everybody." So that was what did it. She let us go.

After I went inland I was not very thoughtful, seldom wrote home. Because, I said to myself, "Well, they're in occupied territory and I'm not … in case they'd get into trouble because of me." But they knew I was all right, I think.

So my friends and I went all the way to Guiyang. My brother accompanied us to Shuiko [水口] about four hours walk from Shanzui, my ancestral village), where we were set to take a sampan ferry to cross a river, after which we were supposed to go by foot to our next destination. While we were crossing the river, a Mr. Liao saw us. It turned out Mr. Liao was one of my brother's former co-teachers at the boys' high school where he had taught. He asked us where we were going. We said, "Oh, we're going to Guiyang to join the Chinese Red Cross." He just couldn't contain his admiration. He was a "smuggler" of sorts. Because goods were in very short supply inland, and the Japanese bombing had cut off transportation supply lines and such, he would buy things in Macau or Hong Kong and smuggle them in through the back door. Things like toothpaste, socks, undershirts, etc., and maybe cosmetics. I don't know if he did cosmetics or not, because at the time Chiang Kai-shek was promoting this New Life Movement. No permanent waves [the hairdo]. No makeup. All these were luxuries, supposedly. Supposed to live a simple life. And in Chungking they were still smuggled in. People bought them in the black market. You could still get a permanent wave on the black market.

But don't you get in trouble, because everyone sees it?

No, you can say you had been over in India and got your permanent wave there. *(Laughs)* That was how I took one of my Army chief nurses in Chengdu when I was in the U.S. Army to get a permanent wave. We went into a barber-shop to ask about it. And then the hairdresser said, "Now, follow me." We went through some back alley and up to an attic. In those days, they used electric clamps. They'd curl your hair up and put the clamps on. When done and the hair was unclamped, all these papers had to be taken off. They were scattered all over the floor. And the operator would go "Pfew!" *(Laughs)* The Chinese used to spit, and my chief nurse would say, "Elsie, tell him not to spit!" I said, "I could tell him, but that's not going to stop him." Anyway that was an experience for her, and for me too. She got her permanent.

Back to the "smuggler" Mr. Liao, who said, "I'm going to write a letter to the pastor of the Baptist church at your next stop in Gaoyao, and ask him to let you folks sleep in the church sanctuary—and to provide whatever assistance you need. And when you leave for the next stop, ask him to write a letter to the Baptist pastor there in Wuzhou asking for the same favor." Actually, by the time we got to Wuzhou we also found a Baptist hospital there. And one of our old schoolmates from high school was the head nurse there. She said, "Well, you people don't have to go to the front. We need nurses here too. Do you want to work here?" We did not.

That was how we finally got to Guiyang—by stopping at various churches for shelter along the way. It was now April. Since my friends had not completed their training to receive their RNs, they stopped at Guiyang's Central Hospital to continue their training. I joined the Chinese Red Cross Medical Relief Corps and was there for several months, assigned to the base hospital there. Then toward the latter part of 1942 there was the prospect of joining a medical service training unit that was going to be in India, to help train Chinese soldiers to be medical orderlies. That was when I signed up for that program.

We left for India on Christmas Day 1942. The first part of 1943 was spent at this training camp called Camp Ramgarh that the British had used previously for Italian POWs they had captured during the war over in Europe. But it was turned over to the U.S. Army to train Chinese soldiers of the Chinese Army.

Oh, the camp was dusty, dry, and seemed to be out in the middle of nowhere. It was really very, very rural. And we slept in tents. There was this infantry training going on, and a motor component for teaching Chinese soldiers how to drive trucks. And then the reason for our being there was to train medical orderlies in the basics of first aid and field sanitation. I was there for a little over a half year. By July, we had completed two training sessions.

There were three women in the unit. One of them was married to the sanitation officer, and she became pregnant. She was sent back to China earlier. Later on, it was thought that the training period was sufficient for the troops to start moving north. So that was when one of the doctors, the other nursing instructor and I were sent back to Kunming.

In the meantime, the U.S. Army had also set up an infantry training center [ITC] in Kunming. The people from Guiyang, the Red Cross people, had also set up a medical service training unit similar to what we had done in India. I was really not all that involved anymore, because the folks from Guiyang were in charge of the training. So we operated the sick call clinic for the Chinese soldiers to come in in the evening, for us to address whatever complaints they had—check their symptoms or give them a pill or change a dressing.

Who was providing all this training? The American military or the Red Cross?

The American military, that is, the U.S. Army, for the infantry training. The Chinese Red Cross, that is, the medical service training unit, to teach medical orderlies how to care for equipment and supplies provided by the U.S. Army as well as train them in first aid basics etc. In Guiyang earlier I had become familiar with similar field equipment sent over from the Bureau of Medical Aid to China before the war. I remember sterilizing supplies in small autoclaves over a coal fire when I first arrived in Guiyang, assigned to the operating room.

Once we had settled down to our new routine in Kunming I came across Major Ernest King, a Chinese American medical officer who had come by to inspect our unit earlier when we were in India. He was posted at the ITC and I saw him often. During one of our conversations, I told him about my visit to the American Consulate in Calcutta when I was in India, to enquire about coming back to the United States. I had told the consular officer about my experience and what I had been doing. that I would like to go back to the United States. Of course at that time I was considered to be in the Chinese Army. He took my Form 430, and said he had to get instructions from Washington.

That was when my new friend gave me the idea to apply for the U.S. Army Nurse Corps. His wife had become a U.S. citizen after joining the Army Nurse Corps. He said, "You're a U.S. citizen. Apply for it, and I'll send your application in through the APO [Army Post Office]." As I considered myself a U.S. citizen, I wrote to the Superintendent of the Army Nurse Corps, and mentioned my experience—nurse's training, what I was doing and working on.

Shortly after that, the reply came back from the Army Nurse Corps, complementing me on my qualifications, but it also said, "You have an obligation to serve your country," meaning China, denying my application. My friend was furious. That was when he wrote back and said something to the effect that "We all came from someplace. The only original Americans are the American Indians. *(Laughs)* And here is somebody born in the United States, who is applying in her capacity as a U.S. citizen." But I didn't know at the time that there was a law that says you lose your citizenship because you served in the armed forces of another country which the U.S. was allied with in war.

Because of my friend's letter probably—well, no one knew at the time that I had lost my American citizenship. So right away the War Department or the Surgeon General's Office sent a cable over which gave me a direct commission as a second lieutenant in the Army Nurse Corps. It said that I was to proceed to APO 210, which happened to be Chengdu [成都]. I was commissioned Second Lieutenant Elsie Chin, Army Nurse Corps, U.S. Army, on June 17, 1944, assigned to the Air Service Command [ASC]. Its headquarters office was operating out of Hostel Three outside Kunming [昆明] where the headquarters personnel of the 14th Air Force was also posted. In the beginning I worked out of an office at the ASC to familiarize myself with its operation. Coincidentally, my friend was also working out of the same office, which dealt with dispensaries attached to a number of Army airbases. He had been transferred out of the Infantry Training Center to the ASC.

Technically, the Air Service Command was part of the 14th Air Force. So I was housed in Hostel Three where the officers of the 14th Air Force and its brass (all the majors and up) were housed.

Perhaps that was when the American Consulate in Kunming finally got the notice stating that I had lost my American citizenship and sent it to me. But I could take an oath of allegiance to get it back. Which I did—took the oath and became an American citizen again.

The only two Army nurses on the compound were a flight nurse and me. The flight nurse usually accompanied the injured Army personnel when they needed to be flown over to India for further treatment. Perhaps I was impatient—not doing much except pushing paper and discovering that locally employed civilian nurses for the airbases under the 14th Air Force came under the ASC. But the order had said "APO 210" and that was Chengdu, and I was in Kunming.

One day at dinner, a colonel walked in with a friend, and introduced me to a general. The general told me he was just on his way up to Chengdu. And I said, "Oh, you're going to Chengdu? I'm supposed to be ordered there." And he laughed and said jokingly, "Well, well, let's see if we can get you there." Months later, after I had already gotten myself transferred to the Army's station hospital, the Surgeon General of the 14th Air Force came by, and spotted me. He knew, because I was the only Chinese American nurse in the whole caboodle. He came over to me and said, "We're sending a detachment of six nurses up to Chengdu.

Medical Service Training Unit ready
for trip over the "Hump" to India

For Ramgarh, a sun helmet
and bush jacket

Would you like to go?" I said, "Of course I'd like to go." So that's how I got up to Chengdu.

We were attached to the small Army hospital located on the campus of the university in town, and a vacated missionary's house also on the grounds became the living quarters for the nurses. There were several airbases around the area, and the general's headquarters was based at one of them. I saw the general again shortly after our arrival and we laughed over his early remarks when we first met in Kunming. I saw him several times, usually at parties at his base headquarters. I think he was impressed by my easy handling of English and Chinese, and interest in what's happening in the world.

Anyway, detached duty up in Chengdu lasted only five months, but I was happy it gave me a chance to explore the city … to shop and meet a couple of high school friends who were studying at the local university. I even had a chance to visit the historical Dujiangyen dam some distance away, at its ceremonial spring opening of water to nourish the low-lying basin. Before I left to go back to Kunming, the general gave me his home address so that I could get in touch with him once I came back. I did, shortly after I came east after returning to the United States. We kept up a friendship over the years, until he passed on sometime in the 1980s.

* * *

I came back to the United States in 1946, right after the war. I was still in the Army and was sent to what was called the "Medical Replacement Pool" at Letterman General Hospital out in San Francisco at the Presidio. Before further assignment, we were given options, "Do you want to stay in the Army for another six months, or one more year?" I chose the shortest, six months, because I thought it would give me enough time to find a school and then go right to school under the GI Bill. It was around February when we came back. But I guess the Army was demobilizing so fast, they shortened it some more, to three months.

When I went back to Stockton after the war, that whole Japantown was gone. No more Japantown. And it had been such a flourishing place. It was bigger than the Chinatown. My Japanese American friend Shizu Abe was also in Stockton. As far as I was concerned, she didn't have anything to do with military warlords of Japan and all that.

So we made arrangements to meet at our seventh and eighth grade teacher's house. During the war, when I had APO privileges, I had my teacher's address and I started corresponding with her. My teacher had also kept in touch with my friend Shizu, who had been sent to the internment camps during the war because they were interring all the Japanese back in those days. So we met and we walked over to Lindsay Park across the street from the old Washington School, where we had our seventh and eighth grades. And we sat on the bench there and just talked about old times. That was after the war, in 1946.

After this short stop in Stockton, I decided to come east. I was on terminal leave (technically still in the Army). I had told everybody, my friends and patients back in the Army, "I'm going to go see New York when I come back." So I did. Stayed with friends for a couple of weeks. The city was so busy! Overpowering. Then on to Washington D.C. to visit another old friend from high school and wartime China days. The city had all these welcoming trees and it did not seem to be so busy. Stayed to share a friend's apartment. Also, a base to check schools out. I had contacted a professor in North Carolina while I was still in Shanghai with the Army. She was the godmother of a friend who had died in Hong Kong shortly after the war, and her mother had asked me to contact this professor friend of theirs, which I did, and received an invitation to visit once I had come back to the United States. I did, and discovered that the Woman's College of the University of North Carolinas had a special program for nurses, whereby we earn a Bachelor of Science in Nursing degree after two years of liberal arts. I was told that the dean devised the program because she was impressed by military nurses at their outposts during the war.

While waiting for school to start in September, I met Joe Yuen. He was a friend of my apartment-mate, and had just returned from out west after some tests of rockets. I was impressed. He showed me around Washington, and I married him after six weeks, just a few days before I started school. He said I could leave him and go to college. So I did. It was not easy, but he did allow me to stay down there for two years to finish and get my degree.

Just before I finished college, I had applied for a job with the Central Intelligence Agency. The CIA was just new then. So, on my winter break, I went there and took an exam. You know, the Chinese language test was no problem. And the people looked at me like they were going to get some relief. But then, I was given this long questionnaire to fill out. You know, about where are your parents living? And where is your brother? And how long had you been in China? And so forth. So, by graduation time, I thought, "How come I haven't received a letter?" My husband had received the letter, but didn't forward it to me. My application was denied due to "unforeseen circumstances." Which meant that, you know, all my family—my parents, my brother, my sister, my brother-in-law—everybody who was in China posed a problem. The only person here in the United States was my husband. So I think they denied me on that. Because sometimes, I—you know, all things happen for the best.

Why was it problematic that your family was in China?

The Communists had taken over mainland China, or were about to, all of it. And you know, they could put pressure on my family if I were found to be working in a sensitive job. It's that kind of thing. They thought I might give out secrets or what-not, you know, forward classified material or that kind of stuff. So I just settled down and raised a family in Washington, D.C.

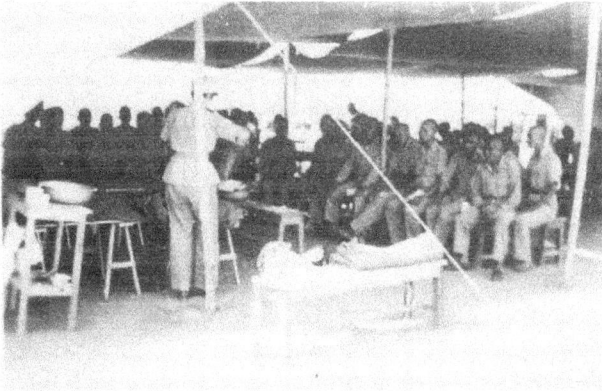

Training session for Chinese Army medical orderlies in Ramgarh

My husband was working at the Naval Research Laboratory. The laboratory was conducting experiments with some captured German V-2 rockets at the time. There were a few left over after the war, and they were brought over to the United States for testing. At that time, it was more upper atmosphere research to see how far they could go up. When all the V-2 rockets were used up, the lab folks went into designing their own rockets. They would go off to White Sands Proving Grounds to see how high they'd go. I forgot which rocket it was that showed the curvature of the earth. It was high enough for the camera to take a shot that showed the curvature of the earth and lower California. That was supposed to be kind of earth-shaking at the time.

Later on in the 1950s I already had two children and was pregnant with the third. My husband said he was going out to White Sands for a month, because the group was going out there to shoot and test two rockets. We thought if I could handle it maybe we could go on a trip down there and make a vacation of it as well. So that's how we got to go down there, and on the way to New Mexico saw some oil wells in Oklahoma City. Stayed at a little town called Las Cruces. He'd go off in the morning with the other guys to work. Some little boys and their mother also came with their father on this trip, and we all stayed at the same apartment complex. So the kids had somebody to play with. Back in those days, security wasn't so tight.

When it was time for the Viking rockets to be fired, we were allowed to go onto the proving grounds to watch. I remember it was on a mound, and I think that was one of the most breathtaking experiences of my life, to watch that rocket go up. It's not like watching it on TV. We couldn't have been more than 50 yards away. Some other families were there too. And here I was holding my two kids, one on each hand, and looking around to see—in case anything, debris or such fell, to run. And then we saw the fire, and we felt the heat. The heat from the liquid oxygen. When the rocket was ready to go, we felt the ground shaking too. That was how it was. We felt the ground shake. Then the rocket started

From left to right: "Muzzy", Elsie, ?, and Jean Lynas

going up. You see it on TV, where before it shoots up, it hovers. It hovers a little bit—hover like that, and then *whoosh*. Then it's gone. But that was before the days of Vanguard and before the days of satellites.

From that, my husband went on with the Vanguard satellite program too. Then he came down with cancer. So when they fired the first little grapefruit of a satellite, he wasn't there, because he had surgery. When NASA was being formed, quite a number of the Vanguard people went over to NASA. Joe, since he was still recuperating and not asked, his feelings were very hurt. I said, "You know, the Navy's not going to give up its finger in the satellite pie." Another fellow, who was responsible for devising the global positioning system that later evolved, also stayed. So after he got well he stayed with the Navy. He went into solar cell–wind power supply.

* * *

By the time my older children were in senior high and my fourth child had started school, I began thinking about outside employment to help with college tuition for them. I had been doing some contract translating for some time as a stay-at-home mom, but it was like feast or famine.

On the spur of the moment, I got a job as a technical publications writer-editor at the Naval Medical School at the National Naval Medical Center in response to an ad in the paper. My job involved revising some of the training materials for Navy corpsmen. Back in those days, some of these manuals done with a regular typewriter just didn't look right, especially when chemical terms for water or radioactive iodine-131 need subscripts and superscripts. Finally, when the IBM Composer became available in the late 1960s, we used it to make the manual into a professional-looking text. I also joined some professional group to keep current about such skills. I went to my first meeting of the Society of Technical Communication [STC] that was held after work at the American Chemical Society building. I also discovered that every year a group called the Federal Editors have a publications competition, and the STC people also have one as well. After months of work, I entered my 300-page X-ray training manual in the Federal Editors competition. When it got an honorable mention, I was elated. It was also entered in the local STC competition, and received its top prize, and went on to the STC's International Competition the following year. It really was more of a national competition, with maybe some entries from Canada and Australia. Even then, I received a second prize for it. It was kind of fun. And it gave me confidence.

But I did not give up translating completely, especially when the topics were interesting and challenging. I translated *The Barefoot Doctor's Manual.* The first thing I was asked was always how long it would take. I would say, "It's so long, it's going to take close to a year." That was an interesting job too. Learned a lot about traditional Chinese medicine and herbs. Did a lot of browsing in a Chinatown bookstore and learned something about Chinese folk medicine. At that time, I was also thinking about changing jobs. I was still working at the Naval Medical Center, but the Navy commander who had given me much responsibility had completed her active duty assignment and left. Shortly after that, I left for a technical information specialist job at one of the institutes at the National Institutes of Health and learned a new skill—retrieving specific information from the medical literature database at the National Library of Medicine.

I finally retired in the mid-1980s, shortly after the IBM personal computer appeared on the scene. Still translating small jobs at the time, but I also started to volunteer at a computer learning center for seniors until the late 1990s when I moved into the retirement community where I now live. I still dabble with my computer and play with digital photography, printing and cropping my pictures.

Photos from a booklet produced by daughter Elaine, for her mother's 90th birthday.

CHAPTER FOURTEEN

Wayne H. Wong 黃榮洪 (1922–   )
U.S. Army

Wayne H. Wong arrived in Wichita, Kansas, in 1935 as a paper son, and went to school while working at his father's restaurant. He describes the people of Kansas as "kind and fair and loving" and was touched when Mrs. Marguerite Wiggins invited him to her home for a roast beef dinner and offered to be his American mother. He served in the 987th Signal Corps Company of the 14th Air Service Group, an all–Chinese American unit in World War II. He talks about building his life in Kansas, finding his wife after the war, starting his own restaurant, and fulfilling the American dream. He is author of a memoir, *American Paper Son.*

My birthday on paper is August 9, 1922. But my real Chinese birthday is December 30, 1922. My paper name when I entered the United States was Wong Hung Yin. My birth name is Mar Ying Wing. When I took my oath of office to become a naturalized citizen, I anglicized Wing to Wayne. (Wing means prosperity and glory.) I combined my paper name and real name for my American name as Wayne Hung Wong. I didn't want to change the surname because my Army papers are Wong. My children's college degrees are Wong. All my real estate is all under Wong. So there's no point for me to change to my real name. So I just keep the name Wayne Hung Wong.

Where did you grow up?

I was born in Changlong village, Baisha district, Taishan County, Guangdong Province, in southern China. I finished grade school at 12 years old and I came to the United States at 13. It was November 1935 when I left Hong Kong. And when I got to the United States, it was December 4th.

What was your family's reason for moving?

Same as everybody else's. In China, if you get to be 13 years old and you—I was not smart enough to go to high school. Didn't go. My father decided he wanted to bring me to the United States to start a life at that age. So that's the reason I left.

I was just about two or three months old when my father left for the United States in 1922. He came to Wichita, Kansas, and became a partner at the Pan American Café.

Left to right: sister Suit Wing, mother Sen Kell, wife Yee Kim Suey, grandmother Soo Shee, brother Henjung (seated on Soo Shee's lap), Wayne Hung Wong, father Tung Jing, and brother Ying Kam. In Baisha, Taishan, Guangdong, China, April 1947.

So, of all the places in the U.S., how come your father ended up in Kansas?

Okay, that's a very good story. Wichita is the biggest city in the state of Kansas, and about 30 miles from Wichita is El Dorado. Oil was discovered in El Dorado. A lot of people moved in, opened up oil-drilling companies, and that makes a good opportunity. So some of the Chinese in Tyler, Texas, which also has oil and coal, came to Wichita and opened up a restaurant they called Pan American Café.

And those people were fairly old. When they got old, they wanted to sell ownership of the restaurant to somebody else and go back to China to spend their golden years. My father came to the United States as a bill collector, because my grandfather was an exporter/importer. You ship merchandise to the United States, and if they don't pay, you need a bill collector to get the money. One of my father's friends in China told him about the restaurant.

You know, in 1882, the United States passed the Chinese Exclusion Act, a law that said no Chinese are allowed to come to the United States as a laborer. Anybody in the world can come to the United States to work, but not the Chinese. However, if you've got money, you can come to the United States doing business.

If you have $2,000 U.S. dollars you can come as a merchant. Some of my aunts' husbands came to the United States as merchants. But my father came as a bill collector. And since he was a bill collector he had no right to bring the children to the United States. If later on you read my book, you'll see how my paper father obtained his false native-born papers.

So you came when you were 13 years old. What was life like in Wichita?

When I came to the United States I went to school at Carleton, which was about six blocks from my father's restaurant. My father's restaurant has three stories. The restaurant was on the ground floor, and on the top two floors were apartment rooms.

So when I got there in January they put me in first grade reading and fourth grade math. And I studied hard. The first semester I was in first grade. Second semester I was in fourth grade. Third semester I was put in the fifth grade. Then in the fifth grade my teacher said, "I'm going to teach summer school. If you attend summer school, I will put you in the sixth grade, so you can try to catch up with the other children." So that's what I did. The following year I attended junior high school.

Were you the only son?

No, I have one brother living in Wichita, Kansas, one brother lived and passed away in Hong Kong, and my one sister still lives in Hong Kong.

Did they all come over too, or just you?

Eventually. The Communists took over China in 1949 and in 1950 we were free. The Communists eased up on rule—cruel rule against the overseas Chinese. My mother paid a certain amount of money. So they left China and went to Hong Kong, I think in 1952. My father owned a building in Hong Kong.

My sister and my mother knew some people at the Catholic mission. So the Catholic mission wrote a letter to my father in the United States and said, "If you will send us the airfare we will get the papers processed for your wife and your children to come to the United States as refugees." My father sent about $1,000 dollars for each one. He brought his wife and his youngest son.

Let's go back to what life was like growing up in Wichita.

Well, in the summertime I worked in my father's restaurant. I worked 12 hours a day, 7 days a week. At the end of the month, they paid me $7. I remember very well the manager—this is a cooperative restaurant—six people owned each share. Every month, they divided up the profit six ways. I remember the manager—every month when they divided up the profit, there was some extra money. He said, "I want to give some of this extra money to these student boys, they've got little money. Give them a dollar." My pay was just $7 a month for 12 hours of work and 7 days a week. So I never will forget that. I said, "Gee, I work so hard, I want to make my money work for me." So I saved money. I invested in real estate, and I became independent.

I was in my junior year when Japan bombed Pearl Harbor. I told my teacher, "You know, I'm 20 years old, and they're going to be drafting any time. I don't want to serve in the infantries. Too tough."

A week later Mr. Yoe, my electricity class teacher, said, "Hey, Wayne. I got a brochure from the Signal Corps and they're looking for high school students to do radio communications. Telephone and telegraph work. If you don't want to serve in the infantry, you need to enlist." So I enlisted in the Army on November 6, 1942.

Was Wichita pretty much all white?

Wichita is mostly white. And I think at the time the black population was only about 7%. But the population at that time was about 75,000. At its highest point, there were 72 Chinese. So that's only about 1% Chinese.

Were people friendly or unfriendly?

They are friendly. The Caucasians eat in the dining room. The black people, if they want to eat, they eat in the kitchen.

Oh, so if a black person goes to your restaurant they eat in the kitchen?

Yeah, most of them. Like the shoeshine boys. The restaurant is downtown. If a painter or shoeshine boy came to the restaurant and ate, they always sat in the kitchen.

So did pretty much people get along together?

Yes.

Black, White, and Chinese?

When I went to the first grade, I remember there were about maybe seven or eight black people. They were segregated, in a different room. They would be in one room. But I was mixed up in the same room with the Caucasians. *(Laughs)* I think there were about four Chinese in the whole grade school.

So did you like it?

Yeah. The teachers were very helpful. I was in the fifth grade when my teacher said, "You know, if you go to summer school with me, I will get you up to intermediate right away." And at summer school the teacher said, "Mr. Wong, you are doing so well, I'm going to promote you another semester." So I became an eighth grader.

If I want to summarize my life in Wichita, I would say Wichita is a good town. Wichita is very friendly, and I could not have been more blessed to be in Wichita. I'm grateful for the teacher. I remember I was an office boy for my junior high school. I helped her make mimeographs and did office work.

Mrs. Marguerite Wiggins, the school secretary, invited me to her family's house for Sunday dinner. We had a very nice roast beef dinner. And then when I was leaving, Marguerite said, "Wayne, you don't have a mother here. Your mother is in China. I want to be your American mother." So, now I have two mothers. What else can you ask for from a person who says that she wants to be your mother?

I thought that was wonderful. That shows you the people of Kansas. They are kind and fair and loving. So I'm very blessed, very grateful, for the people of Wichita, and stayed there and made it my home. We are four generations in Wichita now. So my life has really been blessed and I met a lot of good people.

What was high school like?

I was a junior in 1942. I was elected vice president of the boys' junior class.

What was the election like?

I just declared in the school paper that I'm running for Vice President of the Junior Class, and I was overwhelmingly voted in. I got 75% of the vote. So that's pretty good. So there's no Chinese discrimination whatsoever as far as I know. If there was then they wouldn't have elected me. I was a straight-A student.

After high school, you went into the military?

On November 6, 1942, I enlisted in the United States Army Signal Corps. They had a new program called the Enlisted Reserve Corps (ERC). If a person enlisted in the Corps, he would receive 8 intensive months of instruction at the Mechanic Learner Training School in Kansas City, Kansas. The instruction would include radio theory and radio repair practical training. After the trainee had completed the program he would then be inducted into the regular Army Signal Corps and serve in the communications department.

What was being in the military like?

I went to radio school at Kansas City to study radio theory. I went there for about six weeks, and they paid for ERC. I think at the time they were paying $75 a month for me to go to school before I was inducted into the Army. I rented a room. It ran about $30 a month—a dollar a day for a room. There were six ERC students in this house.

I was just in the Reserve Corps, not in the Army yet. When you finish, they induct you into the regular Army. After I was through with my ERC, I went to basic training in Camp Kohler at the Signal Corps Induction Center, not very far from Sacramento. We did marching and sharpshooting and things like that. After basic training, I went to recruit school. I was sent to Camp Crowder, an old radio signal school. This was very big, near the Ozarks, in Missouri.

I was made supply sergeant. At that time the Signal Unit was already filled. The cook, the radio operator, and the transporter positions were already filled up but they needed a man that knows how to keep records. So I did the ordering for whatever the GIs needed—some requisition to buy shoes, boots, or whatever they needed. I was there from November to June, about eight months. Then we went overseas.

We left Camp Crowder June 1st and we went to Wilmington, not far from Los Angeles, and then we got on a Liberty ship. They're very slow. They only have about seven or eight speeds. A Japanese submarine will run nine.

Wayne Hung Wong in his unifrom in
Wichita, Kansas, circa January 1946.

So I was with the Army Signal Corps 1943 to June '44. We went to Calcutta, India. From Calcutta, we flew over the Hump. We were assigned to radio communications on the French Indochina border. I was in the 987th Signal Operation Company, which was Radio Communications. Our unit was the only unit that was all Chinese American. We were picked because we could read and write Chinese, and they wanted people that knew Chinese so that we could communicate with the Chinese soldiers.

After the United States dropped the two atomic bombs, the Japanese signed the papers for peace. It was the only time I saw Japanese soldiers. They came to the headquarters to arrange the procedure for surrender. So the signing of the surrender was in French Indochina, or what is now Vietnam.

And you saw this?

Yeah, I saw the delegation of five members of the Japanese general staff that came from Hanoi to talk to our headquarters, to the commanding Nationalist officers. They signed the surrender papers in Hanoi. But the preliminary meeting was in our headquarters in Kaiyuan.

How did you feel?

I felt wonderful. The war was over. They surrendered. We didn't have to do any dangerous fighting at all. So that was wonderful. That meant we were going home.

How long were you away from home?

I enlisted November 6, 1942, and I was discharged in 1945, December 21st. The paper shows I got out of the Army in 1945, December 18th. So I enlisted for 37 months.

How did you meet and find your wife?

After the war was over, I heard there was transportation. A ship to go to Hong Kong. I caught the second ship to Hong Kong, the General Gordon. That's when they started the Trans Am Pacific travel.

So I got back to China in '46, I think maybe in July. I told my mother, "You know, I'm 24 years old and I want to find a wife. Not like the old Chinese. They marry and leave their wives in China and they come to the United States to work. But now I have the right to marry and bring my wife, what they call a war bride, to the United States, because I'm a GI." So I took off and that's what I intended to do. So we let the marriage people know that I was looking for a wife, and then eventually we got married and moved to the United States to live and make a living.

Did you get to pick someone or was it like a matchmaking—

Matchmaking. Mostly it's relatives who do this and say, "I got this girl here, you want to meet her?" You meet her, talk a little bit. They match you by your birthday, what time you were born, what day you were born. Do you know that the Chinese—You're Chinese, right?

Yeah.

You born in the United States?

Yeah.

Then you probably don't know this. In the old days, they'd match you by the time and the day you were born, to see if you were compatible. And you'd marry with your counterpart.

Did you believe in it or do you believe in it?

Well, whether I believe it or not, it's the way the custom was, so I just said, "All right, Mother, this is what you said." You did what mother said. Whether they match or don't match, and there's something wrong, that's something else. It was the twelfth interview when I picked Kim, my wife—

Is it usual for people to go to twelve?

I really don't know. I talked to a lot people, and they usually see four of five of them. We came to Kansas, because my father is a part owner of the restaurant. So when I came back, there was a job waiting for me.

Were you happy about it, or—

Yeah, I was happy about it. I was 25 years old when we came to work in the United States. I was married in '46. My girl was born May 1st, '48. And then there are three other children. All four were born in May, even the last one of six years' difference.

What was life like when you returned from the Army?

It's work. It's moving forward to build a family. So I worked and I saved money and I bought a house and the children were comfortable. We just kept saving money. During the Korean War, Wichita was very prosperous. There were four aircraft companies. Three were in Wichita: Boeing, Beech, and Cessna.

When the War broke out, they were open 24 hours a day. Women—a lot of riveters, they all went to the factory. They worked in the aircraft companies making airplanes. A lot of women did this because all the men, the young men, had gone in the Army. There was something like about 18 million women in the U.S. working in World War II.

How about your restaurant?

The restaurant was open 24 hours a day.

Another story I wanted to tell is when I was discharged. The lieutenant said, "Sergeant Wong, your rank is staff sergeant. That's pretty high." Staff sergeant is just above the middle ground, okay? He said, "You really need to enlist in the Reserve in case a war starts again. If you're in the Reserve, you can keep your rank. Otherwise, when they draft you you'll have to be a private and start all over again."

Well, by 1950 I had three kids already. The first one was born in '48, then '49, and '50, all right three in a row. So when they sent me the papers for reenlistment, I just told them "No. I don't want to reenlist." My wife didn't even go to American school. They all depended on me to make us a living. If they drafted me in the Army, they all would be starved.

Then what happened in 1951? The Korean War. So I did the right thing at the time. It saved me and it saved my family. If I had not done that, I may not have lived and may not have been able to take care of three kids. Just to speed things along … There were three children and then we had four children. We worked in the restaurant. And then I changed jobs.

How come you ended your restaurant job?

I worked in my father's restaurant until 1953 as a partner. They paid me $280. Then this man at another restaurant offered me a job. He said, "Wayne, if you want to come work for me, I'll pay you $320 a month."

This restaurant was also Chinese. So for $40 extra a month, I just quit and changed jobs. It was 1954, and I worked there for about two years. And then my son had an accident—somebody ran a stop sign and hit my boy. So I told the owner during lunch hour one day, "My son had an accident. I need to go home." And the owner said, "Hey, this is lunch hour. You can't go." He said, "This is the hour I need you to work." But I said, "My wife doesn't speak much English. My son got hurt by a car. I don't know how bad it is and I've got to go home to see him." He said, "No. It's too busy for you to go. It's lunch hour." So I said, "Look, my children are more important than my job." So at the time I was angry. I left and went home to see how my boy was.

From left to right: Wilma, Edward, Wayne, David, Kim Suey, Linda. Wichita, Kansas, circa 1976.

How old was your son?

He was in the first grade.

Oh, wow.

Yeah. So when I got home, it was okay. Later on he was passing blood, urinating blood. I said, "The kidney must be damaged." I called the doctor, and he said to take him down to the hospital. They monitored the urine and gave him some medicine to heal the damage. And then the third day, the doctor said, "If the bleeding has not stopped today, we may have to operate and see and repair the kidney." But luckily it stopped bleeding. He did have one kidney that was damaged quite a bit.

Because I decided to leave the restaurant in order to see my son's accident—that was September—about two months later, the week before Thanksgiving in November, the owner called me up. He said, "Wayne, you don't need to come to work tomorrow. You don't need to come to work anymore."

He didn't say anything else. He just hung up. So the reason was because I defied him. Because hey, my boy is hurt. I was around the house for a couple of weeks, and then my wife said, "Hey, you need to get a job. *(Laughs)* You've got some children to support." So I looked in the newspaper, found the ads. A nightclub, they needed a chef. So I went down and applied, and he wanted me to work that very day. I said, "No, I got to get things straightened out, and I'll work in a week." So I went down to work for him in 1956.

What club did you work for?

It was called the T-Bone Supper Club. They had a striptease show. You bring the whiskey, and they charge you for the mix, whatever you mix with the

Wayne Hung Wong and Yee Kim Suey,
Wichita, Kansas, circa 1947.

whiskey.

So this is a gentlemen's club?

Yeah, high-class gentlemen's dinner show club. No minors in there, because it's a drinking place. The law says that you can drink, but you cannot sell it, the whiskey. So the owners said, "All right. We'll open up a club, you bring your own whiskey, and then we sell you the mix, 25¢ a cup."

And did that business do well?

It was a big business. They were full every night. I was there 16 years. They expanded three times. It seated 300 initially, then 400, and finally about 520 people. I ran the kitchen as chef, managing everyone and ordering food supplies.

What kind of food did you make?

Filets, chicken, lobster. There were only just two cooks, one salad girl, and then a dishwasher.

In your own restaurant later on, did you also cook or were you a waiter?

The original owner of Georgie Porgie's Pancake Shop was a Lebanese shoe repairman, George. He hired this lady to run the kitchen and everything else. And then this lady had a better job at Beech Aircraft, so she quit. When she quit, she took all the cooks. He couldn't get a cook. So the owner put the restaurant on the market and I bought it.

Finally I had my own restaurant, Georgie Porgie's Pancake Shop was named after a nursery rhyme. I took care of the dining room and hired some Caucasians for the kitchen help and to waitress. It was a pancake shop—it was not Chinese food. However, we occasionally served Americanized Chinese food such as chop suey as specials for lunch or dinner.

I was the cashier and enjoyed seating, pouring coffee, and talking with my customers. I also took care of ordering the food supplies. My wife ran the kitchen, and in the beginning she didn't even know how to speak English or read the orders *(laughs)* and she was washing dishes. In about eight months she learned how to listen to the waitress's orders and bravely forged ahead with everything else. Later on my last son joined us. So we were there 20 years.

And when did you have your Georgie Porgie Restaurant?

In 1972. When I quit the T-Bone.

After 16 years?

In '72 three of my children are in college, and my youngest one is in high school. So my wife said, "Wayne, I'm going crazy at home. I want to go to work. I want to make some money on my own so I can have my own money to spend." And I said, "I don't blame you," and I said okay.

So I said, "There is a National Linen not too far from us, about three blocks." National Linen rents tea towels, aprons, uniforms. So I got her a job at National Linen. So we went to work at 8:00 and got off at 4:00.

The job was folding linen. No skill needed, you see? So she just worked one day. The next day, I say, "Kim, it's time to go to work." She said, "No." Well, I said, "You want to work. Why don't you want to go?" She said, "I don't like the job." I said, "What's wrong with the job?" She said, "Well, I stand there and fold, and fold, and fold. No chance to go to restroom. I wet my pants. *(Laughs)* I don't want to go to the job." So she quit.

You know, I thought that was funny so I put it in my book. Then somebody said, "Oh Mr. Wong, it's a humorous story. But don't print that your wife couldn't go to the restroom and wet her pants on the job!" I said, "It's saying they ought to set a time, a certain time, to cut down the time, so they can go to the restroom." So that's nothing wrong. I thought that was pretty cute.

So I said, "All right. You don't want to work there, then I'm going to buy a restaurant." I looked around. We looked at two, three restaurants, and the pancake shop was the most advantageous.

The owner said he wanted $40,000 for the restaurant. So I told him, "No, from your sales tax, your volume only grosses $6,000 a month. I'll give you $30,000." Then he said, "Okay, I'll tell you what, I settle for half of it. I drop $5,000 and you go up $5,000." So I bought it for $35,000.

And then I worked at the dining room. And my wife had three cooks there, Caucasian cooks. My wife washed the dishes. We worked for maybe six months, and then one time the cook died. He just *(snaps his fingers)* had a heart attack in front of the stove.

He died, the cook. A big, heavy cook. My wife just sat down there and cradled him and then talked to him—I happened to be in the dining room. And then I came back and said, "No, he's gone. He had a heart attack." That was terrible. But anyway, so we worked there for 20 years. I did the buying, and she did the preparation every day. We opened up six days a week. We had Mondays off. After 20 years, my wife said, "I'm tired. I want to quit." I said, "Okay. You're tired. You'll quit." We just quit.

But in the meantime, we made quite a bit of money. So there was a real estate man came in there and he said he wants an investor. "All you need to do is build a building and we'll lease the building for you and they pay your taxes, they

Left: Wayne H. Wong with family and extended family in Wichita, Kansas, 2014
Right: Wayne H. Wong's daughter-in-law Lillian and son David

pay insurance, and they pay the repairs." It's called Triple Net. Triple is taxes, insurance, and repair which the tenant pays. Normally if you rent a restaurant, you pay taxes, insurance, and the repair. So I said, "Okay." Eventually, we did more real estate with QuikTrip, a gasoline company, and a Taco Tico.

Taco Tico?

You know Taco Bell? Taco Tico is a Wichita company. The Taco Tico was going strong in Wichita before Taco Bell was ever built. My son owns it, we own it. They all made good money on the rent. So we retired in 1990. By that time I owned quite a bit of real estate.

So my advice is, really, if you get fired, don't get discouraged. Still better things come ahead. The important thing is that you save your money, invest your money, or triple net. When I first went into business, I took the papers to a bookkeeper to file the taxes and keep track of the profit and loss. The bookkeeper happened to be about two doors from my house. So I gave him the papers and then he figured it all out.

He said, "Well, what I did—I put in some re-sell, they do not have to pay sales tax." So he did about $200 re-sale and saved me 4% sales tax. That's what he told me.

So I looked at him, and I said, "No, I'm running an honest business. I don't want to cheat the government. I don't want the government to come and break my neck. I want you to report exactly what I took in, what I sell, what it costs me." So I fired the bookkeeper and got me another bookkeeper. My philosophy—I was able to sleep. I want that nobody can tell me that "You cheat this." So I get me a bookkeeper, I said, "I want to keep honest books. I want to keep Uncle Sam and everybody away from me." So that's what I believe. I report everything I make. I pay my taxes. And then I invest my money in real estate, and I invest my money in stock. And these days, you know, a lot people lost money in stock. Not me. When I buy my stock I want to make sure they pay me my dividend. So I usually go to a big company. AT&T, utility, light company, all those things. So in this stock market crash I still make a profit.

Wayne H. Wong with grandchildren at National WWII
Museum, New Orleans, May 2013.

Any thoughts on being Chinese American or growing up Chinese American?

You know, in all my life, being Chinese American, I didn't experience any discrimination. Just to repeat to you, when I was in junior high, I worked in the office, and the secretary took me back to her house and have dinner with her. And when we leave her mother says, "Wayne, since your mother is in China, I want to be your American mother." I said, "Good, I'm happy to have two mothers to care about me." So, in my life, I think I have always been doing right, honest, pay my income tax, and all my investments have worked out fine. Later on, they build a QuikTrip for $1.8 million …

So I wrote my book, and the editor was at Wichita State University History department, and he was a very good friend of the library. And the librarian that ran the library told us there were hardly any Chinese, Oriental history books. So I said, "You know what I'm going to do? I'm going to donate some money." He said, "Okay, you donate money, we'll create an endowment for you to buy Asian books, only Asian books." I said, "Okay." So I just went ahead and did it. See? I have quite a bit of money and I do not worry about my children or my grandchildren. They will be comfortable with my money. So the royalties from the book I put to Wichita State. And it's called the Wayne H. and Kim S. Wong Endowment Fund.

And you're the first Asian—

That's what she said, "You're the first Asian to have an endowment at Wichita State."

PART II: KOREAN WAR

Chinese Were Considered a Threat

The Korean War era was marked by McCarthyism and the Red Scare, and was a dangerous time for Chinese Americans. Communist China was considered an enemy to the U.S., especially with stalemate and armistice in the Korean War. Chinese in America, by association, were suspected of being Communist sympathizers.

Everett F. Drumright of the U.S. consul in Hong Kong alleged that almost all Chinese in America had entered the U.S. illegally[15] and that the "paper son" system was devised by Communists to send spies to the U.S.[16]

Any Chinese American involved with any leftist, progressive organizations or unions, or who had ever criticized the U.S.-supported Chiang Kai-shek, was suspected of being a Communist and was questioned and investigated.

Chiang Kai-shek's Nationalists, the Kuomintang (KMT) were funded by the U.S. in the name of "democracy" even though many Chinese Americans hated him and the U.S. was aware of his corruption, widespread killings, and his causing inflation and scarcity in China.[17] However, Chinese Americans in fear of being deported or imprisoned proclaimed themselves anti-Communists and did not speak against Chiang Kai-shek. Banners at the yearly October 10 Chinese National Day proclaimed "All 30 million overseas Chinese support the Republic of China" (which occupied Taiwan, and which the U.S. recognized as the legitimate government of China under Chiang Kai-shek's leadership).[18]

In addition, Chinese in the U.S. were not allowed to leave for the mainland because it was feared their advanced scientific and technical knowledge could be used to aid the Chinese Communists against the U.S. government.[19] One hundred twenty Chinese intellectuals, including Dr. Tsien Hsue-shen, who founded the Jet Propulsion Laboratory at Cal Tech and designed some of America's earliest missiles, were detained and not allowed to leave for years. American customs agents impounded books and films suspected of having originated from Mainland China. Individuals in left-wing Chinatown organizations such as the Chinese Hand Laundry Alliance and the China Youth Club were watched, bugged, and interrogated. To intimidate subscribers of leftist papers like China Daily News, FBI agents visited them and warned them to drop their subscriptions. Virtually the entire Chinese community was under scrutiny and investigated[20]

Confessions Program

In 1956 the Immigration and Naturalization Service (INS) announced the Chinese Confession Program. The government asked that any Chinese Americans who entered the country with fraudulent papers come forward and also implicate others.[21] Chinese Americans were told it was in their interest to come forward, though they weren't promised anything specific. Individuals who confessed had to surrender their documents of citizenship and were required to accept that they could be deported if their confession was denied. Not coming forward warranted being deported. So did being suspected of "leftist political acts." Chinese Americans lived in fear of being watched and reported and this put enormous stress on the Chinese American community. When the program ended in 1965, 13,895 people had confessed, exposing 22,083 others, which resulted in the closing of 11,294 paper son slots. The Chinese American population in the U.S. (excluding Hawaii) in 1950 numbered only 117,629.[22]

Despite the unfair and unethical treatment of Chinese Americans and the psychological devastation to the Chinese community during this period, there were Chinese Americans like Rita Chow and Kurt Lee who served and represented their country.

CHAPTER FIFTEEN

Kurt Lee 呂超然 (1926–2014)
(a.k.a. Chew-Een Lee)
U.S. Marine Corps

Major Kurt Lee was the first Asian American to receive an unrestricted regular commission in the U.S. Marine Corps. This was in 1946, two years before desegregation became a matter of policy by Executive Order in 1948. He was awarded the Navy Cross and Silver Star Medal for gallantry and heroism in combat while serving with the 1st Battalion, 7th Marines in Korea, in September–December 1950, in the Chosin Reservoir Campaign. As the first Chinese American to lead a Marine combat unit, some Americans questioned his loyalty before engaging in battle against the Communist Chinese Forces in Korea. Major Lee also served in the Vietnam War.

Major Lee was featured in The Smithsonian Channel documentary "Uncommon Courage" and the books *The Last Stand of Fox Company*, *Breakout* and *Colder Than Hell*, the last being adapted into a mainstream feature film.

I visited Kurt Lee in February 2010, at his apartment residence in Washington, D.C. At 84, he was practicing tai chi daily. His apartment, spacious and elegantly decorated with Chinese sculptures, scrolls, and many bookcases, had a wall where two swords hung: one was a Marine officer sword and the other a Japanese officer sword.

See this sword on top? It's a Marine officer's sword. Every Marine officer has this sword with his name engraved on it. And the other sword up here is a Japanese officer's sword, Samurai.

Is this sword actually used in war?

No. The Marine sword is only for ceremonial or ornamental purposes, in parades and all that. It is not used for cutting.

From Iwo Jima, a Japanese officer's sword. The Japanese officers used swords to cut, to kill with, and they carried a sword that's sharp enough, tough enough, to cut through a machine gun barrel … very strong. And this is called a K-bar, a Marine Corps fighting knife. It has many purposes, primarily for killing *(laughs)*, but also for eating, cutting saplings, tree branches, and all. But it's very famous, the Marine Corps K-bar. This one was given to me by one of my men as a gift.

Kurt Lee, 1948

Mine was used too much out there, covered with blood, *(laughs)* and all that. So it's better to have a brand new one here, as a gift, nice and clean. Well, there are some things that I'm proud of as far as collecting these items is concerned, and each one of them has special meaning to me. Some of them are pretty valuable, others have primarily sentimental value because they were given to me by my brother, and by the women I married and, you know, people close to me.

The first thing I'm going to ask you is when and where you grew up, what your family was like, and what it was like growing up.

Well, I guess you have to start off with my name, Chew Een Lee, even though later I legalized the name Kurt, primarily because of my admiration for the Germans. To me, they had the most efficient military. I had a lot of admiration for them because they sent a military mission to China to train Chinese troops. And the two best divisions I remember were the 88th and the 89th Divisions. And these were infantry divisions equipped totally with German equipment, German weapons, and all. And they held up very well against the Japanese in the early days of the War. And as far as myself is concerned—

Which period was this? When the Germans trained the Chinese?

This happened before the Sino-Japanese War that officially broke out in 1937, on the so-called Marco Polo Bridge. The Japanese used a pretext to take military actions against the Chinese and start the war—1937, I think. I don't know how old I was then, maybe about 10. But that was when I first took intense interest in the development of the war. I felt a lot of pride with magazine photos showing what the Chinese soldiers did fighting against the Japanese, and was horrified at those gruesome pictures of atrocities committed by the brutal

Japanese army at Nanking, for example. I was quite young at the time, but it just turned my stomach to see those women's mutilated bodies and live prisoners being bayoneted, beheaded, and things like that. But anyway, when growing up, I was a member of a pretty large family, as most families were in those days. And I had three brothers and three sisters. I was the oldest boy, number three actually amongst my brothers and sisters.

I was born in 1926, 84 years ago. My father had gone back to China to marry my mother. My father, and my mother also, were members of—they called themselves Zhongshan [Chungsan 中山] people. Originally I think their ancestral district was called Xiangshan which means fragrant mountain. But because Dr. Sun Yat-sen was born there and he had used the name Zhongshan for his name [Sun Zhongshan], they changed the district name from Xiangshan to Zhongshan, you know, to honor their most famous son.

Most of our people, Zhongshan people, settled in Hawaii in immigrating to the New World, as opposed to settling on the mainland, as was done by the Taishan [Toisan 台山] people. Both were Cantonese, but the dialect is quite different. My name is Lee—Lee Chew Een, but it is not the usual Lee. In our dialect it is pronounced Lee, but in Cantonese proper or Mandarin, I think it's pronounced Lu, and amongst the Taishan people it's pronounced more like Lui. But in ours it's called Lee, so that's what I assumed. We, as kids, were sent to private Chinese school.

In Sacramento, where we grew up—when I was born, my father was starting a new venture, as a farmer. Before he married my mother, he was more a political activist, because of his knowledge of English. He served as a labor contractor with the white landowners who used primarily Chinese labor to grow their fruits and make their profits. But when he married my mother, he had to return to China, to an arranged marriage, in order to bring her back.

And my mother was the most gentle and, to me, the most beautiful Chinese woman I've known. My father—I don't really recall anything. I was about two years old when he moved his family from the Sacramento River delta area to the city because of the Great Depression taking place. You know, crops left unpicked in trees, rolling in the fields and all that, and there were no ways to make a profitable living by farming.

So my father went into business with some family members at a place called Grass Valley, northeast of Sacramento, toward the Sierra Nevada, known for its gold mining activities. And there were a couple of Chinese families up there, Zhongshan people, related to my father's family. But it was pretty rough. He had to drive back to Sacramento, spending all day replenishing grocery stocks and all that. And my poor mother was pretty much left alone with, at that time, four kids aged 1, 2, 3, and 4.

My father was coming back home so late, and my poor mother, without any knowledge of English, was trying to raise the kids, and mind the store. So my father accepted an offer from some Chinese fellow who had an established business providing bulk farm produce to restaurants and hotels in the Sacramento area. My father took over his business. I guess the other guy retired. And so that was my father's livelihood, and he was not happy about it, but it provided shelter, food, and everything for the family. He sent us kids to private Chinese school in the evenings following daytime public schooling.

We were all sent to private Chinese school and we were teased by the Taishan kids. We didn't speak their dialect, which we considered very sing-song. But they were jealous of us, because for some reason, even though I was not the best of students, I can assure you that somehow I and my brothers and sisters always ended up top of the class. In Chinese school, you know, they list the standing of the students, written by brush and ink and placed in a glass frame at the end of each semester. And the first four names were always my sisters, myself, and my brother. And later on Chew Mon, when he came of age. He was just one year younger. Chew Mon was in Korea with me as an Army officer, by the way, and had a tremendous record out there as a good Army officer. But as kids we didn't associate with him. He was too young. And all other kids called him *(laughs)*—I guess he'll never live it down—called him Sweet Pea. But I guess we grew up in pretty normal fashion. At home we spoke Chinese [Zhongshan] to our parents. But with the neighborhood kids and at school, and amongst ourselves, we used English, as soon as we learned English.

You said that in those days Chinese people couldn't own farms, so that's why Chinese people had to labor for—

At that time, oh certainly. I was too young to know the significance of laws and things like that, but we were all operating under the Chinese Exclusion Act of 1882, which was not repealed until after World War II started. And it started with Pearl Harbor in 1941, but it was not until 1943 that the White Fathers in Washington, the politicians, decided to repeal that very onerous, discriminatory Act against only one people, only one race, the Chinese. Everybody else was treated more or less equally as far as being immigrants were concerned. But for some reason the Chinese were considered sub-human. But I did not experience that while going to school, by the way. Our student body was mainly Asian. It was an American school with about 60% Japanese Americans, about 30% Chinese Americans, and the remaining 10% Mexicans, Whites, and a few Blacks, and all. So the competition really was between the Chinese kids and the Japanese kids. Quite frankly I was not impressed at all by the Chinese kids, although as I look back at it now, there were a few bright girls. The boys, to me, were uniformly dumb. And with the Japanese, they were equally dumb, but at least they were good in athletics. And they played baseball, they were all on the Varsity teams, baseball, basketball, and—I don't think we had a football team.

Was the neighborhood and community you grew up in mostly agricultural?

The community, no—it depends. If you lived in the rural areas in California

The First Basic Class, Marine Corps School, Quantico, Virginia, 1946

at the time, along the Sacramento River Valley, which is a very fertile valley where the Zhongshan people settled and built up the dikes to keep the region from flooding, it was certainly agricultural pursuits that these people—they were farmers basically, and people who supplied to farmers, and general stores and a few restaurants and all that, in these older Chinese communities. From urban Sacramento, within a span of 100 miles, there were about two or three little small towns, which were inhabited primarily by Chinese Americans. For example, Walnut Grove, Isleton, and there was a small community called Locke. The Chinese called it "Lockee"; I guess it was founded by a Caucasian named Locke. But it was built entirely by the Chinese, and was inhabited almost totally by the Chinese. And it's become sort of a heritage-type, historic site in California. But those were farmers. I do not recall any of the days when my father was actually engaged in farming.

I recall some things when I was two years old, but it was not until three that things started to register in my memory bank, where we lived and all kinds of little details. And when we moved into the house next door—when I became four, I knew then my two older sisters were sent to American school—kindergarten, first grade, I guess. And when I became five I joined them by entering kindergarten at Lincoln School, and spent my entire childhood attending Lincoln School until I graduated. All my brothers and sisters graduated from Lincoln School, which went up to the ninth grade—junior high was from the seventh to the ninth grade. And then we transferred to what is called the senior high school. It would be either Sacramento High or McClatchy High. McClatchy was perhaps slightly better by reputation than Sacramento High, because there were more rich, white kids living in the neighborhoods around McClatchy High, I guess.

Sacramento High School was where most Lincoln School graduates went and where we Asian kids were first exposed to White mainstream society.

In Sacramento the Japanese kids had their Little Tokyo through which my brothers and I used to walk en route to Chinese school. And the Chinese had their own small Chinatown, but it was not the same thing as Little Tokyo, where they had all these organizations, you know? Black Dragon Society, Bushido, and many shops had the samurai-type dolls dressed in replicas of samurai armor with weapons and all that. And members of our class at Lincoln School were obviously members of these really pro-Japan associations and societies. I remember a guy named George Sakai who always swaggered when he walked. He was not too smart, but he had a strong, robust body *(laughs)* for being just a little kid. But he had two little retainers—I call them retainers. And I knew—I'd read enough at that time—about Japanese culture and all that. And here this guy was swaggering around and the others—I guess in American society they would just be his buddies. But they acted as his retainers, you know? Do anything that he wanted them to do. So that was the society.

The 'retainers' were also Japanese?

Yeah. I got into fights with these Japanese kids. I was open and friendly with Chinese American boys out there, in the class, but I was never buddies with any of them. As I think about it, I don't think we shared much common interests. It started with my personal conflicts with the Japanese, I guess.

Speaking personally—I can't say that about my brothers and all—I consider myself to have been very selfish, a very selfish person, as a kid. I expected something special all the time. I liked to be treated differently. Like eating food that I liked to eat. I liked to be the first, to have first pick *(laughs)* at whatever part of a fish or whatever the food. And really I was not very nice. But yes, surprisingly, years later when we were all adults, my brothers always said that they had a great time, you know, as kids, and don't recall my being excessively selfish and all that. In fact, my brother Chew Mon, who was in the Army—I'd like to talk about him a little bit more in the military sense, because he ended up as a career military officer, the same as myself.

I find surprising the later publicizing of the academic excellence of Asian Americans, for example, that as a group how well they perform. I'm not so sure. One of the kids, Chinese American, to me was a real dumbo. He was sort of big for a Cantonese kid and all that. And he was not particularly good in sports or anything else. He was just a big, dumb kid. But, you know, he was accepted at a dental school and became quite a success. *(Laughs)* I was surprised to hear, when I was in the Marine Corps, that this fellow—we used to tease him and call him Handsome Eddie, because he was not really handsome, at all. Those Japanese kids had a big time with him. I got into many fights with the Japanese and I guess I wasn't bad with my fists. Every time we had a fight—There were actually railroad tracks out there, not far from the school. and the kids after school would all gather around and watch the fight. One time, one of the big athletes—Atsugi, I remember his name, his last name—he was a good basketball player, and I don't think he really wanted to fight me. But he was egged on by some of his—This is a thing about kids, you know. A lot of them would like to do things to me, but they were afraid to. So they'd try to have somebody else do it. Anyway, we got involved in this fight, and I just happened to get his nose bloodied and then while fighting his blood got all over him, and all over me too. But he was obviously beaten by me. When I went home that day, and my father saw me, after he came home from work, and my mother said I had been in a fight, he took a look at me, my father, and got very angry at me. I said, "Now wait, this is not my blood." *(Laughs)* And then he realized that it was the other kid's blood. He gave me a big reward—a big shiny silver dollar. But after that fight, the Japanese kids got one of their real pugs, a guy who was a boxer, to challenge me. He was part Filipino and part Japanese. His twin brother Clarence was a nice guy. But this guy, Conrad, was the one who was the pug.

What's a—

Pugilist. His surname was Floggio, I think it's Filipino. It is not Japanese. He kept challenging me, and I didn't want to get involved in another fight, but in the end I was forced to. And it was the same group of people out there, watching and egging him on, and encouraging him, and all. As I think about it, never had I seen a Chinese American kid watching those fights. Nobody, you know, cheering me on, and all that. And it was sort of a draw, but I knew somehow that I could not beat him, and all I did was to keep him from beating me. And then, something happened, somebody appeared, and it was my big sister, Faustina. She broke up the fight and started to shout at these other kids, "Stop doing this! Stop this!" And I guess, in a sense, Floggio was sort of a relieved dude. He was getting as tired as I was. But that was the only fight that I felt I did not win. But thereafter he turned out to be decent. He never—I think he was initially egged on by all his other buddies and all that. And once they found what he could not do, then they let up on the pressure on him. I was about 11 or 12 then.

In the movie, in the documentary, you mention that your dad had a tattoo.

Yes. My father was a very smart man and physically he's a very strong person, because he had to lift big crates of lettuce, sacks of potatoes, when he delivered these things and stacked them aboard his truck. But what amazes me about my father was ... his wide intellectual interest in different things. He had a big collection of books. It's so sad—When he was dealing with farm produce and all, he had these many boxes of books, at a corner of the big garage where he kept his truck and where he had to do a lot of cleaning—a salvation to some of their sacks of potatoes and what-have-you. So he needed a lot of room to work and his books were always in a corner. And as a kid I used to thumb through them, you know? And they were not protected, they were just kind of wooden cartons, and they got mildewed, and I guess silverfish—not in good shape, but I salvaged a number of them. I realized there were books on every subject. Chinese-English dictionaries, they looked so crude and elementary compared to dictionaries of today. But a lot of his books were on philosophy and a lot on religion, including Christianity. And he did a lot of reading.

My interest in books has been longstanding. As a kid, I remember in the third grade, when we had library classes, the kids could pick up any book and read it. And I remember picking up books on cavemen, you know, anthropology. But the most interesting book was Van Loon's history of the world. It's a big, thick book, but I found it fascinating reading about the history of Western Civilization. I recalled many things later on when I got involved with the world history of this and that. "Oh, I've had this before." So it was very easy. And I used to like mystery books, or the macabre. So we made use of the libraries. But you know, this is the thing about it, that I said I was selfish. It was catering to myself. I never discussed what I read with my brothers, for example, or apparently couldn't care less what they read and so forth. So now I hope I will be able to go to California. I have only one living brother left. He's a year younger than I. Chew Mon, my military brother, is dead and my kid brother Wilbert has passed on too. And it would be nice to ask my remaining brother, Buck, and ask my sisters, What did you do at this point in time when I was doing that? I have no idea. They have different kinds of memories and maybe I—But I felt when I entered the military I pretty much broke off with my family. I did not correspond or do things like that, and it was all in trying to develop myself into a better Marine and all that kind of stuff.

Can you talk a little bit about the documentary? You talked about how you were influenced by Sun Tze and the Three Kingdoms, your dad's tattoo.

I didn't even answer your question about my father, as a young man, before he married my mother. I guess the woman was nice-looking, and he had his own personal life. There was talk that he was interested in some nightclub singer *(laughs)*, Chinese, in the town of Locke. Apparently, they had a dancing girls' house there. And so, he's been around, so that he—I know this—he had two tattoos—one on his shoulder and one on his forearm. They were good, aesthetic tattoos, not like what was shown in that documentary.

Oh, so it didn't actually look like what was shown?

Not at all!

So they just made up something to—

They just got some tattoos from some second-rate tattoo parlor. They asked, "Have you got anything 'Death Before Dishonor'?" Those were the words that I remember emblazoned on a very good artistic tattoo. And the other aesthetic tattoo was of a shield with two flags, the American Flag and over it, the Chinese Flag. But that Chinese Flag was of the early days, I guess, right after the 1911 Revolution, where they had these five colors, the stripes. So the tattoos in that film—my father would never have agreed to have any of these coarse-looking examples. They just weren't very artistic.

So he got them for—to impress a lady, or—

No, I think it's just like the Marines do, and men do, it's more a macho thing. If you have a brawny arm, put a tattoo on it, and all that.

(Laughs) Was he ever interested in the military?

Yes, but he was between wars and all that. He was a little late to get involved with World War I. But I found him wearing, in one of the photos, an Army uniform. During World War I the soldiers were called doughboys. And he looked pretty nice with this Army tunic on. He had the campaign hat. Then he had on leather puttees. A puttee is a covering to protect the legs from thorns, brambles, and all that. We used cloth leggings in the Marine Corps. We used to bind the strips, you know? Then we had leggings which—canvas and all that. But his was made of leather.

Puttees—I think it's an Indian word—east Indian. But you know what? When I asked him about it, he was very embarrassed. He said, "I never served in the military." He wanted to—this is very big—he wanted to so much that he went out and bought the whole uniform, and had his picture taken. But by then the war was over, and so he never did serve. This was before he married my mother, obviously.

But my mother was the one who—strangely enough, my mother was unusual in that she was an educated Chinese girl—woman, during those times. She was an only child, a girl, and her mother took pity on her. Normally people of her class ended up with lily feet, deformed feet, because they were bound. And had to grow up that way, painfully—a horrible custom from the Qing Dynasty. But her mother allowed her to leave her feet unbound so that she could have a happy time playing with the village girls. But she went to school, and the other girls didn't go to school. My mother told me that she was not a very good student, she liked to play hooky. But the fact is that she learned enough about Chinese culture so that she could read novels, opera librettos, and what-have-you. *The Three Kingdoms* is very famous. It was an actual period right after the Han Dynasty, a period when instead of one dynasty controlling, the empire was split up into three kingdoms, and this is part of real Chinese history. But all I remember is that my mother would be reading this aloud to me and to my younger brothers, if they had any interest and patience to listen. And usually they didn't, and I ended up being the only one there absorbing wisdom. Now that, hanging up beside the swords, is a scene from *The Three Kingdoms*, and that is a very valuable piece of true antique tapestry.

In recent years I have been picking up history books on China, and I have *The Three Kingdoms* here. I plan to read through the tome but, you know, there's about 1,500 pages. It comes in three volumes here. So I was familiar with that period from my mother's reading and learned that in Chinese history much was founded by martial prowess. And Americans are familiar with a lot of baloney about the Knights of the Round Table and things like that. But the Chinese far predate them on martial matters, the use of body armor, developing tactics, and all that. I mean obviously the Europeans did not develop or get involved in this until much later.

They had a person that supposedly matched Sun Tzu, who existed centuries B.C. and was recognized as the Chinese genius in tactics and strategy. And the Germans have their Carl von Clausewitz, but today's military scholars consider that the teaching of Chinese Sun Tzu was much more complete because it included what happens after defeating the enemy—not something to be left wide open to descend into chaos, like in Iraq and all that. No, proper war planning including statecraft. And the Chinese rulers have all these different aspects of war well thought out before they embark on military expeditions.

* * *

I personally find it very amazing what the Chinese did in this [Korean] war, because they were pretty much unprepared, you know, with all the equipment and weapons having gone to the Nationalists courtesy of the U.S. Government. And when the Chinese Communists defeated the Nationalists this really started a new chapter in China's modern history, leading through to the two World Wars and the beginning of Gongchandang, the Communists, and Kuomintang, the Nationalists, and Dr. Sun Yat-sen.

There had been over a century of humiliation of China as a nation. At that time it was still a so-called empire, the Qing Dynasty. As a result of the Opium War [in the 1850s], that's when the doors were broken down and the Western imperialistic powers began to carve China into spheres of influence in grabbing what they could of the resources and treasures of China. And they treated the Chinese in a very humiliating way. Even in America, through our laws, we considered the Chinese as inferiors, not worthy of immigration or any type of political or social contacts. And so when China entered the Korean War, I experienced a sense of vicarious pride. I happen to know enough of Chinese so that when we captured Chinese documents from a dead enemy or live prisoners of war, I found it very curious that in their diaries—they seemed to maintain diaries, all the leaders did, even squad leaders—you could see checkmarks. You could see where ... the Communist system was actually being brought into play, even in jotted down diary comments and all that. Apparently entries had to be screened *(laughs)* or approved or whatever, checked by the Commissars, you know.

Commissars: political officers as opposed to the military officers. In the Chinese Communist Army they have a level of supervisory personnel to ensure that people are properly and politically indoctrinated and that they adhere to what is considered proper, under Communism. But what struck me was that the diaries

Kurt Lee and Linda Lee wedding photo, 1960

followed a common format. The Chinese troops loved to sing martial songs for morale purposes. Recently I've been listening to "The Ode of the Motherland," a song, very patriotic. To me, it has the combination of "America the Beautiful" and "My Country 'Tis of Thee." But these diaries all had a section at the forefront of martial songs so that the squad leaders could teach troops how to sing.

I find interesting that in all these diary notebooks the martial songs are preceded by a frontier page showing Chairman Mao in front of two crossed Chinese flags, with no mention of Communism. And all the tenor of these martial songs is strict nationalism, keeping the Imperialists from invading our sacred borders and saving the sovereignty of the nation by defeating what they called the Capitalists and Imperialists. Nothing Communistic was brought out, from my scan of these. I see these little checkmarks that indicated somebody had checked these diaries and all. So what I found amazing was that when the Chinese entered the Korean War, they had just barely got the country together. They had yet to be organized as a nation in any real meaningful way, I would say. Yes, they've had the government structure and infrastructure in place. But there was hardly any Military-Industrial Complex established for making heavy weapons, for example, beyond light infantry weapons—artillery pieces, armor, planes, motor transport, any of the other needed weapons of war. They had not got their industrial capacity together, when they were forced into fighting America. That's what it turned out to be.

So what do you mean when you say the diaries had checklists?

Well, a patrol leader might make a little entry or record in his diary/notebook about what happened on his patrol, a virtual checklist. Check marks would indicate that the Commissar was aware of what took place, and everything that went on. In my mind, what they're trying to detect is whether there were any acts that might indicate less dedication and zeal for the mission, or perhaps a breakdown of morale and discipline within the group, things like that.

And you said that when the Korean War ended, it did not result in a victory for the U.S. You said Chinese Americans here were—

Well, this is true. Now, when the Chinese Communists entered the war there, they knew that they were up against American air power and modern, sophisticated weapons. And they knew they were at a disadvantage. And even more so when they went into the northeast corner of Korea, where the Chosin Reservoir was, where there were rugged ridgelines and steep slopes in a mountainous area, where they could not use any motorized transportation. They had to leave behind all their heavy artillery and equipment. We did not have any of those problems, although the terrain hampered the use of tanks and armor.

So they entered the war with only mortars, machine guns, that they could carry on their backs. And they had no developed logistics supply system. So, other than one or two units of fire—which means the assigned ration of ammunition to fight for the day there—once they got involved in an attack of an American position, they might expend all their allotted ammunition. Unlike the Americans, the Marines—we had developed a strong logistic-supply system moving up. Even though there was only one narrow road for transport, the Main Service Road [MSR], at least they could get trucks in with needed supplies. And if not, if they were blocked by enemy action, we had aircraft dropping supplies, ammunition, food, water, and things like that.

The Chinese had none of that. Once they expended all their ammunition in the assault they had to wait for one of their comrades to get killed, or wounded, and pick up his weapons and ammo, to continue the fight. Their communications were horrible. They did not have radio and adequate communication to issue orders and apply the time-space factor.

Space is the distance from point A to point B, and the proper use of time is essential for success. If you were to attack an objective, you must have all your people at designated positions by a set time for a coordinated assault on point B, for example. And if the time is all used up countering enemy actions or negotiating terrain obstacles, you cannot get there in time to participate in the coordinated attack.

So this was what the Chinese forces were up against. But even with that, they soundly defeated the powerful 8th Army on the western front and, even with heavy casualties, drove the 1st Marine Division out of North Korea on the eastern front. My brother, First Lieutenant Chew Mon Lee, who had just rejoined his unit in the 8th Army after having been wounded at Pusan, was badly wounded again in the western front, but ultimately received the Distinguished Service Cross for heroism.

He told me the Army troops were routed—they panicked and ran, dropping their weapons, their packs, and equipment—and ran! On the Marine side, we fought our way out against twelve CCF Divisions and inflicted heavy casualties on them. The Chinese High Command knew that the 1st Marine Division was the most formidable and potent American fighting unit. The propagandists painted us as a unit comprised of murderers, rapists, and criminals to be stamped out as snakes in their homes. They were convinced that by trapping and destroying the Marines at the Chosin Reservoir area, the news would be demoralizing to the already defeated UN Command, and America would have to sue for peace under Communist terms. The Marines refused to cooperate and the UN Command was resuscitated to fight two more years to a draw in 1953.

The Chinese would walk over everything. That's their strategy, obviously. And so when they forced MacArthur's UN Command back across the 38th Parallel—where MacArthur, as far as I know, never had any authority to cross, and least of all to go smack against the Yalu River, which is China's water—you can see the concern of the Chinese to have an enemy right at the border. And that's why they have always wanted North Korea to exist, to remain a viable, friendly country, to act as a buffer, so that no enemy would be right on the Chinese border.

Oh, you asked about the Chinese considering [the Korean War] a victory, that they drove the UN forces out of North Korea, which is true. They consider the People's Liberation Army as never having been defeated in battle in any war, including fighting against the Marines at the Chosin Reservoir. You know, you can't argue with the fact that there are no Marines there now. They inflicted heavy casualties and yes, they themselves suffered even greater casualties.

I think about 30,000 were killed in action out there. But they have boasting rights to say that they saved North Korea and maintained the buffer, and all that. One thing I wanted to make clear was the fact that we fought so well in Korea, not just at the Chosin Reservoir, it's wherever the Marines were sent—in the South, in the Pusan Perimeter, when the United Nations forces were on the verge of being swept into the Sea.

They sent the First Special Marine Brigade out there to bolster the UN forces. And the North Koreans were planning to make a final push through—push them to destroy and cause the UN troops to surrender. When the First Special Marine Brigade was sent there, it consisted primarily of the 5th Marine Regiment reinforced with other supporting weapons. The Marines always fight as a total integrated unit, so that they can take care of themselves and accomplish this mission with their own artillery, tanks, aircraft, and all that.

And they did save Pusan and created the opportunity for MacArthur to make that landing up in Inchon. He could not have made it without getting the 1st Marine Division reactivated into a total combat unit. And it's been brought out in the films that it wasn't that easy, with many untrained Marine reservists called in.

A lot of the men, reserves that were brought in, had not even completed boot camp training. This included NCOs, corporals, who had never been through boot camp. And that was why I had this big contention with my fellow officer Lieutenant Joe Owen in Baker Company, and I thought his approach was wrong. For example, his men didn't even know how to salute properly. So he says, "Well, we've got to teach them how to employ their mortars, rather than how to salute." But a salute is only a manifestation of courtesy and obedience to orders, and unless you know how to obey orders, you will always be in an iffy situation, in battle. And this is why I said, "Well, I disagree. They'd better know military courtesy so that when the chips are down, they recognize who the leaders are."

But at Pusan, this enclave at the south corner of the Peninsula, when they were about to be overrun, my Army brother, First Lieutenant Chew Mon, a member of the Second Infantry Division that was stationed up in Washington State, was sent over to join the fight. They had a number of other divisions out there, the 24th, 25th, the 1st Calvary, whatever. But my brother's outfit, although it was a duly organized infantry division, had some shortcomings. At that time, the shortcoming was in receiving serious training.

And I don't know why, but the Marines always seem to exact the maximum no matter what training time we have, instead of having the people go out on liberty. The Marines always know what their primary mission for being is, and this is to be prepared for combat. We all like liberty, you know, and Marines have more than their share of fun while on liberty, but when the time comes for them to report back to train, they are there for serious training. Not so with the Army, that accepts minimal training in peacetime.

* * *

So my youngest Army brother Chew Mon Lee got to Korea before I did, and the formidable 4th North Korean Division was preparing to cross the Nakdong River, which forms a delineating border for this enclave—enemy on this side and the UN forces practically with their back against the Sea. And Chew Mon was an Army first lieutenant at that time, had a 75-millimeter recoilless rifle unit. I don't know whether he had a company, or a platoon, or what, but anyway—as with most infantry officers, each one should be qualified to serve as a forward observer [FO]. In other words, being on an outpost to call back firing missions for the artillery, on how to fuse the missions, time on target, and all that.

So he was the FO on this hilltop overlooking the Nakdong River, which coursed along broad and fast. And each artillery shell has a fuse, which could be adjusted to see whether they explode in the air, or upon impact, and so forth. It's called a VT fuse, a variable time fuse. You could time it to explode at set height just before it hits. So he was using the VT fuse against the enemy who were trying to cross the river. And he said from his observation post there he could see the enemy let loose a torrent of tank fire to keep the Americans down, so that they could not fire back at the enemy trying to cross the river.

What they did was hook each other's arms so that maybe 10 or 12 soldiers would form a ring, or a circle, and this way they had many more feet and if one of them went down, you know, the others could hold him up and so forth, in order to half-swim across the river.

Chew Mon was calling down artillery fire to explode on top of the enemy so that "the river ran red with their blood." And they were like clusters of ants, they would break apart and then try to regroup, re-cluster, but many of them were killed that way. But they succeeded in crossing the river.

And Chew Mon's men abandoned him, they deserted him. This is something inconceivable in the Marine Corps, that the troops would run and leave their leaders alone. Chew Mon was wounded at that time, and his men all abandoned him. Even his pack and all that stuff, where he was observing, were still there and he had letters and all that, from his wife Rose, in the bag.

But, to survive, he burrowed—dug into a haystack where he could barely see what was happening from inside. He had to pull the straw down so that the enemy would not see his burrow hole. Well, the enemy established their own outpost at the same location while they sent the troops that succeeded in crossing to circle around the base of the hill to attack any Americans there. And when morning came, Chew Mon awoke—you know, he had passed out, unconscious from his battle wound. Then he heard this jabbering outside, and he very gingerly crawled his way toward the entrance so he could hear and see a little better. And he saw that there were three people there. One was a North Korean officer, who was controlling the thing, his radio man, and an apparent scout or runner, who came up—he was the one jabbering to this lieutenant.

Chew Mon said he was excitedly pointing down at his legs, and the officer barked some orders and immediately all three of them picked up the gear and ran off the hill.

And Chew Mon said the North Koreans were saying—he served as a Korean Battalion Advisor when he was a second lieutenant. This was back in 1948 or '49, so he could speak a little Korean—And what the man was saying was that new Americans were coming and they had yellow legs, they were wearing yellow leggings—they were the U.S. Marines. Many Koreans had fought with the

Japanese Army as laborers.* They were not allowed to form their own combat units, they could not be trusted. But they were pressed into service as military laborers. So many experienced the same thing as the Japanese military, when fighting the Marines in the Pacific.

You mean in World War II?

World War II, the Pacific fighting, yeah, which was just five short years ago in 1950. And a lot of the Korean military people knew something about Japanese military training, because they served as military laborers.

Anyway, so then the Marines came and Chew Mon recognized that they were indeed Marines, so he called out and was rescued by the Marines. And they flew him to an Army hospital in Japan to recover, even as I was aboard ship headed for Korea.

On the radio, as we approached Japan, there was a female North Korean broadcaster, who served as Tokyo Rose did during World War II. She broadcast to Americans troops in the Pacific, giving all kinds of propaganda about how Americans were losing the war and all that. And here was a Korean woman who was doing the same thing, broadcasting misinformation and propaganda. In mock sympathy, she said, "Here is one of your great soldiers. He is now dead, because here is a letter from his wife." She read a letter from Rose written to Chew Mon on the radio, even as Chew Mon was listening while lying on a hospital bed in Japan. The letter was taken from his abandoned knapsack on that hilltop.

So we docked at the Japanese port of Kobe for two days. This was in order to re-juggle and shift some Marine units. We still had people being flown from the east coast to join a unit that was already on its way to war. Shifting of personnel could only be done in Kobe, so that they could shift units before we landed in Korea. And in the meantime the troops were permitted to go ashore for a few hours of liberty. None of my machine gunners were allowed to go on liberty.

I had my men debark with full combat gear, including all the machine guns, and full ammo boxes, to drill on the hard, concrete docks. There were enough spaces to go through machine gun drill, but it was pretty rough on the knees. The drills included setting up firing positions, action taken when taking casualties, shifting gun position while under fire, and so forth. Not wanting to damage anyone's knees while drilling with heavy weapon loads on the concrete docks, I sent a scout out to look for a more suitable drill field. He found an athletic field adjoining the dock area, but it was occupied by a group of Marines playing football.

We use the term, in the Marine Corps, when troops are playing games and not serious, as "playing grab-ass." They had a sock stuffed solid and they were tossing it around like a football. I recognized the unit. It was a Mortar Section

---

* During and before World War II, Korea was occupied and colonized by Japan.

of Able Company. The station leader was a first lieutenant named Bill Davis who was junior to me by a couple of years. When I took my men out there, you know, his mortar section had about 20 men in it—I had 65 men with me, and I told him, "You people are playing grab-ass. We need the field to train." And he said, "Well, we were here first. We finished our training." And I said, "Unless you move your men off the field, my Marines will run right over you." So he cussed and got his men and moved off the field. So we had some training before we went aboard ship. It was our only field training that I … could see what state my men were in, before we landed in Korea to face the enemy.

So, unfortunately, my men never had any liberty, and some of them bitched about it, but that's the Marine Corps, and I had no empathy for that. So we went to war. Chew Mon in the meantime was—Before we went back aboard ship, Chew Mon got the word that the Marines were there—the 7th Marines. He knew I was in the 7th Marines. And he made a great effort to find out where our ship was located, and all that.

He was still very weak—I forgot what wounds he had. I think he was shot through his lungs or something. And he came looking, and just before the Navy pulled up the gangplank—the gangplank or gangway is where you walk to go aboard ship—there was Chew Mon and another officer, a companion he took with him. He was waiting, and the officer of the deck passed the word to the captain of the ship and said, "There's an officer down there on the dock, and his brother is aboard ship." So they graciously gave us ten minutes.

Chew Mon came aboard ship, and we had an impromptu reunion there, and he was telling me about all that happened to him, you know. That was how I learned—he told me about hearing Rose's letter being read over the radio, and so forth. But it was just a brief reunion. He had to leave quickly. So I went to war with the Marines. And after we landed at Inchon, the 7th Marines participated in recapturing the city of Seoul.

We landed about 5 or 7 days after the big assault landing. We went in as the Division Reserve. This was why we became the spearhead in the next big division action, because we were barely bloodied at Seoul. We set up blocking positions outside of the city to keep the North Koreans from trying to escape. And we had a few casualties there, the first being one of my machine gunners. He was shot through his stomach, but he was lucky because his metal belt buckle partially deflected the bullet. So he had only a flesh wound and was smiling and waving goodbye to people on being evacuated. He had a "million dollar wound" and was getting a Purple Heart for it. Yet, he had done virtually nothing at that point.

But anyway we accomplished our mission, incurred a few more real casualties, and came back down to the port of Inchon, to re-outfit, get in new replacements to replace damaged gear and stuff like that.

And lo and behold, who should come in there just when we were about to board ship to go up to North Korea but my brother, Chew Mon. He had just been released from the hospital, and he was rejoining his 2nd Infantry Division, with the 8th Army moving north on the Western Front. And that was where—I was happy to see that he had recovered from his wounds to the point where he could return to action. But I had him forfeit some of his new equipment to me.

You know, Marines always operate on a shoestring, with leftovers, it seems. But he had on new style Army belt suspenders, which can accommodate more hand grenades being hooked on it—but, more important, his carbine. The Marines use a 15-round magazine for their carbines. But the Army has these new, what we call "banana clips," which would hold 30 rounds. And Chew Mon had these banana clip magazines which, taped together, would mean a 60-round magazine!

So I had him exchange magazines, and I took his two banana clips. And I was the only one in the 1st Marine Division with this extra load of ammunition for my carbine. A carbine is a small rifle, and officers carry carbines. Some officers carry a pistol, but this is primarily when you're on a tank or something like that. But infantry platoon commanders carried carbines.

So Chew Mon rejoined his unit and went north with the 8th Army and I went north to the Chosin Reservoir area, initially by sea. When the Chinese hit the 8th Army, this was before they hit the Marines. The reason the attacks were not coordinated was because of the time-space factor. The Chinese on the east front could not get their people into position because of the terrain—rugged mountainous terrain and all that. Well, for whatever reason, they had to leave behind all their artillery. They could not take them up into the roadless mountainous area.

When the 8th Army was hit, Chew Mon was at its vanguard. He told me that had the Army moved up like the Marines, they would never have been trapped like that. Because, before the Marines moved on, they would send men up to the high ground, on both sides, before moving forward, so that they could see what was on the other side.

But the Army people remained road-bound with their motor transport. And I guess their officers didn't want to climb the hills themselves, and didn't have the guts to send the men up there, if they were afraid or too lazy to go up there themselves.

And so, when the Chinese opened fire—using enfilade fire, you know, like this, on my knee here—with many men firing from this side, your bullets will go through and hit a very small number. But if you fire from positions at the front and the rear, your bullets will go through the whole column. And even though I was missed in the beginning, I might be hit by bullets from the other end. Enfilade fire can also be applied from a flank.

So the Chinese had their units dug in to deliver devastating fire, and totally disrupted the columns, and Chew Mon said that the Army troops panicked. They had tanks up there, but the troops dropped their weapons, dropped their packs, and started running to the rear. And Chew Mon said there was nothing he could do, short of shooting them in the back. These men just ran to cluster behind the tanks, and the tanks were blind—they couldn't see anywhere. And they were swinging around, without concern for the troops—running over all kinds of their own men hiding behind their tracks, the metal tracks, and got crushed to death by their own tanks in a scene of horrible chaos. Total disorder! In the military this type of defeat is called a "rout." It's not just a defeat; you know in defeat you could still do many things. You can withdraw in an orderly fashion with one unit protecting another to set up other positions. But if you run in panic without some degree of control, there is no semblance of order; you cannot organize.

Chew Mon said despite shouting himself hoarse trying to stem the rout, he found himself running with these men. So he finally broke loose from them—to cross a river, which was half-frozen at that time, to reorganize as many men as he could to take them back into the fight.

That was where he earned the Distinguished Service Cross [DSC] for "extraordinary heroism." He deserved another DSC back there when his men abandoned him, on that hilltop. Because of the tremendous enemy casualties he caused calling down artillery fire over them, it delayed the enemy from coming across, to enable the Marines to be shifted to restore the beachhead. Otherwise the enemy could have overrun the whole Pusan Perimeter.

But he went back into the fight and did a tremendous job, and he went up on top of a tank, heedless of enemy fire directed at him, and directed the tank, under his control, when and where to shoot and all this and that. And he was shot up very badly, badly wounded, shot through his chest, through his throat, and he was lying on the side of the road. He could not talk—with froth and blood coming out of his nose and mouth. But what he did was to pull out all his military insignia, his rank, and his Army Infantry insignia, so that people could see that he was an American soldier.

He was lying on the side of the road out there, with casualties on and off vehicles. The road was clogged, jam-packed with Army vehicles going south, running away from the pursuing enemy. And then, right in front of him, inching along the road, was an Army major in a Jeep. He was the only occupant in this Jeep, and he had a half-full trailer in which he had his gear and stuff. He must have been a Staff Officer, picking up his maps and stuff.

Chew Mon could not speak but tried to get his attention. The major looked down at Chew Mon and quickly averted his eyes. He stared straight ahead, and refused to help him. His vehicle remained there for a full 20 minutes before moving on—horrible! And Chew Mon was suffering horribly from his heroic battle actions, but couldn't talk or do anything.

And this is how Chew Mon found God in combat. It was the act of Providence that the things that happened, happened. One of the trucks that went by—one of the soldiers looked at him, and said, "That's Lieutenant Lee!" And the soldiers clambered off—the truck was inching along—and put him aboard the truck then and there. They all ended up at some Aid Station or field hospital, where all the casualties were being prepared for evacuation. But then all the soldiers moved on because they were not wounded and all were still with their unit. But Chew Mon was there, on a stretcher, and everybody was picking up the gear and running. They were evacuating that Aid Station.

They were abandoning, or relocating, the Aid Station, and moving and running. And Chew Mon again would be abandoned. Nobody would even look at him. He probably was just a Korean to them. They ran.

How could they think he was a Korean when—

Well, it's easy—he's Oriental.

Even when he's wearing a different uniform?

Well, they were kind of the same type of uniforms—because the U.S. Army provided most of the equipment and uniforms to the South Korean Army.

Oh, so they thought he was South Korean?

Whatever, and they—again, by stroke of Providence, some officer came in, looking for his briefcase, I guess, and found Chew Mon there. He was at the Aid Station before, whether he was wounded or what, I don't know. So he picked it up, and saw Chew Mon there. He was Chew Mon's battalion commander, who recognized him immediately. He barked orders to have him evacuated with the rest of them, otherwise he would have been left there to die. So Chew Mon ended up being evacuated to Japan, and then to the U.S. because of his severe wounds. I stayed in a military hospital longer than he did, six months. I think he was released after three or four months. But my injuries were shattered bones and all that, and his was puncturing of body organs—without much fractures. So he was healed, sent to Chinese Language School at Monterey, and then back to Korea for a third tour to control and train Chinese land-crossers.

Can you tell me again why those people evacuated the Aid Station? They were running away from—

Yes, the Aid Station is usually set up to the rear, away from the front lines—where it's relatively safe, where the enemy action and artillery cannot reach them. This enables medical personnel to treat and care for the wounded and all that. They would perform triage, treat wounds and illness, and classify which ones should be evacuated out, back to military hospitals in Japan. And from there they make a decision whether to treat them in Japan or send them back to the States, if the severity of the wound warrants it.

And they were evacuating it why?

They evacuated because the enemy was coming close, and would soon overrun that so-called rear area, so they had to displace and move. The defeated 8th Army moved all the way back, south of the 38th Parallel Line.

I asked you earlier why you chose to be a Marine, and why you volunteered for it. When you found out Marines are the first to die, and they get the worst job. And you said you volunteered and said, "I'll do it!"

I did say that.

So why is that?

Why did I choose to be a Marine?

Yes.

I always felt that when you enter the military, it should be for the frontline duty, as I said. And at the time when I was inducted into the service, I really was not that knowledgeable about what the Marines were all about.

One day when I was coming home from high school, on my bike, I saw a man in green uniform with red chevrons entering a house. I wondered what kind of uniform that was, because I was accustomed to the drab olive Army uniform while in the Junior ROTC. But when I was standing in line and they were to break up these new recruits into different services, they asked for volunteers first.

The Marine Corps is known to be the preeminent military service, I found out later. At the time, I was not sure, but when I was told that their mission was to land first and incidentally perhaps, get killed first. *(Laughs)* That appealed to me that it is really the cutting edge of all the services. If the Marine Corps is the cutting edge of the Armed Forces of America, then that's what I wanted.

So for that reason I immediately stepped forward, and have had no regrets since, because it turned out to be far more than I expected. If you don't know much about it, they'll certainly teach it to you in boot camp, which included a big dose of Marine Corps traditions and history. This was all part of the program to instill a pride and esprit de corps in a person, to be proud of being such a unique organization that you cannot help but want to contribute your own potential to make Marine Corps history and Marine Corps glory. And the chances are that you may not live to enjoy it, but that's *(laughs)* beside the point. At least you feel some rationale for being from the outset.

You talked about how you at first wanted to be in the Air Force, because you wanted, if you were going to die—

I have to admit not many Marines knew this, but I was initially more interested in what is called the Navy V5 Program. The Navy had a program for training naval aviators straight from high school, and you go directly to the flight school to become a naval aviator.

Again, it has something to do with my being Chinese, Oriental, a fatalist, and in wartime, people get killed. It's all over the newspapers. And if you do your job, then the chances are that you will be killed if you do your job in combat action. I thought of the Navy aviation more as an end rather than as a beginning.

At no time had I ever thought of establishing a career to retire old and grizzled with a bunch of kids, grandkids, and all this. To me, life is such that if you give your fullest at a time of peril, then chances are you'd be killed.

Well, then, how should you die? Well, the glamorous way, I would say, is not in a ball of flame and being shot down, if you're not good enough—by an enemy aircraft or enemy anti-aircraft fire. And, hopefully, in doing so I could inflict the maximum damage to the enemy before I'm hit. But I have no fear of death, really, because to me, if the wound is not severe enough for instantaneous death, then the chances are you will survive. And with unknown consequences, you know, survival could be horrible too, and death is easy in my mind. So I really have no fear of death.

I always felt that some of my men—you know, the Americans are a strange group of people. They have all this religious fervor, being a Christian nation and all that, but most people are hypocrites. And the real God-fearing type—when the chips are down in battle, then you find that a lot of these people suddenly realize that they're not prepared to die. The one thing drummed into them is the existence of heaven or hell, or whatever. So that was why, in one instance, when I was first wounded, and brought into the aid station with my arm in a sling at that time—it was painful, but not a real bad wound. There were Marines at the aid station who were badly wounded, limbs torn and stomach and chest wounds and all that, all waiting for transport back to the Army field hospital 40 miles away. All the Marines had were the Battalion Aid Stations.

Anyway—I resented very much the way this episode was depicted in one of the books. I think it is Martin Russ's book, *Breakout*, and he wrote that it was on the parallel of Army General Patton, who would have made a very fine Marine Corps general. But he was the one who created a sensation, going to war with pearl handled pistols, and all that. If you go to the Fort Myer Officers' Club, you'll see a big portrait of him. He loved war. And when he came across a wounded soldier in a hospital—I don't recall what the true circumstances were, whether he was really not wounded, or had shellshock, but, there he was lying in bed, and the General took his gloves and slapped him, on the face, saying, "You're not a true soldier. You don't have an honorable wound. In fact, you're just malingering up here."

Well, anyway, at this aid station, I saw three Marines—big, hulking Marines—gathered together, loudly talking and blubbering, crying, whining, which annoyed me very much. First of all, all the other Marines were quietly trying to nurse their wounds, maybe groaning every now and then because of pain. But here these guys were loudly talking and blubbering away. So I walked up to them and said, "What's the matter? Were you people hurt or wounded?"

Instead of answering, they started blubbering, "I saw my buddy so-and-so blown apart" and "I saw this and that—this and that." And I said, "You men were not hit in any way? So what are you doing back here? Why don't you go back where you belong with your unit, fighting the enemy?" And they quieted down immediately.

Major Kurt Lee, 1967

It was not my authority or prerogative to direct them, because presumably their unit allowed them to come down to get medical help. I suppose in today's war this would be pretty common and anybody can relieve himself from combat duty by claiming this and that, by blubbering away in an aid station or field hospital.

So I told them to "Shut up, I don't want to hear another word out of you." And so they whimpered and at least followed my instructions, and all. I don't know what happened to them and hope the doctor sent them back to their company. But in that book Martin Russ depicted me as "browbeating one poor, helpless Marine." These were three huge, hulking Marines out there, and "browbeating" them and figuratively slapping them like General Patton *(laughs)* did another "malingerer" and all that. So it got twisted a little bit, and this is why I have launched some sarcastic comments on certain book authors.

I'll show you it before it gets printed.

(Laughs) Joe Owen was reluctant to show me his book *Colder Than Hell.* The only part I contributed was where I got wounded and liberated a Jeep in order to return to my unit—that little escapade. Because I gave him that information, and even so he didn't get it totally correct. But anyway—

Yeah, that's why for me—I can give you a manuscript and you can correct it before— because it's an oral history and ... what matters is getting it right.

It is very easy to be confused about a certain point, and maybe I would feel that oh, that's not important to make a big deal about—a paragraph about, or—

You said you became a Marine also because you wanted to show that a Chinese American can do it too. Because you were the first Chinese American—

I was the first regular, what they called "unrestricted" regular officer in the Marine Corps. A restricted or limited duty officer could be an interpreter, for example, or a translator. Usually they're recruited as Reserve Officers from academia or with other experience they enabled them to contribute in a specialized way.

But knowing something about the dynastic history of China and of the high degree of sophistication of the Chinese military, in the martial arts, in tactics and strategy, I know that the Chinese as a race is second to nobody in military prowess.

But because of the recent couple hundred years of history with the Europeans coming in to defeat and exploit China with their superior weapons—the Chinese have to get themselves up again with new technology and weaponry. And if I'm in the Marine Corps, I would have the same benefits as any other American would have. It would, to me, be a relatively simple thing to show that—I always had confidence that I could do better than the other person—it is a matter of application and perseverance and all. When I entered the Marine Corps, I had the advantage—boot camp was very rough. As they say, even though there's a lot of humor about going to boot camp in San Diego—that makes you a "Hollywood" Marine, whereas the real Marines supposedly came from Parris Island, in South Carolina, where boots have to stand rigidly while sand fleas crawl around you and bite your face, your nostrils, what-have-you. But I was very proud to have gone through the San Diego Recruit Depot. All drill instructors were Pacific War Veterans mainly of the bloody battle of Tarawa.

Marines call them "DIs" and they wore that Smokey Bear hat, you know, and even the Army's copying everything about the Marines. Anything good we have they try to copy. But, as one of the book writers said, "The Marines don't go in with any badges, tassels, to pretty up the uniform, because that doesn't contribute to any efficiency."

The Japanese Nisei made a great reputation for themselves that they're able to fight, and I don't see why the Chinese could not be as good, and as committed to be good soldiers, good Marines, and equip themselves for combat with the very best of them.

And that was my challenge, and I was confident of it. When I went to boot camp, I had this advantage of some Junior ROTC training. At high school they had this tactics book, the "Bible," for the Junior ROTC Program. It's like the Marine Corps Guidebook all boots use. It has a bit on tactics, a bit on marksmanship, a bit on scouting and patrolling, on map reading: everything.

I not only read that book, but I digested that book. I was probably the only one who checked out a rifle to bring home and to practice hitting the deck, running, and how to—they say "hit the deck," the ground, with the rifle extended, while running take up a firing position quickly and all that.

In boot camp they used me as the example and model because I was doing everything correctly while other people seemed to be having a hard time. To keep the heels down, for example, when they hit the deck. The DIs have taught that if you land on the beach and you hit the deck, to take up a firing position, and your heels go up and you don't try to control them, you'll kick up sand, and the enemy could see these sand spurts. So these are things that I already knew. Like marksmanship and all that. I was already in high school an expert rifleman and in the Marine Corps I quickly became an expert in all the weapons that I use—rifle and pistol and carbine.

Did society have doubt in Chinese people, do you think? Did American Society have doubt—

Well, unfortunately I think too many Chinese Americans are intimidated by the loud mouths of Caucasians, and give white Americans a sense of superiority and thinking that always relegates the Chinese—unless they're engineers, professors, teachers, or doctors—as a bunch of laundrymen, or people that don't have the same verve that an American should have. You never hear of a Chinese being called an alpha male and all. *(Laughs)*

Nowadays there are.

Now there are some, yeah sure.

Can you talk about how you led the 500 people out of Fox Hill, the particular episode that you won the Navy Cross for?

Oh, that. Well, I suppose my most productive venture in combat—to me combat is easy: people look for leaders, and if you have the knowledge and have prepared yourself and you can exercise your initiative, leadership is very easy. People like to follow. So, in combat, very quickly all the big, loud mouths aboard ship suddenly become very quiet, because quite frankly they are afraid.

I had the opportunity to show that, where true leadership was concerned, I was never concerned about establishing popularity with the troops. All I wanted was to gain their respect and obedience. I couldn't care less whether they like me or hate me, as long as they respect me and know me to be a good officer, that I'm fair with each one of them. And if I chew them out, they know it was for a specific reason. Of course being an effective leader, one must always look out for their welfare.

So I'm known to be a very direct and even curt officer. It's a funny thing, in combat, you give a combat order—now normally, a formal order has five paragraphs—it includes something about the enemy and basic mission and breakdown of the mission for your various units, the communications and everything else at the end. But in combat you don't have the luxury always to give complete orders. So we gave what is called "frag orders"—fragmentary orders.

One thing is that I was a past master in giving frag orders. When I took over that rifle platoon—I eliminated all the unnecessary verbiage that goes into an order—unnecessary articles, prepositions, pronouns or adjectives and things like that. So bing-bing-bing, you don't have to say, "That tree there, the tall one with red bushes beside it," you just say, "Direct-front, tall tree, red bushes, right side, machine in position." You know? And when I gave orders like that, I didn't stand around making speeches about—just the essentials for understanding the plan for attack.

And you know, long after the war, in one of our reunions, one of my squad leaders made a comment that "Lieutenant Lee speaks in Pidgin English," that I didn't know English. It was hilarious to others, but that was the impression that he got, after I took over the platoon—because I didn't use complete sentences in speaking. Well, anyway, coming back to this point here—

Actually, which episode did you win the Navy Cross for? Was it when you went on the recon mission and spoke to the Chinese?

The Navy Cross was before the Chosin Reservoir Campaign. It was our first encounter with the Chinese at Sudong village in North Korea. That was the episode where—I personally do not think that our company acquitted itself uniformly well, and yet we had some people who thought they could brag about stopping the 124th Chinese Division with heavy losses. No, that was our very first encounter with the Chinese in the Korean War, as far as the 7th Marines were concerned. Many mistakes were made even though we emerged victorious.

Can you give a brief description of that episode?

Yeah, that was our first encounter with the Chinese and we had been alerted by the South Korean troops who had reached that point before the Marines did, and they were very relieved to leave the hills out there, because they encountered "many, many Chinese" there.

So we went up there and established our defensive positions by nightfall, we had come in very late—and my machine gun sections were attached to each rifle platoon. That means instead of my directly controlling the machine guns, the officer who had the attached machine guns would control and employ the machine guns attached to his platoon—subject to my approval as the MG platoon commander.

This was done because of the terrain. Normally if it's more wide-open, we'll keep the machine guns under my direct control, so I can coordinate the fire of all six machine guns that we have. But anyway, my only function at that time was to be sure that the guns were properly employed and, as a machine gun officer, I would visit each rifle platoon sector in order to assure that the machine guns were properly employed.

And if the platoon leader objects, then too bad, I'm the machine gun officer, and this gun should be not there, but over here. Well, after nightfall, and nearing midnight, everything seemed quiet, and then I was half-dozing when, precisely at midnight, everything hit the fan.

It was the Chinese who were attacking, with bugles and whistles blowing not just our company positions, but it was a coordinated attack against virtually all rifle companies holding other hills. To me, it was a marvelous show, all the noise, staccato of machine gun fire explosions, and the ricocheting of bullets and tracers off the rocky hills.

You could not tell in the darkness which side was Marine or enemy from the distance, because they were all using red tracers. I hate to say it, but it was a spectacular live fire show, you know, despite the casualties and intermingling of gunfire and all that. It created such vibrations and noise echoing upon echoing with red tracers ricocheting and bouncing into the air off hill after hill. It was like we were in the middle of a quivering bowl of jelly, really. The cacophony seemed to have quivering substance, and that's why I described it that way. But the significant thing I noticed was that the Chinese were using our ammunition.

The red tracers from the enemy probably came from stocks captured from the Nationalists—who were supplied by the Americans. It's quite different from fighting the North Koreans, whose tracers came from the Russians, I guess, and they were a bright bluish-green, quite different from ours. So we could always distinguish who's doing the firing. When the attack commenced at midnight, my runner—my radio man—immediately came to me and tried to say, stuttering all the time, that we were under attack *(laughs)*—I was already up, not having taken my shoes off and all—and I was all ready for combat.

And then suddenly everything was quiet, like someone turned off the spigot of battle pandemonium. All of a sudden everything was silent in our sector. I didn't know where the enemy was and neither did others apparently. All I knew was that the report came back to me that they had overrun one of my machine guns. And this was from a certain machine gun section leader attached to one of the platoons up there.

The worst thing in combat is the unknown, the fear of the unknown. Where is the enemy? What is the enemy doing? And unless we knew, we could not take any counteraction. I had my gunnery sergeant—gunnery sergeant is called a gunny. He's a five-striper—chevrons. A good reliable man—my right arm in helping to organize and train this machine gun platoon. And the gunny, I had him remain in position and get all the stragglers and people and form a new defensive line, at that point.

I wanted him to have the men observe where the enemy was by when they opened fire, and at least know how far they were, or whether they were right on top of our people. But in order for them to disclose their position, one has to provoke the enemy into action, and so I appointed myself to be the provocateur. I intended to move forward of the Marine lines. The enemy would not know where the Marines were either, and they would not know how many were attacking them and so forth. So what I did was to move forward toward the captured position, on the ground, and by firing. I did not use my banana clips' load of 60 rounds until the very end for the assault. But I wanted to create an impression that a Marine force was moving forward—perhaps to counterattack.

I picked up many of the weapons that were left, by the Marines who were wounded and evacuated. They had left the weapons in the foxholes. Carbines, and a few M1s and a BAR, which is a Browning Automatic Rifle, which is like a shorter hand-held machine gun.

So I moved from one position—it was dark—to another—but, with just enough moonlight from a quarter moon so that I could identify the positions as I closed in there. So I picked up another carbine and fired it one or two rounds, maybe a short burst—staggering the rate of fire. Alternating the carbine with an M1 rifle, to fire a few rounds at varying rate—and then picked up a carbine and fired a few rounds.

And then when I found a BAR, I used that to unload a few magazines of 20 rounds at slow or rapid rate, moving always toward the enemy. And I kept moving forward, alternating weapons picked up along the way. I would anticipate the enemy returning fire at my gun flashes, so I would immediately roll over to a side and fire from another position, and all that. I kept doing this, and at one time—I wasn't sure whether it was a man or an animal—something suddenly broke through the thick brush out there, like it was really running, and I fired a few rapid bursts in its direction.

But I didn't realize how long I'd been there doing this, and it was at midnight when the first attack took place, but suddenly I heard voices—Chinese voices, you can tell—like they heard something, and then suddenly opened fire in my direction. And then I realized that I was right where the enemy positions were. They had occupied the high ground, and I was right there *(laughs)* on one of their flanks.

The thought is whether the enemy would defend or attack or send a patrol out to search you out, or what? And what about the Marines out there—where do they think you are? And I'm caught in between there, but it's what I teach in tactics—that to survive, you must take aggressive action. You've got to be moving forward all the time, and your safety lies in your aggressive movements and effective use of fire.

I still had two hand grenades left with me—in moving forward, I would pick up hand grenades and toss one in this direction, and toss one in that direction, punctuating it with fire at that direction, and all. But when they opened fire and I knew that they were in my presence anyway, that's when I first shouted *(laughs)* what's considered to be Mandarin "Don't open fire. I'm Chinese!" (不要開火。我是中國人!)

But they kept firing. And so, there was nothing for me to do but to go forward, I didn't want to go backwards. So I took my two hand grenades and with my carbines set on full automatic, and timed it, with the grenades armed, and tossed one and then two seconds later tossed the other one, so that they would explode not simultaneously, you know, but like they were being tossed by two people, and jumped up and charged directly into their fire, spraying my carbine fire set at full automatic—while shouting for other Marines to follow me, and all. Sprayed all the areas where the gun fire was coming from—it wasn't too far, it was just about 15 or 20 feet away. I was right on top of those people.

And suddenly the sound of whistles or something, suddenly, very abruptly, all enemy fire stopped—but I kept moving forward and kept firing, and there were dead Chinese on that hilltop, dead Marines were there, and some of the badly wounded Chinese were propped up against the rocky backdrop there, with automatic weapons placed in front of them, and I had to kill two of them, because they were still alive, by spraying them.

The others were so badly wounded that they apparently had just died in the position there. And what happened was that many jumped over the low rocky cliff there—that's how they came up to attack the Marine positions, by forming human ladders and pushing themselves up there.

So, at that position, there was my lost machine gun with a couple of my dead machine gunners. The machine gun was taken from its position, but the Chinese had not totally captured it. I went all the way to the end to make sure that there were no enemy there, and then waited, because dawn should be breaking soon.

I guess it must have been close to 5:00 or so, because day was beginning to break and I assumed that my men, back in the woods, way back—saw this little fire fight going on up there. And it was good that they did not open fire because there's no telling what they would be shooting at.

But I stood up on top of the hill there and, very eerily, the quarter moon had come up to a position where it made everything seem gray but visible, and I could see all these bodies and the overrun position by a machine pit. The best thing to do was to wait for daylight to come so that my vision could be extended—to see beyond a certain distance.

I stood up on that hilltop and shouted to the Marines, took off my helmet and waved it, and you know that was still a risk because regardless of being born and brought up in this country, I still have a trace of Oriental accent. But nobody came forward until finally—and I kept shouting, "All clear," and "This is Lieutenant Lee." The enemy heard all of that too.

So out of the woods' edge—that was down about a couple hundred yards from the more open hilltop there, where the positions were—I saw tentatively a couple of Marines appear. Then the tall, slim form of Gunny Foster leading the deployed line of Marines out of the woods, coming toward me, standing on the skyline, waving. It was no longer my show when the gunny quickly deployed his men to reoccupy the lost position recaptured by my action. It was the 1st Platoon's position, but where was he? I later learned that the platoon commander had abandoned his platoon before the enemy attack.

So I walked back down the ridgeline and saw one foxhole with a dead Marine in it. He was the squad leader. He was our only black squad leader and apparently was killed with a grenade and bayonet slashes and all that. He was trying to get out of his sleeping bag, but got out only his arm trying to pull the zipper. By his chevron there was no mistaking who the guy was. It was a black arm with three stripes on the sleeve. I thought without pity that he almost deserved to die for being zipped up in a sleeping bag without being more alert with reported enemy around.

When daylight came, and I walked down past the company commander and executive officer's foxholes which were together, the captain stood up there in his foxhole and looked at me. You know what he said? He said, "Pretty rough, wasn't it?" And I just looked at him and didn't say anything. I just sort of sneered at him and walked on down to my own position, which was further down the hill there. I suddenly felt very, very tired and took off my equipment, my suspenders, to hang my carbine up on a small shrub. Then I got hit! A sniper round found me. Picked me up, spun me around—and I twisted my knee when this happened.

But what happened was that that bullet—well, I won't say "through the grace of God" and all that kind of stuff, but had it been a fraction of inch in another direction, it would have shattered my whole arm. Instead, the bullet just tore off a strip of flesh, exposing my bone all the way to my elbow there. But it felt like *(laughs)* a big sledgehammer hitting me—like hitting your knee or something with a big rock. So immediately the Marines came to help me, and got me off to the aid station, where I got involved with this *(laughs)*—these big crybabies. And then I was trucked out to the Army field hospital 40 miles away in Hamhung City, near the coast. And from there I took a Jeep and got back.

That's when you stole the Jeep with the other person, and were followed by an ambulance.

Well, they credited me in the documentary film made for the Smithsonian Institution as leading the 1st Battalion 7th Marines in the night operation to relieve a Fox Company that was being attacked by the Chinese Communist forces for three or four days and nights. The unit was on top of a very vital pass that had to be held, because all the Marines north where I was, toward the town of Yudam-ni at the Reservoir, we had to pass through that pass to move down to the coast.

Fox Company had suffered heavy casualties in these constant attacks by two full regiments of Chinese troops. The Battalion had tried two times to go by road to relieve Fox Company. And the third time was when we had orders, and I didn't know it at the time, from the regimental commander to our battalion commander to take the battalion behind the enemy lines, up across a trackless, mountainous area, to reach Fox Company before it was overrun. But in order for our company to reach the attack position—where the jump off point is, and this was on high ground that the enemy held—they apparently moved in after we moved on up to Yudam-ni, and they moved in and established very strong positions there.

We had to fight starting from 8:00 in the morning to clear the Chinese from terrain spurs, fingers, ridgelines, and what-have-you. It was a virtual honeycomb of enemy positions up there. We were in the attack preceded by Able Company. Baker Company's mission was clearing the side of the MSR there. But when Able Company got stopped by the Chinese, we had to go up to help Able Company to seize this jump off position.

At that time I did not know that we might continue the attack at night. It was around 5:30 when we finally seized that position. I and other officers and NCOs were setting up what is known as a "hasty defense" to provide security for the night, and rest, before continuing the attack, jumping off early in the morning. Then the officers were called to a meeting.

We were told that the Battalion would continue the attack at night, without any rest after fighting all day long, and that we were to relieve Fox Company by taking a back route behind the enemy concentrations blocking the road. I was told that the battalion commander wanted "Lieutenant Lee to take the point in leading the attack." Baker Company would be the lead company for the operation. By the time I got that order it was around 7:30 and already dark. The company commander, Lieutenant Joe Kurcaba, relayed the complete order issued by Lieutenant Colonel Ray Davis, our battalion commander. I was immediately concerned because some aspects were unworkable.

And I thought that sort of strange, because when I was at the point in moving up to Yudam-ni from the south, I also led my platoon, and the whole battalion without relief. Normally, they would rotate the platoon commanders after so much time, maybe every two hours, then another one would take over, and so forth. But in my case the company commander, whether it was Captain Wilcox or Lieutenant Kurcaba, always chose me to lead. Maybe it was because I never complained. But I think it was because I relished the assignment of leading Marines in combat. They had full confidence in my judgment and capability, perhaps more so than in the other platoon commanders, for accomplishing the mission.

This night attack was a high-risk proposition because of the confluence of a number of negative factors. When you have a confluence of all these negative factors together, they render it a virtual mission impossible.

One big factor was the exhausted physical shape of the men. They were all fatigued from fighting all day just to get to the jump off point. And to go on this attack we must carry even heavier loads, because we don't know how long we're going to be out there, or whether we will ever reach Fox Company. Everyone had to carry double loads of ammunition, rations, grenades, and everything else to sustain us on this mission. And in addition to all this load, certain units were assigned to—besides carrying their own weapons and all that, as a rifleman, for example, you may have to carry a box of machine gun ammo or maybe a single mortar round. You know, these are both heavy ordnance items. And I got rid of a couple of my field manuals that I took to Korea, because to me they became added weight—two little books. And a hand grenade weighs more than just a few copies of field manuals, so the priority to me was to carry an extra hand grenade.

So there was this added load to aggravate our exhausted physical condition. And another negative factor was the weather condition: horrible, sub-zero weather—going down to 20° and then 30° below zero, freezing solid everything. People tend to swathe themselves with woolen mufflers, pulling down their parka hood, with their helmet on top. I didn't do that, because, as a Platoon Leader, I need to listen to hear enemy activities in the wind.

So I never had my hood on, and my ears would freeze, and it became so painful that I had to put the hood on—just to relieve the pain. With heavy gauntlets on, one could not massage the ears. But once the pain was relieved, the hood was pulled back down because I cannot hear with that hood on. Okay—horrible weather, and then there was the lack of visibility—one could not see the terrain features. You orient yourself by studying the actual terrain features that you could see with your eyes. If you look at a map, it shows all these terrain features by map-contour lines. But these maps were useless. The scale of the maps was too small—1 to 50,000—for tactical use by small units. Contour lines were readable in daylight but not at night.

All the principles of land navigation taught in military schools were inapplicable in the combat environment at the Chosin Reservoir. I challenge anyone to read a 1 to 50,000 scale map with a flashlight under a poncho. Even if one has microscopic eyes to do so, what good was the exercise? You still could not see the terrain features outside. And you have destroyed your night vision doing so.

And the final negative factor—perhaps the most important one—was the unknown enemy situation. Without knowing where the enemy is, you have to be prepared to fight in any and all directions. At nighttime, control of battle formation is difficult; hence, we try to have rehearsals before the actual operation.

Okay, the enemy is very important and we didn't know a thing about the enemy other than that the location of the Chinese divisions—20,000 men—was unknown. Were they preparing to finish off the Fox Company? Everyone down to the last private knew the urgency of the situation. Prepared or not, we had to go. So with me at the point of the tight single file column, we moved off from the point of departure in a blinding snow storm. The time was about 9:00 and Baker Company was in attack mode form beginning to end of our daunting mission.

So the only reliable guide that I had was the Lensatic compass, but the instructions I got for the compass were wrong. A lot of the signals in the instructions were wrong. I knew this, and yet no leader sought to correct them.

For example, the battalion commander said, "Providence has provided two stars to shine over Foxhill—" where Fox Company's position was. "And all you have to do is to follow those stars to Fox Company." Because the earth rotates and the only celestial constant was behind us, and not south. It was the North

Star. So when I hear ridiculous info like this I wonder, why didn't somebody raise his voice and point these things out to the battalion commander?

This is one thing I have against the military, and that is the reluctance of anyone to contradict his superior despite obvious errors. In my leadership classes I encouraged people to speak up in a tactful way. Because sometimes an exhausted commander—in this case, Lieutenant Colonel Davis was very fatigued. He said that he had to "go under cover (a poncho) to look at the map," Then, when he came out he promptly forgot what he did and had to go back under again, because his mind was so fatigued, you know? Clearly, he needed the opinion and judgment of a clearer mind that he never got. I don't think that this poncho episode ever occurred. He could not have oriented himself any better than I could and I couldn't see anything. It was like shadow boxing blindfolded inside a closed box.

The killing effect of the brutally cold weather cannot be overemphasized: fully one half of the 8,000-plus casualties at Chosin was caused by cold weather injuries serious enough for evacuation. With this constant wind blowing down from Siberia, the temperature was closer to 50–60° below zero, because of the so-called wind chill factor.

Another thing that upset me very much when I got the attack order was that I knew it was unworkable. Indeed, if implemented, it would lead to disaster. The idea was to fire artillery-illuminating shells into the air periodically to guide the battalion. Two things wrong: one, it would destroy night vision; two, it's unreliable—the wind blows this parachute flare this way or that way. One time you're looking at it it's in this direction, next time it's in that direction. But the worst thing is that it would destroy your night vision.

Before going on a night patrol, for example, we have to seclude ourselves in a darkened room first. So that your eyes adjust to the darkness in order to see in the darkness without lights. So here, looking at a flare, a burning light in the sky, it would instantly destroy totally your night vision, and yet you're responsible for detecting the presence of the enemy on the ground in the darkness. So the basic concept was beyond ridiculous, it was dangerous! Still, General Davis, to the day he passed on, still thought that the success of his mission was based on the implementation of the unworkable plan. I rejected it totally. None of it worked, and I never used any of that. But it was still my responsibility to lead. I did so using my own intuitions, my own judgment and perseverance and luck to overcome all challenges and obstacles—both friendly and hostile—to accomplish the mission.

The only thing I had was this compass and a very dim light, and to trudge along in the snow—step by step, in front of you. Sometimes when you felt the ground give a little bit, you had to physically touch with your foot, whether or not it's going to break, or be at the edge of a cliff. We were wary.

So this was what I had to do. Normally, an officer will have two scouts move out a little further ahead, for safety. But here, I was leading the scouts and directing them because we had to go almost within touching distance. So that was a difficulty and I realized that the people following have all the gear. The canteens had to have a sock over them so that they would not rattle, because there has to be silent movement by 600 men. I don't know where "500 men" came from, but it was probably more like 600 men.

But those people had to follow each other with extra heavy loads, and each step that you take forward, the ice melts because of the pressure and it became glossy, slippery ice again. I didn't envy those heavily laden troops going up the hills. At least when I was moving it was over virgin knee-deep snow and I could fix my feet, by moving step-by-step. But these people had to follow a trace, and people were slipping and sliding, and the heavy weapons would be dropped—I don't know how much of this extra ammo they carried was left on the trail, but I was fully conscious—They could not warm themselves, and if they stopped they had to remain silent, they couldn't stamp their feet—and merely stood in place freezing. I was fully aware of their predicament. So I and my scouts had to move as quickly as we could, and we traversed double what these people were marching, because we had to scout out the terrain out there.

We encountered some enemy patrols out there and we tried to keep quiet to avoid alerting them. But they heard us because some of the Marines couldn't stop from cussing after banging their knee against a rock or something like that, and falling. The Chinese patrols were very aggressive, I can tell you that, and I could hear some of the conversation.

I remember one case where for some reason—maybe a drop in wind velocity—the voices came across very clearly, even though they might have been quite a distance away. I heard one patrol leader say something in Chinese— "你聽到嗎?"—"You hear something?" "Yes. Shhh!" And then there was a discussion and I couldn't catch it—in Chinese, but they didn't conceal their voices. Then, you know what the leader said? "打了!" He said, "We attack!" instead of, you know, easing away from situation.

We were trying to avoid getting involved with people like that, because we wanted to have our full fighting strength at Foxhill, in case we had to fight the surrounding Chinese out there. We came across Chinese patrols. They reminded me of these Harper seals up there in Alaska. Like pictures of the Arctic and these people half-frozen to death and very sluggish in moving. But we overran one of their positions like that, and we had to kill anyone found alive like that. And then at about—we had started out at 9:00—and about 2:00 we were relieved of our strenuous responsibility.

The 3rd Platoon commander told me that the company commander wanted his platoon to take the lead, but my men were to remain following them in column. And then, for just another hour, the battalion commander halted the battalion—everybody was too physically exhausted and people were beginning to fall asleep on their feet. So we stopped on some hilltop there and set up a hasty defense, and the Chinese knew we were there because they were shooting random fire at us. And the battalion commander said a bullet went through his poncho, his helmet. Every Marine, in his own situation, had a different experience. One was shot through his butt. I rested peacefully on my back—without taking off my heavy pack—gazing up into the clearing skies—so lovely, that snowy scene!

So what happened with that guy? A bullet hit his poncho and then what happened?

He was not hurt. But he could have been killed or wounded. And I saw, when we were up there on the hill, the skies were clear suddenly, and everything was so peaceful. And I could actually see beyond—no snow was falling down. And I think that's why the enemy could at least hear us.

I was so tired and fatigued that all I did was lean back on my pack, on the side of this steep hill, and you would be looking up at the heavens—lovely, really—and the stars and everything else out there. But the enemy continued to fire at us and hit one of the Marines very close—oh, about 20 feet away. He got shot in his rump, and I saw him clutch his buttock, and thrash around in the snow. It must have hurt very bad—he was gritting his teeth. "Ooh"—grunting, you know—trying to stop making noise and all that. In that episode, that night attack, we had a number of people killed and about 23 wounded. But the big fight was yet to come when we got orders to continue the attack.

I thought, Did anyone say we should change the formation? Daylight would come very soon and we can't be in a single file. This is where the commander has to be exercising his initiative all the time to adjust to the situation on the ground, including light conditions. But we were still in a single file, moving out just at daybreak. And as we were debouching from this wooded line—*debouching* is moving from a closed area out to an open area—debouching from the tree line out into the more open area, we were sighted by the enemy. The 3rd Platoon was in single file ahead of my platoon, but I was up close to their last man. And they came under fire from a rocky hill mass to our right front, which would be the southwest direction. And that was where I got really angry at the 3rd Platoon commander for not taking immediate action.

In combat, you have to take instantaneous action to keep the enemy from seizing fire superiority—in other words, have greater fire power—shooting at each other, so you have to keep your heads down, while they have the initiative in killing you. And all his men in that column hit the deck without returning fire, and kept their heads in the snow, like a bunch of boots and all. I was looking for him, but I couldn't identify him, you know, with everyone's face in the snow. But I was already formulating an attack plan.

I felt that we've got to eliminate the enemy that, from my field glasses, I could see several different positions up there, some were delivering heavy automatic fire at us. I quickly have my platoon sergeant assemble my squad leaders. What I want to do must be done rapidly. We've got to regain fire superiority and quickly move to seize the rocky hill mass. I have no idea what's on the other side.

They may have a lot of troops ready to augment their defense unless we quickly seize that position.

But I feel we could do it. I have the one machine gun left, on the flank, and the men quickly assembled in straight line—it's called Skirmish Line—everybody facing forward with their weapons forward for maximum fire effect, and to open fire on my signal. They would open fire simultaneously—machine guns, BARs, all rifles. With this massed and sustained fire power, the enemy would have to keep their heads down. And when this was done, the assault was launched. And we were all carrying our heavy packs, I'll tell you. Even I was carrying 60, 70 pounds, and at the time do you know how much I weighed?

118?

How did you know? I was 118. *(Laughs)*

I did my reading.

One-eighteen, yeah—that's a lot of weight for that. And I had the men fire as they were marching, moving without stopping. And they've got plenty of ammunition because of the overload—double loads of ammo that we had. But some of these men were carrying close to 100 pounds of combat gear in the attack.

Normally, in battle, you like to dump all that stuff before going up a steep hill—just pack up there with your weapons and ammo without a heavy pack, and then pick up their packs after the battle. But because we were always moving forward, we didn't have time, the luxury of going back to pick up our packs. So we had to carry them with us going up this steep hill.

That was when I almost got killed. I always moved with my skirmish line, but I was on one flank so that I could see the rest of the people to be sure that they kept up. I had my platoon sergeant egging, prodding people on, in case there was anybody slow. We want to have all the fire, the weapons pointed up toward the crest. As you converge on the top, the fire would be more concentrated too. But I'll tell you, it's natural for one to become tired, after all that went on—the day before, the night attack, and all that.

So when I neared the top there, I felt very fatigued. My thighs were like two pillars of lead and I had to will myself to lift my legs to move forward and all. And this strange thought entered my head: Why didn't an enemy soldier get up and push me with his finger and I would topple backwards *(laughs)* down the hill, relieved of all this physical torture. It was very painful with my legs, but I kept moving. And when I was near the crest, two enemy soldiers stood up with their weapons and they were very close—in heavy, quilted uniforms, and both of them with burp guns.

I don't know whether they wanted to surrender or what—but, too bad they had their weapons with them. So I opened fire with my carbine, and I wasn't sure if it would penetrate their heavy clothing. You know, the carbine round is a fairly small bullet—but, they did, because I fired bursts of two or three rounds into both of them to kill them.

And I later found, much later, that a third soldier that I did not see had his rifle aimed right at me—the same distance—he couldn't miss. But one of my sergeants, following up there, killed him before he could pull his trigger. *(Laughs)* I never knew this until 20 years later—in a reunion, they were talking about these things. But anyway we reached the top of this crest and I realized we had overrun a strong point. We saw a couple of soldiers try to slip over to the other side—go back to the other side, there on top of a hill.

The enemy on the reverse slope were already 300–500 yards away, floundering in the snow, running in staggered line, about 18 or 20 of them. They had abandoned their positions, even though they had foxholes all over the other side of this rocky hill mass, because they were expecting Americans to be coming up from the road side direction, you know, down the hill there. And we just stumbled across them from the rear, and I was very proud of my men. Even winded as they were as we neared the top, they started shouting and whooping it up and all, and actually ran with their heavy packs on to the crest! And you know, they each were men who started out with me at Camp Pendleton. We had some new replacements that joined us, very unhappy people, for that night operation. Now, a few days later, they were an integral part of my platoon. They were up there, many of them on the hilltop with me, but some were strung out halfway up, too exhausted to move further.

And I felt very exhilarated and flushed in victory. We had minimal casualties and routed a larger enemy force. We showed up the 3rd Platoon, whose men were still at the bottom of the hill—and did not do their job as far as I was concerned. We had put on a demonstration of how to do things right. But as I said, when we got up there, some of my newer replacements were still strung out halfway up the hill. It was too steep for them to climb further. And here I thought that at 24 I was an old man or something. Was this why these young Marines at 18 or 20 could still shout and run the last few steps while I was still huffing up there? But what the heck. And from there, we pursued the enemy by fire. We didn't go after them because we were still headed toward Foxhill. There was one final ridgeline, about 300–400 yards ahead of us, that was known as Rocky Ridge. The hill mass we just captured—the rocky hill mass—was not named, and except for us who were involved in that fight, it was never mentioned anywhere. And yet, that was a very crucial battle, because we routed the last enemy force that stood between us and Fox Company.

And we were on course toward Fox Hill less than 800 yards away! It was about 10 a.m. when my platoon took this rocky hill mass. Rocky Ridge was about 400 yards ahead and beyond that was Fox Hill. By then Lt. Col. Davis was able to make contact with Fox Company from the hill we took. Along with preparatory fire by battalion and company mortars, he wanted an airstrike called on Rocky Ridge before we moved out to take it. We didn't have the right communications, but we did have communication with Captain Barber at Fox Hill. So he helped us—by then, we had contact with him. Up to that point, we did not have contact with Bill Barber up there. That was when he had called the aircraft down to make some rocket and strafing runs on Rocky Ridge. Following the mortar barrage, we moved forward to take the Rocky Ridge—nobody was there.

But Rocky Ridge was the attack position from which the Chinese had mounted many of their night attacks against Fox Hill, because all the dead Chinese were beyond Rocky Ridge, toward Fox Hill, and they were mowed down by the hundreds. Dead Chinese soldiers, all of them facing their objective, nobody running away. This shows the courage of the Chinese in their unsuccessful attack mission to take Fox Hill.

In the distance, about 500 or 600 yards away, all the Fox Hill people were on the ridge line, cheering—they finally realized that we were Marines, on the Rocky Ridge, out there—and cheering and waving pieces of colored parachutes that they picked up, from airdrops and all that. And we moved up there, still in combat-formation, but this time, the 3rd Platoon was on the left and we were on the right—both on line—and this time, I relinquished the lead to my men.

I let my men be the first to go up there. And you know, Marines greet each other in very crude, obscene manner, but showing brotherly love, great friendship and camaraderie, and telling how each other looked like hell or worse, and all that.

A couple years or so ago Fox Company had a reunion—Dedication of the Marine Corps Museum Opening. And they invited me to be the guest speaker at their banquet. So that was when I had the opportunity—most of them never knew what the 1st Battalion did to save them and they all were very cocky and smug. All the big publicity was on them, and so I told them, "Before you get too cocky, let me tell you something—it's unfortunate that people get killed, but you actually had it pretty good sitting in those foxholes. You always had hot chow, in that they had a big 55-gallon tank that they boil water in, so that the C-rations—all of us couldn't eat ours because they were frozen like rock. The Fox Company people had a 55-gallon drum and they boiled water in it, like a big, deep tray. They had water there, boiling constantly, full of C-ration cans in there. And that's how those people ate out there. They had hot food, whereas, where we were up at Yudam-ni, in the hills and so forth, we could not—we didn't have time to heat up, to melt—it's very difficult to eat a frozen-solid can of food.

When we reached Fox Hill, after all this welcoming, we were indeed treated to hot food and each one of us picked up a can of hot solid ration—spaghetti and meatballs, or lima beans and ham, or chicken—it's not too bad when it's heated up. And somebody said we had some hot meals, but that was when we stopped briefly at Hagaru and Koto-ri.

I was the first officer from Baker Company up there at Fox Hill. And Joe Owen likes to say that he was, but hell, his mortar men were always in the rear supporting us. I was up there and I was looking for the company commander and was pointed out where he was. He had been shot through the leg, shrapnel or something. And he was half-reclining on some sandbags and looked at me dourly as I approached—sizing me up, you know?

And my right arm—I could not salute with my right arm. It was still in a sling. So I extended my left arm and said, "Lieutenant Lee, Baker Company, Sir." And he extended his hand and said, "Glad to meet you, Lieutenant." He seemed rather gruff. But I was wondering what was going through his mind when I was approaching him. He was a veteran of the Pacific fighting and had been wounded on Iwo Jima.

While looking at me, he must have been thinking that I looked like the guy who shot him on Iwo Jima. *(Laughs)* Sort of a joke, you know? But Bill Barber became a very good friend of mine. He was the only officer who would stop a Marine on the road walking by and get him squared away before I did. If a Marine comes by and his salute was sloppy, I would correct him on the spot. If his field scarf was askew or something, I'd have him corrected before he moved on.

Field scarves—This is an illustration on how particular every officer should be in order to maintain the required standards of Marine Corps dress. And some officers didn't bother probably because they needed a shoeshine themselves. But a few like Bill Barber and I were very strict on matters like this. And the word got around so that Marines always straightened themselves out when they saw either of us coming by. Barber was a good officer, no question about it. But he was too direct to be a general, and it's too bad. We lost many good potential flag officers like that.

One thing you mentioned that was really interesting—you said that usually if people follow the rules they either are at least a corporal or become a general by the end of their military career. But it's the people who take risks—

Well, yes, I did make a comment that you can get along with minimum effort. There are some who do that. They never question their superior, or never offer anything—a typical "yes man." And strangely enough, even without initiative and all, and without contributing anything new or anything good in the running of their units, they get enough good reports so that they would end up with a successful career which, in my mind, is to retire as a colonel. Whereas others who take risks are considered controversial—but there are ways to work the system.

People who don't take risks can still survive and retire with a good rank, whereas some who take risks, or perhaps are outspoken, are considered untactful or too forceful. But it is right that those who take risks should be rewarded for it, if the risks turn out right, of course. And some who take risks are penalized for it, but again this could be the shortsightedness of the commander, because it did not work out. But were other benefits gained from taking this particular risk? And did this officer benefit from his experience, whatever marking he ended up with in his risk-taking? So anyway, this is why I'm quite cynical looking at some of the senior officers, knowing that their service never included risk-taking. I'm talking about in promotions, and my case is a very complex story that I shouldn't be involved in for discussion at this point.

When your men felt that you deserved the highest honor, was it for any specific episode or just for your entire performance?

My men thought that when I received the Navy Cross—it was presented in 1951. At the time, I was very unhappy that I had to be involved with the premiere of *Retreat Hell.* It's not a very good movie about the Chosin Reservoir. And because, at that time, when I got the Navy Cross, it was presented to me by my regimental commander, Colonel Homer Litzenberg, who was by then a brigadier general. What was your question?

The question was when your men thought that you deserved the highest honor, it was for a specific episode, or just for overall performance?

What they were trying to push was for this night action—they thought that the Navy Cross was presented for the night attack. I call it a night attack—other people may be justified in calling it a night march, *(laughs)* because they never committed to any combat.

Baker Company alone was involved in actual combat from beginning to end. So my evaluation of that situation was that we were in attack mode from the beginning to the end, even though our attack formation was by company column. Of course, upon enemy contact, I deployed my men in other combat formations. And when I got the Navy Cross many felt that it was not high enough—that I should have gotten the Medal of Honor. But this was—most did not know it was not even for Chosin but for Sudong Battle, back on November 2, 1950. They thought it was for the Chosin Reservoir Battle. But little did they know that I did not receive anything for the Chosin Reservoir Battle for seven years, except a Purple Heart. And my role in the night attack was not played up by anybody, and this was my personal bitterness against certain people in the Marine Corps Historical Section. They operated by personal politics for favored individuals.

But anyway, I received the Silver Star, seven years after the qualifying event. General Litzenberg wanted to upgrade the recommendation from the Silver Star as written to another Navy Cross. When, years later in reunions, the men found out that what I got was the Silver Star, then they wanted me to be recognized for the Medal of Honor. And they wanted the citation to be amended, with witness statements on what took place in that historic night operation.

And those who made the decision for the Silver Star were not veterans of Chosin. But I let it be known, by the 21 men who did sign a petition, that I did not want to compete with my battalion commander, who received the Medal Honor for that operation. He was a tremendous and inspiring battalion commander, I can tell you that. I have unbounded respect for him—except for what was to be done in this particular case. I told my people that I don't mind their pushing for a second Navy Cross rather than the Medal of Honor. So they put in for that and General Davis, our former battalion commander, wrote an endorsing statement.

The fellow who was the head of this department lied to me by saying that he got the word late to check into this situation, yet he's been holding that petition for over a year. The crux of the problem was that this fellow had no concept of what went on in Korea, and particularly the significance of the major campaigns and battles. When I sought information for my men, he was evasive, disingenuous, dissembling, and openly lied to me about preparing his PowerPoint [presentation]s to have the commandant reject the petition for Silver Star upgrade.

* * *

Vietnam was the first time in which I was open to being assigned to an intelligence billet, because I was on the verge of leaving the Marine Corps. I thought it would be nice to have the experience so that I could join some "think tank" involving intelligence, particularly in the China area. I have enough friends in the Marine Corps who recognize my value. So there were no objections when I just suddenly appeared on the intelligence scene when I was assigned to the 3rd Marine Division. We landed on Chu Lai Beach in May 1965.

As a major, I requested and was assigned as the division combat intelligence officer, and established what was called the Division Translation Center, to interpret and translate captured Viet Cong and North Vietnamese documents. And *(laughs)* working for me was a Japanese American gunnery sergeant named Tanaka, and under him, for translating, were some Vietnam soldiers—all excellent men of Chinese ethnicity. And one thing about me was that I was able to pick up certain words. I was never trained in the Vietnamese language, but I always seemed to hit the right word—I guess I did have some talent—so that the reports, many of them, I sent back to check more on this or that area.

And I guess they were all impressed and convinced that they couldn't slip anything by me. Being the division combat intelligence officer, as I said, had more to do with the division-level mission of seeking intelligence, as opposed to the front line units—the regiments and battalions—that send out their own reconnaissance patrols to obtain intelligence more for immediate use, such as location and size of enemy dispositions, terrain obstacles, and things directly affecting their work operations, in their area, and so forth. As the division combat intelligence officer, these reports all come to me anyway, so that, if necessary, we may have to upgrade to a higher mission, use other resources, and all that. So it was an interesting position there and I served a year doing that.

My intelligence experience didn't help me any, after I retired, in trying to join a think tank. I found that you've got to be politically correct in supporting the administration's policy. I know we still have some old adherence to the Taiwan Lobby, for example, as opposed to opening with Mainland China. And it was clear to me that—I felt that we should be more involved with developing good relations with the People's Republic of China. *(Laughs)* We can easily make it a self-fulfilling prophecy for war by demonizing the Communists all the time and make them into a de facto enemy.

Right now we are at a point where they can go either way, and my personal interest is in—and there are many good thinking Marine Corps officers in the senior ranks who agree with me—that we should have better contacts with the Chinese military and be open so that we can know what each other's motives or grand schemes are all about.

Because I'm convinced that the Chinese will never be an aggressive predatory nation like the Soviet Union was, with a clear desire to expand their territory and the spreading of Communism. It's going to be an interesting year on that front. In Vietnam, I was involved with none of that—about the Chinese helping the North Vietnamese, the mining of Haiphong Harbor, and high level things like that. But it was strictly on the contacts of front line units and with Viet Cong units and their movements and training and all that. So intelligence really was of interest to me. My office was spread with captured Viet Cong slogans and banners. It seemed like the Viet Cong had opened up a propaganda office in the middle of the Marine Corps General Staff, but people knew me pretty well and accepted my sardonic humor.

There's one last thing: You mentioned that you stayed in military life, so you didn't really face discrimination, but you said that some people who did service who came out couldn't get houses in white neighborhoods?

Yeah. I was shocked. I was shocked to learn this because when I entered the military I never got—it became my life career and identity. Whereas most of my

Kurt Lee and Linda Lee en route to Hawaii, 1960

friends—Chinese Americans, I'm talking about—virtually none of them made a career of the military like I did.

And I never knew until very recently, reading an article from the *Sacramento Bee* sent to me by my brother, I think, about how some of these World War II veterans were reminiscing about their military experience and mentioned emphatically—many of the people that I personally knew—complaining that when they came back to civilian life in Sacramento, they were given no priority for government jobs, for example. They could not find places to live where they wanted to live. They could not buy property because they happened to be Orientals—Chinese. And I was surprised to hear that because I thought when the war ended in 1945, the Chinese Exclusion Act had been repealed in 1943. But yet, there seemed to be this lingering discrimination that took longer for things to work out. Today it's quite different because of education and progress, but people still remember vividly their discriminatory treatment despite having served in combat in the military.

* * *

I had a relative who was a Flying Tiger pilot, Pershing Lee. My father's brother's son, Pershing Lee from the little town of Grass Valley, California. It's just about 40–50 miles from Sacramento, close to the mountains. In some of these towns, now, they may have been the only Chinese American family there. His father, I think, ran a restaurant, a very popular one, there. And they were very well thought of in the community. They were treated just like any other American family there. He joined the Flying Tigers during the—in fact before *(laughs)* World War II started. I don't know him well. My sister, Betty, of course, knew his wife and knew him. I remember Pershing was one of the pallbearers when my father died. This was in 1966, just about a couple of weeks after I came back from Vietnam. My father had a heart attack, two weeks after I saw him.

Betty would say, "Oh, Pershing is an ace in the Flying Tigers." I said, "Let me check it out. But I don't see his name listed anywhere at all." And I recall seeing the picture of him in flying togs standing beside one of these Flying Tiger P-40 fighter planes. So he was there, no question about it. But unfortunately now he's gone and I don't know how to pick up his history. He must be registered someplace. He was a flyer, a fighter pilot. The P-40 is a fighter plane with one occupant, the pilot who was also the gunner, and everything else.

CHAPTER SIXTEEN

Rita K. Chow 周蓮翠 (1926–   )
Army Nurse Corps, U.S. Army Reserves

Rita Kathleen Chow served from 1998–2012 as Director of the National Interfaith Coalition on Aging, a constituent unit of the National Council on Aging in Washington, D.C. Dr. Chow attended Stanford for a BS in Nursing, Case-Western Reserve University for an MS in Teaching Surgical Nursing, Columbia University Teachers College for a Professional Diploma in Nursing Education Administration and Doctor of Education, and George Mason University for a Bachelor of Independent Studies in Public Health and a Gerontology Certificate. Chow first served as Deputy Chief Nurse Professional Officer of the U.S. Public Health Service, then became Deputy Director of the Office of Long-Term Care. Subsequently she served in the U.S. Dept. of Health and Human Services; as Chief, Quality Assurance Branch, Health Standards and Quality Bureau; and was Director of Patient Education at G.W. Long Hansen's Disease (leprosy) Center in Carville, Louisiana. Also she was Director of Nursing in the Federal Bureau of Prisons' Medical Center, Fort Worth, Texas.

I was raised in San Francisco and Dad was thrilled when he was brought over from Guangdong, China to have a better life in America. And he was taught to be a tailor in a garment factory. I thought he was pretty smart in that he was able to be on his own after he got married. At first we were raised in Chinatown. He thought we really needed to move away from Chinatown, where he could set up a tailor shop in the Mission District—Peter's Jacket Shop—jackets and pants made to order. We were among the very few Chinese families in that district. And there were three children: my brother Ronald, sister Ruth, and I, the youngest. And we were all given special roles according to our abilities. For example, Dad would send us on an errand to take deer skins to the tannery, and we would bring them back in our red enameled wagon after they were tanned. But since I was so young, he tried having me operate the button and buttonhole machines. But I wasn't very good at it. I could hardly reach the pedals and did not have the strength required. He decided I was breaking too many needles, and I was given simpler essential jobs like ironing and steaming seams. My sister did more household chores, like the laundry.

What year did your dad come to the United States?

We're not sure about the year he was brought to the U.S. He said he was

Rita Kathleen Chow, recipient of the 1969 Federal Nursing Service Award from the Association of US Military Surgeons, Washington DC, for outstanding accomplishment in professional nursing and for writing the winning essay entitled "Intensive Cardiac Care—A Study of Professional Nursing Practice"

born in 1900. The picture he showed us looked like he was about 12 years old.

So you're not sure how he came over?

All we know is he said he was brought over as a boy. And because there was a devastating earthquake and fire in San Francisco everything such as documents was destroyed at that time. Lacking proof, we just had to accept whatever he said.

What year were you born?

1926.

And how about school? What was school like?

We were usually the only Chinese in Le Conte Elementary School. At Horace Mann Junior High, there was one other family. And we went to both Chinese and English schools. So when I was about 8 I started Chinese school too. My brother and sister started earlier because they were older and able to commute using public transportation provided by the Valencia Street car and the Powell Street cable car lines to reach Cumberland Chinese School in Chinatown.

What was the town you were growing up in again?

Well, being in San Francisco, all three of us went to Chinese school for 9 years. In Cantonese the education level was known as Sui Joong Hawk [Little Middle School]. So it was expected of us to study there, but I didn't finish until

I was about 17. And we didn't go on to Chinese high school. I told my parents that I really didn't think I could continue simultaneously going to two schools, if I was going on to college.

So Chinese school was difficult? What happened in Chinese school? Was it after regular school?

It wasn't difficult; it was just two hours long—4 to 6 p.m. Practically every Chinatown church had a Chinese school. So we would get home by 7:00, have supper, and do two kinds of homework. Each weekday our Chinese teachers consistently required us to submit a page of Chinese calligraphy—carefully rendered at home in black ink with a Chinese brush pen. I wasn't a brilliant Chinese scholar at all. I decided I really needed to concentrate on English. So I tried much harder in English school. I did receive the Chinese school graduation prize for good character attributes—whatever they are.

Your achievements are phenomenal. Do you attribute it to your family upbringing, or your Chinese culture, or just being an independent personality?

Oh, I think it is family, the environment and the drive that was inherent in the way we were brought up, because Mom and Dad worked really hard. Mom would go up to Chinatown to shop for fresh food and get orders for twill work coats for butchers and grocery men. She would ensure that their work clothes were personalized with their names and the name of the grocery store or fish market embroidered on them. And Dad would work almost 'round the clock managing the shop, performing sales and tailoring tasks, and creating a customer-friendly setting. And when sales increased he employed seamsters and seamstresses too.

I think that the inner drive to serve and please others started very early—exemplified by our parents being polite to customers, and teaching us the value of listening to them and teachers. Although they had limited education, I think my parents were very diligent and intelligent. I always admired them for their creativity and brightness. For example, when our Cumberland Presbyterian Chinese Church needed an interpreter for a guest speaker, Mom could interpret for worship service speakers from English to Cantonese with rapidity.

She married your dad in China? Or here in the United States?

It was a matched [arranged] marriage, probably in San Francisco.

And she was brought up in Monterey?

Yes, she grew up in Monterey, California, in a very big family and, being the oldest daughter, she was asked to work on the farm rather than go to school after attending the third or fourth grade. It was tenant farming where the family worked for a farmer, but didn't own the land. Apparently, she was pretty good at horseback riding and capable with such tasks as tossing hay.

Did your mom's parents come in the Gold Rush or before?

My maternal grandfather was a fisherman and that's why they were in Monterey. I have no idea what year he came from China to the United States. And grandmother said that she was born in Monterey. But I never heard her speak a word of English; I just accepted what she said.

So your family goes back four generations in America—

On Dad's side, we're first generation, but on mother's side it might be the third.

I think you mentioned somewhere that your family lived in the back of your tailor shop.

Yes, the shop was in front and we lived in the back between stacks of corduroys, tweeds, cowhides, and pigskins.

And the leather was for cowboys, or clothes, or—?

Oh, Dad was an excellent designer of leather jackets. The jackets would be very attractive with buttons and zippers in different places. There would be a white leather piece in the back over the shoulder, so the motorcyclist could be easily, safely seen from a distance.

This was in the '20s or teens or—?

This would be in the '30s and during World War II. At that time tailored jackets for motorcyclists were very popular, and few others thought of having tailor-made pants, slacks, and leather jackets. And when leather jackets needed new zippers, my job was to remove the old ones, and Dad would replace them with new ones.

And was your family—were your parents strict?

They weren't strict. They had certain expectancies that we would study as hard as possible. There was nothing more important than education. They said, "Since we didn't have much, we expect you to get as much as you can. We'll support you until you finish your Baccalaureate, and after that it's up to you." So I took that challenge.

You talked about Girl Scouts and how the Girl Scouts did a lot of nursing stuff too. So was nursing a very big thing in those days? How did you know that you were going to go into nursing? Or, when did you know?

I started Girl Scouts at age 12 or 13. And I'm still a lifetime member of the Girl Scouts. But what was important is that I found additional English-speaking role models. I knew I needed to hear English spoken as much as possible, because I didn't hear much conversation except with customers in our store.

As a teenager, I began to realize that I really needed other role models, and Girl Scouting eventually had many for me. I started admiring the leaders. And they were very liberal about how much I could do. So I worked on as many badges as I wanted to, and just kept going up until I received the First Class Scout badge—the highest for intermediate scouts at that time. And my parents didn't mind my choices at all; they said, "You may take piano lessons and go to Scouts on Friday afternoons, but you need to keep up with Chinese school." They enabled me to do what I wanted to do, and still accomplish what they thought would be important—that was education.

Were there other Chinese Americans in the Girl Scouts?

At that time I was always the only one in the troop, and it was the same when I got to the Girl Scout Mariners at the Senior Scout level.

So, when Pearl Harbor happened, how old were you?

I was in my teens doing volunteer work as a Girl Scout; what I did mostly during World War II was to study and volunteer. I'd go to the Red Cross Blood Bank and help run the elevator or type. I had already learned how to type in high school, so, I would interview people and record their personal data, so they could donate their blood. I also joined the American Women's Voluntary Services Juniors. We did such volunteer work as preparing bandages or packing gifts such as for the Merchant Marine. And I started going to Girl Scout camp at that time too. My sister and I were the very first Chinese to ever go to Camp Sugar Pine in the High Sierras.

At camp, and in the town where you grew up, was the general atmosphere pretty friendly for Chinese Americans?

Yes, yet there were times of tension during World War II. I think most San Francisco Chinese will tell you that, because people couldn't tell the difference between Chinese and Japanese. But even though the Japanese had been forcibly relocated away from San Francisco, people still had such fear that there were incidents of people breaking the window glass of store fronts. So to prevent possible vandalism we put up a sign in the front, "We're an American-Chinese store," so we never had any break-ins. But people still seemed uncomfortable with differences in appearance. In grammar school you'd be ridiculed with some name-calling. That's part of being tested as a minority member. So you'd have to put up with that and not get upset.

So it wasn't a big deal, it was just like a nuisance. But did World War II affect you socially? Other than having to put up the Chinese sign?

We had to put up black shades that could be pulled down. And I would make sure we got a bucket of sand and a shovel. We were instructed that if a chemical bomb came, to cover it with sand.

I'm not familiar with this. What's the—

They asked everybody to put a bucket with sand and a shovel in their homes.

And black shades?

And all the window shades had to be pulled whenever the Civil Defense test alarm sounded. It was important for all homes to be dark. When the siren was set off, Defense officials asked everybody to pull their shades down, if possible have black ones, and be quiet.

What was the rationale for that?

We were told that if the bombers came, the enemy would look for lights. And with the city dark, it would be harder for them to pinpoint the targets.

And then you went to [college]. So after you graduated from college, what happened?

Well, after I graduated from Stanford, the Director of Nursing, Grace Ringressy, learned that I was studying toward a master's degree. And she said, "Go to the very best graduate school you can find. Don't stay here." So I kept studying part-time, scanned college catalogues and, of course, was still very active as a Scout leader.

By the time the Korean War came, my savings were really low. So I said to my parents, "I think I have to join the Army—unless you don't want me to. They're short of nurses and looking for RN students. They will pay for my master's studies. And I think I can do it in a year and a half, depending on how many requirements they say that I have to do." So I selected Western Reserve University, now called Case Western Reserve University in Cleveland. It was known for being the very best in the country for the master's study. I just thought that would be wonderful, so I applied and got accepted into the Army Nurse Corps. However, the one drawback was my entry rank. The Army intake official said, "The only thing is that since you are coming into this program you'll have to start as a second lieutenant, even though you could be much higher in rank. You might make captain easily, with all your teaching." [She had already taught at Stanford and had been teaching two years at Fresno County School of Nursing.] I said, "All right. I'll do that."

As a result, after October 11, 1954, under the Army's RN Student Program, I was able to use my second lieutenant's salary to pay for the lodging and tuition expenses at Western Reseve University. And I graduated in September 1955 with a Master of Science majoring in my favorite subject of Teaching Surgical Nursing.

How did you know—Since when did you know you wanted to be a nurse?

Well, guidance counselors in the ninth grade asked us to pick an occupation or profession to go toward.

Wow, so people then knew from ninth grade what they were going to do for life?

Yes. Every student had to decide what to do in the future in order to decide which track to take in high school. There were commercial tracks, the professional curriculum, or the academic track. And those that wanted carpentry and hands-on kind of activities could pick a third vocational track. At that time the only options for women were teaching or nursing.

Upon graduating from Western Reserve University, I was assigned to the Orientation course at Fort Sam Houston, where I noticed I was the oldest among the second lieutenants. Also I was awarded a teaching MOS, a Military Occupational Specialty in Medical Surgical Nursing. My first assignment was to Fitzsimmons Army Hospital to be a Staff Nurse in the Medical/Surgical wards to care for GIs in various stages of tuberculosis.

And this was where? What city?

In Aurora, Colorado, a suburb of Denver. They later had me work in a surgical ward, which was really tough because of the shortage of nurses. We had tremendous patient loads. To fill staffing gaps, I would be assigned to rotate from day to evening to night shifts.

Why were they in Colorado? They were sent back from—

Fitzsimmons was the first stop from the Korean War zone for GIs who needed specialized pulmonary care. One of the fortunate things that happened was that the nurse administrators decided that I might do better in the Intensive Pulmonary Surgical Unit. And that was where they were doing unusual life-saving pulmonary surgery for patients with very diseased lungs.

So it worked out well. This was very first intensive pulmonary care that I know of, in the military where they were able to manage well with just simple equipment. In 1955–1956 there was no automatic plug-in electric pulmonary suction for underwater drainage. So we had to set up suction bottles and connect the tubing to a faucet. After adding a T-tube, based on the physics of Bernoulli's Principle, when the faucet is turned on and water passes straight down through the T-tube, suction will be created.

So I was impressed with how scientific principles were contributing to a very efficient kind of postoperative care. I felt very fortunate to get to work in a setting where there was creative thinking and the newest kinds of surgery being done at that time—years before all the automated electronic medical equipment was created.

After persistently asking nurse administrators when I was going to receive orders to use my MOS and teach, I eventually got my orders to go to the Medical Training Center at the Brooke Army Medical Center in Fort Sam Houston, San Antonio, Texas.

The Medical Training Center, where all the Army medics are taught, was a wonderful assignment. In six weeks they were able to effectively and efficiently teach essential Basic Patient Care to the medics. With carefully written lesson plans, the teaching teams taught a few thousand soldiers each week—each class size varied from 30 to 300, depending on the subject being taught.

I was very impressed in being part of the teams. Colonel Katherine Ball, the

Director of Basic Patient Care, was a kind, capable nurse administrator. She had such an open mind about new ideas to improve the teaching there. One eventful day she said, "We're going to have the Army Surgeon General coming for an inspection visit. We're going to have him watch you teach the venipuncture class. That just happens to be on the schedule for the day he's coming. He only has these few minutes to be in your class." I said, "Okay." In fact, the Surgeon General was so impressed with the way we were teaching that he pitched right in and helped the students with the technique. We all enjoyed that very much. It was just one example of how easy it was to teach when the latest audiovisual equipment and the newest ideas are we put together.

So your military years spanned about 14 years?

Yes, 14½ years in the Reserves, including three years active duty.

How come you decided to stay in for so long? Just because you liked it?

After completing the first three years of active duty, as required by the RN Student Program, I discovered that I was faced with a continuing 20-year Army duty obligation to be a member of the Ready Reserves by attending two-hour weekly drills with a Hospital Unit. Also, as a Reservist, each summer I was expected to participate in Annual Active Duty Training for two weeks. So from 1957 to 1968 I was employed as well as studying in graduate school and partici-pating in the Army Reserves. The Reserves offered a Medical Services Training course. And after moving to New York City I was chosen for that course and went to those weekly classes instead of attending most of the drills at the Hos-pital Unit in the Bronx.

Upon completing the 4-year Medical Services Training, I was selected for Army Command General Staff College [C&GS]. Unexpectedly, I was the only nurse and woman in my classes at C&GS. There was also mandatory 2-week summer annual active duty training for Reservists when the military courses were especially intensive and concentrated—culminating in written exams. The C&GS course during summer active duty in the '60s at Fort Knox was a tough course, with subjects focused on battle logistics. Everyone was at least a major, and so it was appropriate for those in the higher rank to decide on fire power—where and what guns were needed, supplies, and men and materiel, in order to win a battle. C&GS College is normally a 5-year course in the Reserves, so over time you can absorb and really apply the concepts.

In looking back—Before I began graduate studies at Columbia University Teachers College, I taught at Wayne State University College of Nursing in Detroit, Michigan and left after a year. It seemed to be an opportune time to make a change in 1958. One reason was because I was chosen to represent the Girl Scouts of the USA in Switzerland for three months as an exchange visitor-observer, all expenses paid, to do training and to represent the United States in all the different activities of the Swiss Girl Guides. I also had received a federal traineeship to study for a Professional Diploma in Nursing Education at Teachers College, Columbia University in New York City.

So after the summer in Switzerland, I went directly to graduate school at Columbia University's Teachers College and started in '59. By '61, I had finished all the course work for the doctorate. One of the things I learned in the Army was systems research. And that was precisely what I had been focusing on, as to how to apply systems research to nursing and how to use that approach to improve nursing care. Fortuitously, the Army provided that theory through the battle logistics. And that's why I was using that knowledge and combining it with my medical knowledge to see what I could do to improve nursing care, particularly post-operative care. And I decided to analyze the most complex care of cardiosurgical nursing.

In 1961, unpredictably, I found that my struggle with professional writing in English was about to be over. In the past, I almost failed an undergraduate English course. I didn't have the level of English on a par with other students. So during graduate study my doctoral advisor said, "There's something wrong with your English. You've got to go take English." So she sent me off to Columbia University to take Professional Writing and I received a B-plus. And she said, "All right, now you'd better go back and take some more." Popular Writing really encourages creativity, and I received an A-minus. At that point, when I'd completed the Professional Diploma requirements at Columbia University Teachers College, I needed a job.

Unexpectedly, I got a phone call from the editor of the *American Journal of Nursing* who said, "We'd like to talk with you. I have been talking with a Lieutenant Colonel Haylow in the Army Nurse Corps, and she talked about your writing and how unusual it was. Please bring your samples with you." So I did, and she said, "Oh, it's obvious. You know the King's English." And she hired me right away as an Assistant Editor for the *American Journal of Nursing*, which at that time was the official magazine of the American Nurses' Association with about 200,000 in circulation. After a year I was promoted to Associate Editor, so I decided that my English wasn't too bad after all.

Okay, there was this interesting part. You wrote a textbook and it says that "During the Nixon Presidency the staff was given the responsibility to collaborate with the Social Security Administration and other parts of the government."

Okay, I'll tell you about the textbook first and then I'll jump to Long Term Care. The textbook was a product of the three years at Ohio State University [OSU], doing the Systems Research that I was so interested in. When I went there for an exploratory visit, OSU Professor Howland said, "We don't have a penny for you, but we'll give you a desk. Here's a little spot for you to sit, and it's up to you to find some monies if you're going to be here." I said, "Oh, all right." So I got two funds rescuing me, to bring me through that first year for the pilot study that needed to be done.

I needed to demonstrate that it was feasible to videotape patient care in a surgical intensive care unit, since nobody had done it yet. The OSU Foundation and OSU Hospital's Nursing Service administrators supported my proposed study. I thought my research team could analyze 4 hours of continuous recording of each patient's care via videotape. And from that analysis we would know what should be done, and be able to identify what scientific principles should be applied to that care. I thought that if we could document what the nature of nursing is, then we would be able to teach it—to teach what should be done, and the scientific reasons for that care.

The fact that such an approach was not in any nursing textbook at that time motivated me. It seemed so difficult and expensive. And it was expensive. But there were volunteers who came while I was working on the project in Ohio. Videotape was just being created at that time by the 3M Company. They supported the pilot study by donating the first reel of tape and sending a camera man too.

So I was able to record and show that tape to the United States Public Health Service [USPHS] Division of Nursing staff. And there were a couple of people there that looked at the tape and said, "Do you know that you are solving how to analyze the quality of care?"

I said, "All I know is that this is what I'd like to do, and—if it's possible to get some support." And so that's how I got the start of the 3-year funding support from USPHS—through various administrators, staff, and faculty members who perceived what was possible. The funding made it possible for me to proceed with plans to select a nurse research team as well as a technical team—because I needed audio and camera experts, an engineer and a studio.

So in 1965 I contacted Medical School faculty at Ohio State University. They said, "Well, we don't have any TV yet, but we're building a studio, so we'll let you use it when it is finished." I said, "Okay. I'll pay for my camera with the zoom lens, the videotape machine, and cables that I'll need. And I'll give it all to you when I'm finished with the project because I won't need them." They said, "Fine." So that's how the Medical School staff pitched in, laid the groundwork and cables, and connected their studio with my project's research site in the University Hospitals' Surgical/Intensive Care Unit. Eventually, my textbook based on this postoperative study of 23 patients was published.

That's wonderful. Can you talk about long-term care? Nixon? And Social Security?

You probably know the Surgeon General, together with the U.S. Public Health Service, have always addressed various national health issues. They included the extended role of the nurse and the need for nurse practitioners, and concern about chronic diseases and care of the aging. When Nixon said he was going to change long-term care and improve the nursing homes of the nation and a group of us in the USPHS were given the responsibility for the Office of Nursing Home Affairs, we gathered on a Sunday for brain-storming. Our very imaginative colleague Florence Reynolds said, "We know nursing homes need change. What we need is a campaign." We decided to create this campaign. The campaign was to conduct the first unannounced nationwide visit to nursing homes.

Up to this point the nursing home administrators knew when state surveyors were coming to inspect their facilities. The results of the survey determined whether a nursing home was going to qualify to receive Medicare and Medicaid funds. Our campaign focus would be on health and safety but completely on the actual care being given instead of the potential for care, using a research-validated assessment form.

We surmised that we needed to select the essential survey forms to use, assemble a surveyor's guide book, and train the survey teams. In essence we said, "Let's call for federal volunteer workers for fifteen teams that will be divided among the ten regions. We have a Director for every region. And let the Director decide where the team should go to survey the selected nursing homes. Nobody will know except the Directors. The teams will consist of eight disciplines, including a medical records person, an administrator, a pharmacist, social worker, the nurse (of course), physician, and safety engineer. The specialists selected had to have been already screened and must promise to keep secret where they were going all summer until the fact-finding survey is completed. The findings will need to be published by November. And I was assigned to be the editor of the reports.

In brief, through extensive collaboration with the ten Regional Directors and many organizations in the federal government, the Office of Nursing Home Affairs (later renamed Office of Long Term Care) staff conducted the first unannounced survey of a statistical sample of nursing homes throughout the nation and published the findings in several reports and through multi-media. The results served to stimulate regulatory changes that have progressively improved the quality of nursing homes.

Any final thoughts or things that you'd like to add about your military experience, being a veteran?

Well, the transfer from the Army Reserves to enter active duty with the USPHS Commissioned Corps was a good step, because I had learned decision-making from the Army, The military training can provide a kind of critical thinking that's very unusual, that you can still use any time, wherever you are. So I think whenever I was faced with a life situation—what I call a gamble—each time I tried to learn from the past and hopefully acquire an attribute or stamina, thanks to the Army.

One of life's gambles happened after I had been Chief of Quality Assurance and involved with Long Term Care facility regulations in the Health Care Financing Administration in Baltimore. I received orders assigning me to the Rosebud Indian Reservation because they needed an evening nurse in the

At the Organization of Chinese Americans in Washington, D.C., 2010

USPHS Hospital in Rosebud, South Dakota.

It was an interesting challenge in management with limited resources in health manpower and equipment. And it was an old hospital. Unquestionably, they needed a new one, but first they needed to make some improvements in order to be recertified and qualify for Medicare and Medicaid funds. After three months, they said, "We're wasting you" and asked me to set up a quality assurance program, and I agreed. And they immediately changed my job to Assistant to the Administrator to initiate the program. My goal was to empower them to take leadership. I said, "You'll have to do the work, though. I'll give you the ideas, do your paperwork, and give you the guidance you need, but you're going to have to all do the leading." And they said, "We'll do it." And they did. They did very well, and I was able to leave in six months and take another new assignment.

The USPHS Commissioned Corps also provide health personnel for the Federal Bureau of Prisons [BoP], but I was surprised in 1989 when I received a letter from the BoP Medical Director asking me to consider being the Director of Nursing at the Fort Worth Correctional facility because of my administration and gerontology background. Before accepting the assignment, I made a site visit with BoP Chief Nurse and learned that there was no long-term care facility in the BoP for aging prisoners. Fort Worth was designated to be the site where there were already 50 to 60 inmates there using wheelchairs.

Again, I was glad that I had prior Army experience because I had had rifle training annually as a Reservist. And I learned that every nurse who was going to be on the BoP staff had to be able to shoot off three weapons accurately: the rifle, shotgun, and pistol—before we could be part of the staff.

Was it frightening working in a prison?

No, because BoP sends all new employees to three weeks of orientation at a Training Center for firearms training and to learn from didactics and demonstrations, and aikido for self-defense. With the ability to defend ourselves, we weren't afraid, and they knew it. The inmates knew that we all knew how to shoot and use aikido movements when needed. They've seen staff in action before. So there's mutual respect, and we talk to the men as gentlemen. And they always call you "Miss," "Doctor" or whatever, and they're always very polite.

What are the prisoners in for usually? What kind of crimes?

Oh, the ones we had at Fort Worth were in mostly for drugs. So we had a large drug program conducted by clinical psychologists to help them overcome that problem of habituation. There were some who had really done some pretty bad things. But most of them were non-threatening. In fact, from 1989 to 1995, we were able to not only design and build the very first long-term care facility for the Bureau of Prisons, but also be innovative in selecting state-of-the-art patient care equipment. Through interdisciplinary professional collaboration, we created BoP's second inmate-to-inmate hospice program and started an Inmate Volunteer Caregiver Program. Finally, we even became fully accredited for long-term care by JCAHO [the Joint Commission for Accreditation of Health Care Organizations].

Is there any most memorable experience from in your life that you think might be interesting for younger people who want to just understand how things might have changed? Before, you said that there wasn't too much discrimination. But do you think there has been substantial change for Chinese people in America?

I don't know how much. It varies so much depending on the number of us and where we are. There are large numbers in California, so people don't notice any impact. If they're not used to seeing you, they might look at you twice. But I've never had any difficulty, partly because I try to prepare for it.

But one of the interesting things that happened is when I had to drive through the South, down to Texas for six weeks orientation to the army. For a companion, I took along my dark-complexioned friend from Zamboanga, Philippines, who was living in the same dorm I was in and wanted very much to see that part of the United States.

While we were on the road, I said, "Please let me know what you're going to do so we won't have any difficulty." Well, she wasn't quite sure what I meant, so I said, "When we get to Chattanooga, Tennessee, we're going to go on the Incline Railroad because it would be fun to ride and see the Falls." She said, "All right." So we entered the Incline car and everybody stared at us because there was a sign, "Colored people to the rear." And she looked at me and I said, "We'll sit in the middle." And everybody smiled and nodded. They thought that was just fine.

Right before that, while I was loading gas at a station, she left and tried to buy some fried chicken as a treat for dinner at a carry-out, but the sales persons refused to sell food to her. She came back crying. And I said, "I was trying to spare you of that. They just don't know who you are and what you are and so their fear is just to a draw back and not to do anything. We can try it again when we go have coffee, and I'll show you what we can do." She said, "Oh, all right."

So we went to a counter in a coffee shop, and when the servers saw us, they all rushed back into the kitchen, disappeared, and could be heard yelling at each other back there. And I said, "Now you just go ahead and speak up and ask for what you'd like, in your coffee, and I'll speak first." She said, "Oh, okay."

Soon a young waitress came out timidly, and she really looked afraid. She asked, "May I help you?" I said, "Oh, we'd just like some coffee. It will help us wake up." And then my friend she said, "I'd like some coffee too, with cream in it." When we smiled at the waitress, her mouth just dropped open. She probably thought to herself, no Southern accent and it was a different accent. So she relaxed and seemed so pleased to serve us. She had no idea what we were like, and it was all right. We knew it was just a matter of time that they'd understand that we're not so strange.

PART III: VIETNAM WAR

Emergence of Asian American Identity

A new Asian American identity emerged alongside the protests against the Vietnam War, the civil rights and Black Power movements, and as women and the gay community pushed for equality and social justice. Prior to this, Chinese, Japanese, Korean, and Filipino Americans saw their cultures as distinct. However, their common experience of being seen and considered by the rest of America as all the same bound them as a cohesive group. The term "Asian American" was coined by Yuji Ichioka, a founder of the Asian American movement, to replace "Oriental" which was now deemed outdated and evocative of European colonialism.[23]

Racism In The Military

While each individual had a different military experience, and many Chinese Americans did not experience racism, harassment did occur for some. Generally, officers experienced less racism than enlisted men. The Winter Soldier investigation into U.S. war crimes in Vietnam revealed that Vietnamese and other Asians were called "gooks" and considered subhuman. In January 1971 in Detroit, Scott Shimabukaro of the Third Marine Division testified that "military men have the attitude that a gook is a gook. They go through the brain washing about the Asian people being subhuman ..." and "I saw how Whites were treating the Vietnamese, calling them gooks, running them over with their trucks. I figured I am a gook also."[24] Even a U.S. general, General Westmoreland, announced, "The Oriental doesn't put the same high price on life as does a Westerner. Life is plentiful. Life is cheap in the Orient." When a Chinese American GI objected to verbal abuse, he was put to two years of hard labor in the stockade.[25]

Radical Political Movements

Inspired by Red Guards of Maoist China (who revolted in the Cultural Revolution against elders and the former establishment) and by Black Panthers (revolutionary socialists who fought against police harassment and brutality), a Chinese American radical youth group called the Red Guards formed in San Francisco in 1969. They defied the Chinatown establishment, spoke against genocide in Vietnam, against government injustices and police brutality, against U.S. recognition of the Chiang Kai-shek government as the "real" China, and against miserable conditions in Chinatowns. They advocated militancy, called for ethnic studies programs on campuses, developed social programs such as free breakfast and lunch programs for the poor, and organized tenants against landlords. They wanted to improve conditions for Chinatowns and Asian Americans. They did not gain much support from their community, and ultimately dissolved due to internal issues.[26]

John Gerald Miki speaks about the Secret War, the protests and the turmoil of the 1960s, and the new exciting changes happening; David Louie and Gabe Mui talk about the draft; Randall T. Eng, Fang A. Wong, Frederick Pang, and John Fugh about being "firsts" as Asian Americans in their fields; Richard Wong about growing up in old New York, and Thomas Wing about growing up in Newark. David J. Louie also speaks about new icons like Bruce Lee and mainstream interest in China being piqued after Nixon's trip to China.

CHAPTER SEVENTEEN

John Gerald Miki (1938–   )
U.S. Air Force

John Gerald Miki went to Indiana University on a swim scholarship, was an All-American, co-captained the swim team that placed third in the 1960 NCAAs and was on the medley relay that broke the American record. The Air Force sent him to the Air Force Academy to train for the 1960 Olympic Tryouts for Rome. Inspired by his uncle who was in the 442nd Infantry Regiment, Jerry served thirty years in the Air Force, seven in Europe and nine in Asia, including two combat tours in the Vietnam War. He was an H-53 squadron commander in Germany, and United States military Air Attaché to Switzerland and Singapore and Chief of Project Stony Beach in Thailand from 1988–90 charged with tracking reports of live PW/MIAs in Southeast Asia. He was awarded the Air Force Legion of Merit, three Distinguished Flying Crosses, the Bronze Star and seven Air Medals. He retired as a colonel in 1990.

You could say that I was born to war. When my third-generation Chinese American mother and my Nisei Japanese father married in Hawaii in December 1937, Japan was engaged in the Rape of Nanking. They were warned the marriage would never work, but they were young and stubborn. Four years and three kids later, on December 7, 1941, my newly divorced mother was stuffing us under a bed as anti-aircraft shells from the Pearl Harbor attack rained on Honolulu. That night the FBI arrested my Japanese grandfather because he was a leader in the Japanese community and an interpreter in the Territory of Hawaii Court System. Other relatives were held in the Manzanar Internment Camp in California for the duration of the war.

Before the war, I remember sleeping to the comforting click of mahjong tiles as our Chinese clan laughed and gossiped in Hakka dialect through all-night mahjong sessions. My great-grandfather was Lau Ah Leong, who controlled the opium trade when Hawaii was a kingdom, and later when it became a U.S. territory. Opium was the after-work relaxant of Chinese after long days of heavy labor in rice and taro fields. Ah Leong smuggled it into Hawaii with his grocery shipments from China while bribed officials looked the other way. He grew so rich that he paid the government to let him keep his five wives and numerous concubines.

Everything changed after Pearl Harbor. Martial Law, where one could be

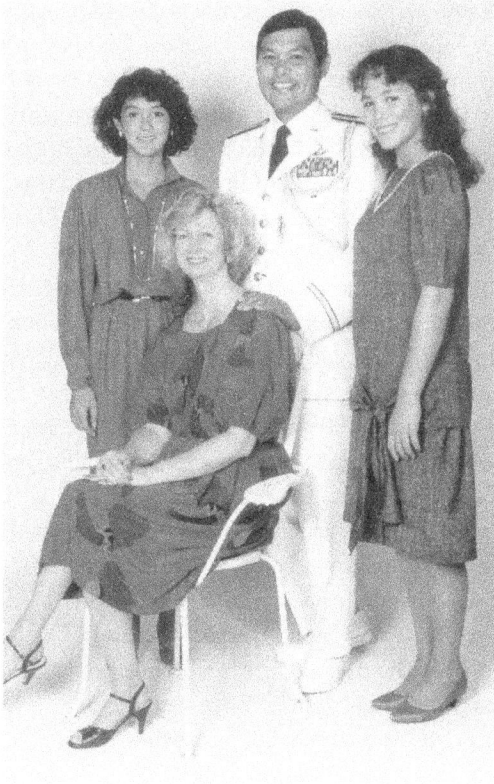

Family portrait in Bern, Switzerland, 1985
Jenny Rebecca, 18, left; Misha Juliet, 19, right

shot in the street by military authorities, was imposed. There were blackout cur-
fews, barbed-wire, and tank and truck convoys everywhere. Soldiers and sailors
with money and fatalistic "anything-goes" attitudes filled Honolulu streets. We
lived in Waikiki where pilots bound for Iwo Jima and Okinawa would scream
in low at treetop level to scare their buddies in the Moana and Royal Hawaiian
hotels that had been converted into Officers' Quarters. The fighters pulled up
sharply to practice dogfights high above Waikiki beach, silver aircraft twisting
and glinting in the blue sky. It was then that I vowed to someday become a pilot.

One had to be one thousand percent American in wartime Hawaii. Japanese
and Chinese language schools were closed. We spoke English to avoid upsetting
jumpy FBI agents. Kids were ashamed to be non-Caucasian and wanted to be
American as apple pie. I was never taught to speak the Japanese, Chinese or
Hawaiian languages that my family spoke before the war. It was a subtle form
of cultural genocide.

As kids we spent summers at my Chinese grandparents' home in Kona
on the Big Island of Hawaii where the army manned scattered garrisons. My
grandparents worked from 3:00 in the morning to 11:00 at night running a

general store, gas station, bar, pig farm, coffee mill, and poi factory. I remember them phoning the Military Police for help to clear their bar at curfew whenever a young soldier, thinking he was back in the Wild West, would slap a .45 pistol or live grenade on the bar and drunkenly shout, "This bar ain't closing!"

My Japanese uncle, George Miki, fought in the segregated 442nd Regimental Combat Team in France and Italy. He returned after the war and starred in the 1950 movie *Go For Broke*, which depicted the heroics of his unit. He wanted to be a Hawaii Air National Guard pilot but was told he was too old. Uncle George helped raise us kids and was more of a dad than our real father. He died of cancer at age 39 in 1960. I wanted to become a pilot for him, too.

From 1956 to 1960 I attended Indiana University on a swim scholarship. I was an All-American, co-captained our team that placed third in the 1960 NCAAs, and swam on the 400-yard medley relay that set a new American record. I also took AFROTC to qualify for pilot training. Just before graduation, the Air Force informed me that they were sending me to the Air Force Academy to train for the 1960 Swim Trials to qualify for the Rome Olympics. I reported to Colorado Springs on June 9th, 1960, and trained myself, since the athletic staff was on summer leave. Two months later I placed third in the 100-meter breaststroke at the Olympic Trials in Detroit. The first place finisher went on to Rome, where he won a gold medal. The next day I was on my way to Marianna in north Florida for primary pilot training.

Other than passing through en route to swim meets, it was my first time in the South. One evening as I sat watching a movie in downtown Marianna with my roommate Val Bourque, a girl came up and punched me in the face. Everyone in the theater turned around and laughed. Val, who was to become the first Air Force Academy graduate to be killed in the Vietnam War, could only laugh and say, "Welcome to the South, roommate. You're supposed to be in the colored patrons' balcony." I smiled through my bleeding nose, not letting the crowd think they'd gotten to me. Being raised in multi-racial Hawaii and wrapped in the protective cocoon of the Indiana University swim team when we traveled, I was naive about the reality of race in America.

But I learned fast at Craig Air Force Base in Selma, Alabama, where I spent 1961 flying jet trainers in Basic Flight School. After we students were assigned flight instructors, I found myself at a table with one black and one effeminate white student, and our instructor was a rebellious surfer dude from California who the base commander wanted to kick out of the Air Force. The hierarchy at Craig Air Force Base seemed to aim at discouraging minorities from staying in the Air Force. If you objected to any perceived prejudice, your military career was over. My black tablemate and myself, along with a Jewish American student in another flight, ended up at the bottom of our class, which meant we received helicopter assignments while top students got slots to fighter school. By graduation, the white student at our table had washed out of training and the instructor pilot left the Air Force. This was the way of life at Craig Air Base in 1961.

The South was besieged by Freedom Riders arriving by bus to integrate lunch counters and register voters. Restaurants told me to line up outside at a window with "the rest of them niggers" when I tried to eat downtown. Some of my classmates from the South boasted about how teenagers flung whiskey bottles from speeding cars into the faces of Blacks walking along the roads at night. Ku Klux Klan signs were prominently displayed. I was in my Air Force uniform when I was ordered to move to the colored waiting room in the Montgomery bus station.

Each day after flying and academics I volunteer-coached the Selma YMCA children's swim team and took them to weekend meets in Birmingham and Tuscaloosa. The YMCA head introduced me to Sheriff Jim Clark who, along with his deputies in 1966, I would watch beating Freedom Marchers on the Edmund Pettis Bridge with clubs on national television. When the YMCA head told me to jump into the pool to show the sheriff how "a Ha-wai-yan" swam, I refused, saying that the kids had to begin practice. The YMCA head was embarrassed and angry that I declined to be his Hawaiian performing seal for Sheriff Clark.

After earning my pilot wings I spent six months as an assistant Varsity swim coach at the Air Force Academy en route to Helicopter School in Nevada. My first duty assignment was to Hill Air Force Base in Utah in 1962, where I flew helicopters, 4-engine transports and the T-39 executive jet. I married a girl who had been on the swim team with me back in Hawaii and was attending the University of Utah. In 1966, the Athletic Director of the Air Force Academy offered me the swim team head coach position, promising that if I accepted I wouldn't have to serve in Vietnam. But, eager to test myself under fire before the war ended, I turned him down.

* * *

I was as an advisor to the Vietnamese Air Force from July 1966 to July 1967 in the II Corps Central Highlands, flying in Pleiku, Kontum and Quin Nhon districts where there was heavy fighting. The pilots were in their twenties like I was, but they had a lot of combat experience. We trained them in logistics and tactics so that someday they could defend their country themselves. Since I looked like them, I was often mistaken by our own military advisors as being Vietnamese. When our advisor's compound was attacked at night, I knew I could be shot by trigger-happy Americans who took me for Viet Cong, so I remained in my room with my .38 pistol. War can be both deadly and ha-ha funny.

From my helicopter I saw wild elephants crossing jungle streams, spectacular waterfalls, and flocks of multi-colored parrots that burst like rockets when we flew low over the treetops in Vietnam's Highlands. If your aircraft crashed into the rainforest it was swallowed up by the triple-canopy trees standing at 250, 150, and 100-foot layers over dense foliage that concealed Viet Cong and North Vietnamese troops. The jungle soil is so acidic and corrosive that when

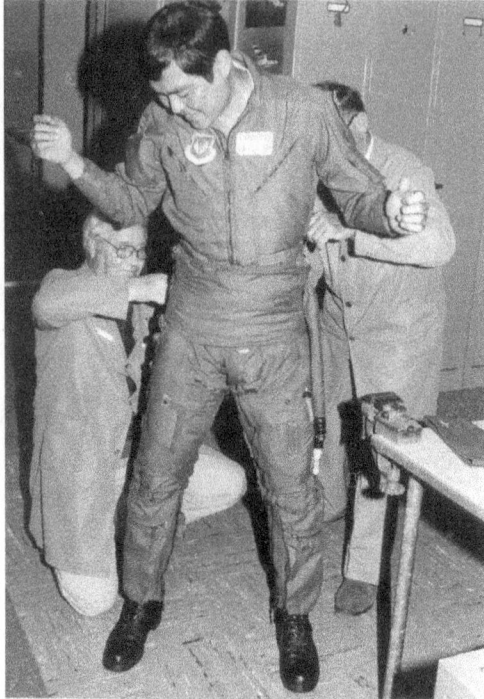

Donning a g-suit before flight in Swiss Air Force
Mirage fighter, Switzerland, 1984

U.S. recovery teams excavated crash sites in search of American crew members' remains after the war, they found only bits of belt buckles and aircraft parts. Bodies had literally dissolved and vanished and become part of the jungle.

When I saw that we were flying over the same villages, fighting the same battles that we'd fought four months earlier, I knew that we were losing the war. Peasants in the countryside resented Americans and the South Vietnamese military. I learned that our Vietnamese pilots were taking money from refugees we carried aboard our helicopters and saw other instances of graft and corruption that would eventually cause the downfall of South Vietnam. We gave them our guns, money and blood but were unable to change their culture. So much for our missionary zeal to spread freedom and democracy in Vietnam.

Upon returning stateside, I was assigned to the First Helicopter Squadron at Bolling Air Force Base in Washington, D.C. Although we were criticized by the press for transporting VIPs throughout the D.C. area, our primary classified mission was to transfer military personnel to remote command posts outside Washington where they would direct America's retaliatory strikes against Russia from submarines, missile silos and B-52 bombers when World War III started.

Vietnam War protests were raging across America when I arrived in Washington in 1967. One evening, after attending a lecture at George Washington University, I picked up a carload of college anti-war protestors seeking a place to sleep. I took them home, fed them, and drove them to their rally the next morning. Then I went to work and flew the helicopter which filmed them as they marched on the Pentagon that day, 27 October 1967. Like a schizophrenic, I understood both sides of the Vietnam War and was struggling with my own doubts.

Most of my fellow pilots were politically conservative. When I commented on the My Lai massacre and shootings at Kent State, I was told, "If you don't like it, get the f--- out of America and go back where you came from." It was hilarious. One squadron pilot called me "Hop Sing," the name of the Chinese cook on the then popular *Bonanza* television series. I laughed because these people really wanted me to return to China.

The Year of the Monkey, 1968, was a dangerous time in America. After Martin Luther King's assassination the smoke-filled skies made Washington look like World War II Stalingrad burning. Rumors that rioters were firing at our helicopters proved false. There was also North Vietnam's Tet Offensive, LBJ's decision not to seek a second term, the murder of Robert Kennedy, chaos at the Chicago Democratic Convention and the election of Richard Nixon as president.

In 1969 I was passed over for promotion to the rank of major, even though I wore a Bronze Star, Distinguished Flying Cross, two Air Medals and had a clean record, while my squadron mates who had never served in Vietnam were promoted. An officer's military career depends on whether they get promoted or not. I requested a transfer to Hawaii to position myself to leave the Air Force if I was passed over again the following year. Since helicopter pilots in Vietnam were in short supply, the Air Force informed me the only way I could be stationed in Hawaii was to take another combat tour in Vietnam.

By September 1970 I was flying Special Operations helicopters dropping Green Beret reconnaissance and sabotage teams on the Ho Chi Minh Trail in Laos. We flew out of Nakon Phanom Air Base, Thailand, in what was called a "Secret War," since the 1961 Geneva Accords had proclaimed Laos neutral and no Soviet, North Vietnamese or American military forces were to be in the country. Nevertheless, fighting raged on, with the Americans directed by the CIA from the U.S. embassy in the Laotian capital of Vientiane. The war was secret only to the American public; if you were killed in Laos, your family was told that you had died in Vietnam.

Our choppers airlifted Hmong tribesmen to fight the North Vietnamese and Pathet Lao. We flew out of Long Cheng, a secret CIA base in north Laos shrouded in fog and clouds and surrounded by fantastic limestone karst mountain formations that one sees in Chinese scroll paintings. It was a strange, surreal war. The United States persuaded the Hmong to fight on our side with money, arms and vague promises that if we won the war they would be granted some form of recognition by the Lao government.

The Hmong were fierce warriors who had defeated the communists in guerilla hit-and-run raids in the jungles and mountains of northern Laos. But after the CIA converted the Hmongs into a conventional garrison force defending fixed positions such as forts, roads and weapon depots in the mid-1960s, the North Vietnamese artillery shredded the ranks of these proud mountain fighters. By 1970, our squadron's pilots were surprised to be airlifting 10-year-old Hmongs into battle. When we inquired where the older Hmong were, the CIA handlers told us that their fathers, uncles and brothers, an entire generation of brave warriors, were dead. So it goes in war.

Later when asked what I, as an Asian American, thought of killing other Asians, I answered that we were just trying to keep Communism from imposing its will on Asia. There were Asians on our side and Asians on the other side. If, in the end, Asians rejected Democracy and chose Communism, so be it.

But I was questioning whether the war was worth it. One night on a flight along the Mekong River I glanced 100 miles to the northeast and saw the Mu Ghia, Nape and Ban Karai mountain passes, that fed trucks, men and weapons from North Vietnam onto the Ho Chi Minh Trail, burning like Dante's circles of Hell. Cries of Mayday and wailing beepers jammed the emergency radio channel as American aircraft were downed by enemy missiles and anti-aircraft guns guarding the passes. A red moon rose out of the South China Sea above the killing and madness.

I was busy fending off my own snipers. Frustrated that America was about to lose its first war to "gooks," and "monkeys," some bosses called me, "Hey, boy," and gave me their Jim Crow stare, as if I was an uppity Chinaman who was somehow happy we were losing the war. Hell, America was my country, too, and I wasn't any happier about the situation than they were. But I'd always been an outsider and didn't let their taunts get to me. After all, hadn't I beaten their best as a swimmer, and didn't Ah Leong and Miki blood flow in my veins? Besides, on appeal, the Air Force had rescinded my pass-over and I was promoted to major with a date of rank backdated to when I should have been promoted.

Our squadron lost several aircraft and good men that year, but I survived the enemy green tracer bullets that hammered our aircraft. I found that during combat it is possible for one to live more in 20 seconds than most men live in a lifetime. It's when you begin to crave the adrenaline rush from danger that you risk turning into someone you don't recognize in the mirror. I never grew to love war.

There was a price to pay for my second combat tour. Soon after reporting to my new duty station at Hickam Air Force Base in Hawaii, my wife divorced me and took our two young daughters, ages five and six, to live with her sister in California. Her father had been an Army Air Corps fighter pilot during World War II who was killed during a flight test accident in 1947. She told me that she couldn't take the uncertainties of military life any longer. Losing her and my daughters was the great heartbreak of my life. Now alone, I decided to remain in the Air Force.

For three years I flew SH-3 helicopters out of Hickam Air Force Base, spending a third of that time aboard converted Liberty ships, tracking satellites around the Hawaiian Islands. Photo intelligence was of the highest priority for America. U.S. spy satellites could spot a tennis ball on the ground but until the mid-1970s they lacked the capability to transmit photographs to ground stations. Instead, a button was pushed in a relay station in Adak, Alaska, and the satellite would eject a photo package that would reenter the atmosphere, then descend by parachute from 50,000 feet over the Pacific to be snagged by C-130 cargo aircraft from our Air Group. The photos were then rushed to the Pentagon and White House. Since 5% of the packages fell into the ocean due to torn or malfunctioning parachutes, our helicopters were to pluck them from the sea before the Russians, who shadowed our ship, got to them first. Our satellite recovery range stretched 2,000 miles from Midway Atoll to 500 miles east of the Big Island of Hawaii.

From 1974 to 1977 I was at Yokota Air Base in Japan where I was in charge of the Flight Operations Division that flew T-39 VIP jets, H-1 Huey helicopters and DC-7 four-engine transports to Taiwan, Hong Kong, South Korea and the Philippines. I was promoted to lieutenant colonel in 1976. While in Japan, I was able to visit my Japanese relatives in the small village where my grandfather was born before he sailed to Hawaii as a 4-year-old in 1886.

After Japan I spent 1978 to 1982 in an H-53 heavy-lift helicopter squadron in Germany. Since NATO's line of fixed radar sites on the West German border could be destroyed by the first wave of Soviet aircraft, the Pentagon's solution was to form a Tactical Control Wing that would deploy sixteen mobile radar units which could be moved like chess pieces by H-53 helicopters as the European battlefront ebbed and flowed. Each mobile radar unit consisted of ten vans the size of small house trailers that contained radar dishes, power generators, communications equipment and command-and-control modules that were manned by about 40 airmen. Their mission was to guide our fighters to intercept enemy aircraft for a time before shutting down to be moved by our helicopters to another location to avoid destruction by enemy fighters. Roads could not be used because of the threat of saboteurs and the crowds of refugees fleeing the war zone.

This plan had existed on paper for over ten years but had never been tested due to Vietnam War demands and the crashes of two of the Wing's H-53 helicopters that killed 39 airmen before I arrived in Germany. When I took charge of the H-53 squadron, I told the wing commander I could move all his radar units if he backed me; he overrode the objections of wing personnel who feared another catastrophic helicopter accident. Within ten months I safely airlifted the wing's sixteen mobile radar units without an accident or incident.

For this and other accomplishments, the wing commander was promoted to major general and I was elevated to the rank of full colonel in 1981. More importantly, I restored the pride and morale of my squadron, which had been damaged by the previous accidents and the Vietnam War. But for me the happiest event in Germany occurred in 1978 when I married Bonnie Hildebrandt, whom I had met in Japan while she was teaching at Yokota Air Base high school.

After my promotion, the Pentagon asked where I wished to be assigned. I wanted to be the military air attaché to China, but since that slot was already filled, Bonnie and I chose Switzerland. We attended military attaché school and the Foreign Service Institute in Washington, D.C. for 18 months, studying French and German and learning how to become a military attaché. An attaché's mission is to determine the military capabilities of a country [not only the host country] and to gauge its political will to use that capability. A country may possess effective military strength but not the political will to use it, or vice

On tour of a Swiss Air Base with the assistant Russian
and two assistant PRC military attaches, 1986

versa. Military attachés gather raw intelligence to be analyzed and used in their country's intelligence reports. After being an operational line pilot for 21 years, this proved to be an interesting career change for me.

I was the military air attaché at the American Embassy in Bern from June 1983 to June 1986. To cultivate contacts, we hosted foreigners at dinners and cocktail parties in our home several times a month. Bonnie was my unpaid partner and accomplished this with style and grace. The fact that I was from Hawaii and Bonnie from Wisconsin fascinated the diplomatic community. We did our best to represent the strength and diversity of America to Europeans who, in the 1980s, could be judgmental in their attitude toward America's mixing of class and races.

The Cold War power game in Bern was an elaborate diplomatic minuet in which each country tended to its own interests. Of the 40-plus military attachés accredited to Switzerland, nearly half were from the Warsaw Pact. It was a critical time because the Kremlin, realizing that Russia was falling behind in its economic and military capabilities, was pressing their leaders to invade Europe. Fortunately, reason prevailed. To ensure that the neutral Swiss tilted toward the West, we hosted exchange visits between high ranking Swiss and U.S. Air Force officials. We also initiated proceedings that led to the sale of a squadron of F/A-18 fighters to Switzerland.

For my next assignment, I was named Air Attaché to the Republic of Singapore in 1986. Chinese comprised 77% of the population, with Malays and Indians in the minority. It was a Confucian-style meritocracy that ruled with Orwellian benevolence. In contrast to Europe, diplomatic receptions and dinner parties were informal in the tropics. Bonnie and I sensed the wave of energy and optimism in Asia as we watched Singapore and other governments work to meet the rising expectations of their people. Economic momentum was swinging from Europe to Asia.

The Singaporean Chinese traditionally groomed their sons to assume careers in business, medicine and academia. One's first loyalty was to the family; a career as a soldier was considered wasteful. When I arrived in 1986, Tom Cruise's movie *Top Gun* was changing that attitude just as Singapore was about to receive its first squadron of American-made F-16 fighters. I helped set up their F-16 training course at Luke Air Force Base in Arizona and sent their first cadet to the U.S. Air Force Academy. Today he is the commander of the Singaporean Air Force. Their best young minds had come to accept that a Confucian-style career in government, industry and the military could indeed be honorable and rewarding. Today Singapore's economy reflects this drive for excellence.

In June 1988, the Defense Intelligence Agency transferred me to Thailand to lead a team investigating reports of American servicemen from the Vietnam era believed to be still held prisoner in Southeast Asia. Con artists were scamming American families with promises that for money they could rescue their missing sons, fathers, or brothers from jungle prison camps. The belief that Americans

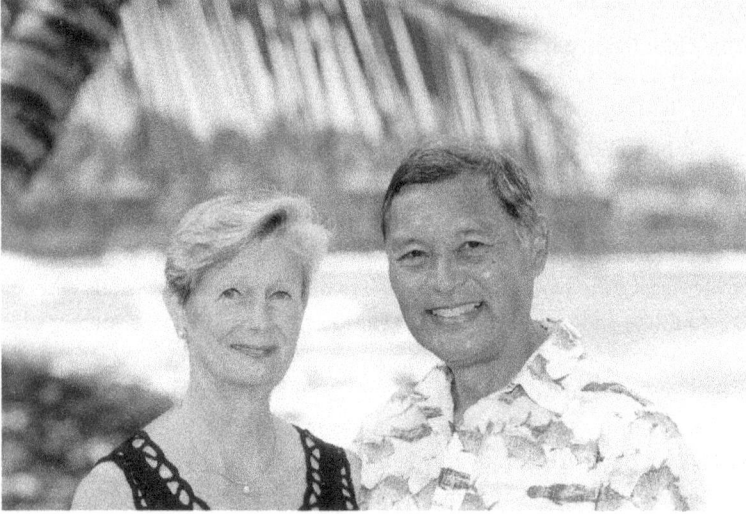

Bonnie and Jerry Miki happily retired in Kona on the Big Island of Hawaii

were left behind in Vietnam after the War ended was such an emotional issue that President Reagan formed a team that fanned out over Southeast Asia to question refugees on whether they had seen or knew of any Americans still held in captivity in Cambodia, Laos or Vietnam. Working out of the U.S. Embassy in Bangkok, our team gathered much intelligence but found no evidence of any American being held against his will in Southeast Asia.

Bonnie and I departed Bangkok in September 1990 to out-process from Bolling Air Force Base in Washington D.C. and retire on the 31st of October 1990, after over 30 years in the military. Together, we had spent seven years in Asia and seven in Europe. Plus, I had logged two combat tours and three years flying in Hawaii for a total of 19 years served outside the continental U.S. Today we live in Kona, not far from Kealia village where I spent childhood summers with my Chinese grandparents.

I was fortunate to have served my country during the last half of the American Century. I recall, in 1985, the wife of the South African attaché to Bern angrily lecturing me that we had no right to push for Nelson Mandela's release from prison after our genocide of American Indians and enslavement of Blacks. And in Singapore, in 1987, the Chilean military attaché told me, "How dare America criticize President Pinochet for imprisoning and torturing Chileans" when we had such a dismal human rights record. I replied to both of them that yes, America had committed missteps, but we tried to do the right thing and could not stand by in silence when we saw wrong being done, even by our own government. Wasn't I, an Asian American in an Air Force uniform representing America, proof that we were trying to be a positive force for what was right? We often take two steps forward and one agonizing step backward in our quest to do right, but America is moving forward, away from beatings in Selma, away from the Massacre at Wounded Knee, and away from the Saturday night lynch-ings of Chinamen in California's gold fields.

I was blessed to be born in America, for where else could I have come so far? That doesn't keep me from protesting against my country's willingness to engage in a continuous state of war without considering the price that must be paid. Over 2,000 years ago, the warrior-philosopher Sun Tzu said a nation must carefully weigh the cost involved before entering a war. If Americans choose to fight, they must be prepared to pay with their blood and treasure and understand that there are limits to what power can achieve.

The boy who once delighted in watching aircraft dogfight in the skies off Waikiki Beach during World War II had taken a lifetime to learn that there is no glory or winner in war.

CHAPTER EIGHTEEN

Randall Eng 伍元天 (1947–   )
U.S. Army National Guard

The Honorable Randall T. Eng is Presiding Justice of the Appellate Division, Second Department, of the New York State Supreme Court. In his judicial career of nearly 30 years, he was appointed Administrative Judge of the Criminal Term of the Supreme Court in Queens County, and appointed to the Appellate Division in 2008 by then-Governor Spitzer. He was also a trial judge, having tried many serious criminal cases. Justice Eng was also a judge of the New York City Criminal Court and was appointed by Mayor Koch in 1983. He was also Inspector General of the New York City Department of Correction from 1981 to 1983, and Assistant District Attorney in Queens County from 1972 until 1980. I first met Justice Eng at an American Legion Kimlau Post meeting and interviewed him in February 2012 at his Chambers in the Supreme Court of Queens County, New York.

You have a very prestigious career. I'm supposing you're one of the first Asian Americans or Chinese Americans in your field?

Yes. I was the first Asian American, first Chinese American, to be an Assistant District Attorney in New York State. I was appointed by the then–District Attorney of Queens County Thomas J. Mackell. I was also the first Asian American to be a judge anywhere in New York State when appointed to the Criminal Court in 1983. In my military career, I was the first Chinese American to serve as the State Judge Advocate of the New York Army National Guard, which meant that I was the Chief Legal Officer of the Army National Guard in New York. I assumed that position in 1993.

Can you talk about what your childhood was like and what it was like growing up Chinese American?

I was born in China, in Guangzhou, then known as Canton, in 1947. I was brought to the United States, to New York City, at the age of six months. So even though I was born in China, my entire life has been shaped here in New York City. We've lived in Queens County since I was brought to the United States in 1948. I grew up, as a matter of fact, within a mile of this Courthouse, right here in the Jamaica Briarwood section of Queens. I went to the New York City public schools.

Judge Eng in uniform as colonel, with his eldest daughter
at 10 months, on Family Day, Camp Smith, New York.

I graduated from Brooklyn Technical High School in 1965 and from there I went to the State University of New York in Buffalo. Then I came back to go to St. John's Law School which then was in Brooklyn. I graduated in 1972. Upon graduation, my first legal job was as an assistant district attorney here in Queens.

So my life was shaped and formed in New York City. Growing up Chinese American in that period was … an experience that I don't think anyone residing here in New York can be particularly familiar with because it was very different. There were very few Chinese families in New York at that time. The number of Chinese families in Queens was so few that I think we knew all of them in the immediate area here, as I was growing up in the 1950s and 1960s.

How many Chinese American families were here?

I would say that in the Jamaica area there were fewer than ten families. There were single men who were in the laundry business that we also knew, but families were very few. I'd say that in the six years I was in elementary school my sister and I were the only Chinese Americans in the school at the time.

So that's what I mean when I say it's a unique experience. Now, Asians are over 10% of the population in New York City. I don't think anyone today would have an experience like that where they would be the only Asian Americans, the only Chinese Americans, in a school for that long a period of a time.

I must say that we had our share of hardships regarding being minority group members, but nothing that we couldn't overcome with perseverance and

Left: Judge Eng's father in England serving with U.S. 8th Air Force, servicing a B-17 Bomber. Right: Judge Eng in Basic Training during the Vietnam Era. Both 22 years old.

Judge Eng and father, present day at ages 90 and 65, at American Legion Post 1291

study. And I must say that many opportunities came our way as well, because after the Civil Rights Movement came to pass in the 1960s, we benefitted from that. Having a good education, having a good foundation, we were able to avail ourselves of the opportunities that came at that time. When I was growing up in the 1950s and 1960s we found that, employment-wise, Chinese American men were limited in mainstream occupations to technical occupations. There were persons who were engineers, draftsmen and physicians, but aside from that there was very little mainstream employment opportunity. So it behooved us to study hard and prepare for these opportunities that came along. Other than that, growing up, the majority of Chinese men were in restaurants and laundries at that time.

Did you ever expect you were going to be a judge when you were a kid? Was it something you were aiming for?

No. But I knew that I wanted to do law from very early on and that is because I was preparing for mainstream employment in a technical area. As I mentioned, I'm a graduate of Brooklyn Technical High School and I thought I would become an engineer. However, I found that though I did well in the courses, I didn't like it. I didn't like engineering. I'm glad I have the foundation because it's been useful in my life. But I didn't want to make a career in it. I thought that lawyers could make more of a difference. Lawyers could affect people's lives more and it was better suited to my personality. That's why I began to study law after graduating college even though there were very few Chinese American lawyers then. I must say that, in my own experience, I think until about 1980, I knew every Chinese American lawyer practicing in New York City.

How many Chinese American lawyers were there in New York City?

There were probably 25 or so and most of them were doing real estate, small business matters, and immigration. They were not in the mainstream, they were not in the law firms, they weren't in the corporations, and they weren't in government service. Because, as I said, upon graduation, I found that I was the first Chinese American, the first Asian American, to be appointed as an assistant district attorney anywhere in New York State. So it was something that few had attempted.

Now, with being on the Appellate Division among our duties, we admit new lawyers who have passed the Bar Exam and we admit them in person in our Court. And in my experience, it looks to be like 10% of the classes now are Asians, male and female. So the demographics of it have changed extraordinarily in my lifetime, in my experience. And now Chinese Americans are everywhere in law. They're everywhere in the government, they're everywhere in law firms as partners and associates, in corporations, and they're representing every phase of the law. It's just something that is revolutionary. It's a tremendous change from when I started.

You mentioned that your joining the military was an easy choice because of your dad. Do you want to talk about it?

Well, let's say that he had a very positive experience in World War II and that he was able to give good and meaningful service. He came to this country as a teenager, when he was 15 in 1937. He came to join his father in New Jersey at the time and he attended several years of school here. Coming to the United States as a teenager, as a 15-year-old, is very difficult because, of course, you have a language barrier. You're close to being of working age so it's very difficult to acquire an education when you come at that age. But my father managed to get some school and he was drafted along with everyone else in World War II. So in 1943 he was drafted and served the United States Army Air Force. He served in the 8th Air Force overseas in England.

He was assigned to B-17s. He was a mechanic and a gunner. He had several combat missions in B-17s over Northern Europe, bombing missions over Germany, France, the Netherlands, and he was trained as a mechanic as well.

So that was one of the great experiences of his life. He was trained in many bases in the United States, traveled all over the country, and he did a year of service in England.

For lay people, can you explain what the gunner does?

A gunner has a defensive position in a large bomber. The B-17s that he was assigned to had a 10-person crew; a pilot, a co-pilot, a bombardier, a navigator, an engineer and gunners. The gunners would assume a defensive position. They would man machine guns because, of course, German fighters would try to shoot them down over occupied Europe. So his position was a tail gunner, he told me, a turret gunner. Those things would revolve between machine guns, so he did that.

Because of that, he had a very useful and meaningful service and he had always been very positive about it. So because he was positive about it, I suppose he imparted that to me. And I served in the Vietnam Era. I didn't serve in Vietnam, but I served in the Vietnam Era so military service came to me very naturally.

Your dad must have been one of the very few Chinese Americans in his unit, right?

Just a handful. Of course, the Army, at that time, was segregated. The Armed Forces in the United States were segregated. African Americans served in their own units. They were not permitted to serve in combat. Chinese Americans, there were too few to segregate in the units, so they were distributed everywhere, in that sense.

However, there was a unit that was largely Chinese American and that was, I believe, the 14th Air Force that served in the China-Burma-India theater and there were many Chinese Americans who served there, but my father had no connection to that. He was with the 8th Air Force in England.

Who was the first in your family to arrive in the U.S?

That would be my father's father. He came in the teens. I am not exactly sure what year—1917, 1919, something in that range. My mother's father was actually here even before him. My mother was born in the U.S. and is nearly 90 years old now. She was born in Cleveland, Ohio, in the 1920s.

Well, my parents met in China. My father, after World War II, went back to China to bring home a wife. So in the village they were actually introduced by matchmakers, as I understand it. And of course they had an affinity because my father had come to the United States as a teenager. My mother returned to China with her family at age 11. Yes. Her family returned to China from Cleveland during the Depression when things were very, very difficult. They had a large family and things were easier in China, so they went back there and she lived in China from the 1930s until the end of World War II.

But getting back to the affinity that I mentioned: well, of course, they're a natural, right? You have two persons here that have lived in the United States and they both speak English, so it was natural they got together.

They met and married in China. And they lived there for a year. After they were married, I was born then. They had intended all the time to come back to the United States but there were some family issues to work out. Travel was difficult because of all the persons desiring to leave China during the Civil War in China. So that's why I was born in December but I was here by July of the following year.

Your mom's family was in Cleveland. How did they choose Cleveland?

Well, it's the typical immigrant experience. You just go where your other relatives have gone before. So my grandfather (my mother's father) joined his relatives who had a restaurant in Cleveland. After he came, he brought my grandmother over and they had a family in Cleveland.

Did you speak Chinese growing up?

Well, my parents are bilingual and they spoke Chinese with each other and they taught it to us. So we all have an understanding of household Chinese, learned in the home. Actually, I am not fluent in speech. I speak words and phrases. I have very good comprehension, though, and the same with my sisters. Because my parents are bilingual, we just ended up speaking English when we were at home. Of course, growing up here in Queens in a totally English-speaking environment, we spoke English. We never lived in Chinatown so we didn't have that experience and our grandparents didn't live with us either. Usually, that's how everyone becomes multilingual and that is because of family needs, environment. Our grandparents weren't with us and we didn't live among Chinese neighbors. My wife, who was born in Brooklyn and who is Chinese, had non-English-speaking parents, so my wife is fluent even though she was born and raised in Brooklyn. But because of family needs, she is bilingual.

What kind of work did your parents do when you were growing up?

Well, my father had cleaning businesses; dry cleaning and laundry. And that's what he did throughout his whole career. He worked until the age of 78 in his own cleaning business.

And your mom helped your dad?

She did. And, well, in those days people were able to be stay-home spouses more easily, so she spent maybe half of the time helping him and half of the time at home. So we had a very stable home environment.

I know this is a silly question but, as a Chinese American, do you feel more Chinese or more American?

No, that's not a silly question at all. I'm a blend, of course. But I have to say that my own inclination is, probably, more mainstream American, from my own perspective. I think that's the way I approach issues because I was raised here.

Before the Civil Rights Movement happened, was it almost unfathomable for minorities to—

Well, you talk about unfathomable. The Chinese experience in New York is always been such that, in my own experience from childhood, we were never the lowest of the underclasses, so to speak. You know, we were always somewhere in the middle. There were always groups who had it harder, of course, than Chinese Americans. Because of family stability and because of a stable economic base, we didn't have the hardships other groups had, in that the restaurants and the laundries, although not glamorous, although not overly lucrative, were a firm economic base. Having that firm economic base is a great advantage in preserving family stability, I think.

Because of that, we had a stable upbringing and our relatives and our friends had very similar experiences because everyone else had humble origins. And yet we were able to become doctors, lawyers, engineers, and teachers. Everyone in my generation that I knew achieved in that regard, and entered the professions, or started businesses that were successful ... because of that stability that we had in our lives.

And of course, regarding opportunities as I was growing up, as I said, there were mainstream opportunities. Men could become engineers and other technicians. And women, at the time, seemed to have access to mainstream occupations in clerical, retail, things like that. Of course, all that has changed, all that has improved, but they did have opportunities. There were peers of my parents who had those. I saw it. They were bank tellers. They were secretaries in law firms. They had that access. Women seemed to have easier access to the mainstream than the men. So it was there. But, again, all of that evolved and improved in the decades that followed.

So in college you studied—

I was a Political Science major. I knew after high school I didn't want to pursue a technical education. Then I realized that even though I did well, I didn't like it. So from that point on I went into a legally-oriented pre-law curriculum.

And at that time you were one of the first Chinese Americans to go into law?

Yes. In my law school class at St. John's we had sections. In my section there were 150. There was only another Chinese American male and myself.

One other and yourself.

Yes. Only one other one among 150. But the demographics then were all different. There were 150 but there were only six women all together in a class that size. Today, Law School enrollment is 50% women.

So pretty much what was in the school reflected the population, and also who wanted to—

Well, yes, because when I started law was a man's field. The opportunities for women lawyers were not nearly what they are today. Today the opportunities are limitless. There are women in the highest positions everywhere now in law and half the judges in this building are women. That wasn't my experience when I started here.

I'm assuming there were never instances of discrimination or anything when you reached this level.

Well, it never got to the point where it was really a career stopper. I knew that there were positions I didn't get because of my origins, but I think I also *got* positions because of my origins. It cut both ways and I can't really say that I've suffered from invidious discrimination. No, in my experience, that didn't happen. And in growing up I don't think that I had the persecution that some of my other contemporaries had. I know that some people from other neighborhoods were always being beaten up and always being abused. I had my share of name-calling and social snubs and everything else but nothing really much beyond that. But that was an experience, and a formative experience.

Can you talk a little bit about when you decided to do the military?

Well, it was a practical decision, and that is that I had finished law school in 1972. I started in 1969 but the Vietnam War was at its height and they were drafting everyone. And I had an educational deferment from the draft until I graduated from college. So from that point on I had to make a decision: Do I want to be drafted and not be able to make choices regarding what I wanted to do in the service? Or do I want to get involved in the service proactively? So what I did was I enlisted in 1970, while in law school, in the Army National Guard. The Army has two reserve components and those are the Army Reserve itself and the Army National Guard. I enlisted in the Army National Guard. The Army National Guard has two service elements and it is the reserve of the Army. It is a part of the Army, or it can be utilized as part of the State National Guard. There are many of our units that have served in Iraq and Afghanistan. So I have a lot of experience in dealing with State emergencies. I've been involved in prison disturbances, floods, hurricanes, snowstorms, and events of that nature, wildfires. So, when I enlisted in the Army National Guard, I then received an exemption from the draft because I was already in the Army.

When these things happened, what were your duties?

Well, depending on what my grade was at a given time, I was usually involved in giving legal services in support of those missions, and that is working with local authorities, harmonizing the kinds of services that our troops could deliver, the limitations of their activities, dealing with claims in these operations—and these operations always have some kind of property damage or personal injury involved—and also in justice issues. There are always disciplinary issues. So what happened was that I had enlisted as a soldier in the Army National Guard, but upon graduating law school I was offered a commission in the Judge Advocate General's Court, so I became a military legal officer from that point on.

As a military legal officer you are involved in advising the Command regarding legal issues that arise. I mentioned some already regarding interfacing with all the authorities in these operational settings. There's also a military justice component because the military justice system is separate and apart from the civilian justice system and our soldiers are subject to court-martial. A court-martial is a military criminal justice proceeding so, as such, military legal officers have to be involved in the prosecution and in the defense of soldiers that were charged with offenses. So that's a big component. Then I was also involved with military contracts, with legal assistance matters. Prior to deploying, our soldiers who are going to Iraq and Afghanistan have to get their personal affairs in order. We prepared wills, powers of attorney, and advised them on family law issues: the whole range of things that are associated with being deployed. So we support our soldiers in that regard. When I was the State Judge Advocate of the New York Army National Guard with the rank of colonel, I had 27 legal officers that reported to me throughout New York State.

How many years did you do that?

I was in the New York Army National Guard for nearly 35 years. I was enlisted for the first 5 years and for the last 30 I served as a commissioned officer in the Judge Advocate General's Corps.

And when you had these responsibilities, you still had your civilian position at the same time?

Yes, because I was a reservist at the time which meant that I had an obligation to perform 48 drills—48 meetings a year plus 15 days of annual training in the summer.

I did many, many tours at Fort Drum, our large training facility in the Watertown area, and the entire units of the New York Army National Guard, we trained together at the time. And we supplied thousands of troops to the Army in the first Gulf War and, of course, in Iraqi Freedom, and now Afghanistan. So thousands of our troops in New York had served. I have not been deployed, though. In my 35 years, I did not deploy overseas to any of those but I certainly supported the deployment of thousands of our troops then.

When you had people under you and you were one of the first Asian Americans or Chinese Americans in such positions, was it something that everyone took in stride?

In all candor, I don't think I have any real horror stories to tell there because it has always been a diverse group of lawyers that I work with. We've had African American lawyers; in my time we've had three Asian lawyers that I can recall now, two Chinese and one of Korean origin. And there's always been a lot of diversity in the service. There always has been, so you're accustomed to it.

Do you have a most memorable moment from your military experience?

Yes. The most memorable in my particular service was following 9/11. When 9/11 occurred, I was a colonel and I was the State Judge Advocate of New York Army National Guard and that's the position that I achieved progressively. I started up as a lieutenant, as a trial counsel's lieutenant, and then I got promoted to become a captain, a major, a lieutenant colonel, a colonel and … with each of those promotions, I had a greater responsibility in those positions. So I had different roles in each of those ranks that I held.

But in 9/11 I can recall that we mobilized immediately 3,000 of our Army

Justice Eng when he was an Assistant District Attorney, summing up to the jury in the case of People v. Morales in 1978. Sketch by Libby Dengrove.

National Guard soldiers. We had about 11,000 at that time so we mobilized 3,000 immediately to guard the World Trade Center, and I was assigned and I was there from the beginning. I was there from the beginning of those operations that started out as the Search and Rescue and then Search and Recovery and everything else that went on there. I was on active duty for just about a month in the first phase until I stood down, but then I was reactivated after that for more tours. And that was probably my most memorable assignment following 9/11.

In those assignments, what were some of your duties?

Well, in the support of other first responders, we provided perimeter security. We provided transportation assets. I was involved in advising the commanders there, essentially, regarding the rules and regulations that were applicable to this. There were a lot of issues of first impression, as a matter of fact, because this was an unprecedented disaster. And of course, as with any other operation, we have our disciplinary issues. So I was involved in that … the whole range of services that we provided as legal officers. It certainly gave me an opportunity to serve usefully in the aftermath of that. I was very grateful that I was in a position to be able to offer that kind of service in support of our country, state, and city following that.

Do you have a most memorable moment from the Vietnam era?

Well, the most memorable is probably on the active duty. I was on active duty for training and seeing the return of remains at that time. We had lost some 56,000 Americans who were killed in the Vietnam War, so you can imagine the impact on the country at that time, the negativity toward service at that time.

There were no parades that followed the return of veterans in Vietnam. There was tremendous conflict, there was tremendous animosity toward the war and toward the people who had served, and it took many, many years for that to be undone.

Serving at that time was a mixed experience, because I was motivated to serve, but it was not appreciated at the time. I am very happy to see now that the veterans of Iraq and Afghanistan are receiving better treatment and better appreciation, although I do observe that there has been nothing regarding parades and other large recognitions for the thousands who have served. We've given large parades to baseball teams and football teams and whatever else but the veterans of those conflicts have not had their day yet, have not had their recognition.

Legally speaking, is there a most memorable case that you're able to tell us about from the Vietnam era?

Well, at that time, I was an assistant district attorney and I tried some significant cases. As an assistant district attorney, I tried a terrorist—a FALN* terrorist who was involved in a Puerto Rican liberation movement. He was building bombs in an apartment in Queens. After one of them accidentally detonated, he was arrested with his bomb-making equipment, and he was severely injured himself and he survived.

That was my first experience in the 1970s in dealing with terrorism. And I was surprised at the willingness of persons to serve as jurors and the dedication that the jurors had in this—what I would call a political trial—because it was used as a platform for the defendant regarding his views. But I think we got a fair and just resolution in the trial.

Is there anything that you would like to add that we haven't covered?

I would just like to say that law is still, after 40 years, a very exciting and dynamic field. I would encourage anyone who is interested in doing good, in making a difference, in being involved at all different levels, to consider a career in the law. There are many people who have studied law who don't necessarily practice in the courtroom or even practice in offices but who have found a legal education to be very useful in other pursuits, in business, in other professions. So if anybody is so interested in a legal career, I heartily recommend it to them, because for over 40 years it's been very good to me personally and very satisfying and rewarding.

---

* Fuerzas Armadas de Liberación Nacional (Armed Forces of National Liberation) was a terrorist group which fought to transform Puerto Rico into a communist state.

CHAPTER NINETEEN

Fang A. Wong 黃宏達 (1948–　　)
U.S. Army

Fang A. Wong was the first Asian American National Commander of the American Legion, the largest veteran's organization in the United States. He served with a military intelligence unit for the U.S. Army during the Vietnam War and retired from the U.S. Army in 1989 with the rank of chief warrant officer. He talks about meeting his father for the first time when he immigrated to New York at the age of 12, living in Harlem, and his experiences being the first Asian American national commander.

Can you talk a little bit about how people have received you as the first Asian American National Commander of The American Legion?

I don't know if you heard about the story of when I started traveling and campaigning in a state in the Midwest. I talked to the legionnaires, the guys there, and after a while, they wanted me to talk to the auxiliary members, the wives. So I was joking about how they can't vote for me, as auxiliaries and all that, but in the end, I said, "I need your help." I asked them, "When you go home, convince your husbands to support me." And they all said they'd do that.

Then the next day, one of the husbands walked up to me early in the morning and started telling me he heard my speech and he liked it. And his wife heard my speech, and she thought it was okay. But every time they talked about me, the wife would say, "But he's a Chinese, but he's a Chinese." And so that made me feel kind of uncomfortable. That was at my first outing.

I went back and I thought about it. From there on, wherever I went, I told the story but I also made it a point. I say, "I'm from the Northeast—New York. And in New York, you have to be politically correct." I said, "The correct statement should be that he's a Chinese American." I said, "You know, being a Chinese doesn't give me any rights here. But being a Chinese American gives me the right to serve the country, protect the flag, and do all these other things." And people basically loved it. They accepted it because I was saying I choose to be an American.

A few months later, I went to a state in the Deep South. Not too many years ago, they burned down buildings and fought with the National Guard to keep Blacks from going to the same schools and the like. I didn't think about it, and I relayed the same story, and at the end of it, just when I was walking down the

Fang A. Wong, National Commander, The American Legion (2011–2012)

stage, two guys approached me and basically cornered me.

One guy said, "You're not a Chinese American." And I thought, "Oh man, this is bad." So finally I summed up my courage. They're too big for me, but I said to them, "Well, if I'm not a Chinese American, who am I? What am I?" He said, "Two words describe you." I said, "Okay let me hear it, what is it?" He said, "The first word—you're just an American." And that just hit me right there. I felt, wow, I'm not a Chinese American; I'm just an American. So then I wanted to know right away the second word. "What's the second word?" He said, "You are a veteran. So we can call you either a veteran or an American." I was crying. I was crying because I realized it right then and there; I knew I was truly accepted. They look at me with no distinction and that happened in a state in the Deep South, and it's unbelievable. I said to myself, "You know what? That is a true indication of whether you've been accepted by the mainstream." People look at you and see just you. You are just Fang. The other part is insignificant. And that's how they made me feel.

You are the first non-white national commander? What is that like?

Yeah. As the first non-white I did notice something. Almost everywhere I go, when I run into any minority members, it doesn't matter where—it could be in the Northeast, the West, South, anywhere for that matter—they seem to be very upbeat and happy that I'm the national commander. Some of them seem to be happier than I am, and they'd squeeze my hand and say, "About time that we made it." I mean I get the message, I understand where they're coming from.

Same thing in the Chinese community—people seem to get excited. I went to Boston's Chinatown; they threw me a big party. Went to Los Angeles' Chinatown, San Francisco's Chinatown. It seems viral. People are happy. They want to be taking a bow now.

I used to think that being the national commander is no big deal but after I visited all the states, after I went overseas and I'm being received by different people at different levels, different places, I realize that whether or not I like it, it is a big deal to a lot of people. It's the office and it's the position that you represent. I used to take it very lightly and joke about it. I still do that, but in the meantime I also know who I represent, what I represent. And you feel that your shoulders are a little bit heavier and you've got to be careful you don't embarrass yourself—that you don't embarrass your organization and, of course, [being] from Chinatown, you don't want to embarrass your own group.

After you see how people react to you, people that you don't even know, you wonder, "What business do they have to give somebody they just met for the first time such respect, such courtesy?" Well, not you—they're treating the office of the national commander with that respect and courtesy. You just happen to be the body that wears the uniform and fit into that position. I mean after all these years there have only been 93 of us that could say, "I'm the national commander." So it's an honor. But, me being me, I like to have fun too. So I don't let it go to my head. You just do what you have to do. You try to do the right thing and in the meantime you enjoy.

Can you talk a little about your childhood?

I was born in 1948 in Guangdong, China, after the Communists had taken over. The Communists at that time didn't have as tight a control in Southern China as far as people moving around. So we were able to escape. We moved to Hong Kong when I was three. I came to the U.S. with my mother and my older brother in 1960 when I was 12 years old. That was the first time I got to meet my father. He had come to the United States in the 1930s. He worked at a farm in Long Island. Then he went back to China after World War II to visit my mom, my grandma, and my older brother, because they were left behind. So he stayed in China for, I guess, over a year and then he returned back to the United States, right before the Communists took over China.

Finally we made it here in 1960. I think it was November 13th—two weeks before Thanksgiving. I was a 12-year-old boy. I didn't know anything. I didn't speak English. I mean, I knew my A-B-C-Ds, just the alphabet, and that was it. My father operated a laundry at the time, right in the middle of Harlem, 148th Street and Eighth Avenue. The first couple of years, we lived in the back of the laundry, because that's the way the laundry operates, you know? The family lives in the back of the laundry.

I started sixth grade in January 1961, and six months later I graduated *(laughs)* and I still didn't know much English. But it was fun. In the whole school, I was the only non-black, from the students and teachers to the janitors. It was right in the middle of Harlem. I was kind of a novelty for everybody, because they never had a chance before then to really see a Chinese boy up close. I felt a little strange, but then you know, you don't have a choice.

Were you scared when you moved from Hong Kong and saw people who looked completely different?

No, I was kind of excited, because you hear so much about The Golden Mountain. You hear all these nice things, and you get hyped up, because you finally get to meet somebody that you call Father. *(Laughs)* As a young kid, you learn things and you absorb things. You don't have time to be scared or worried about anything.

You know, people would say "You were in Harlem? Weren't you scared?" What's there to be scared of? Everybody is just like everybody else. In the eyes of a kid, there's no difference.

But you were the only one who was Chinese. You didn't feel like—

At the sixth grade, yes, I was the only one, but everyone treated me like I was someone special. You can feel it even if you don't know what they're saying. The teachers and everybody, "Oh, the Chinese boy." But the one thing is you can't get in trouble because if you get in trouble you'll never get away with it. *(Laughs)* Because they all know you. You're the only one.

After I graduated I moved on to the junior high school, around 130-something Street. I was one of two non-Blacks. There was another Chinese boy there. He was a year ahead of me. And the good thing was he practiced kung fu. In the year that he first attended, they picked on him, and he just wiped them out. When I arrived we hit it off and Eugene basically protected me. "That's my cousin. You don't mess with Fang." So I kind of rode on his coattail.

That was good for a couple of years, and then I moved down to Chinatown. My father finally got an apartment and said, "Why don't you just move down there," because my grandmother arrived from Hong Kong at that time, and obviously not everybody could live in the laundry. So we got an apartment, and I lived down there with my grandmother for a few years.

After I finished high school, I went to Pratt Institute night school and worked. I got my draft notice in '69. At that time, I was working in a restaurant on Pell Street. Someone at the restaurant who retired from the Army said, "You ought to consider volunteering instead of just going as a draftee." He said when you volunteer, you have some control of the field you'll be assigned to. So I volunteered to be in the Army.

Are there highlights from your military experience?

I was stationed in Germany doing personnel work. Then I transferred to Vietnam. President Nixon announced that we were going into Cambodia. This was early 1970. Up until that point the United States Military was not allowed to chase the Viet Cong or the North Vietnamese into Cambodia, although secretly we had people in there, but openly, no. So in the spring of 1970, it was necessary for us to attack the North Vietnamese force across the border. One morning we got an alert: "Stop everything you're doing. Let's screen through all personnel records." They were looking for Chinese linguists because the Chinese Communists were providing advisors to the North Vietnamese and they needed people to interrogate when they captured people. Well, out of the whole group at that time, they found two guys. I was one of the people who spoke Chinese. I didn't get to go to Cambodia. They sent the other guy because he had M.I. [Military Intelligence] training.

A few months later, an officer called me up and wanted to meet me. I went over to one of the clubs to see him, and all of a sudden he starts speaking Chinese to me. He was white, a lieutenant, mid-20s, a real nice guy. He studied Asian Studies, and they sent him to Monterey, to a defense language school, and he studied Mandarin over there. Then he went to Hong Kong and started picking up Cantonese. He spoke very decent Mandarin and Cantonese. Basically, he interviewed me. He wanted to know if I was willing to help them. He was the A.I. [Area Intelligence] officer. Their job is to go out and collect information from the enemy or run agents. So I agreed to help him. They yanked me out of the personnel shop and they put me on civilian status. We went undercover and we worked downtown. There were a lot of Chinese people who worked for the U.S. Government at that time. I went with them and I did the interpretations. There were a lot of sailors, Chinese, in ships coming into Saigon. They worked for the U.S. Government and they brought information. We can talk about this now because this was, like, 40 years ago. They worked for the U.S. Government and they wrote reports of what they observed in various ports in Southeast Asia, on Chinese Communist activities or the local whatever. We would translate these.

Sometimes they came in, and a warrant officer would strap them down and give them a polygraph test to make sure they were not lying and still working for us. *(Laughs)* You know, not a double-agent somewhere. When things like that happen, I have to go and repeat in Chinese what the technician asks, because it's easier if you use their native tongue to get their true reaction.

Later in my military career, I became a warrant officer and did personnel work in Germany and Korea.

When did you first learn about the American Legion?

I first learned about the American Legion when I was about 15 years old. I was taking Chinese classes at the Chinese public school on Mott Street. I traveled from uptown and would spend two hours here [in Chinatown]. At our graduation, the Vice Commander of the American Legion Kimlau Post—I think it was Dick Chiu—he came on Graduation Day and handed envelopes and boxes to us. The envelopes had scholarship money—$15, good enough for tuition for the next semester, which was great. Then there was a scholarship medal inside the box. And that made a big impression for a young kid at that age—that somebody would actually come in and show their appreciation and reward you and honor you with a check and a medal.

I had no idea what the American Legion was about, other than the fact that they gave each of us this gift. But I said I like their style. I said, "If I have the opportunity one of these days, I would like to be a member of that organization." So after 20 years of service, when I finally retired, that's one of the things I remembered I needed to do: come here and join. So that itself was what motivated me to be a member of the American Legion.

As the National Commander of The American Legion, I testified on September 21, 2011, before the Joint Senate and the House Veterans' Affair Committee. I finally got to meet the President at the end of our Washington Conference, the 1st or the 2nd of March. I went into his office and we had a little visit.

CHAPTER TWENTY

Frederick Pang (1936–   )
U.S. Air Force

The Honorable Frederick Pang talks about growing up in Honolulu in the wake of the bombing of Pearl Harbor. He served in the Air Force from 1959 until 1986, ultimately attaining the rank of colonel, and was the first Asian American to be named Assistant Secretary of the Navy, appointed by President Clinton, and later appointed Assistant Secretary of Defense for Force Management Policy. In 1997 he left government service and started a consulting firm, ViStar, which provided services to the Department of Defense and other governmental agencies. He lives with his wife in Virginia.

Who were the first in your family to come to the U.S.?

My grandparents are of Hakka heritage and came from China as indentured servants, contract laborers, around the late 1800s or the early 1900s. They lived and worked on the Big Island of Hawaii, where there were huge sugar cane plantations. They did not go back to China when their labor contracts ended, but stayed in Hawaii. My parents were U.S. citizens from birth and were educated as Americans. They had known each other on the Big Island, but they went to Honolulu separately after they graduated from high school and fell in love and got married. It was not an arranged marriage. *(Laughs.)*

What was it like for you growing up?

It was pretty idyllic. I was fortunate. I'm the first male child. That was significant, I found out later, and I'm sure my parents were very happy. I have a brother and two sisters. I had a third brother, but he died when he was 12 years old. My father, at the time I was born, was a machinist for the Navy. He started out as an apprentice, went on to become a master machinist, and that is what he did as a career for over 30 years. He was working at Pearl Harbor when Pearl Harbor was bombed. He was not physically there when the bombs were dropping, but as soon as the bombs dropped, they called him to work.

As I recall, we didn't see him for several days. He went back there and his job was not to fix ships. There were a lot of dead people after the attack, so his job was to help police up the dead and get the machine shops in order. I remember when he came home. He washed up outside and threw his clothes into a fire pit we had in the backyard, where he burned them.

Since my father worked at Pearl Harbor, he had sailor friends he would bring home from time to time. I used to play with them so I was comfortable around military people early in my life. Right after the bombing of Pearl Harbor, the National Guard came and some of the soldiers were in our yard. They were there for a couple of days because there was a fear that Hawaii would be invaded by the Japanese. So I got to play with the soldiers too and found that I liked them too.

And so that definitely helped influence you.

Yeah, I was also lucky because my parents really wanted me to get a good education. They insisted that I speak English, and speak proper English. In Hawaii, at the time, the immigrant people spoke Pidgin English. The social distinction was how you spoke English. So they insisted at home that I speak proper English. When I was getting ready to go to the elementary school, at the time in Hawaii, there was what they called English Standard Schools.

These were schools that took children that spoke proper English. The other schools took all the other children and basically when I look back on it, it was just like English as a second language sort of school for those kids. I think the assumption was that those who spoke Standard English were destined to white-collar jobs and those who didn't, to blue-collar jobs. I went to Royal School. Royal School was the school, you could tell by the name, where the Hawaiian Royalty was educated. I was born after the monarchy was already gone. The United States had already taken possession of Hawaii. Nonetheless, the school still remained and retained its status. I started school back in—let's see, I was born in 1936—I must have been six years old, so about 1941. It was fortuitous, when I look back on it, being able to get a good education and potentially a good career in life.

Can you talk a little bit about what the population was like in your time? Were Chinese Americans a minority in Hawaii?

Yes, we were a minority, and also a minority among minorities. When the first wave of Chinese immigrants came to Hawaii, they were brought there for labor. Sugar was a valued commodity and demand for it was growing. The United States had moved westward aggressively and California was booming. So a small group of businessmen in Hawaii, all white people who were from the Missionary class—whalers, shippers and other entrepreneurs—they started the sugar business. They said, "Hey, there is a demand to be filled and we can make lots of money filling it."

The sugar business requires a lot of labor. So the question is, Where are you going to get the labor? At first, the planters tried to enlist the local population, Hawaiians, the indigenous people of the Islands, to work on the cane fields. They had two problems. The first was that the population was limited and the second—that kind of back-breaking field work day in and day out was simply foreign to the Hawaiian way of life which was subsistence-based. They had a sea that was rich with fish and other edible sea life, taro, various fruits, and so forth that were readily available to gather or farm for food. So you didn't have to actually get into a commercial type of work to survive. So the planters had to look for another source of cheap, dependable labor.

There was already trade going on between Hawaii and China at the time, mainly in sandalwood that was harvested in the Islands. So the planters were familiar with the conditions in China and saw a huge labor pool of field workers scrabbling for survival, as there was a famine going on there. From that pool there began a wave of immigration of Chinese to both Hawaii, for the planters, and to the mainland to work on the transcontinental railroad that was being constructed. The initial Chinese immigrants to Hawaii were the ones who worked the cane fields, and later the pineapple fields, to grow these into large, profitable enterprises.

Socially, were Chinese people accepted? Did they ever really assimilate?

Well, the Chinese laborers, when they first got there, were set aside in camps. Most of the plantation workers lived in barracks-type quarters that were provided for them by the planters. The living conditions were pretty bare. The laborers were all men. They didn't bring in any women. The idea was that the indentured servants would come and work for whatever period of time their contract called for, and at the end of that period they would return back to China.

Well, a lot of Chinese came and a lot of them went back. But some also stayed. Of those who stayed, some got married, and they married mainly Hawaiian women. There was discrimination at the time. White people were the aristocracy and they were the bosses. They were the owners. We at the other end were the servants, the people that worked the fields and other menial jobs. So there was a huge gulf between the Whites and the laborers, the Chinese.

How about in the case of your grandparents? Did they marry—did they bring wives?

They brought wives later.

And they were allowed to?

The main reason they were allowed to stay and bring wives was now there was a need. For what? Well, somebody's got to farm to provide food to sell, do the laundry, all the service-type work. There was a need for that. So they filled this need. Somebody needed to provide these services to a growing population. You're not going to bring in indentured servants to do it. You want them in the plantations to prosper your business. So those who stayed filled that void, and a necessity at the time. So you now have restaurants, laundries, barbers, tailors, vegetable farmers, and so on.

So they make a good living from that?

Yes, and they gradually began to evolve from immigrant laborers into a bud-

ding middle class. A few became quite wealthy and even married into the aristocracy. Even way back then, Hawaii began to become a "melting pot" despite
the racism that existed. I'm talking about the wave of Chinese labors who were
brought over to put in the transcontinental railroad. It's incredible if you look at
the story of what they did under conditions in which they worked.

The same thing that happened here in Hawaii was also happening in the
mainland. Now you have a booming San Francisco connected to cities like New
York on the other coast. Service businesses are in demand and those Chinese
who stayed began to fill that void, and you begin to have communities that
became Chinatowns. As these thrived and grew, there was consternation in the
white population. They said, "Look, we've got all these people settling here.
What are we going to do to control this?" This fear of "the yellow peril" grew so
strong that it eventually led Congress to enact the Chinese Exclusion Act, one
of the most significant restrictions on immigration in U.S. history.

Because of the growing population of Chinese and the Chinese Exclusion
law, what the planters did was they quit bringing in Chinese. They still needed
to find labor so they settled on the Japanese, and brought them in huge waves
to the point where they eventually became the majority population in Hawaii.
The theory was that Japanese are more loyal to their homeland and would leave
to return to their homeland when their indenture was over. That was the reason
why Chinese only reached about 7% of the population when I was in grade
school, so I would guess that less than 10% of my classmates were Chinese.

That's fascinating. What was attending Royal School like?

Well, I went to grade school and I had very good teachers. I mean if you
taught at Royal School you had to be a good teacher. In those days *(laughs)* there
was corporal punishment and if you were bad, you could get hit on the knuckles.
It was a very strict, but nurturing education. We were taught respect for elders,
respect for the flag, and our country. We would, every morning, line up when
the bell rang, and we went in order, into our classroom. You stood at attention,
pledged allegiance to the flag. Then you would hear the morning announce-
ments, and then class would start. It was a pretty strict school system.

Then I went to Kawananakoa Intermediate School, and right at that time
my father had acquired enough money to build a house. We were renting up
until then. We moved only about three or four blocks away, but when we did,
we were in a neighborhood that was completely different than the one that we
had lived in.

The large majority of people who lived in this particular neighborhood were
of Portuguese, Puerto Rican, Japanese, Filipino, and Hawaiian ancestry. There
weren't very many of Chinese ancestry there. Our next door neighbor on the
left was of Portuguese ancestry, the one on the right was Filipino, the people in
front of us were mixed Hawaiian and Chinese race, and the people in the back
of us were Portuguese.

How did the Portuguese enter Hawaii?

The Portuguese came because, in the early days on the plantations, they would never let an Asian be a foreman. Because *(laughs)* there's this idea that you don't want to let them do that—it's not their station in life. So it had to be a white person. So they brought in the Portuguese because the Portuguese would take the lower pay. They were white and they were the foremen. They ran the plantations. They called them "Lunas."

They brought in Puerto Ricans too. And it was because of race. They said, "We are not going to let any of the Asian labor run things." There was a fear, I think, to some extent that "If you put these people in management they'll forget their place." What was interesting is that, from a racial standpoint, the Portuguese and the Puerto Ricans were discriminated against by the upper-class Whites. Most of the businessmen, the people who had control of the Island, were white people from the Northeastern part of the United States, who initially came as missionaries. They came to bring Christianity to the heathens. And they stayed to become the aristocracy of Hawaii—the powerful businessmen who made Hawaii into what it is today.

After you finished high school, you went into—

Well, let me tell you how I got affiliated with the military. My father worked at Pearl Harbor and because he worked at Pearl Harbor I was able to meet servicemen. There was kind of a general distance from anybody that was a serviceman, because the working class people tended to be insular within their communities and didn't interact much with the military. You had Hickam Air Force Base, Pearl Harbor and other large military bases in the Islands. The military has always had a very influential place in Hawaii. The admirals and the generals were actually part of the Hawaii aristocracy. Obviously most of the soldiers, sailors, and Marines that were there were white. So there was not a lot of intermingling or relationships with people in the military, except for those who worked there like my father.

When I went to high school, there was mandatory ROTC, because McKinley High School, where I went, was a land grant school. And for the first two years in high school, if you were physically able, you needed to—you had no option, you had to take Junior ROTC. And the Junior ROTC was Army. So when I was in tenth grade I was issued an Army uniform. And part of my schooling was to learn about the Army, in the Junior ROTC. So I had an M1 rifle—

When you were 15? (laughs)

Yeah, that's right. So I learned how to fieldstrip an M1 rifle. This was right at the time the Korean War was going on. So my ROTC instructors were people like Sergeant Cabral, Sergeant Mailolo, Sergeant Chun, and Captain Herrin who was in charge of the high school ROTC. All of the sergeants were from Hawaii, and the captain was from the mainland. All were Korean War veterans.

It was a good experience for me and I think all who were in it. There was a discipline that we learned individually and as a team. We also knew if there was any kind of trouble, all the principal had to do was go to the ROTC instructors. If there were fights, they were the ones that broke it up. And people paid attention to them. Why? Because Sergeant Cabral was a Korean War veteran whose arm was a bit crooked because of a wound he had sustained in battle for which he was awarded the Purple Heart. Sergeant Mailolo was awarded a Bronze Star for Valor. Captain Herrin walked with a slight limp due to a wound he had sustained from battle and was awarded the Purple Heart. So we knew that these were tough guys. *(Laughs)* So you didn't fool around with them. If they told you to do something, you did it. But they were also very good, caring people.

Was there a fear that you might have to participate in the war, in the beginning?

I never thought much about it, because it was too distant for me.

You weren't afraid that the War would keep going and eventually you would have to—

I think it would probably be fair to say that I did think about it, but I never worried about it. It was something I couldn't control *(laughs)*, okay? So I didn't worry too much about it.

Can you also explain—You said your school was a land grant school. What does that mean?

The land that the school was on was granted by the federal government. So if you were at a public land grant school, at the time, you had to have Junior ROTC. The only way you could not take it is if you were physically not capable. You had to have a doctor's statement to that effect. Otherwise, it's like the draft. I mean you were drafted *(laughs)* into Junior ROTC and you had to do two years. So I did the first two years. In my senior year, one of the ROTC instructors suggested that I take a third year, because after a third year you're an officer. You get to carry a saber—

Sabers?

Yeah. You're dressed in the same uniform, but now you had what they call a Sam Browne, which is a leather strap which came over your shoulder and around your waist to carry a saber, a ceremonial saber. You were a cadet, lieutenant, captain or whatever rank you achieved. You were in charge of other cadets and led them in a military hierarchy.

I was a decent high school and ROTC student. I was not one of the best and brightest. *(Laughs)* My attitude when I was in high school was work as hard as I can to get a "C." If I got a "C," that was fine. I had friends who were good kids, but non-achievers. We just liked to enjoy ourselves, to the consternation of my parents. However, I could take exams well, so I must have been somewhat smart.

When I graduated from high school, my father insisted that I take the exam to go to college. I took the exam, passed, and went to college as my father wanted.

But before then, I had a different idea. When I was in my senior year of high school, some friends of mine said that they were going to join in the Naval Reserve because at the time there was a draft. I thought to myself, at some time I'm going to serve in the military. And I thought, Well, I've had experience in Junior ROTC, I carried a rifle, I did all the things that a person in the Army would do, and I liked it well enough.

But then I also met sailors, and my father had taken me to work a few times and I saw Navy ships and what sailors did. And I thought, Gee whiz, if I'm going to serve, maybe it would be a good idea for me to serve in the Navy. At the time there was a big recruitment program to get people from Hawaii to join the Naval Reserve. The way it worked was: when you finished boot camp you'd go into the Navy for two years, and then when you were done with your two years you'd come back out and remain in the Naval Reserve for six years. I thought it was a good idea, so I signed up. I asked my father. He said, "Yeah, you go ahead and do that." Because he also thought, You're going to have to serve in some service, so you might as well sign up for the Navy.

So your parents, your mom and dad, weren't at all scared about you going?

Here's what I think they thought: Look, you have to go into the military anyway. It's probably safer to go in the Navy than it is in the Army. What appealed to me about going in the Navy was I could go in with a group of people that were all from Hawaii, and they were going to form an all-Hawaii company and go to boot camp and train together. So I signed up and, lo and behold, I'm shipped off to mainland United States. I end up going to boot camp at Naval Training Center in San Diego. It's the first time that I've ever left home for any length of time. I'm 18 years old. We fly to Moffett Field, and then we get a bus that takes us to San Diego.

When we get there, they begin to form these companies. Well, they had oversubscribed the *(laughs)* Hawaii Company. There were too many people, and they started from the As and the Zs. And guess what? I fell out.

You were P?

I was a P, myself, and I think maybe four other sailors fell out. *(Laughs)* So now they've constituted an all-Hawaii company, but I'm not a part of that. There were companies from other states in the same situation. Those who fell out like me were organized into what they call a Rainbow company. *(Laughs)* When this happened I was sad. I was placed with a whole bunch of people, kids from Texas, Wyoming, Ohio, and other states. And these were places I had only read about. I could look at a map and kind of know where they were, but it was my first chance really interacting with people from the mainland. And it was the first time in my life where I was now put in a group that was predominantly white.

Our drill instructor was not really happy having a company like us, so he was tough on us. But what was interesting was we came from all different cultural backgrounds. *(Laughs)* And we were pushed together, and it was amazing what happened, because we won the Outstanding Company. We were the Outstanding Drill Company of that session of boot camp.

It was my first exposure to accents from the South. *(Laughs)* There was this kid from the South and when he spoke, I had a hard time understanding what he was saying. And I'm sure when I spoke to him he had a hard time understanding what I was saying. Did race have an effect or did I feel any of it when I was in boot camp? No. I mean, you know, people looked at me—they knew I was different, because of how I look, but we were in the same boat and it didn't seem to matter.

It was mostly white? There weren't any Blacks or—

Yeah. There were no Blacks there at all, in the company that I was in. In fact, I saw very few Blacks at the time. So—

And this was 19…

It was 1954. When I completed boot camp, I had a feeling that I was now a man. I was not afraid of anything. I had come to the mainland as a boy. I was nervous. [Then] I go to boot camp; we finish boot camp. I'm a sailor now, a real sailor. *(Laughs)* At the end of boot camp I went down to Mexico with some of my sailor mates. It was the first time I had been in a foreign country. It was an eye opener, because it was pretty wild down there.

After boot camp, we went up to Moffett Field to wait for a space-available flight back to Hawaii. After a couple of days, I caught a flight to Barbers Point, and I think I had *(laughs)* 20¢ in my pocket or something like that. When I got there I walked out to the bus stop and got on a bus that stopped right in front of my house. I was happy and my parents were happy to see me. They noticed that I had matured a lot just in that brief time. But, as it turned out, I didn't go into active duty because I had passed the College Entrance Exam. I got a deferment to go to the University of Hawaii. And guess what? The University of Hawaii is also a land grant school. It's a land grant college.

And so that means every male in the college whose—

Must take ROTC *(laughs)*—must! I mean if you're physically capable, you've got to take ROTC. So you had a choice between Air Force ROTC and Army ROTC.

Well, I had already had Army experience in high school, and Navy experience. So I said, "Let me try Air Force." So I went into the Air Force ROTC Program in the first two years, mandatory. At the end of two years I did well in my ROTC studies because I'd had all the background before, in the military.

So I was encouraged to go into Senior ROTC, and if you complete Senior ROTC, you get a commission in the Air Force. I said to myself, "Well, I've seen how enlisted people live and work, and how officers live and work, in the Naval environment, and it's a much better life if you're an officer." *(Laughs)* So I said to myself, "What the heck, I'll become an officer in the Air Force and besides, I get to fly. That would be fun." So that's what I did. In my junior year, I went to an ROTC summer camp. I went to McChord Field in Tacoma, Washington. We went there and the ROTC detachments from different schools were all congregating there for the big, huge Air Force ROTC summer camp.

When I went to summer camp, there were sports activities you had to engage in, and I also got to fly. I got to fly in a T-33, which is a jet airplane. They had different flights. When the plane is full of gasoline, it can't do extreme maneuvers. The plane went up three times, and if you were in the third flight, the tip tanks are now empty and so the plane is a lot lighter and it can do the more extreme maneuvers.

Fortunately, that's the one I got. So I got to fly with a pilot—he made me feel comfortable because he had been stationed at Hickam Field before, which is in Hawaii. When he heard my name, he said, "Are you a local boy?" I said, "Yes," because I knew what that meant. He said, "I was stationed at Hickam. I'm going to give you a good ride." We took off and then he let me handle the controls of the airplane. He showed me how to do it. I did rolls, loops, all kinds of maneuvers, and I did well. *(Laughs)* I had a really super grade. He said, "This man has very good hand-eye coordination and could be a very good pilot." So I had a good rating. There were sports and I was a decent athlete. We played softball and the group I was playing in, we won our flight.

The flight selected certain players and I happened to be one of them—to play in an all-star championship game for the whole summer camp. Well, I was nervous. I was probably just as capable, but some of them were a whole lot better players than I was.

But then the coach says, "Okay, Pang, you are a pitcher, but you don't have the speed. Other people can throw the ball harder than you. So you're going to play second base." I never played second base before. *(Laughs)* But I said, "What the heck." So I played, and—the purpose of me bringing this part out is there were a lot of things that happened that were just pure luck. *(Laughs)*

We're playing a game—boom, this guy hits the ball. I could barely see it. I knew it was going to my right so I just stuck my glove out and the ball popped in there. I caught it. Everybody cheers.

I get up to bat. I'm a decent hitter, but not a home run hitter. But the ball comes and I take a swing, and I hit it just right. Boom! Gosh, man there it goes. I mean it was over the fence. Home run! So people think, Hey, this guy is a good player. So when you get rated, it's how you perform. And it's peer ratings; I'm a good teammate. So I get a great peer rating.

When I go back to Hawaii at the end of summer camp, the Professor of Air Science calls me in and says, "Pang, you got an outstanding rating for your summer camp. You represented us extremely well and we are all proud of you."

Frankly, up until then I was not one of the standouts in my class. I was just a regular cadet. I think the roster of leaders for the senior year of ROTC was already set and when I came along out of summer camp the way I did *(laughs)* and you have these good scores, what are you supposed to do? I got called in and they said, "Okay, you're going to be the wing commander."

Wing commander?

In other words, you're going to be in charge of the whole darned Air Force ROTC Cadet Corps, and I had no aspiration for that. I thought to myself, I haven't got enough time for this. I've got to practice teaching. I've got to do all these other academic things to get my degree in Education.

So your mind was really still on the Education track.

I just wanted to finish college and go on to serve my commitment in the Air Force. So when I was called in and told that I would be the cadet commander for the wing, I told the Professor of Air Science, "That's an honor, sir, but I'm in Practice Teaching and I think there are other cadets that aspire to the position more than I do."

And he cut me off and said, "No, you're it," and I said, "Yes, sir." And he said, "What I want you to do is address the incoming class of freshmen, and encourage them to take Air Force ROTC." Because the Air Force ROTC was the smaller of the two, as most people went into Army ROTC. I would say Air Force ROTC was at about 40%. The Professor of Air Science wanted 50-50 or better, and told me to address the freshmen class and make this goal.

So I got up before the incoming freshmen. I gave speeches to encourage them to join our Air Force ROTC. As it ended up, it was the first time in the University of Hawaii's history that the Air Force ROTC Class was larger than the Army ROTC Class. *(Laughs)* So the officers that were in charge, the Professor of Air Science, Colonel Green, were very happy.

I was the cadet wing commander for the first semester of my senior year. Then the second semester, I sort of went into an honorary status to allow another cadet the chance of leading the Wing.

I graduate from college and now I'm commissioned in the United States Air Force, and head off to Lackland Air Force Base in Texas for pre-flight training to be a pilot. I did well, but toward the end of pre-flight, I had to take a final physical before I went off to primary flight training. I had my oxygen mask, all of my gear and stuff like that. So I went in, you know, fat, dumb, and happy for my medical review. They did all this stuff and they found that I had scar tissue in my eye and therefore disqualified physically from flying. So I could not go on. It was a terrible blow and I cried.

All my friends went on to fly. I didn't. I was held back and now they had to find something for me to do. So, as it turned out, there was a class that was opening up and it was in Personnel. I took this class—I mean I didn't know what to do. I was distraught. I said to myself, "Okay, here's what I'm going to do.

I'm going to stay in the Air Force, and in four years I'm going to get out when I fulfill my commitment." And off I go to school, and then I was assigned to Kirksville Air Force Station in Missouri, where I spent—

When they give you these tests, they don't give you physical exams in the beginning?

They do. I passed them all until I got there.

So your eyes were okay up until them?

My eyes were not okay, but they never discovered it until later. *(Laughs)* I guess it's the way the chips fall. The scar tissue I have is on the cones in the back of your eye that you use for night vision. And I think they were particularly thorough on the exam I took, because the class I was in was going to be the first class that went right into jets. You didn't train on propeller airplanes. I was not the only one. I mean there were a number—I think there were five of us that were washed out. So I didn't get to become a pilot. I became a personnel officer.

I got to Kirksville Air Force Station. It's in the Air Defense Command. So I'm there for a year and I get an assignment from that unit to a place called Resolution Island, which is up in the Northwest Territory of Canada. It is remote, in the North Atlantic right off Frobisher Bay, and latitude-wise, north of the Aleutian Islands on the other side.

So here you've got a kid from Hawaii being sent up here to Resolution Island. I was up there for a year, and it is a very, very remote place.

I flew in with a bush pilot, landed on a short dirt runway. There were about 100 people on the island, and there were five officers. I was one of them. While I was not happy about being assigned there, it turned out to be a terrific training ground for me. The mission of our unit was aircraft control and warning and construction of a ballistic missile early warning system right in the height of the Cold War. So we constructed these big antennas while at the same time operating our radar and communication system 24/7 to detect Soviet aircraft that would try to penetrate Canadian air space and fly down to our country. So it was exciting. It was a high priority operational assignment, lots of responsibility, and all I did was work. There was no civilian population, no women, no wild life to speak of, nothing. You're just up there. I was up there for 11 months and 14 days, exactly. When I left, the project was just winding down, and it was amazing. I learned about teamwork, cooperation, overcoming challenges, and the value of strong, ethical leadership.

I also observed the hardships endured by military personnel and their families even in peacetime. Can you imagine being away for a year from your family for a year and the only way you can communicate is by letter? And sometimes the weather would get so bad that you wouldn't get letters for a month?

People would be cooped up. They would be nervous. There were occasional family issues. Wives would run off from their husbands and things like that. I was a second lieutenant—I was the adjutant of the squadron. My job was to deal with these matters.

So I was counseling people that were old enough to be my father, and try-ing to help them get their lives in order and things like that, and at the same time making sure that they were working. In other words, we had a mission to accomplish, so that was my duty. Then from there, I went to Oklahoma City Air Force Station for a couple of years. And that's when I got married. I knew my wife—we knew each other from college. And the pact we had was when she graduated, because she's three years younger than I am, we would get married. We got married. I brought my wife to Oklahoma, and she was not used to the military. There was kind of like a pull to go back to Hawaii. So I thought about it, and I said, "Well, I think I've put in my time. I've got the four years just com-ing up. I think I'll just get out of the Air Force."

So I wrote a resignation and sent it in, and right at that time the Cuban Missile Crisis happened. And if you were a regular officer you weren't allowed to get out. So I stayed in. The major that took my paperwork asked me what it would take for me to stay in the Air Force. And I said, "I would like an assign-ment back in Hawaii." I was just kidding. I didn't think he'd do it. But, the next thing you know, he was able to work a deal and I got assigned back to Hawaii. I was there for three years, and I completed my assignment there at a headquar-ters unit, and then I went from there to Japan.

That was a good assignment too. When I was assigned to Japan, they were establishing something called The Far East Communications Region. And so I was the first one in to set up the Personnel Office. We had units in Korea and Japan and Okinawa. And I was just a young captain, so it was a big job and great experience for me. I had good bosses. They gave me a great deal of latitude to do what I wanted to do, and it was fun. I did that for three years.

While we were there, we had our first daughter. As I was completing my tour in Japan, the Vietnam War now was near its height. I was assigned in June 1968 to be the Director of Personnel for the 1964th Communications Group, which was in Tan Son Nhut, the main headquarters base in Vietnam.

Tan Son Nhut Air Force Base was in the outskirts of Saigon, Ho Chi Minh City now. And the 1964th Communications Group had units, squadrons, at all major bases in Vietnam. And I got to go to all these locations. So in my tour in Vietnam I went to every major location in Vietnam. I traveled a lot. My job was to make sure that we were properly manned, with the right skilled people in all these different locations. We had requisitions that we sent to the higher head-quarters. They would fill them and I would review them. It was a very important job for a captain, a big job. So I was fortunate in that regard.

And you volunteered to go there? You weren't afraid?

No. I was about 32 years old, and so I didn't think much about it. I said, "Well, okay, there's a war going on here. I'm in the Air Force, this is what I'm trained to do." And you know, I said to myself, "Better to go now than later," because our daughter was newly born, not yet even a year old. So I figured she wouldn't even miss me.

Your family stayed?

My family went to stay in Hawaii among family and friends. And I went. And again it was an exciting, good assignment. Was it dangerous? Yeah, of course. But not as dangerous as for our soldiers and Marines fighting in the jungle. *(Laughs)* They were out there in the bush. I was in a headquarters unit. I did go on combat missions, but not many. I think maybe five.

I flew in the back seat of an observer aircraft flying in South Vietnam and we were interdicting enemy river traffic. So I flew in an O-1 single engine airplane that has fabric wings. It looks like a Piper Cub. I mean a small airplane. And there was myself and a pilot. We took off, and we would fly along the river. And I had binoculars and I would be looking down to see if there was traffic on the river. When we spotted traffic, we would call down to a liaison post, because they knew what traffic was authorized on the river. So we were looking for unauthorized traffic on the river.

On one of those missions we caught unauthorized traffic. We were flying and we spotted them. They were right near the tree line. There were several sampans. And when we called, the liaison people said, "No, they're not authorized there."

There were two jet airplanes that were circling. That's how this thing works. We told them we spotted these bandits down there. And so we dived down and marked them with smoke rockets, and then they [the jets] came down and bombed them and shot them up. And I was worried, because when you look down there you say, "Gee whiz, I hope these are not a family of people who got lost or something like that." But then when I saw the secondary explosion, I knew that they had ammunition or something bad. I also went on a Swift Boat mission one time on the Mekong River in the delta.

So I did that, and then when I finished my tour in Vietnam I went back to Hawaii on a special mission there, to help put together a consolidated personnel system. I did that for about two years, and then the Air Force sent me to get my graduate degree at the University of Hawaii. I got a Master's in Business Administration there. When I finished that I was sent here.

To D.C.?

Yeah, the Headquarters of the United States Air Force. I was the lead officer programmer. My job was to help plan the reduction of Air Force officers in number, because the War was coming to an end. So that was a good assignment for me and exposed me to a lot of senior-ranking people. When I finished that job, they gave me an assignment to the Office of the Secretary of Defense. My job was to help enact a comprehensive legislative proposal to make uniform the management of officers in the separate military services. It was called Defense

Officer Personnel Management System. You had the Army, Navy, Air Force and Marines, and you had officers in all these branches of service. But the rules that governed appointment, promotion, retirement and career development weren't uniform and some of the rules were dysfunctional and needed to be corrected.

There was this notion that said, "Hey, look, you know everybody that is of the same grade, commissioned officer grade, ought to be treated generally the same way. There might be nuances, because of the needs of your particular service, but these rules—a lot of them are policies—should be embodied in law. So you have these protections." It was a precursor to more joint operations, an effort that had been languishing for quite a while. I mean, 6–7 years. So when I came aboard there was an urgency that gave this initiative priority.

At the time, we had an Assistant Secretary of Defense for Manpower and Reserve Affairs—his name was Robin Pirie—who was dedicated to try to get this through. On the side of the Congress, it was Senator Sam Nunn of Georgia. He was the Chairman of the Personnel Subcommittee of the Senate. He was the big advocate for getting this particular piece of legislation through. It was a huge piece of legislation, terribly important to the military, but he and the military were at loggerheads. Senator Nunn had ideas and principles that he wanted to see in the legislation. But you had a military that wanted to maintain more separation among the services. He wanted more uniformity.

So they'd been going at this for years. When I came aboard, and was onboard for maybe about a year or so, I got promoted. I was asked one time, almost fortuitously, by Secretary Pirie, why we remained at odds with Senator Nunn. He said he was tired of being lectured at hearings about the military's intransigence. I told him that I thought there was a way to bring compromise between the two sides such that both sides will be basically satisfied. His response was "Well, what are they?" I said, "Okay, let me think it through and I'll write it down." So I did. I wrote it down—this is the honest to God truth—on a legal pad *(laughs)*, a yellow pad of paper. And I went in to see him and told him how we might be able to do it. He looked it over and directed me to work directly with him, to try to work it out to the satisfaction on both sides.

What happened was this particular piece of legislation all of a sudden gained new life, because Pirie said, "I'm committed to doing it. Work with the Senate and House staff people to see what we can do to come up with a good piece of legislation and I'll handle the military services." So, given that authority—this was senior authority entrusted in me—I worked on it with focus and zeal. In the end, the Defense Officer Personnel Management Act of 1980 was passed. And it still exists today.

The Act embodies the laws that govern the appointment, promotion, career development, retirement of officers in all the military services. So that was a big, huge accomplishment. What was my role? I was a colonel and a point person in doing this.

The major players were the Secretary of Defense, the Chairman of the

Senate Armed Services Committee, the Chairman of House Armed Services Committee—really big, powerful people. And their subcommittee chairmen, there were two: on the Senate side, the key person was Senator Sam Nunn, of Georgia and on the House side was Congressman Bill Nichols, Alabama. And these were very well known, highly regarded people.

When the Act passed, these people knew that I was the working point person in the Defense Department for it. So that was significant for me, very significant, and I'll explain later on why.

As I approached 27 years of service in the Air Force. I knew I had to retire fairly soon. Thirty years is all you're allowed to serve in the Air Force as a colonel. So I said to myself, "What should I do?" I was kind of uncertain. A friend encouraged me to take the job as Professor of Air Science and Tactic Science at the University of Maryland. He was a general and we had served together as colonels. I remember him saying to me, "I know you like to run and play tennis." I was a very fit, athletic guy. He says, "You'll love it out there." So I said, "Okay, fine. I think that's what I'll do." I thought it would be a good way to end a 30-year career.

However, in the meantime, the boss I had in the Office of the Assistant Secretary of Defense didn't want me to leave. I told him, "Look, you know I've got 27 years in. You want me to stay here, for me to work for you. I could retire and go into the private sector, because at some time that's what I'm going to do anyway. Let me serve that way if that works for you." And he said, "Okay, fine. Let's work it out."

So it was arranged that I retire and come back to work for him. When I retired, I was hired by a defense contractor and the defense contractor had a contract with his office. I was detailed there to work. I worked there for about six months and enjoyed it. But, as it turned out, in the elections of 1986 the Senate changed hands.

It went from a Republican Senate to a Democratic Senate, and Senator Nunn became Chairman of the Armed Services Committee. So he had oversight over all the Defense Department. I got a call from his staff, right after the elections in December, and was asked if I would come to work for him, and that's what I did. I became a professional staff member on the Senate Armed Services Committee. And I was on the Senate Armed Services Committee staff for 6½ years.

My portfolio was Manpower, Reserve Affairs, and Health Affairs. So it was a big portfolio. Fortunately, the knowledge I had acquired, both in substance and process, from my experience in the Office of the Secretary of Defense, stood me in good stead. I was assigned as the senior professional staff member on the Subcommittee on Manpower and Personnel of the Senate Armed Services Committee. My Subcommittee Chairman was none other than Senator John Glenn, the astronaut.

I can say that today, both of them, Nunn and Glenn, remain friends. They're some of the best public servants I've ever had the pleasure to work for, because they put country first. Are they politicians? Of course. Were they partisan in some areas? Of course. But when it came down to doing the right thing for the men and women in uniform, and for the country, they would put aside their partisanship and work with the Republicans to get things done. As it turned out, the ranking minority member on the subcommittee that I served was none other than John McCain. So I know him too. But anyway, I did that for 6½ years.

As a general rule, the Administration proposes legislation, the Congress disposes. You have huge responsibility given to you as a staffer. I'm not elected, but I serve my masters, who are Senator Nunn and Senator Glenn, within the context of the Senate Armed Services Committee. That was a profound responsibility. I was able to use my military experience to help me in that job. But I think the most significant thing that was accomplished on my watch as a staffer there was the passage of the laws that provided for the transition of military personnel from military life to civilian life after the collapse of the Soviet Union.

When the Soviet Union came down, the military reduced in strength by over 30%—it was about 35%. So how do you take an all-volunteer force, and reduce it by that amount, over a period of time, without breaking it? All previous draw-downs after wars, conflicts, and the like, were disastrous.

After World War II they just let everybody go. They didn't have a good plan of action of how to do it. So when we had the Korean War, it was a disaster. I mean, never learned the lesson. Same thing—after Korea, let everybody go. Then when Vietnam started up, you know? We never were prepared.

So the question was: Okay, all those things happened in the past. How do you do it this time, in such a way that that doesn't happen? You transition the military in a smart way so that the smaller force you have remains prepared. It has a distribution of people, in terms of grade, years in service, and experience that makes you ready for any eventuality. And I'm particularly proud of having worked on that, because it proved that we did the right thing. Just look at how the military has performed in the conflicts since then. So from that standpoint, it was probably one of the most significant accomplishments that I was involved in.

When this task was completed, I was pretty burned out and I felt it was time for me to leave and try my hand back in the private sector. This was at about the time President Clinton was elected to his first term of office. When he took office there were a number of personnel issues in the Navy that his Administration inherited, namely the Tailhook problem, a cheating scandal at the Naval Academy, and a number of other matters involving both racial and gender discrimination.

I don't know if you've even heard about it, but the Tailhook problem involved a bunch of Naval aviators who were out in Las Vegas at a big conference. It was the Tailhook Conference, and there was drunken, unruly behavior that involved the touching and grabbing of women. This, plus a big cheating scandal at the Naval Academy, needed to be resolved.

My bosses felt that these problems needed to be dealt with properly and promptly. They suggested to President Clinton that I could help the Administration do that. So in coordination with the Secretary of Defense, at the time Les Aspin, I was nominated, confirmed, and appointed as Assistant Secretary of the Navy for Manpower and Reserve Affairs. It took me a year, with the help of a lot of people, to solve the Tailhook and Naval Academy cheating scandals. The solutions were not perfect because they involved human judgment, or lack thereof, and they were inherited with flaws that were not possible to correct. Nonetheless, justice was served.

There were also some discrimination cases that had to be concluded. And one of them, which made the press, was the Bruce Yamashita Case. I don't know if you've ever heard of it. Bruce Yamashita was a Japanese American who wanted to join the Marine Corps as an officer. He was too old. Senator Inouye from Hawaii convinced the Marine Corps to bring him in under an age waiver. So Bruce Yamashita goes to officer training in the Marine Corps. The first day he gets there, one of the drill instructors talks to him in Japanese and makes fun of him. Through the course of his training there, there were several incidents of discrimination, blatant. He complained. It was investigated and the investigators found that there was indeed discrimination, but they concluded that it was not serious enough to have affected him in a negative way.

As it turned out, Yamashita did not get commission as an officer in the Marine Corps. So he filed suit. This thing was all hanging out there when I took over. People were looking at me to see how I would act. My course and principle was to discern the facts, analyze them objectively, and act fairly on that basis. I knew if I did this, we would arrive at a just result. What I found was that there were blatant acts of discrimination during his training that prevented Yamashita from being commissioned as an officer in the Marine Corps. I concluded this not just out of the clear blue sky but from reading through very thoroughly and carefully the investigation that was conducted by the Marine Corps itself. So I went to see the commandant of the Marine Corps.

The commandant?

The highest guy in the Marine Corps in uniform, General Mundy, and I said, "General, I've reviewed this report. It was written by your Inspector General and it says discrimination occurred. It was blatant." He says, "No, no. I don't think so." I pointed out to him that the report describes among other incidents the first day of Yamashita's training when he was called out by his drill instructor and spoken to in Japanese in front of all the other officer candidates in his class. When Yamashita could not respond, he was ridiculed for not knowing how to speak "his" language. So, from the first day, Yamashita stood at the bottom of his class and among his peers because the drill instructor put him there and then continued to keep him there. Another incident was when he was getting ready to meet a board of officers who would determine if he would be allowed to graduate. As the report showed, Yamashita dressed in his proper uniform to appear before the Board. As he was leaving to go to meet the Board, he was ordered by his drill instructor to change into a uniform that was wrinkled and not suitable for Yamashita to wear before a Board. He complied with the order and of course it had its desired effect.

So anyway, the short of it all was that I saw the commandant. He knew what the report said and he knew my conclusion. I asked him to take the initiative to do the right thing. He demurred for reasons of his own. So I told him that I would take the appropriate corrective action. He said he understood my position and would fight it. So I ordered the Marine Corps to commission Yamashita as a captain in the Marine Corps Reserve, because with all that time that had elapsed, he would have been a captain by then. And that was the resolution of the case as fairly as I could do it.

So the commandant said he wanted you to—

I gave him the opportunity to fix it himself. He wouldn't do it, and I did.

And why did he say he wouldn't do it?

I can only speculate, and I think that he just didn't want to overrule a previous decision that there was no discrimination.

And that would put him in a bad light among people who don't consider those acts discriminatory?

Well, I think he was more concerned about that than doing the fair thing. I know the man. He wrestled with it, and in the end couldn't make himself do it. Because he would have had to admit he was wrong. Because he had come to a different conclusion, right? Now, he's got to overturn. And senior—I found this to be true—senior people, way at the top especially, have a difficult time admitting error, and he was in error.

After serving as Assistant Secretary of the Navy for a year, I was asked to come on and be the Assistant Secretary of the Defense for Force Management Policy, which basically means I was in charge of all manpower and personnel policy in the Defense Department, military and civilian.

The biggest accomplishment on my watch was a quality-of-life initiative that we programmed and funded for the military that involved better childcare for families, better military housing through public/private ventures, and a first class overseas schools system for military children.

My job was to also oversee the drawdown of our forces over the same period of time. So it was interesting. I had a big hand in drawing up the laws. Then I had a big hand in taking those laws and putting it into effect, so that when we drew down our forces we didn't create great harm to the force.

So when I was done with that—it took about three years to do all of that—I said to myself, "Well, I can either stay on and seek something else at a higher level position …" And they had talked about potentially making me the Secretary of the Air Force, which I would have taken, by the way. But there's a lot of politics that gets involved.

At this point I felt I was at the high water mark in what I was doing and thought it was a good time for me to try my hand again in the private sector. I felt good about what I had accomplished in government and wanted to explore opportunities in which I could capitalize on my background and experience. So I left office with satisfaction and looked forward with anticipation toward private enterprise.

When I left office, I started out as an individual consultant, on my own. I picked up a couple of consultancy contracts. And in the course of doing that—because, I think I did real good work *(laughs)*—people asked me if I could do bigger jobs and put together a team to help us do A, B, C, and so forth. So I did. At first, very small, just maybe 4 or 5 people. Then, next, 10 to 15 people, and pretty soon some of the jobs were big ones. And instead of using consultants like I had, now I needed employees.

So I went from being an individual consultant, Fred Pang and Associates, to ViStar Corporation, a defense contracting company that grew quite rapidly. Some of the things we did included supporting the deployment of personnel to the Coalition Provisional Authority in Iraq and later to Afghanistan, supporting the Office of the Assistant Secretary of Homeland Defense, supporting the Army's Readiness System, and supporting a number of other high priority missions. In exactly eight years a venture capital company in New York bought us to be merged into another company. So in eight years I went from being an individual consultant to a company with revenues in the millions.

Oh my gosh!

Yeah, so I smiled and decided to retire, at least for a while, so I can spend more time with my family, especially my granddaughters. I know I am a very fortunate man who has never had to go it alone. I've had wonderful mentors, co-workers, friends, and associates who have helped me get to where I am. And of course I cannot leave out the most important person who put up with me for all these years, my wife Brenda. It all would have not been possible without her. *(Laughs)*

CHAPTER TWENTY-ONE

John Fugh 傅履仁 (1934–2010)

U.S. Army

Major General John Liu Fugh became a staff judge advocate in the U.S. Army in 1963, and rose in rank to be Judge Advocate General of the U.S. Army from July 1991 to September 1993, becoming the first Asian American to attain rank of general in the U.S. Army. With 35 years in the military, Fugh served as legal advisor to the Army Chief of Staff in the Persian Gulf War. After retiring from the Army, Fugh joined as a partner at the law firm of McGuire, Woods, Battle & Booth in Washington, D.C. He later spent five years serving as Chief Representative for several U.S. companies in Beijing and was Chairman of the Committee of 100, an organization encouraging constructive China-U.S. relations and full participation of Chinese Americans in all fields of American life.

There is a saying, 好铁不打定, 好汉不当兵, this kind of Confucius bias passed down, how "Good metal shouldn't be used to make nails. Good men do not become soldiers." So I joined the military really almost out of necessity because I graduated from law school in 1960, and before that I was being haunted by the Draft Board. I was student deferred. So finally after I graduated from law school, before you can get a commission in the Judge Advocate General's Corps, you've got to pass the Bar and be admitted to the Bar. The percentage for passing the D.C. bar is about 40%. There was a lot of pressure on me because I was engaged to be married, and June was not willing to marry just a soldier to be drafted. Fortunately, on my birthday, September 12, a law school friend who was clerking for a judge in D.C. District Court called. He said, "John, congratulations, you passed the Bar." He saw my name. So that was real good news.

So I enlisted as a soldier and entered the Army. I really liked the Army, the atmosphere was quite good, and my first assignment was a choice assignment at The Presidio, San Francisco. That's a beautiful spot, you know. Then I took a break from service at which time I was working for the Atomic Energy Commission in San Francisco, Operations Office. Then the people in The Presidio asked me to come back. I was interested. A retired colonel in the JAG, the lawyer for the Stanford Linear Accelerator Project, asked me one question.

He said, "John, what does your wife say about your interest in returning to the Army?" I said, "She's in favor of it." Then he said, "Do it, because, once

John Fugh on the USS John F. Kennedy (CV 67), 19 May 1993

you've got clearance from your wife that's the main thing. Otherwise you'll be miserable." And that's good advice.

I was given my assignment of choice at Heidelberg, Germany, where we arrived in 1964, and my son was born in Heidelberg. We stayed there until, knock on wood, I made it to the top. There were a lot of challenges.

People usually ask, "Did you face any overt discrimination?" I say, "Not really." I think being Chinese in the American Army does something. They'll remember you well, one way or the other. If you're good, they remember you. If you're bad, they remember you. There's little in-between.

So I was tested in different assignments and did very well. The biggest test was when they sent me to Germany in 1976. The assignment was to be the staff judge advocate of an armor division. It was a very tough job, because there were a lot of courts-martial. There were a lot of drug cases. I had a very tough commander who kept on testing me. He would call me on the weekend, and want me to go to the office, just to see how quickly I respond to his request. Or he'd call me and say, "We have a request for the 3rd Armored Band to perform for a recording company." And I'd happen to remember there's a statute banning military bands from performing commercially. So he knew the answer, but he was just trying to test me. Once you pass the test, it was fine.

We had a lot of cases to be tried. Murder cases, rape cases. It was very trying. I think I lost about 10 or 12 pounds because day in, day out, there was a lot of pressure.

Can you talk about growing up, what it was like?

I was born in Beijing in 1934. It was a very traditional family. I had grandparents, Ye Ye and Nai Nai, and I guess the person that had the largest influence on me was my mother, who was a teacher and also a Protestant. I say she's had the largest influence on me, because my father was always away. So she brought me up. She always told me, "Whatever you do, you must be able to look at yourself in the mirror. Do not try to take advantage of a situation. Always do things that stand up under the light of day. 正大光明."You know?

At night, I knew that she would pray with me. She was a very, very devout Protestant. She didn't wear it on her sleeve, but it was in all the things she did. She ran the family household. Even my wife, June, is very close to my mother. She's not close to her own mother, but she's close to my mother. I'm the only boy in the family. I have three sisters, and my father's brother also had girls. And being the only boy, you can imagine—you get, not spoiled, but sheltered. I remember when they used to go to Beidahe, I didn't go. I got kept home and everybody else went. Beidahe is a sea resort. Nowadays, Beidahe is where the Communist leaders meet. So I was brought up in a very sheltered environment. In fact, when I started school, I went to a girls' school, because I grew up with women. Even today I feel more comfortable with women than I do with men. There's something—

Interesting, especially because you went into the military.

Yeah. Well, today it's a little different. I mean I can get along with men too. *(Laughs)* But it's just that I remember, when I was growing up, they sent me to a girls' school first, until I got acclimated, then sent me then to a boys school. At first it was a cultural shock, but I grew accustomed to it.

My father always worked for John Leighton Stuart, who founded Yenching University. That's a Christian university that became very famous. And a lot of people went there, including later on some Communist leaders. Like—I'm trying to think of the Foreign Minister of China. Stuart was born and raised in China of missionary parentage, and he actually spoke Chinese, I guess before he spoke English. *(Laughs)* Stuart wrote a book called *Fifty Years in China*, a copy of which I still have. He lived a life of Christ. He never had any desire to have money or anything, he just—he was an educator, a Christian educator.

My dad worked for Stuart for many, many years. It was almost like father and son. My dad helped him with all the Chinese protocol things and later on, when he was Ambassador, my dad was very instrumental in helping him do his job with the Chinese government.

When you talk about protocol do you mean like legislative protocol or like customs?

With Chinese protocol. More with what are the right things to do, I guess an advisory role.

In interactions with the Chinese people, or government?

Yeah, with the Chinese government. It was very funny because here my father was a Chinese National, not an American citizen, who resided with the American Ambassador to China. There was a lot of speculation. Even later on there was an American general I became acquainted with who said, "You know, we always wondered whose side was your father on!" You know, either on Communist side or Kuomintang side.

I said, "He wasn't on anybody's side. Okay?" He was just devoted to Stuart, and tried to help Stuart get his job done as Ambassador. It was a very difficult time. It was really, if you think about it, it was mission impossible. General George C. Marshall was the one who picked Stuart to be the Ambassador, thinking that he was respected by both the Communists and the Kuomintang, that he would be ideal. But, first of all, if you look at what they wanted to do, it was impossible. The Communists would have to give up their Army, to be integrated with the Nationalists' Army. That's a nonstarter to begin with, right? And so they had all these meetings and so forth, but it all broke down, and then the Civil War started.

I remember I went to Nanjing in '48, I think. My mom came out, on the last airplane, in '49 from Beijing, and joined us. Then we went to Shanghai, where we stayed for a while. Before the loss of Shanghai, my dad wanted to know what my mom wanted to do—to go to Hangzhou, or to Chongqing—in those days Taiwan wasn't even mentioned—to kind of retreat with the KMT. My mother said, "No, I want to go back to Beijing." My grandfather was still alive. So Shanghai was lost in May in 1948. Yeah, because in '49 the founding of the Republic of China started. We went back, and my grandfather was still alive, and they were very tough times. There were a lot of local informers. They would come and take my mom away and then kept me separate from my mother, and asked for secret documents and ammunition, and threatened, "If you don't tell us where everything is, you'll never see your mother again." You know, here I was a teenager, and that scared me.

Was it the KMT or the Communists who put you away?

Communists. It was so desperate. I remember my mom and I, we were playing the Ouija board, to see if we should leave. My grandfather said, "You've got to leave. You've got to leave!" So finally—

Was this a Chinese Ouija board?

It's a fortunetelling thing, I don't know. I don't even know who suggested that we try that. You know, we used to have power outages, and I remember doing this by the candle, the Ouija board. I don't know whether it moved on its own, or if we were subconsciously moving it, I don't know. Whatever it was, my mother got so frightened, she became very ill. I remember we got into a rickshaw and went to a friend's house, because her father was a doctor, and tried to get some medicine. I got some medicine and came back. It was raining so hard.

Finally we were able to get an exit permit. I still have it, by the way. I'll show you; it's kind of interesting.

In 1950, we arrived in the U.S. Stuart had already suffered a stroke. My father and Stuart were living in the Fairfax Hotel, and they needed my mom and me too, because my mom could help cook and stuff like that.

With President Barack Obama   With President George H.W. Bush, Oval Office, May 1991

Your sisters stayed in China?

Well, my eldest sister was in New York. She went to Fordham University. My second sister was still in Japan. My third sister came later. She married an American-born officer.

We moved out of the Fairfax Hotel, we rented a place on Waterside Drive, by Massachusetts Avenue, and then I started at Western High School. My English was okay, but it was not that good. I remember I took a test. I think I was equivalent to a moron, because a lot of words I didn't understand, like blush, you know, redness in face. So there were challenges, language-wise. Even today, I think sometimes I still have a little hesitancy, you know? But anyway, those were the days that I managed to overcome.

In the military, I really didn't have any setbacks. People often ask—did you suffer discrimination? Not really. Also, don't forget, I was in a professional group, lawyers. If I had been an infantryman, maybe it would've been different. But people joke sometimes, you know. They use a racial slur every once in a while, but they don't mean it. In terms of overt discrimination, I never really experienced any.

When I was undergoing training at Fort Benning, which is an infantry school, that was pretty close to the Korean War, and the cadre was called The Chinks, and they used words like that. Outside of that I really didn't experience any overt discrimination.

So during the Korean War and Vietnamese War, when the enemy was Asian, were they ever suspicious of your loyalties or anything like that?

It's interesting. *(Laughs)* When I visited China for the first time, in 1988, I went with a group of American generals and we went to a Shanghai Friendship Store, and this little salesgirl starts following us. We were all wearing summer uniforms, and she was asking "How come you wear the same thing they do? Are you a fraud?" She said, "If there's a war between U.S. and China, whose side

Xi Jinping 习近平, Zhejiang Party Secretary,
Hangzhou State Guest House, 9 November 2006

will you be on?" You know, Chinese people have that very deep feeling. If you're Chinese you don't fight the Chinese. That kind of—if you think about it, there were the Japanese [Americans in the] Second World War. How many Japanese [Americans] served and served heroically in the [U.S.] military, even though their family members were interned, right? And that concept is very hard. In fact, the same question was asked of me by a reporter when I was in China. I said, "Which side do you think I would be on?" I then finally explained to her that your allegiance and loyalty is to the country, it's not the color of your skin. That is something I think Chinese have difficulty accepting, at least some Chinese. I don't think the Americans have too much trouble with that. It's—have you ever experienced anything like that? People ask—

Yeah, people ask that all the time.

Still do?

I think so. I remember it mostly in the '80s—I think that times have changed now. But when I was a kid, during the Olympics, people would ask, "Who do you cheer for?"

Yeah. But I'll tell you, there was a sense of pride during the Korean War. Remember China and U.S. fought, and China didn't lose. There was a sense of hey, you know, we could fight and didn't lose, you know, a sense of pride.

Pride for Chinese Americans or just Chinese?

Chinese Americans. I think nowadays, times have changed. You know, China is labeled as an upcoming world power and sometimes you read in the papers, even here [in Washington, D.C.], they're talking about, "Don't let China get too big for their britches," you know? I was reading that the other day. There are a lot of things—tension could be building up, and that could be very difficult, I think, for Chinese Americans. Don't you think? It could be challenging times.

Yeah, on one hand, China's considered our friend, and then they're also an enemy and rival.

You know, there are groups I work with right now. I'm working with Brzezinski and Brent Scowcroft. They're starting a roadmap of how to fashion U.S. relations in a positive way. This is part of a spinoff of the Atlantic Council of the United States, of which I'm a director. I think this is important; the relationship has got to keep on an even keel. Because China in a way is ... sometimes getting a little too strident in the position they take. This arms sale to Taiwan, they've known it for a long time. It was approved by the last administration, and they were rattling their saber. And this about the Dalai Lama's visit. I think China should learn to be a little more magnanimous about things like that.

And I told the Chinese, "You know, you consider the Dalai Lama a splittist, an enemy of the Chinese people. Don't forget, in the Western world he is considered a holy man, a man of peace." It's how you look at things. I don't think it's in China's interest to be too myopic. You've got to look at the long term. But recently there were some indications that are not very good. So China is saying, "You know, I'm big enough. You don't push me around anymore." I understand that feeling, because I was one who always felt since I grew up that China was 東亞病夫, the "sick man of Asia." Everybody took advantage of us. The sense of humiliation is ingrained in me, even today.

I think the Olympics did a lot to sort of pull us up. We all have that feeling, but I don't think we ought to let that blind us to what overall is the best interests of not just China, but the world. That's why I work on a lot of these issues here and continue to try to improve U.S.-China relations. I think it's important. If you talk to people like Kissinger and so forth, they all tell you the most important bilateral relations today is U.S.-China, and Brzezinski and all those people feel the same way. So it's about how to make that relationship continue to be constructive. Because it can easily go the other way. Like this RMB [renminbi] devaluation—the undervalued RMB, there's some truth in that. But China would say, "Oh, that's internal business." I think China should take a more realistic, far-sighted view about things. I think they will. You know, all these people, the players we know, like Yang Jiechi who is now the Foreign Minister, they know how important the U.S. is, but because recently you begin to see some sliding back from that position. Well, we can only hope for the best.

Do they come to you for advice?

Well, I work in the—not for advice, but I'm very frank with them. I think last time we were there, with the Committee of 100, we met with people who were in the NPC, the National People's Congress. We were talking about the Dalai Lama. I just told them, "You cannot persuade Americans to look upon the Dalai Lama the way you look at him. True, he is doing a lot of things to try to encourage—but he has never said that he wanted Tibet to be autonomous." But then some Americans told me that what he wants is almost half of China because they're all Tibetans, you know? So those are really tough issues, I think, for Chinese Americans.

You're considered a veteran of the Vietnam War.

Yeah, I was in the Vietnam War, '68.

You were also involved in the first Persian Gulf War?

Yes. We were the only ones who sent in a War Crimes Team. We did a lot of investigation about wars crimes committed by Iraqis when they went invaded Kuwait. They did a report too. I sent in an international law team.

Was there a most memorable moment in your career?

Yeah, we had a scandal.

A scandal?

Yeah, a big scandal. In fact, the guy who was nominated to be Judge Advocate General was not confirmed by the Senate. As a result, I was confirmed and he wasn't.

There was somebody who was nominated to be a brigadier general in the JAG Corps, and this guy had baggage. He was involved in command influence. Military justice is supposed to be in a neutral environment. When you have somebody who is trying to influence it in a certain way, it's called unlawful command influence. And this general basically passed word out saying if you recommend a soldier to be tried by court-martial that could result in his dismissal, you should not then testify for him, saying he should be retained, because it's not consistent. Well, in the purest way it made sense but it really is telling people when you recommend somebody for court-martial that could result in him being kicked out, you do not come and testify for him. That word got out.

The Court of Military Appeals, the highest court, said that this colonel was either unwilling or unable to do anything to stop this. So as a result they did not confirm him. And then this guy who was supposed to be the Judge Advocate General was carrying the water all throughout the Pentagon saying he was really the best one and he should have been promoted. There's nothing wrong with it. We have an opportunity to disclose all the information, okay? He failed to do it.

So basically they did not confirm him because of this withholding of material information. I still remember when he called me. He said, "John, I just learned that you were confirmed by the Senate, and I wasn't." I didn't quite believe it. I said, "Are you sure?" Later on the Senate came out with a report saying what he did. That's why they withheld him. I would say that's a very memorable time for my career, because the bottom line is that we, as lawyers in the military, like somebody said, we're the keeper of the flame. You have to keep

With Governer & Mrs. Ronald Reagan
10 October 1971, Taipei, Republic of China

With President George W. Bush and President
Hu Jintao 胡锦涛, White House, 20 April 2006

good. They thought Chinese Americans were more loyal to China than to the

straight. You got to be able to say what is right and what is wrong. And if you know something is not right, and you try to make it right by telling people it's right, that's a big sin. And that's what cost this guy, who always wanted to be number one, to be not confirmed by the Senate, the first one I can think of. And he still has a very responsible position today as the Clerk for the Supreme Court of the United States.

Shouldn't he not be there then?

Yeah, I think he squeezed by in there. If this thing had blown up earlier, it would have cost him that too. But, anyway, that's a highlight in my life. We have to have the courage to say what is wrong and what is right. If we don't do our job, then the whole system collapses.

It goes back to what my mother used to tell me, "不要取巧. Don't try to play tricks or take shortcuts with trying to get a little advantage over people. Do only things you are willing to have examined under daylight. 做正大光明的事情." That kind of talk, ammunition, stayed with me.

I was reading through the American Legion Journal, for the Kimlau Post in New York. You wrote a letter to the veterans and said in the early 2000s the Committee of 100 did a report. It asked people how they would feel about having a Chinese American president. Most people feared such a thing, and thought that a Chinese American would be more loyal to China than the U.S. Then in this year's new report by the Committee of 100, Chinese Americans are considered much more favorably in the eyes of Americans.

The survey?

Yeah. Do you have thoughts on that?

Things are changing. You know, the first report came out—it was not very

United States. The second report, I think was better. That kind of image, we've got to change. Matt Fong, when he was running for the Senate against Barbara Boxer, some newspaperman asked him, "If you're elected will you be more loyal to China than the United States?" That's insulting. I remember that. Matt Fong talked about that too. Some people hold the belief that because you're Chinese, you therefore must be more loyal to China. That doesn't really compute if you think about it. I always talk about the Japanese Americans—their properties were confiscated and they were put in basically concentration camps, and they still fought for the United States. That's an outstanding story. That's why I am on the Japanese American Memorial Foundation. I'm the only Chinese who belonged to that—I'm a director—because I admire Japanese Americans for that. And they not only fought, like Senator Inouye. They fought heroically, and he lost his arm as a result of that. That kind of deed earns people's respect. The things I believe in, I will support them.

CHAPTER TWENTY-TWO

David Louie 雷光達 (1949–   )
U.S. Army

David J. Louie was Sergeant-at-Arms of the American Legion (National), Chairman of the Chinese Chamber of Commerce, Co-Chairman of the Chinatown BID Steering Committee, Charter Chairman of the Chinatown Partnership Local Development Corporation, past Chairman of Chinatown Manpower, and a board member of the Chinese Consolidated Benevolent Association, The New York Chinese School, Chinatown Day Care Center and American Legion Kimlau Post. He is a charter member of the Chinese American Insurance Association, and past President of the Chinatown Lions Club.

I met David J. Louie at his insurance office in Manhattan's Chinatown in 2012. Upon entering, one is greeted by his collection of antique slot machines, including hand-carved wooden Indians from the '30s and '40s. Hanging on the wall are pictures of David Louie with illustrious individuals including Warren Buffet and New York City Mayor Michael Bloomberg.

[*Showing pictures*] That's Warren Buffett. He owns two insurance companies. I'm an agent of one of his insurance companies. This is me meeting Mayor Bloomberg through my work with the Chamber of Commerce. This picture is me as sergeant-at-arms with the USO girls, at probably the Fourth of July Parade. You know I'm the national sergeant-at-arms, right?

Tell us what this is.

Okay. The American Legion today is the largest veterans' organization in the world. It was started in 1919 by Teddy Roosevelt, Jr. Each year they elect a new commander. This year, as you probably know, in 2011–2012, the national commander of the American Legion, for the first time, is an Asian American—Fang Wong, from the Kimlau Post. The commander chooses his own commander's aide and sergeant-at-arms. Fang was gracious enough to choose me to act as his sergeant-at-arms for the American Legion. I'm very humbled by it. I try to do the best I can to serve Fang Wong and the American Legion.

What does a sergeant-at-arms do?

The sergeant-at-arms maintains order at functions and at meetings, specifically at the conferences of the annual convention.

Let's start from the beginning of your life. Where did you grow up? What was your family like? Who was the first person in your family to come to the U.S.?

My father came to the United States in the 1920s. He was born in 1902. In those days, they had what they called the Chinese Exclusion Act. It was still very difficult for Chinese women to come over, and even for a Chinese male to come over. My father was single all the way up to the beginning of World War II. In 1942, he was already 40 years old.

Now they weren't drafting 40-year-old people, but 40-year-old people could enlist. He and a whole bunch of other Chinese people enlisted in 1942. After the war, he was able to bring a wife. Remember, in World War II we were fighting the Japanese and the Japanese were occupying China and Hong Kong. So a lot of Chinese did volunteer. Many Chinese were drafted, but many Chinese also volunteered.

Where were you born?

I was born in Coney Island, in Brooklyn. We lived in Coney Island because my father had a restaurant there. I went to Abraham Lincoln High School. Then I went to Kingsborough College for one semester, but I wasn't the best student. I was just having too much fun as a waiter.

In those days, I was working in American nightclubs making good money. I wasn't just working in Chinese restaurants. I decided to drop out of college after one semester. Then I bummed around for a year, working as a waiter here or working as a bartender there, making money.

Then I got a notice to go for a physical to see my draft eligibility. If you're not going to school—college or high school, then you're not what they call a 1-S, 1-Student. That's a student deferment. Then you're classified 1-A and 1-A is the first to go. You're not 1-A until they physically check you out and see that your body's in good shape.

Then they say, "Okay, you don't have asthma, you don't have flat feet. You're a 1-A." Then they'll call you. When I got the notice, I said, "Well, gee. What's 1-A? What's the physical?" They explained it to me just like I explained it to you. I said, "What happens after that?" He said, "After the physical you go home." I said, "Yeah, but when are you going to call me?" He said, "When we're ready to call you we'll call you, but you just go home, go about and do whatever you're going to be doing." I said, "Right now, I don't have a girlfriend and right now, I don't have a particularly great job. Take me now." He says, "No. That's not the way it works. You just go home and when we're ready, we'll call you, assuming your physical is well." I said, "If you call me in six months, I might have a girlfriend. I might have a good job." He told me, "I'm sorry. That's the way the system works, unless you want to join." I said, "Okay, what if I join?" He said, "If you join and you pass the physical, they'll take you right away." I said, "Let's go."

You weren't afraid of—

No.

What stage of the war was happening at this time when they called you?

It was pretty tough I guess, because they say the Tet Offensive was 1968. I enlisted in May of '69, which was after the Tet Offensive, but it didn't matter. If we're going to go, we go, right? I remember the enlistment station. In Coney Island, right next to Nathan's, in the middle of the street is a trailer. The trailer is a recruiting station. It's on Stillwell Avenue. I enlisted. I went to the trailer and—

How old were you at this time?

Nineteen. One week before my 20th birthday.

Did your mom or dad try to intervene?

They didn't know. *(Laughs)* They didn't know until after. I went home to my mother and father and I said, "Eh, I signed up. What the heck?" My mother said, "You crazy kid."

My father didn't really care. My father figured, what the heck? It's all right. He thought it was okay because I'd dropped out of college. You know what I mean? You can't be a Chinese kid and drop out of college. That's the worst thing that you can do, right?

Part of the reason I signed up was because if you're drafted they could put you anywhere. Obviously, the more glamorous and more attractive stuff would be four years. I wasn't prepared to give them four years, but I didn't mind giving them three years. I said, "What have you got for three years?" They gave me a whole list of things.

I did go to Kingsborough for one semester. I did have some sort of illusion of being an accountant or something like that, so the classification was stock control and accounting specialist. I said, "Okay, stock control and accounting specialist, that's for me. I'll take that. Three years." He says, "Fine. Actually, it's three years active and three years reserve. It's six years." I said, "Fine." So I signed up. Stock Control and Accounting School is nothing more than just supply. *(Laughs)* You're out in the field and they need bandages. They're going to order bandages. They need rifles. They need bullets. They need beds. They need blankets. You're in the supply area.

Did you stay Stateside or did they send you off to Vietnam?

Oh, no, no, no, no. Like I told you, my mother was upset. I told my mom, "Mom, don't worry. We're fighting the Vietnamese. They're not going to send Chinese people over there; they'll mistake us for the enemy." My mother said, "Are you sure?" I said, "Yeah, don't worry. They don't send Chinese people over to Vietnam. We look too much like the enemy. They won't send us over."

I enlisted May 16, 1969. I went to Fort Hamilton. I passed the physical. Once I passed the physical, I raised my hand—bingo, I'm in the Army. I called my mother. I said, "I'm not coming home. I'm in the Army. I passed the physical."

I went to Fort Jackson, South Carolina, for basic training. Then I went to advanced training at Fort Lee, Virginia. Then I went to on-the-job training; 90-day on-the-job training at a supply depot in Georgia.

Then, bingo, we went to Vietnam. Actually, before you went to Vietnam they gave you 30 days at home. First week in January, I was in Vietnam.

I spent eleven months and one week in Vietnam. Then I spent 30 days at home and then I thought I was going to get stationed in Oklahoma or Texas or somewhere. "No, no. You're going to Germany."

They sent me to Frankfurt, Germany and I was there for the next year and a half, and that was it. That was the end of my time in the service. I spent a little bit less than three years in active service. When we came back to New York, then we were in the Reserves, but my unit wasn't activated.

In Vietnam, I was very, very fortunate. I was managing the officer's club because I had restaurant experience. I did not get involved with any combat, fortunately.

In the beginning I had to do guard duty from time to time, like once a week, but, all told, to my memory, I don't think I did guard duty more than 3 times. Guard duty meant going out to the perimeter with your rifle, going up to the guard tower and watching out there to see that nobody—that the enemy's not coming. Fortunately, my base never came under attack.

My base was called Qui Nhon Depot. It's a seaport. Supplies come in by ship and they get unloaded in the depot. Now obviously the enemy would love to get to the supplies, but it was too well protected. I personally never came into any sort of enemy fire. I just say that's by the grace of God.

After you returned, what did you do with your life? Did you use your GI Bill?

That's very important, because I'm very, very appreciative of the United States Army and the U.S. Government. The GI Bill of Rights allows us to go back to school. If we go back to school, they give us what they call a subsistence allowance. That helped cover your expenses.

It wasn't a lot. As a matter of fact, from what I understand, the World War II Vets and the Korean Vets got a better deal. In other words, part of their tuition was paid. They never paid any of our tuition. We just got a subsistence allowance.

They didn't pay for your tuition?

No. Remember, Vietnam was a very unpopular war and we didn't win that war. I went back to Kingsborough. Subsistence was $80 a month. [It covered] food, that's it. You couldn't do housing with $80 a month, but it was food. Some food. It was $20 a week. Granted, a quart of fried rice is only a buck and a quarter, but you've only got $80 a month so it's not much food. The monthly subsistence allowed me to go back to Kingsborough. I did finish college. I certainly would say I matured from the three years in active duty. I wised up a little bit.

What were you like before?

Pretty wild.

When you say "wild," what do you mean? Were there a lot of war protests?

No. I never did a war protest. 'Wild' means I'd go out drinking at night. I would gamble, drink. Finish work at 1:00, drink or gamble, play cards or go out dancing till 4:00 in the morning, 5:00 in the morning. How the hell are you going to go to school the next day? It's impossible.

You said the nightclubs you went to were American nightclubs, not the Chinese ones?

Yeah. There were only two Chinese nightclubs, if you want to call it that, but they weren't really—it was a different time. You had, you can say, one Chinese nightclub in Manhattan, but it was owned by Koreans. We had another one, maybe a couple of small nightclubs, but not like it is today. Today, Asians represent 9% of the New York City population. In those days, it was nowhere near—2%.

Racially, were things integrated by then or what is it still kind of divided?

People didn't feel bad about associating with us, but there just weren't that many of us. The graduating class of Lincoln High School was 1,500 students. Class of '67. Only four of us were Chinese.

How about other Asians?

No, no. Hold it. In '67, there was no such thing as Thai people or Cambodian people or Vietnamese people, at least not in Brooklyn. Vietnamese people were in Vietnam. Here's my high school yearbook. This book has got all the students in '67. If you're not Chinese ... there might be four or five of us in here in a class of 1,500. If you're not Chinese, the closest we got was Filipino. In this graduating class, there might have been two Filipinos. That's it.

What was the majority?

White. In Lincoln High School, because of the neighborhood, there weren't that many Blacks either. There were Blacks in New York City, but not in this particular school. Which is impossible today. How could you have 1,500 students and only have five Chinese or seven Asians? Impossible.

It was easy to integrate because there were so few of you?

Yeah. We got along with the other people. There were some real dummies. Remember, this is '67. That's 20 years after the war. They're still calling us Japs. I said, "We're not Japs, we're Chinese." They call you Chinks. "Oh, you want to call me a Chink? Let's go outside and fight," but it wasn't terrible. Other minorities, the Blacks had a harder time. The Puerto Ricans had a harder time getting accepted by the mainstream Whites.

I finished Kingsborough Community College and got my associate degree in accounting. I was still working all the time. As a matter of fact, here's my hack license. See, it's '73. I was driving a cab. I was tending a bar, whatever I needed to do to make a living. I finished Kingsborough and got my accounting degree. I came to work in Chinatown, in a bookkeeping firm. I did that for about 6 or 7 months and I realized, "My goodness," I don't think I will become a CPA for several reasons. I decided—

It's hard.

Yeah, it's hard. It's hard to be a CPA, but I was doing the general ledger for all these garment factories and all these businesses. I see that every one of them needs insurance. They all pay their insurance broker, pay their insurance company. I said, "Okay, let me try insurance."

How old were you now?

Now, I'm 22 or 23. I asked around and they said, "Yeah, you can get your license in four months. You just have to go to school and get your license." I said, "Four or five months. That's not too bad. Okay, let me try it." As a matter of fact, the school was in Times Square area ... in the Loew's State Theatre building. I went to the trade school called Sobelsohn School. I was lucky to pass and I got my insurance broker's license.

And then you opened your business.

That's it. I worked out of my bedroom as a one-man show. Remember, now, I grew up in the restaurant business, so a lot of my friends about the same age, they're waiters or what they call haksam. Haksam is a maître d'.

Does that mean black clothes?

Yeah. Haksam is black jacket. They were my friends. We grew up together. I said, "Hey, introduce me to your boss." I would tell him I'm an insurance broker.

Now, in those days, in the 1970s, there weren't that many Chinese insurance brokers. There were only six of us in Chinatown. There was no Sunset Park. There was no Flushing. There was only Chinatown. We've got plenty of Chinese restaurants all over. Most of them had quite a lot of insurance brokers: Italian, Jewish, Irish, whatever. As long as you were Chinese and you had a broker's license, "Yeah, why not? I'll give you a try."

The restaurants would give me a try. I picked up a customer here, I picked up a customer there. Eventually, I was able to afford an office in Chinatown. It took about 2½ years.

That's fast.

There's my first license right there on the wall. That was November of '76. By '78, I had my first office. I had a part-time secretary. Actually, she was a college friend of mine. Meanwhile, I was still driving a cab at night to pay for the rent and pay for things, and that's it. I started from one worker to a full-time worker.

You sold insurance in the daytime and then you drove taxis at night?

Correct. Taxi or waiting on tables or bartending, whatever. It was good money. Then I met my wife and married her in '79. We had our first kid in October of '80. When she was pregnant with our first kid, she asked me not to drive a taxi anymore because it was kind of dangerous.

I said, "Okay, I'm not going to drive a taxi anymore." That's when I went back to waiting on tables or tending a bar. It took me till 1983. By '83, the businesses built up enough. I didn't have to do it no more. I just concentrated on insurance in '83.

Now you were also the president of Chinatown Chamber of Commerce?

I was chairman of the Chinese Chamber of Commerce in New York for six years. I've been on the Board of Directors of the Chinese Chamber of Commerce for more than 10 years. Today, I'm the chairman of the Chinatown Business Improvement District.

I support the BID.

Thank you. We finally got approved. I'm the first chairman of the Chinatown Business Improvement District. I don't mind. I've given back a lot back to Chinatown. I enjoy it. It's a lot of work, but I'm glad to help.

People here in your office are speaking so many languages.

I have workers here who speak Cantonese, Mandarin, Tagalog, Spanish, Vietnamese and Korean. I have a pretty well-rounded staff.

Your clientele is mostly in the Chinatown area?

No, my clients can be all over. They're primarily in New York, but I also have people from New Jersey, Pennsylvania, and Massachusetts. We're licensed in all those states.

I want to ask you a little bit about what things were like for Chinese Americans. In history books it says that during the Vietnam War, that was the first time that the Asian American identity came to be—

Pretty much.

That's when Asian people first became political. Before, they weren't.

Correct.

The Asian people came together because they had to have a political voice.

They didn't really come together. They didn't go together. We kept to ourselves. In my father's day and even in our day during the Vietnam War, we more or less kept to ourselves. Yeah, we were the baby boomer generation. We're Chinese, but pretty much, we didn't get involved in politics too much.

What really was the awakening of what it means to be Chinese, and who cares, was after Nixon came back from China. President Nixon went to China and shook hands and had dinner with Mao Zedong. Now, everybody was wondering what's this Chinese about. Whatever year it was that Nixon went to China was also about the same time that Bruce Lee became popular. Now, he became a big star and everybody says, "Wow. What's Chinese?"

When Nixon went to China they printed his menu because they had a nice big banquet dinner for him in China. Maotai, that's a type of Chinese liquor. Maotai was served and now, man, that was selling like crazy in Chinatown.

All the white people wanted it. Maotai, typically I think, is bottled at over 100 proof. In those days, most spirits were bottled at 86 proof. Today, they're bottled at 80 proof. And Peking Duck was served at the banquet. All the restaurants here were serving that. Everyone became more curious about it. That's when it became more active. Then when Nixon opened up China. After that, immigration was easier. We had more Chinese coming over from the mainland. That kind of changed the atmosphere a little bit. That's why now you say, "What? How can it be? You only had five Chinese in your whole entire high school. That's impossible." Yeah, it's impossible for you to imagine today, but all that immigration happened after Nixon opened up China.

Do you want to talk about maybe the BID or your work with the Chinatown Commerce or what it is or how it helps Chinatown?

We lost a lot of businesses. The garment industry has partly disappeared. There's a few left. It started happening in the '90s. We lost it to foreign competition. Now, it's cheaper to do the garments in India or in the Philippines or in China. We lost some of it already in the '90s. But 9/11—9/11 really choked us all. It went on for a month or at least three weeks, trucks couldn't even get down to Chinatown to pick up the garments. Factories were closed for a month. The suppliers and manufacturers had to use alternate sources. Once they went to alternate sources, it was difficult for them to come back to Chinatown when Chinatown did open up again. We've lost a lot of businesses in the garment industry in Chinatown.

It used to be, no matter where you are, you have to come back to Chinatown to do your shopping. Now you don't have to. You've got Sunset Park, you've got Edison, New Jersey, you've got Flushing. Who's going to go to Chinatown to buy vegetables? Who's going to go to Chinatown to see their doctor? Now you don't have to go to Chinatown to see a doctor. Your Chinese doctor is in Staten Island ... in Edison, New Jersey ... in Flushing.

What's the attraction for Chinatown? Tourism. Tourism is a big attraction. We've got to keep them coming. One of the missions of the BID is to generate business. You've got to improve businesses. That's one of the big jobs.

Now, how're you going to get people to come down to Chinatown when it stinks? You've got to clean it up and you have to teach people how to clean it up and maintain cleanliness. Teach people how important it is. That's what people in Oklahoma care about, that it's clean. Education of the shopkeepers is very important, and that's one of the missions of Chinatown BID.

Has Chinatown gotten better now after its decline post-9/11?

It's certainly better than it was in the immediate year after 9/11. We've still got a ways to go. It's hard to say it's gotten better, because now with this economic recession I'm seeing more empty stores than I ever saw before.

These medals on the wall, what are they?

This is a National Defense Medal. This is the Vietnam Campaign Medal and this is the Vietnam Service Medal.

Were you also involved in the Kimlau Post for many years?

At the Kimlau Post, I've been the sergeant-at-arms for certainly over 15 years and I've been a member of the color guard for more than 25 years. I started with the Kimlau Post because my father was a World War II veteran. The Kimlau Post was created after World War II. My father was a member in the 1950s. The Kimlau Post was very considerate of children, to be sure. I was a child and my father would take me up there for Christmas parties and Thanksgiving parties. That's how I got to know the Kimlau Post.

After the Vietnam War, I got involved with the Kimlau Post by just walking by. Some World War II veteran was soliciting donations for poppies, little paper red flowers that look like poppies, on a wire. You used to stick them in the buttonhole of your lapel and they've got a little tag there that says American Legion. It shows that you supported the American Legion. There's a certain period in the course of the year when the American Legion, as their fundraising, sells poppies. It's like how Girl Scouts sell Girl Scout cookies. I said, "Sure, I'll make a donation. I'm a veteran too." Right away, he said, "If you're a veteran too, you should be a member." He got me in to become a member and that was sometime in the early 1980s.

CHAPTER TWENTY-THREE

Gabe Mui 梅本立 (1946–   )
U.S. Army

Gabe Mui, who has served as Commander and Adjutant of the American Legion Kimlau Post in New York for 12 years and still going, volunteers after his full-time job every weekday to do work for the organization, which has been culturally, socially, and legislatively essential to the vitality of the Chinese community in New York. He is part of the backbone of New York's Chinatown American Legion Post.

I was Commander of the American Legion at Kimlau Post from 2007 till 2009. Basically, I represented the Post when we participated at veterans' functions and traveled to conventions. Elaine Chao, the Secretary of Labor under President Bush, invited us to Washington for the Lunar New Year celebration in those years, and I attended. I was also invited to attend the Asian Pacific Islander Month celebration at the White House. It really gives me good memories.

And does the Kimlau Post have one of the biggest memberships for an American Legion post?

It's the biggest for Chinese American membership. At its peak, the Kimlau Post had 620 members for the two years that I was the commander. There are quite a few Chinese American Posts around the country: San Francisco, Boston, Houston, Philadelphia, Seattle, and Chicago. But the Kimlau Post here in New York is the biggest and most active one. We participate in all Legion Functions and serve veterans.

How did you get involved with the Kimlau Post?

I joined in 2000. I was asked to join quite a few times before then, but with my kids being small, I had to take care of them. They participated in sports so I would travel all over the place and really had no time. In 2000 [when my kids were grown up] I finally decided it was time to join.

I live in Plainview, Long Island. I'm here at the Kimlau Post six days a week. I drive to the train station, park the car and then take the Long Island railroad, and then I take the subway here.

I retired [from work] two years ago, in 2009. Even before I retired, I came here almost every day because I worked on 14th Street. During lunchtime I came down. After work I came down. So basically I've come here almost every

day for the last seven years.

Wow. So this Post is a big part of your life.

Yes.

Can you talk about where and when you were born? What was it like growing up?

I was born in China back in December 1946. I left my village when I was 8 years old and spent about six months in Canton [Guangdong] in the city of Guangzhou. After that, my family moved to Hong Kong.

What was your village?

Long Hung Ley [龍騰里].

What was your family's reason for moving?

For a better life. Actually, at the time, my grandfathers on both sides were already here in the United States, in Chicago. My sisters were here. My mother's side of the family was all here because my uncle served during World War II and he was able to get his wife and family over, long before we came. Everybody was basically in the laundry or in the restaurant.

When I was 18, we came directly to New York from Hong Kong because China was under Communist control and we had a chance to leave. We came for freedom and better opportunities for work and education.

When you were in high school did you already know that you would be going to the U.S?

Yes. As a matter of fact, we knew in Hong Kong that our stay was just temporary but temporary turned into 10 years because it was hard, at that time, in the early '60s, to immigrate. Then Kennedy made it easier for all immigrants.

That's when we came over.

When I first arrived, I was very fortunate that someone took me into the restaurant business. I only spent weekends there and I was able to continue going to school. During summer I worked full-time to support myself.

Where did you go to school?

I started an associate's degree at RCA Institute. RCA is Radio Corporation of America. They had two separate curriculums. One teaches you the trade: you major in electronics, you learn to repair televisions, whatever. But I took the college credit course so, basically, I learned electronics and all the theories, and later on I was able to complete my bachelor's degree somewhere else.

Radio Corporation America needed technicians so they partnered with some educators to open their institution so they could train people the way they wanted.

How did you get involved with the military?

I was drafted. When I was still working at the restaurant on the weekends, going to school during the day, I was able to obtain deferment. If you were going to school, they didn't draft you yet. Near graduation time, they use a lottery system based on your birthday, and after graduation you can't defer anymore. My lottery number was number 3, so I knew I was going to get drafted. I found a job at Con Edison after I graduated. About six months later, I was drafted. That was in 1970. I was 21 or 22.

Were you scared to death?

No, not really. My mother was but I wasn't. By then, so many of my friends already got drafted or volunteered so I wasn't scared. On television, we hear reports every day of how many people died, but I didn't have a choice. Draftees are only required to serve for two years, you know. When I was drafted, I had been living in the U.S. approximately four years.

I reported to Fort Dix for basic training. My AIT [Advanced Individual Training] was also at Fort Dix. My MOS, the Military Occupation Service, was transportation. My training was to drive a medium truck, the regular 18-wheeler, and I got assigned to the Transportation Unit in Germany.

My total military service was only 19 months because in 1972, President Nixon passed a law. The war in Vietnam was basically coming to an end and they were drawing troop levels down, so they just let people leave early. So I left about four to five months earlier than I was originally scheduled.

What did you carry in the trucks?

Sometimes it was a whole truckload of boots and other supplies. Sometimes a whole truckload of ammunition.

Any first impressions or special experiences in Germany?

Well, I actually liked it because I was not confined to a base or the camp. My barrack was basically in the middle of the city. When we were not performing in our travelling, we went into the city often. And because my job was to deliver stuff, I was able to travel and see Germany, a lot more than other people. And also, whenever there was a 3-day pass, we would go visit places. I went to Paris, Amsterdam, and Switzerland on my own.

When you started basic training, how many Chinese Americans were there?

In my unit, I was the only one. My company was about 150 people. In my platoon, there were 40-some people. I was the only one.

Since the Vietnam War was a war against an Asian country, did you get insults because you're Asian? Did they treat you or see you differently?

No. I wasn't treated any differently than everybody else. I did whatever I was told. I did whatever was required of me. Even though I was the only Chinese, I was not treated differently.

The only time I felt that they noticed I'm Chinese was once in basic training. One of the exercises involved a long stick. This is hand-to-hand combat and you try to fight the other guy. My drill sergeant wasn't happy with the way people were fighting. They had no form. Obviously, at that time, everybody knew about kung fu. So me being Chinese, he said to me, "You! Go out there and show them what to do!" But I didn't have any kung fu training either so I just did the same thing they did. So I'm not any different. But that was the only time I noticed that they may have thought, "Hey, there is a Chinese here."

What happened when you returned?

Before I was drafted, I already had a job at Con Edison. At that time, the law required that when I came back from the military, I'd have my position back, so I went right back to work. I stayed there until I retired. I got married and had three children.

For the longest time, I didn't even know about the American Legion's Kimlau Post. Because when I first came out from service, Con Edison had their own Post. I'd have belonged to the Kimlau Post a long time ago if I'd known about it earlier.

You served so much time here and did so many things for the American Legion. What are some of the biggest achievements that you're most proud of with the Kimlau Post?

A lot of it is routine. A lot of events we do every year. So we just maintain and try to improve every year. That's all.

What you are doing these days, and what brings you to the American Legion Kimlau Post here every day? Because it's such a huge commitment.

I was asked to serve as commander, so I made myself available almost every day. Whenever I had time, I came. In fact, I even changed my work schedule because we have flexible schedules. So I moved my hours up. Usually, I was the first one at the company. I was there at 6:00 every day. I got out at 3:30 or so and after that, I spent my time here until 5:00 or 5:30 and then I went home. Sometimes, I even came during lunchtime because I feel that if I commit or agree to do something, I want to do it well. So in two years that I was the commander, I came here basically every day.

Can you talk a little bit about how the American Legion came to have such a big role in Chinatown [in New York]? Do you want to talk about its early history?

After World War II, Chinese American veterans returning from World War II felt there was a need to help [our community] and started this American Legion post. So our post, at that time, through the American Legion, with the help of congressmen and senators, eliminated the Exclusion Acts. So that's why Chinatown is more vibrant, because families were able to come over from China. Now in Chinatown we have kids and young people. We were pretty much the leader in that.

And there was another incident, in the 1960s, when they tried to build a jailhouse in Chinatown, on Baxter and Walker Streets. Well, the building's actually there, but originally, they wanted it bigger, to extend it all the way out. They wanted the whole block. So, at that time, our American Legion Post, together with the CCBA [Chinese Consolidated Benevolent Association], fought against it and so the city compromised. Instead of the whole block being a prison, now you also have a senior home over there.

There were many other times when we helped our community. Because most of our members speak English, and also through the American Legion, we're able to get help from outside. So we are very respected in Chinatown because of all the work we have done. Even now at the CCBA, when we go to the meetings, we are prominent and get elected to the Executive Committee. And when a resolution comes up that we don't feel is right for Chinatown, we stand up against it. We speak our mind and overturn it. A lot of associations are afraid to speak up. They probably don't have any opinions but we're basically the ones that do that.

And then the Kimlau Gate at Chatham Square was built by this Post.

Yes. The Memorial Arch. We built that to dedicate to the veterans who sacrificed their lives in World War II and all the wars. That was dedicated in 1964 or 1965.

CHAPTER TWENTY-FOUR

Richard Wong 黃復興 (1935–   )
U.S. Navy

Born and raised in Manhattan's Chinatown in the 1930s, Richard Wong became one of the earliest Chinese Americans to practice law in New York, specializing in immigration law. He was appointed by Governor Hugh Carey to the New York State Human Rights Appeals Board in 1976, and taught at St. John's University School of Law as adjunct professor of law in 1980. Before becoming a lawyer he was an engineer. He shares his family's history in the U.S. and memories of growing up in Manhattan's Chinatown, including rough encounters with kids from Little Italy on his way to Stuyvesant. He is married to Mae Wong and has two children.

Education is very important. My two grandfathers, in the late 1800s, were both able to read and write fluently in Chinese. In those days very few people were able to do that. Most people had to come illegally as paper sons and laborers. But my grandfathers were able to overcome the Exclusion Acts with their education. Because of that, education became very important in our family—that's what allowed us to come into this country as merchants.

My maternal grandfather had an uncle here in the United States and my paternal grandfather had a brother here [who was in Cleveland] in the 1800s. And the money sent back home allowed them to learn how to read and write Chinese. So they were able to get around the Exclusion Acts by coming to America as merchants. Because of that, my grandparents were very anxious for us to get as much education as possible.

I was the first grandson to finish college. Both of them were alive to see me graduate from college in 1956.

I was born on July 23, 1935, at 36 Mott Street. My mother was born in the United States. My father came when he was five from Sun Wei [near Taishan] in China. I have five sisters, four older, one younger. I was the only son. I was special.

My mother was a housewife and later worked for the Bank of China. My father worked at my grandfather's grocery store, Kung Jung, at 20 Pell Street. My father drove a truck to make deliveries throughout the city, which was uncommon, because few Chinese Americans had licenses or could drive.

My grandfather could write Chinese and had a business, so as a merchant he could bring my grandmother. She came over around 1908. That's when my mother was born. My other grandfather also came to the United States as a merchant.

In the 1800s Chinatown was just half a street. Pell Street, Doyer Street, and Mott St below Canal. Mott Street was always Chinese. Then I lived on Bayard Street, which was also Chinese. I went to P.S. 23, which was across the street from where I lived. Every day American school was from 9:00 to 3:00, and then Chinese school was from 5:00 to 7:00. Chinese School was on Mott Street, at the Chinese Benevolent Society.

Going to two schools is what all the kids did. I didn't get good at Chinese. I learned how to cheat or get through without learning. I got hit with a ruler a lot at Chinese School. When I got home, my grandfather would see the red on my hands and give me another couple of swats because he saw I was bad. Hitting was permissible then. Being naughty, I never got a diploma. In American School, public school, it was about three-quarters Chinese, and one-quarter Italian.

We lived in a cocoon down here because we were pretty well protected. The people who ran the stores knew all the kids in the neighborhood. If they saw we were bad they reported us to our parents.

The teacher who flunked me out of Chinese School gave me an honorary degree 20 years later when I became a lawyer and translated in Chinese to my clients. On stage, to an audience of 12-year-olds, I said "I have three degrees: a bachelors in engineering, a masters degree in business, and a juris doctor of law, but this is the most meaningful for me because it was the hardest to get." It was in the papers.

After sixth grade I went to P.S. 130 on Baxter Street for junior high school, seventh and eighth grade. That's when we crossed Canal Street and left China-town and went to Little Italy. We had to always worry about Italian kids; they were tough kids. We went to school in a group for self-protection. But then some of the Italian kids got to know some of the Chinese kids and stuck up for us, and then the rest of them stopped bothering us. If I was late and missed the group, and had to go to school alone, I had to run to school and run home to avoid getting beat up.

Then I went to Stuyvesant High School. I was very good at math and science. I was bad at English, history, and language, which was true of most Chinese kids. That's why I decided to go to engineering school. There were a lot of Chinese kids and Jewish kids at Stuyvesant. Jewish kids didn't pick on us. They were very tolerant. We always took off school for the Jewish Holidays. Stuyvesant was on 15th Street. I took the elevated train from Canal Street to 14th Street. Chatham Square and South Ferry were the last stops.

I graduated high school in 1952. I went to Rensselaer Polytechnic for college. I became a mechanical engineer in 1956. I worked for a company, Ebasco Services, and they designed and built power plants and steam electric generation stations. So I worked for them for a couple years, and I started getting bored, and I thought I wanted to see the world, do something different.

I wanted to fly jet planes off a carrier, so I went to the Navy to take an interview. I did very well on the written part of the test, but couldn't pass the eye test. I thought my eyes were good but when they put drops in, I couldn't see the small letters.

Since I couldn't fly, I still decided to go into the Navy. I was in the Civil Engineer Corps, which does engineering work for the Navy and also Seabees. CB stands for Construction Battalion, and then they made the Seabees mascot.

I was stationed first on Guam as an assistant for a year and a half doing what's known as Public Works engineering—maintenance of buildings and grounds. I also took care of transportation—buses, trucks, cars. Then in the last year and a half, I was the Public Works officer in charge of the whole department, doing the same kind of work in Stockton, California, at what is known as Stockton Annex of the Navy Supply Center. One of the highlights of my experience was being the head of the department, with 250 employees. I was the top leader of the department when I was just 24 or 25 years old. Then I was released from active duty in 1972. After active duty, I continued in the reserves for 20 years. That's how I was able to retire as a commander of the U.S. Navy.

After active duty, I went back to Ebasco. When I had first started at Ebasco, I was doing an MBA at NYU in the evening. It was one block from where I worked, so it was easy. I got a degree from Stern [School of Business] in 1969.

In 1964 I married Mabel Wing, known as Mae now. We met at a dance. Interestingly enough, I found out that we were delivered by the same midwife even though she grew up in the Bronx.

I got bored of Engineering, and there was discrimination. I went to Law School, where there were only two Asians at NYU. Even if you graduated from

Richard Wong with his family

NYU you couldn't get a job unless you opened your own practice.

I entered law school in 1966 and graduated in 1969. Then I worked at Simpson Thatcher & Bartlett as a summer associate attorney. That was the first time they were hiring Chinese. At that time, my law professor Judge Irving Younger was running for office as judge of the Civil Court. I helped in his campaign. I was on law revue with Rudy Giuliani [Judge Younger was his mentor]. Judge Younger got elected and because I was on the law revue and helped with his campaign he offered me the job of law secretary, which I accepted.

It was unusual then, because law clerks were usually picked by the local political [Democratic or Republican] club that helped them win the judge election. At that time the salary of a law clerk was $10,000, as opposed to law firms paying $15,000. My intention was to go with a private practice by myself in Chinatown. As law secretary, I could start my practice at the same time too (but you couldn't appear in court). Now it's considered a conflict of interest.

The judge resigned after a few years to go into private practice and teaching. So that ended my job as law secretary. So I devoted myself full time to my private practice in Chinatown. At that time, there were only four or five Chinese American practicing lawyers.

I started working with Benjamin Gim and we became partners. Ben Gim was a nationally known immigration lawyer, who was also President of the National Immigration Lawyers Association.

While I was working at the practice, I was trying to lose weight. When I got suntanned and thin, people said to me, "You used to be white and fat and now you're dark and skinny." To the Chinese, being white and fat means prosperity. Being dark and skinny means you're poor.

Ben Gim taught at Columbia and I taught at St. John's Law School. When I taught at St. John's and the teacher evaluations came back, I got two or three students who said I was "best teacher at St. John's." That has always been a feather in my cap.

Then I was appointed to the New York State Human Rights Appeals Board by Gov. Hugh Carey in 1976. I was going around the state, hearing appeals. In 1980 I was adjunct professor of Law at St. John's Law School in Queens. I was appointed as a trustee to Beth Israel Medical Center (the only Asian American on the board to this day). We are pleased they now have an Asian Services Unit. Then in 1985, I retired from the practice of law.

My advice is make friends, never make enemies, because enemies never forget and friends sometimes forget. Always give encouragement and support. My philosophy: We believe in giving, and giving back to the community. Whatever you give always comes back in double. That's why I feel very blessed that I have good fortune.

It's the theme of our lives—being active, going on boards, giving back. I sat on the board of the NYU Law Alumni Association and for 25 or more years. I was the only Asian. Now my daughter Boji is on the board. I am an Honorary Trustee at Beth Israel Medical Center. Mae was always involved in PTAs [Parent Teacher Associations] and built up the PTA at the schools our children attended. She got air conditioning for our children's grade school. We believe in being involved with the community and giving back.

CHAPTER TWENTY-FIVE

Tom Wing (1934–   )
U.S. Army

Thomas Wing was a colonel in the United States Army. He completed 30 years of active duty service in the Field Artillery, serving in the U.S., Thailand, Vietnam, and Germany. In civilian life, he was a senior military analyst working for Science Applications International Corporation and developed and conducted simulations for the Department of Defense, Department of the Army, and the United States Marine Corps. He lives in Maryland with his wife and has three sons, two daughters-in-law and three grandchildren. Colonel Wing talks about growing up Chinese American in Jersey City, New Jersey in the 1930s, and making his career in the military.

My father was born in the United States in 1882. My mother was born in Canton, China in 1897. My father brought my mother over from China and they settled in the vicinity of Sacramento and he became a dairy farmer. And after so many years on the farm, the both of them moved to New Jersey and that's where they finally settled and raised their family. My three older brothers and my three sisters and I were born in New Jersey.

My father was born in Seattle, Washington, and he was quite an entrepreneur. In his lifetime, he was a restaurateur, a grocery store owner, and a laundry man. And all during this time, in addition to raising the family, my mother was there helping him.

So do you know who was the first in your ancestry to settle in the United States?

Well, it would be my father's father, in the mid-1800s, since my father was born in 1882 in Seattle, Washington.

My brothers and sisters and I were all born in Jersey City, New Jersey. Raised there and went to school there and essentially that's where I grew up.

When were you born?

Do I have to tell you?

Please?

1934.

And what was it like growing up in Jersey City in the '30s and '40s?

Where we lived, in Jersey City, in retrospect, it was truly amazing. Within a two-block radius, my parents, specifically my mother, never had to leave that two-block radius to shop and do the normal things that mothers did when they were raising their families. In our neighborhood we had two grocery stores, two restaurants, a barber shop, a fish store, a candy store that sold newspapers and candy and goodies and other things like that. We had a theater. So essentially there was never [a need] for venturing beyond that two-block radius for shopping to buy family necessities. There was public transportation within walking distance.

My neighborhood was truly a melting pot. We were the only Chinese American family in that neighborhood. There were Italian, Scandinavian, Polish, Greek, and black families. And growing up, all the kids hung out with each other. And the nice part about that two-block radius, with all of the families in it, was that all the parents knew the children of other families. When anybody got in trouble, there was no such thing as calling the police. It was mother to mother, mother to father, and the parents settled it all. And the children knew that. The worst thing growing up was to be reprimanded or punished by your parents because of something that you did, that they heard of from another parent.

All the parents got along together also?

Yes, and they all knew one another.

And so school was a really nice experience then?

School was a good experience. Being the only Chinese American family in the neighborhood, in grammar school I was the only Chinese American student at the time—of course, preceded by brothers and sisters. But when I was going to grade school, I was the only Chinese American student. Similarly, in high school, I was the only Chinese American in my class, again preceded by my brothers and sisters. And in college, similarly, I was the only Chinese American in my graduating class.

You went to college before the military?

Yes, I went to college before the military. I participated in the Reserve Officer Training Corps program, and I was commissioned a second lieutenant upon graduation, and then started my military career. I majored in Chemistry and upon commissioning I was called to active duty, and I never left the Army.

I attended Saint Peter's College in Jersey City, and I graduated in 1955. I was commissioned in 1955, upon graduation. And I was called to active duty early in 1956, and spent the remaining 30 years in the United States Army. When I was in college, from 1951 to 1955, the Korean War was ongoing.

Then I graduated in '55; there was peace at the time. And I pursued a military career and was assigned within the United States and to an overseas assignment to Thailand. Then the Vietnam War broke out and I was assigned to Vietnam from 1968 to 1969. There were further assignments in the United

States and the Federal Republic of Germany.

Maybe you can talk a little bit about how you decided to do ROTC. Was there any specific event that made you decide to do it?

There was always an attraction to the military in my mind. The only person in my family who served in the military was one of my brothers, who was in the United States Navy during World War II. So, although I did not come from a family that has a military lineage, my brother was in the Navy. Once his tour was completed he left the Navy. So he did not pursue a career in the military.

But there always seemed to be an attraction to the military for me. It was the structure, the organization, the discipline, traveling around the world. So when I matriculated at Saint Peter's College, and they had an ROTC program, that presented an avenue for me to pursue the military, not knowing that I would really pursue a career of 30 years, at the time. So I entered the ROTC program and when I graduated and was commissioned and called to active duty, early in 1956, my first assignments were rather interesting in that they sent me to school to learn about air defense missiles.

At the time, the air defense of the United States was a high priority because it was during the Cold War. There was always the threat of aircraft bombing, invading the coastal cities, as well as interior cities of the United States. So the United States Army developed an Air Defense program to help counter that threat. So when the Army sent me to a missile school and subsequent assignments in Air Defense Artillery Units, that was very interesting.

Did they ask you what kind of specialty you were interested in, or was that something that they decided?

Well, when I graduated from the ROTC program, I was commissioned in the Artillery. Every graduate from the ROTC program is commissioned into a specific branch of the Army, and my particular branch at the time was Artillery.

And were you happy with this—their selection for you?

Yes, I was pleased.

What were the favorite divisions or specialties that you were interested in?

I was not familiar with the Army other than the fact that it was a very large organization. So, as a second lieutenant, your eyes are really wide open, you're trying to absorb a lot of information and the environment. The priority for me was learning my job and not looking too much beyond that. At the time, as a 21-year-old second lieutenant, I was assigned to schools, so I studied to learn everything there was about Air Defense Artillery, and subsequently I was assigned to a unit in the vicinity of Chicago, Illinois, which was one of the cities identified for Air Defense protection.

I found the assignment challenging and interesting. Challenging not only from a technological standpoint, but challenging from the standpoint of having

Cpt. Wing, 1962

to deal with men—as a second lieutenant, I was in charge of 30 men. And when I look back at the composition age-wise of those 30 men, and there were no women in the Army at that time, I was probably the youngest person among those 30. And so, as a second lieutenant, I had to wrestle with the age difference, me as lieutenant, dealing with sergeants and specialists, as part of my organization of the platoon, in directing and convincing them to do things that had to be done, meanwhile recognizing that some were much older than I was. It was a challenge in learning how to deal with men in the military, and I would imagine it's the same thing as a young supervisor dealing with older people in a private company.

Being a Chinese American second lieutenant never presented a problem to me. Again, in my unit, I was the only Chinese American person, whether an officer or an enlisted person. Race never came up. In fact, throughout my military career, race was never an issue. I have no negative experience concerning racial issues from other people toward me or me toward other people.

How about in the Vietnam War?

I was in the Republic of Vietnam during 1968 and 1969. I was a major at the time and during that year I was assigned to the 1st Infantry Division Artillery, more specifically the operations staff officer or the S3 of the 1st Battalion, 5th Artillery, which provided direct support to the 1st Infantry Brigade of the 1st Infantry Division.

Again, I was the only Chinese American officer in my unit, and fighting the North Vietnamese and the Viet Cong, even though they were of Asian ethnicity, that never bothered me. I was assigned, as others were assigned, to fight the Viet Cong and the North Vietnamese. So, in my mind, they were the enemy, and we were sent there to defeat the enemy.

What did your job involve while you were in Vietnam?

The first part of my tour in Vietnam I was assigned to the G3 Section of the United States Army Vietnam. I was an operations staff officer, or assistant G3. And as a staff officer I was dealing with force development issues that involved keeping track of the units that were being assigned to Vietnam.

The last half of the tour was, as I previously mentioned, I was the S3 of the 1st Battalion, 5th Artillery. As a direct support artillery unit to the 1st Infantry Brigade, it was our job provide artillery support to that infantry brigade during their combat operations in Vietnam. Whenever the 1st Infantry Brigade was maneuvering throughout the terrain, we had to provide the artillery support to protect the infantry, as well as defeating the enemy when they called for fire support. So it was my job as the S3 to ensure that those fires were timely and accurate during combat missions.

Can you explain a little bit what artillery support means exactly? Is it getting weapons, or to make sure—

Sure. The 1st Battalion, 5th Artillery consisted of three firing batteries with a total of eighteen 105-millimeter howitzers. In the battalion, each firing battery with six howitzers provided direct support to at least one battalion of the 1st Infantry Brigade. For example, when the infantry battalion was out on a mission to reconnoiter an area, they always had the fires of at least one firing battery of 105-millimeter howitzers.

What were some of your most memorable experiences in the military? A best moment, or the scariest moment, or worst moment?

Well, let's start with the—I wouldn't say scariest, but threatening moment. It occurred while I was in Vietnam. The Viet Cong and North Vietnamese attacked the fire base where I was located. And it started with a heavy mortar and

Maj. Wing, Mrs. Wing
and son Chris, November 1967

Promotion to colonel, 1 June 1977,
Fort Monroe, Virginia

Colonel Wing, 1985

rocket attack at night. The attack lasted through the early morning, and in total the attack must have lasted some 8 or 10 hours. And although I was directing artillery fire support, the infantry was defending the fire base. It was the first time that I had experienced heavy enemy fire with rockets and mortar rounds exploding on the fire base. So it was threatening. The attack was defeated. During the morning hours when the infantry went out to recon and survey the perimeter, there were enemy in the barbed wire. So that was the most threatening experience in my military career. This was in '69.

The most important event in my military career happened in the Federal Republic of Germany where, as Lieutenant Colonel, I was selected to command a field artillery battalion. As an officer, one of the goals is to be a commander, at any level: platoon commander, battery commander, company commander, battalion commander, brigade commander, division commander, corps commander, and so on. When you're lucky enough to put "Commander" in your signature box, it represents a lot. And that's what virtually anybody who pursues a military career wants to become. Because then you're responsible for a lot of things, most of which is the health and welfare of the men and women in your command.

In my military career, I never thought that I had to do things extra special or harder, because of my ethnicity. I had my individual goals, and I knew what I wanted to do, and I knew that I would try my darnedest to do it. And there was never in the back of my mind that I was going to try harder because people are watching, because of my ethnicity. Going back to my earlier comments, I never experienced any undue pressure from anybody because of my ethnicity. Any pressure was self-imposed, and those pressures were to succeed at whatever I set out to do.

And how about when you came out of the Army, after your 30 years?

Well, after I retired, I went to work for Science Applications International Corporation. It is a science and engineering company that does a lot of work for the federal government, state government, and private companies. And when I joined that firm I came on as a Senior Military Analyst, and during my time with SAIC, I conducted and formed a lot of studies for the Defense Department, the Department of Army, and the Marine Corps.

And if you could sum it up for me—because you traveled a bit, all the places you were stationed?

Early on in my career I was assigned to Chicago, Illinois; Fort Worth, Texas; Fort Sill, Oklahoma; Fort Wainwright, Alaska; Fort Dix, New Jersey; Fort Leavenworth, Kansas; Fort Benjamin Harrison, Indiana; Fort Benning, Georgia; Thailand; Vietnam; Germany; and Washington, DC.

Can you remind us what happened in Thailand?

In Thailand, this was 1963 to 1964. I was a captain at the time and I was assigned to the Joint United States Army Military Advisory Group as a Field Artillery Advisor to a Royal Thai Army Artillery battalion, stationed in Udorn, which is located in the northern part of Thailand, just south of Vientiane, Laos, some 50 kilometers.

What is life like from wartime to peacetime to wartime to peacetime? How does that factor in to your personal life? Did your family travel with you?

Okay, let me take the family life. Family life in the military is not an easy situation. There are a lot of hardships that are placed on the family. And how

Col. Wing and family, retirement, 1985

The Wing Family, 2009. Not shown: a daughter-in-law and two grand children

well a family does in the military is so much dependent upon your wife. The wife is the glue.

As a bachelor in the military, it's easier because it's just you and your responsibility is only to yourself. But when you have a spouse then there are other responsibilities. And as your family grows, there are even more responsibilities. The least of which, with children, is education. And the moving around throughout a military career can be positive to some families and negative to others.

I was lucky. My family supported me and they survived. I have three grown sons, who are now on their own. And my wife has been with me all this time. During my career, there were a couple of times when families were not allowed to travel. And in my career, when I went to Thailand, it was an unaccompanied tour, which meant that although I was married, I was the only one who could go to Thailand, to where I was assigned. And of course the other time was when I was in Vietnam.

During those times, because we were separated, my wife took care of our family. The best time, as far as our family is concerned, was my assignment to Germany. My travel was limited because of the Cold War era, [so] my wife and oldest son at the time had a better time than I did. And then with the birth of twins and coming back to the Washington D.C. area, watching the twins grow up and my oldest grow up as they went through the public schools in Montgomery County and on to college—that was nice. That was great.

PART IV: PERSIAN GULF WAR

Victory After Vietnam

The Persian Gulf War was considered a flawless war, with few American casualties and use of high-precision bombing for five weeks and four days of ground assault. Iraqis were driven out of Kuwait and Saddam Hussein retreated.[27]

Broadcast footage on television, in programs such as CNN's *Desert Storm: The Victory* (1991) and CBS's *Desert Triumph* (1991), presented the Persian Gulf War as a clean, clearcut U.S. victory, not another Vietnam War.[28]

"If there must be war, I promise there will not be any murky endings," President George H.W. Bush stated in a televised speech. "I've told the American people before that this will not be another Vietnam, and I repeat this here tonight. Our troops will have the best possible support in the entire world, and they will not be asked to fight with one hand tied behind their back."[29]

A Murky Ending

Analyses after the war showed that the U.S. might not have been as successful in its operations as touted. There were at least 35 deaths from friendly fire. The anti-missile system credited for saving Israel, according to Israeli intelligence, shot down only one Iraqi Scud missile. American aircraft and Special Forces units which Colin Powell and Norman Schwarzkopf credited for demolishing most of Iraq's fleet of mobile scud launchers destroyed none. The hit rate of stealth bombers and of American smart bombs dropped by F117s, according to the General Accounting Office (GAO) in a report in 1997, ranged from 41 to 60 percent—about the same effectiveness as bombs without expensive high-tech guidance systems.[30]

Many Gulf War veterans reported symptoms of fatigue, moodiness, muscle and joint pain, shortness of breath, memory loss, and rashes upon returning home.[31] They sought help from Veterans Administration (VA) hospitals and doctors, but many patients' symptoms were relegated to the category of "psychological stress."[32]

Vietnam War veterans had already set a precedent in demanding that the government and military acknowledge that toxins such as Agent Orange, used to clear the jungles, caused serious illnesses, including cancer. As a result, the VA was compelled to issue disability and death compensation. Even so, Persian Gulf veterans had to go through a parallel situation of having to convince the government that their illnesses were real.[33]

Recognizing Gulf War Syndrome

With intense lobbying from veterans' groups, a presidential advisory committee was formed in 1996 to investigate Gulf War Syndrome. In hearings in

1998 before a House subcommittee, health officials finally acknowledged that 15% of those sent to war (more than 90,000 Gulf War veterans) were experiencing more than just psychological stress and had been exposed to something serious while on active duty.[34] Whether it was from exposure to chemicals when Americans bombed Iraq's chemical and biological facilities, or from vaccines provided to help soldiers survive nerve gas or anthrax, or contamination from the fallout of antitank shells and bombs used against Iraqis, is unclear.[35]

In this section Tony Lee talks about discovering he was sick after returning home, and how he now does all he can to teach veterans about their rights to medical benefits.

CHAPTER TWENTY-SIX

Tony Lee (1962–   )
U.S. Air Force

Tony Lee is a Chapter Service Officer of Disabled American Veterans at Herald Square Chapter 126 in New York City. He trained for the Army Reserves as a medic and was activated for Desert Shield/Desert Storm in the Air Force. He served in the Reserves for 17 years. He received his MBA and is now working on a second master's degree to become a licensed Mental Health Counselor in New York State. He talks about coping with war-related sicknesses and advocating for rights and benefits for veterans.

I was born in New York City, in 1962. I'm first generation, born here. I've been living in Chinatown, New York, my whole life, except during the time I was in the military. My home has always been in New York, Chinatown.

We lived in a tenement down on Madison Street. My father worked in the restaurant. My mom was a seamstress and then later she stopped working—became a homemaker, stayed at home with us, when I grew up. I studied business at Murray Bergtraum High School. Two days after I graduated, I went to basic training at Fort Leonard Wood, Missouri. I'd never been out of New York before then. It was in the early '80s. They had a very strong anti-military sentiment during that time period because of the Vietnam War. So I was post-Vietnam era and I wanted to make a difference and there weren't too many Asian Americans that did that.

You talked about boot camp in the Army; do you want to talk a little bit about that?

Yeah. Basically, back in 1981 when I was 18, I graduated high school and about a week later I was at boot camp or basic training in the Army. I was waking up at 4:30 every morning for training. And I spent about nine weeks there. Believe it or not, there were quite a few Asian Americans in my unit. There were two guys from California, and I was the only one from New York, and it wasn't as isolating.

Was there any hazing?

No, there was no hazing; it was a very different era. During basic training I didn't encounter any kind of discrimination or any kind of racial remarks. It was only when I went further in my Army career, when I went for training with the Army as a medic, that I encountered racism and I got into a fight because of it.

Basic Training, Fort Leonard Wood,
Missouri, July 1981

I had a Special Forces staff sergeant in the National Guard who was attending classes with us who got the guy to apologize. He was also from the South, from Alabama, and he got this guy from Mississippi who called me names to apologize. The guy was drunk, he started calling me all kinds of names and I hit him once. I was dead asleep and he woke me up. We stayed in open bays. This was down in Fort Sam, Houston, Texas and that's when I encountered a form of bias I never encountered in New York.

I didn't get punished because I was dead asleep, I was defending myself. I didn't know who was attacking me. And it wasn't an enclosed room, it was an open bay. It was 50 guys in that room, bunk beds. People could approach you from anywhere and I was dead asleep, and it woke me up and I was confused. I knew where I was but I didn't know who was attacking me. He was drunk, he was calling me all kinds of names. But he apologized. He was apologetic, very apologetic. I said, "You really don't like Asians." He goes, "No, no, no. I have relatives that are Vietnamese, married into the family." I said, "Okay, whatever."

What did you have to do in active duty?

I worked at Womack Army Hospital at Fort Bragg in North Carolina for several months on temporary duty as a Reservist. They needed full-time help. So I had a job for six months, working in a ward, which is equivalent to a being a Nursing Assistant or Practical Nurse. I gave out medication. I did all the medical care in the ward for half a year.

What was your job while you were a Reservist? What was your job in regular life?

My job as a Reservist in active duty was as a 91 Alpha which is medical specialist. I always stayed in the paramedic EMT-type area. In my civilian life, I was a student most of the time. Eventually I graduated from Baruch College. I got my Bachelor of business administration in public administration. And then I went to work for the city. I was trying to go back on active duty again. And back in the middle of the '80s it was harder for the enlisted to go back on active duty as a Reservist.

What do you do for the city?

I work as a staff analyst, an administrative analytical person that does general management and administration. Right now I'm at the top of my career field as an administrative staff analyst, which is supervisory. And I've been on leave from them since last October, for sick leave. I have many injuries from the medical problems that originated from the Gulf War, which manifested to other medical problems as time went on.

Right now I have cancer. I hate to use the word. I'm a cancer patient. I'm not a victim but I'm a patient and I'm still under evaluation. I'm finishing my treatment in March of this year. My medical conditions from the Gulf War prevented me from serving from '95 to '99. And it disqualified me from my military reserve career.

Let me talk about the moments during Desert Storm. They mobilized me October 1990, I think. They called me on the phone that day and told me that I've got a couple of days to get my business together, to go to my job, tell them I'm going to take leave, do whatever I have to do. I'll be expected to come down there soon because we're being mobilized. Kuwait had been invaded and they wanted us to go there to do medical support, and that's all they said to me, and I went there.

Kuwait was invaded August of 1990. I went to Saudi Arabia in October of 1990 to do medical support. They had a few assignments for me to go on in Germany. But when we got to Germany they amended our orders to go to Saudi Arabia.

My unit was at King Khalid Military City. Then I got there and they put me back in the Dhahran Saudi Arabia King Fahd International Airport for medical support. Basically I was responsible for the shift that does medical transportation. You get hurt, you're treated, they go fly you back from Germany for future or more medical treatment. I'm the one responsible for making sure you're all right to get on the plane. And I'm like the holding area. They call it an aerial medical holding area at the Air Force Base, where you hold people until you can get them on a flight. They went to Wiesbaden mostly and Landstuhl Army Regional Hospital and a couple of other places for treatment. Most of the injuries weren't war-related, they were industrial—accidents that happen a lot. When you're [at] a fast operating tempo, people tend to get into accidents.

Accidents from ... ?

Cars, car accidents. Weird things: the tank hit you, a truck hit you, you've been working 16-hour shifts, you broke your arm. We had people with firearm injuries—their firearm accidentally went off and they shot themselves by accident. Injuries, but they weren't war-related. They were just related to the military, the tempo, whatever. Things happen.

What do you mean by tempo?

That's a military term for being fast-paced. How much work there was involved and the volume of work. A lot of these guys were in very boring areas but some of them were very busy and when you're very busy you tend to get careless and hurt yourself. So, basically, when you have a major injury they usually don't keep you in the area of operations, they ship you out to a safer zone.

You take care of their basic needs when they're there because they're there under your jurisdiction, under you, for the time they're there until they leave. The biggest thing I did was dealing with dead bodies.

Dealing with dead bodies?

Yeah, mortuary services. They got an overflow of people being hurt during major operations in Kuwait and they were shipping bodies back for identification. It wasn't our people. It could be anyone, so they were just throwing it back to us. Usually, not that many service people got hurt; most of the people that died were civilians and Iraqi military people. We basically kept them around and there was a mortuary service unit that worked with us and we gave them a hand.

I'm used to dealing with people being alive; it's kind of hard to deal with people that are not alive. So it was an eye-opener for me. When the war started it was hard—you didn't know what to expect, who was coming in. They could come from anywhere and it was all different branches of the services coming in. A lot them were getting out, they were relieved, getting out of the war.

What kind of stuff went through your mind when you had to deal with bodies?

My own mortality. Death. I'd never really encountered death up close. I'd seen cadavers before in training but I'd never really had to deal with people, deal with their personal information, know when they were born. Lots of times you didn't know; a lot of bodies we dealt with were unknown. But they had to be put in that ward, put in a body bag. They had to get refrigerated. They had to decide what the Kuwaitis wanted to do with them. A lot of administrative issues were involved. I was doing the actual, practical work. I didn't do the administrative work.

I think a lot of the bodies got shipped back to Iraq, believe it or not, and a lot of them got shipped back to Kuwait. If they're not an allied coalition member we don't keep it.

They used the Air bases in Daharan as one of the transit points. It's the major, closest departure point to move people out of there. They want to move all of the hurt people and all the coalition people that were dead out of there as soon as possible. So we just happened to be the closest air base near Kuwait to do that. It wasn't an air base, it was really an international airport, but it was set up as a military base for the duration. So they had full facilities. It was basically an airport like Kennedy. It was a little different, weird, because we had air conditioning. It wasn't a standard military base. We kept our people on the passenger terminal because the airport was technically shut down for all civilian traffic.

And at this point did you have personal feelings about the war, when you weren't dealing with all those bodies?

Oh, not really. I mean, we knew that he [Saddam] shouldn't be there; it was an invasion outright of another country. The Iraqi Forces and people that invaded Kuwait shouldn't be there. But I never expected myself as a reservist to get activated to fight a war outside our country. I always expected to stay in the country. It was part of the expectation that I won't go anywhere where I could get into harm's way. The normal protocol in a peacetime base is you're never armed, you don't have any firearms on you. So I knew it wasn't normal protocol. It was a wartime situation and everything operated very differently. I carried a side pistol. But Air Force people are not normally armed at all.

What really wore me down was just constantly being at work. Even when you sleep you still think about work, and it was constant. And like I told you, it's very emotional. We had TV sets around us, so in a fixed facility we actually watched CNN TV on satellite dish. Everything that everybody got [for] the general public, we were watching on TV.

They have two shifts, 12 hours: 6 a.m. to 6 p.m. and 6 p.m. to 6 a.m. I was on the overnight shift. I was the overnight supervisor there.

You said when you go to the desert it's not like Lawrence of Arabia, it's not white sands everywhere.

Yeah, well, basically, every day they sprayed us with DEET, which is bug spray to get rid of the bugs. The airstrip we were on and the international airport was very insect-infested. We'd get sprayed and we go further out. It's a desert environment but it's not white pristine fine sand. There's a lot of life in the desert, you just don't see it. And the perception was basically the *Lawrence of Arabia* movie—pristine sand, there's nothing there, except sand. It wasn't like that. It was humid because we were near the coastline, so the humidity was horrible sometimes. And sometimes it was all right. It fluctuates. The only thing that saved us was the air conditioning.

During the daytime I couldn't really be out there. It's 110° in the daytime during February. At night it drops down to 40° or even 30° so you actually have to have winter clothes with you at night. It was amazing, the extreme ranges. In the daytime you can't go out because it's so hot. But during the daytime I'm mostly asleep, but it was really difficult for me to sleep with the hour reversal. But thank God they kept me on the shift for a while. Sometimes when I switched to do other things on the day shift I had to readjust.

What kind of bugs were there?

Sand flies, huge mosquitoes. Insects I'd never seen in my life. You get bitten up a lot. Fleas; sand fleas they call them, people got Leishmaniasis from it. Very tropical, Third World kind of illnesses you get. We had people with allergic reactions from some of the bug bites.

It was very stressful because you're constantly at work. You don't really have relief. And the biggest thing is when they started ground war in February. We expected a lot more casualties coming in and a lot of people leaving. It was kind of great that that didn't happen.

What does 'ground war' mean exactly?

Ground war means when we actually invade the country, not bombing them, where we actually had tanks and infantry that went into Kuwait. Before we were bombing them forever, so that was an air campaign. Ground war is actually what they now call "boots on the ground," actually, physically going in there. That's when we expected a lot more injuries coming back. And that didn't really happen.

Oh. Why is that?

Very different war during that time. We didn't have improvised explosive devices like they have now. And back then they knew where everything was because they had a lot of new reconnaissance, and I think it was a different era, different mentality. I mean, we weren't fighting a terrorist, we were fighting another country. It was clean, there was no vagueness.

You told me that you were shot at but didn't know it at the time.

I turned around, I looked, and the guy was on the floor. And it was like, wow. And I said, "Why the hell is he on the floor?" The guy says, "I got shot, something hit me."

We didn't even hear noise. The next thing I knew, the person was on the floor and he said he got shot. We had no idea where it came from. That's the scary part. You're walking around; you think you're pretty safe. All of a sudden someone behind you gets hurt.

That was on the airbase. And we were in a secure area and we had no idea. They investigated. The bullet was a standard M16-type bullet; they just don't know where it came from. So we had no idea what happened but we treated the guy. We brought him to the hospital. It was scary. That means you're not really safe. We thought we were safe; we're out of sight, thought we were out of harm's way. They investigated but we never found out the outcome. We still don't know to this day. We don't know if it was a sniper or it was an accident. The biggest

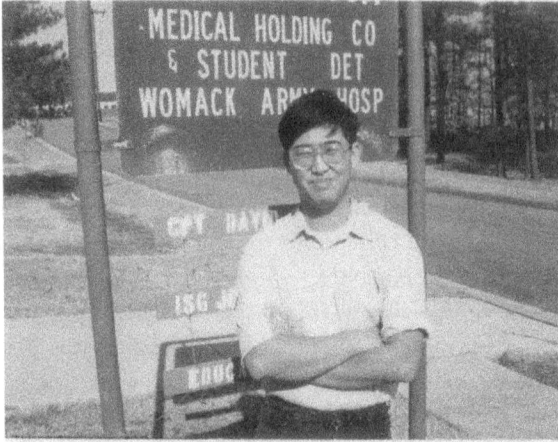

Practical Nurse School, Fort Bragg, North Carolina, March 1984

thing is the unknown. And it's not like the movies, there's no music to it. You get into a very hyper-vigilant mode.

Were there other memorable things that happened during this time?

Mostly it was very routine. Most of the time you get very bored and some-times you get a lot of work and you no longer remember the boredom.

I was assigned out there for six months but I was actually in and out of there all the time. I was technically a flight medic. I could go on planes, work on planes also. I would fly with them if they needed help but my duty assignment was to be on the ground. But that wasn't always the case. I went in and out to other countries, mostly Germany, to Frankfurt International Airport. Usually, I left the area for a couple of days, maybe Monday through Thursday. I'd be out because they needed me to give a hand. Basically once a month I got out of there. And also I got sick, so I was out of there for a little while when I got sick.

When did you start to get sick?

I really didn't start to get sick until I got back home.

And when was that, half a year later?

Yeah, back around Christmas time in '91. I was home since April of '91. About Christmas time I started to not feel well. I started having problems sleeping. I started having memories, bad dreams about the war, being hot, being out there, being irritated, being agitated. But when you're in an area where you don't feel safe, your adrenaline is always going, you're always very hyper-vigilant, you think you could get hurt. I understand the feelings when soldiers say when they're deployed, especially in Iraq or Afghanistan, they always feel ill at ease. A lot of times I felt that way. I mean, I felt calm but there was an uneasiness about it. And the whole time you're there you really never shake that feeling. When I came home somehow that feeling came back with me, that ill at ease. It wasn't

New York Army Guard Summer Camp, July 1987

depression; it was more like you're tired, you just don't know what's wrong with your body. Eventually they found out that I had chronic fatigue. I have Post Traumatic Stress Disorder. I have tension headaches and that's all on my record now and I get compensated for it.

But I'd rather be healthy. I would give all the money back to have my health back. You don't realize how it feels to be feeling good all the time until you don't feel good most of the time. And that's when I realized something was wrong and it wasn't just psychological, it wasn't just a feeling. It was also physical. I got written up in the book called *The Irritable Heart*. The author met me when I was going through the evaluation program in '97.

It was a Phase II Persian Gulf Comprehensive Examination Program they started up for veterans of the Gulf War. They would recall you back to active duty to evaluate you and treat you, you'd be going there full-time and that's where your duty is. It was a month of in-house training to cope with your illnesses. They'd actually have you staying in the dormitory for the whole month while you're getting evaluated and addressing 40 different medical issues. And back in '95 I knew that once I started the medical evaluation process, that'd be the end of my military Reserve career. It would be the end of my military career totally, but my health comes first. I didn't know what was bothering me and what was wrong with me. I was very sluggish at work. I didn't feel good, I was tired a lot, and most of the time. It was multiple ailments and I didn't know where it was coming from but I knew wasn't healthy.

How long did it take you to discover you were sick?

Several years. I thought it was just a feeling but it wasn't just a feeling. Maybe because when I was younger I was in denial. I didn't think it was related to my service. When you're sick you don't always think straight. I didn't believe I had Post Traumatic Stress Disorder but I guess I had it because I had a hard time sleeping and had a hard time focusing. I had a hard time relating to people. I didn't have a relationship for years after the war, after I broke up with my girl-friend. You don't feel very sociable, you just don't want to do things. It impacted me at work. I couldn't even go to graduate school. After I went for the initial evaluation in '95 they came out with ailments I had and the VA rated me with Post Traumatic Stress Disorder in '95. I filed the application as soon as I came out and then they gave me a rating for Post-Traumatic Stress Disorder.

Rating?

In order to award you a service connection for injuries from your military service the VA has to give you a rating, 10% to 100% rating of being service con-nected. Based on that rating you will get a monetary payment. The minimum monetary payment is $150 for a 10% rating. The maximum monetary rating is 100% when you get $2,500 a month tax-free. But that's really for the extreme cases of people that really can't work. Their injuries prevent them from ever having a meaningful, gainful employment. That wasn't my case initially. I was able to go to work but it was a struggle. I also got a documented claim that I have Chronic Fatigue Syndrome.

This war caused me disability that impacted me. I just don't know how se-vere or how light. It's not light but not as bad as it could be and I'm very happy for it. Being involved with the Legion Post here, and being involved with other veterans' organizations, gives me personal relief, happiness, that I could advo-cate for the veterans. There's a lot of things that people, when they're sick and not thinking clearly, don't think about. They don't think that the illness could be related to the service, related to other things; you think it's you. And that gets isolating. I realized it's not me. There were triggers and other things that caused my illness. I'm not blaming them, but it wasn't voluntary either. For the treatment that I have, chemo and radiation, that says a lot, and I'm able to still function and I'm happy. But now I don't know if it's triggered by the war or not. I don't know if there's any relationship to it.

Were a lot of other people affected from the Persian Gulf War? I know there's a whole book that was written about it.

There's a whole book that shows you. Well, I told you one person committed suicide in my unit after the war; he served with me. He was a paramedic too but also he worked in the field and went back to being a paramedic through the city for EMS. A few mentioned to him it may not be really healthy to go back into that kind of work, but he went back.

Because it's high-stress work.

Very high stress. You don't believe how draining it can be. People say it's not combat, but it's very high physical work. It's like working in trauma center constantly, day after day. After a while you get burnt out. It's beyond a normal human experience, encountering traumatic events and injuries constantly.

You don't mind if people are sick, but it's hard when you see people with broken bones, injuries that require extensive treatment, and burns. It adds up. At first it didn't bother me but eventually it will bother you, slowly.

You're dealing with emotionally agitated people who got injured, messed up. They come in and they've been stabilized and they're being shipped home, but they're still angry, a lot of them. They're all right physically—they're being shipped for treatment—but the emotional component never really gets addressed. You have to deal with a lot of aggravated people, frustrated people. They may have painkillers but they're feeling very distraught. They may seem relaxed but it's burning them inside. Sometimes you get lashed out at and you have to be empathetic, you have to listen to them. But you're not a trained counselor, you're trained to treat the physical ailments. You've never been trained to treat the emotional ailments, so you just treat them.

Is there a unit that treats the mental aspects?

We have the mental health technicians with us but they get overwhelmed. There's X amount of it, there's mountains of people 50, 60 people. They cannot get access to every one of them. You have to give them a hand. But everyone that got hurt, there's always an emotional component to it too. And it's because they're tired, they feel drained, or they've been constantly working 18–20 hours every day for several days. Things trigger problems and, getting very specific, these problems are part of the larger issues. During wartime and during contingency operations, a lot protocols in the peacetime military base are not always adhered by. You cut corners, you start taking short cuts, and those short cuts cause you to have injuries. People are not following protocol because they're tired or getting absentminded. These injuries are not always caused by being shot at by your enemy; it's caused by disorganization, your health, your feelings.

It's easy to treat the physical component of it. The hardest thing is dealing with the person, their feelings about things, and that's straining. You have people having all kinds of questions about What's going to happen to them? What are they going to do? They're glad they're out but they have a lot of frustration and agony and it becomes difficult.

I was a chapter service officer in the Disabled American Veterans. I'm the commander of the chapter that belongs to the 23rd Street VA Hospital.

You talked about the stigma of being disabled, getting benefits, etc.

Well, it's this bait-and-switch. How would I explain this? They will sell to you that you're entitled to it, but then we have the paperwork, we have to do the processing, and the system is not very friendly toward veterans. It's supposed to be non-adversarial. The VA by federal [law] has the duty to assist you, but sometimes when you deal with them there's a resistance—like they're giving welfare money to you, or an indifference? It feels like you're applying for welfare benefits but this is not welfare, this is not entitlement.

This is a benefit and a privilege you earn, a difference. It's like being a mem-

Medical Retirement from U.S. Air Force Reserve, July 1999

ber of Congress. A member of Congress, as soon as they do their 2-year term, is entitled a pension, from what I heard. We did our time for our country. We're entitled to what they said. And yet we still have to fight to preserve the money, to give that privilege for everybody else [who needs it]. It shouldn't be that way right now; they won't cut money to the VA. Why do you want to take money away from veteran affairs now—the VA deals with their illnesses—when more military people are coming back home and trying to get help now? Where's the logic to it? "Oh, we don't have the money." Yeah, you have the money. You just put it in everything else except what you have to do. Someone has to make money off of it so you'd rather have a defense contract making multi-billion dollar planes—right?—than give it to the average person that served the country. You don't have a pile—You get very cynical about what their ulterior motive is when they try to take away an earned privilege.

You talked about how a lot of young people coming back today, they don't—

When you come back from war you really don't care about your benefits. All you care about is you got out of it. You have to get your desperate feeling or whatever feelings of sadness, frustration, anger out of your system. It doesn't go away just being at home. It erupts; it could stay with you for years.

One day you'll be fine and all of a sudden something triggers memories, you get really angry. I mean, you're frustrated. You feel like you've been robbed, you feel that you've been displaced.

When I came back from the war I felt like everything went on without me and somehow I got left behind. The music changed, the movies changed, the newspaper articles changed. All the events that I was current with I wasn't really current with. That's pre-internet era. The cell phone wasn't a cell phone, it was a brick. It was pagers—The communication technology when I went to war was not the same as Facebook, Twitter. They've got a whole different infrastructure to keep in contact now. You know what my infrastructure was? Writing a letter, maybe. Getting to call home at $10 a minute, from Saudi Arabia, and they may not be home to answer the phone. Their answering machine clicks on, no one's home. Guess what? You blew your $10, right? That's the worst feeling, when you get the chance to make the call and no one's there to answer your call.

How many years did you end up doing?

I ended up doing 17 years in the Reserves, about a year-plus of active duty, totally combined.

If you're medically retired you get benefits immediately. I was medically retired. In 1999, as soon as they gave me my orders to retire, I had my benefits. I just don't have *all* my benefits because I'm drawing VA compensation. I can't get my retirement benefits, monetary benefits, not the health insurance.

I've been losing my military pension money since day one, from '99 until 2012. I haven't gotten paid for that at all. And I earned that money. That money was for my time and service, not for my injury. But the way the law is written you could take either-or; it's considered double-dipping. It's very unfair.

I'm going to tell you 90% of the veterans won't use [programs available to them] because they're too damaged to use it initially, and they have a 15-year limitation.

You talked about how you're studying to be a counselor now.

Yeah, one reason I did counseling—I already got my MBA, this is my second master's, but I want to get a license for mental health counseling. I'm going through a program and after another year and a half, two years, and I do all my training, I should be a licensed mental health counselor in New York State. I could counsel anyone from substance abuse to mental hygiene, the whole gamut. I could do private practice.

I'm hoping to learn the skills to help more veterans. Informally I've been helping them. I've been counseling them, not just giving them benefits information, but being empathetic, listening to them, letting them vent themselves out. But I've never had really good formal training in it. I'm doing formal training now in order to become a better advocate, be a better counselor, have better rapport. Everything I've been doing has been based on what I learned in the military as an NCO. They teach you, in their leadership school, but I'm looking at a softer approach because it will make me a better counselor.

How did you get involved with the American Legion Post 1291 [Kimlau Post] in Chinatown?

Back in 1991, when I got out of the Gulf War of '87, the National American Legion sent me a free membership to be a member-at-large for the national organization. Eventually I kept paying them big dues and all of a sudden one day they asked me, "Do you want to join a post?" I said, "Why not?" So they volunteered me for Post 1291, the Kimlau Post, three years later. I didn't even know I was transferred and I started getting notices from them, "Oh, you're a member here." I said, "Oh, they transferred my membership out of that large group. Oh, well."

I came up here for the meeting and it was very ritualistic. And I said, Oh God, you've got old World War II veterans talking about World War II issues, and I'm like, That's not for me. That was in the early 90s ... '92. There were World War II veterans in control of this whole Post. They were still vibrant, active, so I said, "Well, fine, no problem." I didn't really come to the Post, it wasn't—I didn't have any relationship to the demographic here. I mean, I don't like to play mahjong and sit here all night. They do. I don't like to talk about old war stories. They do. This was before the Xbox generation. A lot of the things they do I'm not into. It's hard, I mean, I could relate to their experiences but they came from a different era, different time. It was hard being Asian or Chinese American in the military. They had different standards for what constituted discrimination, so it was very hard for me to relate to them.

I relate to the Vietnam veterans easier than the Korean War and World War II veterans because I'm so—Everything's historic to me. Now I've gotten to this stage in my life and realize I could make a contribution to the Post. I have more time. I'm not worried about a career. I'm not worried about getting married. I'm still single, but that's not my thinking. If I find the right person and get married, fine, but if I don't, I'll live with it. When I was younger I seemed to want to try grabbing everything at once. And I realized that's not me now. I want to give back.

Being part of the Post, whatever I can do, I do it. I did it by giving a lecture—that you said only 19 people attended, but hey, I don't care if 2 people attended as long as I know I impart them with knowledge. I'm happy because I don't want to hear from them, "I don't know anything about it. No one told me," because I get that from veterans all the time.

People don't research until they really need it and then it's harder than when I explain all the little different benefits to them. And a lot of vets are under the myth that the benefits they're entitled to don't apply to them. Until they tell you absolutely no, then it's not true. And the problem I find is if you don't go for your benefits they're going to take them away from you.

The mood of this country now—Everything is austerity, so I don't even know how we will come out of this minor recession, or whatever they call it, we're still in a recession. I mean you graduate college, and right now the kids get out of school and have to take unpaid internships just to get work. When I graduated, that was unheard of. If you didn't get paid, you had a developmental disability or something was wrong with you. But now it's a whole different ball game, and I'm young enough to fight, and I'm healthy enough to try to advocate for the younger kids and whoever's left. Because if they attack what we earn we never will get it back. And that's why I do it.

CHAPTER TWENTY-SEVEN

Mimi Wang 卞嘉音 (1949–   )
U.S. Army / Veterans Administration

Mimi Wang was born in Taiwan. Currently she is the Chief of Nutrition and Food Services for the Veterans Administration, New York Harbor Health Care System. She was the first female commander of the American Legion Kimlau Post 1291 in Manhattan Chinatown, New York City. She offers advice for fellow Chinese American veterans and talks about balancing motherhood and serving her country.

I was born in 1949 in Tainan, Taiwan. My father was a physician and mom was a registered nurse. They served in Tripoli, Libya for nine years prior to coming to the U.S.

During those nine years, I was in Taiwan attending junior high and high school. In 1969, after my high school graduation, my parents decided to send both my brother and me to the United States for further education.

I attended the University of Maryland for my bachelor's degree in food and nutrition. After graduation, I completed a 1-year internship at D.C. General Hospital and then moved to Staten Island, where I met my husband, Ho. Ho had helped me look in the *New York Times* every week and eventually found my first job as a director of food services in a 400-bed nursing home in Staten Island.

What was your path to the military? What did you end up doing in the military and how did you get there?

In the early '70s I completed my master's degree in food and nutrition from New York University and was married with no children. One of my girlfriends had joined the Reserve and told me about various benefits of being in the Reserve as a dietician.

Since I had every weekend free, I figured I had time to serve my country. My father retired from the Chinese military, Kuomintang, with the rank of colonel. Maybe this also had given me the incentive to serve in the military. In 1981 I was sworn in and joined the Army Reserve at Fort Hamilton, Brooklyn, as a dining facility officer (dietitian). Our unit was called 1208 USA Hospital. That hospital's mission was to replace active duty staff with reservists in the hospitals in the event of war. During Desert Storm, that's what we did.

When the 1208 USA Hospital was activated in December 1991, we went to

First female commander of Lt. B.R. Kimlau
Chinese Memorial Post 1291, October 2011

Walter Reed Army Medical Center in Washington D.C. to fill in for active duty personnel who had gone to Kuwait. At that time I was assigned as the dining facility officer to oversee the hospital staff feeding. Many reservists were called up to support the first Gulf War, and the total number of staff to be fed therefore increased significantly.

During Desert Storm, I was away for a total of six months from my regular job and my family. For the first time I had to leave my 7-year-old daughter, which was very difficult. I was not sure initially whether I would be sent overseas.

My active duty away from home put a lot of stress on my husband as well. Not only did he have to work long hours on Wall Street, he also had to drop off and pick up our daughter from the babysitter, prepare meals, and check our daughter's homework every day. After a few weeks into my assignment, I was able to drive home on weekends, which made our life a little easier.

What was your regular job while you did Reserves?

I was the food service director at Mary Manning Walsh Home, a non-profit long-term care facility located in the Upper East Side of Manhattan. I oversaw the daily operation of the Nutrition & Food Services for 362 residents and 500-plus employees. We were able to pass all the federal and state inspections every year during the 22 years I was there. It is a Catholic facility and had many well-known residents living there.

When did you first get involved with the Kimlau Post? How did you learn about it?

When I retired from the Army Reserve after 22 years of service. A Staten Island legion friend asked me to join the Kimlau Legion Post 1291. At that time, I had no knowledge of the American Legion. After many visits, I found out the Kimlau post consists of over 600 veterans and provides many activities to Chinese American veterans. As my daughter got older, I had more free time for myself; in 2003 I officially joined. Gradually I got involved with different committees—and eventually I became an executive board member, vice commander, and then the first female commander of the post from October 2011 to June 2014.

Do you have any thoughts about being American, being Chinese American or thoughts about being Chinese American in the military?

Some people will say Chinese are very humble. I want to give advice to all Chinese that in the U.S., people respect you when you know your stuff. First I have to emphasize the importance of getting a good education. Successfully completing formal education will enable one to find a job more easily. Persons with steady income and medical coverage can have a higher chance of getting a great quality of life.

Number two, don't be so bashful. You have to learn how to sell yourself. Whatever you know, share it, not to be showy, but to do it in a nice way, because Americans respect whatever you know. However, if you don't speak up, then people may walk all over you.

Third is to build up individual character through training. Chinese grandparents and parents often say to their children, "Don't rock the boat. Be humble and do not show off." In our society, when you know something's right or wrong, you have to speak up. While planning your career, you also need to learn how to play the right politics. You need to know your organization's culture and the type of people in your organization, so that you will not directly confront the powers-that-be.

These techniques you can only learn through working with people, getting involved with different organizations, and then you can mold your own character and personality.

When you've just come out from school or from a traditional Oriental family, you may not have this type of know-how, but I strongly encourage Chinese to go out and get involved with organizations and volunteer in various committees. We should encourage our youngsters to be brave and participate in different volunteering activities. I believe it will mold youngsters into becoming better citizens.

My parents were Christian. They believed in giving. Both my daughter and I learned a lot from them. It is important to have good role models in family and friends during one's formative years. When one has compassion in one's heart, one tends to pour out support and help others. Compassion should not be just staying within one's family, and it should be passed on to our society.

PART V: IRAQ AND AFGHANISTAN

Toppling Saddam

Those who watched the famous televised toppling of Saddam Hussein's statue in Firdos Square broadcast around the world saw that it was a Chinese American corporal, Edward Chin, who placed the flag over the statue's head before it was brought down by a crane. This image suggested that America was fully victorious, that the war had concluded, and Iraqis were grateful.[36] However, civil war continued in the region, and what we saw was just an intermission between invasion and insurgency.[37] A similar story played out in Afghanistan, where a seemingly short war lasted far longer, with greater casualties than expected. Veterans in this section speak of the humanitarian works they performed in Iraq and Afghanistan. Wilem Wong talks about conducting anthropological research to better understand Afghani's views and communicate why we were there.

Hazing

While many Chinese American veterans like Welton Chang, See-wan Szeto and Cliff Chen had positive experiences and never experienced discrimination in the military, others witnessed and experienced abuse.

In 2011 two Chinese American military members committed suicide, prompting activism from Chinese American communities. On April 3, 2011, Lance Corporal Harry Lew, a Marine from Santa Clara, California, committed suicide in Afghanistan after being abused—he was punched and kicked, forced to do push-ups after digging a foxhole for two hours without anything to drink or eat. Sandbags were placed on his legs as he did leg lifts, and when he stopped, a lance corporal ripped open the sandbag and sand got into Lew's mouth. His colleagues did this supposedly because Lew fell asleep on watch.[38] Harry Lew was the nephew of U.S. Rep. Judy Chu, D-Calif. (the first Chinese American woman elected to Congress). In a court-martial, the lance corporal responsible was found not guilty of hazing. Congressman Chu introduced the Harry Lew Military Hazing Accountability and Prevention Act, asking the military to make hazing a crime, and requiring the Department of Defense to come up with an anti-hazing plan and create a tracking system for hazing incidents.[39]

Six months after Harry Lew's tragic death, 19-year-old Private Danny Chen from New York's Chinatown shot himself to death on October 3, 2011 in Afghanistan after being hazed and harassed with racial epithets by eight fellow soldiers.[40] He suffered physical abuse and ethnic slurs by superiors who dragged him out of bed and across the floor when he failed to turn off a water heater after showering.[41]

Legislation and Aftermath in the Asian American Community

Elizabeth OuYang, an attorney and head of civil rights group Organization of Chinese Americans (OCA)'s New York branch spoke at protests and said minority members in the military "must decide whether it is worth the risk to fight for your country when your country will not protect you." [42]

Anti-hazing legislation sponsored by Rep. Nydia Velazquez and Sen. Kirsten Gillibrand, both New York Democrats, was proposed to Congress. [43] The New York Chinatown community came together. In a march on December 15, 2011, 36 community groups and 5,000 petition signers demanded justice for Chen's death. [44]

Part of Elizabeth Street at Canal Street in New York City was renamed "Private Danny Chen Way" and an opera about Danny Chen called "An American Soldier" was written by David Henry Hwang in 2014, raising awareness and reminding us of the Chinese American tragedies that have resulted in civil rights benefits for all Americans.

The U.S. Marine Corps in May 2013 launched an effort to bring diversity to its enlisted and officer ranks. Marine recruitment encouraged enlistment from Asian Americans and Pacific Islanders, linking Marine discipline to family honor and the concept of self-betterment through education, key values of Asian culture. [45] These values were exactly what many of the veterans in this book sought when they joined the military, and got.

CHAPTER TWENTY-EIGHT

Chi-hung Szeto 司徒志恆 (1975–   )
U.S. Army

Chi Szeto was born in California, went to high school in the D.C. Metro area, and attended West Point for college. He has also lived in Singapore and Hong Kong. He currently lives in Los Angeles where he runs a small business that designs and distributes promotional items and premiums. He shares his perspective on the privileges that come with being American, and our involvement in war.

While deployed in Iraq, what were your jobs? What did your duties entail?

I started off as the deputy S-3. This meant I was an assistant staff officer who helped my boss [a major] run the operations for a brigade-sized element [about 5,000 soldiers]. We would have to track the missions of all the subordinate units and also prepare for future missions based upon the guidance from the brigade commander. While in country I assumed command of a company of about 140 soldiers. We had many different missions, from security, reconstruction, logistical resupply, humanitarian, to dealing with local tribal leaders. In the end I was tasked to turn our abandoned airfield into a forward operating base that would support over 4,000 soldiers.

We lived in very spartan conditions during our time overseas. Going through these hardships and danger helps people grow close. We didn't have much shelter and our area of operations was very dangerous. Unlike places like Baghdad, we didn't have many luxuries [dining facility, morale and welfare visits] for most of our deployment. But there is a bond created with people who you have been in combat with that is as close or closer than any familial or marital bond. I did feel at that time that we made a lot of progress in rebuilding the area we were responsible for, but also knew that threats were constant. I lost two of my best friends during the deployment and there isn't a day that goes by that I don't think about them and all the other people I know who have fallen.

What made you decide to apply to West Point?

It was completely random. My whole life I wanted to go to UCLA. I didn't apply to any other schools initially. I was on my way to turn in some scholarship forms with my guidance counselor. There was a long line so I was just waiting around for him to be free. I saw all these books about different colleges and saw

Cpt. Chi Szeto and Cpt. George Wood (KIA 20 Nov 2003)

information about the Naval Academy and West Point. I had no idea what West Point was about but I was bored and filled out the info card. I got a call a week later, did some interviews, and visited West Point. I really loved the traditions and history and the values of the school resonated with me. And I thought it would be nice not to have to take loans out, so I applied, and the rest was history.

Did any friends or family object to your decision?

My grandfather was very worried at the time since our family was having some financial hardships. He didn't realize that West Point was a college, and prestigious. He only knew it was the Army, which in China was basically the last resort for people.

What was it like as a Chinese American at West Point?

No real difference, from my perspective. There were a few Asians in class but things were more differentiated by seniority and not race.

How many Chinese Americans/Asians were in your class, and what was the racial or geographical makeup of your graduating class?

I think there were about four or five Chinese Americans. Probably about 20 Asians total, mostly Korean Americans. The class started at 1,250, and graduated about 980. Maybe 15% minorities, 10% women.

Were there any obstacles or tension of any kind that were cultural?

Not that I saw.

Did you experience any cultural/philosophical clashes, being a Chinese American in the military?

I'm not sure if it was part of my upbringing, being Chinese, or just my personality, but I tend to be more quiet and not as full of bravado as many people. And I was an infantry officer, where there tends to be a lot of chest thumping and trash talking. I like to let my actions do my talking for me. When you are the best everyone knows it, you don't need to tell everyone. Though sometimes people can confuse calmness with being meek, and you have to ensure that it isn't construed as weakness.

What made you decide to join the U.S. military?

I never thought about it. It was just part of the commitment that came with attending West Point. I decided it would not be a bad career for some time after college.

How did you feel when you were deployed to Iraq?

Excited, a bit depressed since I was in a staff position at the time and didn't think I would have a chance to command a company in combat. I had some concern about the preparedness of my unit and the equipment we had.

When I was there (toward the beginning of the war, in April '03) things were quiet for a while, and then things started getting bad around late August. There were many more attacks, shellings and roadside bombs. 20% of the people where I was at [Baqubah] hated us, and 20% loved us. The remainder of the people were like most people in the world, just hoping to live their lives and improve the future for their children.

I did not see much face-to-face combat. I was shot at a few times and had hundreds of shellings and multiple roadside bombs. It was very frustrating not being able to tell who the enemy was. We were not prepared to fight the insurgency battle. But as always, soldiers are amazing and found ways to accomplish all their missions despite all our limitations.

Did you feel that the U.S. should or shouldn't be there?

It's inconsequential whether I think we should be there or not. We were there and there were no good exit strategies. It's a very different perspective to be overseas and see the difference you are making. The media is usually biased with their reporting, whether it is positive or negative. I met very few reporters interested in telling the story. Most had an agenda and only wanted to hear things that fit that agenda. I know that I lost a lot of close friends, classmates and some of my soldiers. They were irreplaceable as sons, fathers, brother, and friends. But they believed in what they were doing and would not have accepted a lifetime of safety to trade their fate. I believed in my mission when I was deployed and I miss my friends. Everything else is for armchair quarterbacks to discuss.

What obstacles (if any) did you face as a Chinese American, either from the Chinese or the American communities, for the choices you made?

None. I think there have always been expectations for me to do great things. Sometimes I was my own worst enemy and obstacle. I think many Chinese are surprised that I was in the Army, but liked that I went to the Academy.

Cpt. Szeto and local Iraqi children

Did you ever think that you were denied a dream or opportunity (whatever it may be) because you are Chinese American or Asian?

No. I lived in the South for almost 10 years [Texas, Louisiana, Georgia], visited all but five states, and have been around the world and never felt discriminated against. I've seen a lot of ignorance but not blatant racism. Many places treat outsiders funny until they get to know you. Then it doesn't matter what color your skin is—you belong to the community and no one can mess with you. I am blessed to consider myself part of many different families and communities around the country. I haven't had to concern myself with race issues as much as many other friends in different industries, but still feel it necessary to correct people when they have the wrong idea about something to do with my Asian heritage.

Did you always feel like a "real American," and if so, is there a moment that epitomizes it?

I've always felt like an American, and have always been proud to be an American. Every time I travel around the world it reinforces my pride, despite some animosity toward Americans around the world. The reality is that almost everyone that complains about America really only hates our leaders, but typically likes Americans and the American lifestyle. And they'd go to America in a heartbeat if it were a possibility. It's still one of the few places in the world where people can choose their future. No matter how hard that road may be, it is still a possibility, whereas in 80% of the world there really is no way to improve your lot in life. The pride I felt when I looked at my soldiers who came together through very hard times to accomplish our missions is probably my greatest accomplishment in the military: soldiers who came together from different social and economic backgrounds to get things done. Veterans are poor, rich, white, black, young, old, male, female and everything else you can think of. Many classifications leave people out but anyone can be a veteran.

CHAPTER TWENTY-NINE

Pakee Fang 方柏基 (1982–)
U.S. Marine Corps

Pakee Fang was recruited as a Marine in his high school before 9/11. He was part of the first wave of Marines sent to Iraq to provide engineering support and humanitarian aid, and to search for improvised explosive devices. His adventures around the world also include him translating with a Chinese French soldier for their units in Africa, and being offered a bride in Kenya. He has a BS in Electrical Engineering from City College of New York and works at the U.S. Patent and Trademark Office.

I was born on September 2, 1982, in Dongguan [東莞], Canton in China. My mother was an elementary school teacher who taught literature. My dad worked as a construction consultant in Hong Kong. I came with my family to the United States in 1993 on July 5th, one day after Independence Day. I was 10 years old and knew only two words in English: yes and no. My family moved into a cramped two-room apartment that housed eight people on Chrystie Street in Chinatown [New York].

My parents spoke no English. But they had chosen to move to America because my mother strongly felt that America was the land of freedom and opportunity. She was pregnant and carrying my sister, and was forced to hide from the Chinese government in fear of being forced to have an abortion. She didn't want to have to get an abortion, which was what led her to want to live in America. She gave birth to my sister, Shu Juan, in 1988. My aunt, who ran a daycare in Chinatown, petitioned for her family to come to America.

In 1993, my family started our life in New York. I was sent to bilingual class at P.S. 42 on Hester Street for elementary school, and then to I.S. 131, also on Hester Street. Years went by and everyone tried their best to adjust to the new life. My mom experienced a dramatic career change from a teacher of literature in China to a dimsum lady at the HSF restaurant in Chinatown. My dad worked in a meat store and handled meat processing. Everyone was getting stressed out, especially my dad who thought that working 12-hour days six days a week was not worth the move to America, and ended up spending lots of time at mahjong clubs. I rebelled and didn't put much effort into school. I didn't see a point to it. I was getting a C-minus average and just getting by. My life as an adolescent was not harmonious.

The bad thing about spending so much time in Chinatown is that you don't pick up true American culture. Chinatown is isolated, it's an island. I realized that after I went into the military. The military exposed me to a lot of experiences and foreign cultures, taking me to 14 countries.

Before the military, I couldn't really speak English because I'd lived in Chinatown for so long, and didn't generally have to use English to communicate, to get by. People in Chinatown are stuck here. They can't ever leave town due to lack of English.

My relationship with my father grew tense; we argued and got into fights. I didn't really have a dream. Somehow when I was young I had this dream of wanting to move out due to the struggles we had to face. I was 16 in my junior year at my high school.

It was a really tough time. My dad and I would argue dearly. Then one day I saw a recruiter who came to the school. He asked me what I wanted to do, what my dream was. And at that time I didn't even know what I wanted to do. I had no ambition, nothing. I didn't even know if I wanted to go to college. I think because—right now I think that back then, I didn't have a role model—someone I could say "I want to be like him."

I wasn't extremely close to any of my relatives here in America, not even with my relatives in Chinatown. Here, everyone works 12 hours a day and only gets one day off. On the day off, nobody wants to do anything.

I talked to the recruiter at school but didn't sign up right away. It was not until I had a big fight with my father and the neighbor called the police. Then I gave serious thought about joining the military. It was because I didn't know what to do with my life—let's put it that way.

One day I walked up to the recruiter's office and asked what opportunities, in terms of education and travel, there were. This was 1999, when there was no war. The recruiter told me that if I joined the Marines, I would not only travel a lot, I would become independent and gain experience—life experience, while serving in the military. So I took the ASVAB [Armed Services Vocational Aptitude Battery] test. I passed, and enlisted December 24, 1999. I was 17, and did the delayed entry program. Although considered "in" right after signing the contract, I was allowed to wait until after graduation to start boot camp. I got my parents' consent because I convinced my mom and told her there was nothing to worry about because it was peacetime. My mom in turn persuaded my dad. I was looking forward to going. I was just trying to leave my life here in Chinatown behind. I finished high school in June 2000, and was shipped to boot camp on September 18, two weeks after I turned 18.

Boot camp was very frightening. It was the first time I left the Chinese American community, and I realized I didn't really speak fluent English. If you live and grow up here [in Chinatown] you don't become Americanized because you're keeping to your tradition and the Chinese cultural way of doing things. When I left Chinatown I was exposed to the real western way of life and philosophies.

My friend and classmate Qi Peng also signed up for the military in July 2000. We went together to boot camp at Paris Island in South Carolina. I was in Platoon 3106 which consisted of between 67 and 72 recruits. It was physically and mentally demanding. It's hell for an 18-year-old. A lot of people didn't make it through boot camp and had to drop out or got recycled. Most of the Marine recruits were in their early 20s. Three men were in their 30s, and at least six of us were 17 or 18 years old.

For the first three days we slept only two to three hours per day. After that, normal training started and we got to sleep 8 hours a day so long as we weren't assigned night watch. The recruits are assigned different shifts to guard the barracks. For each hour, one person is assigned to guard. The worst shift is for the people who have to sleep a few hours, then get awakened to stand watch for a while and then have to go back to sleep.

They treat you like crap and break you down mentally and physically. It's really hard to describe. You have to live through it in order to know the experience—they impose military doctrines on your soul and mind. In some sense you become more disciplined, but it's the kind of discipline where you just follow orders without second-guessing. Boot camp taught us the military way of life and how to behave like a Marine.

They teach you what previous veterans had to go through in combat. They impose hardships on you so you can grow and get used to it. If you get captured, or face the same kind of hardships again in combat, you don't freak out.

We got yelled at every single day, had practically no free time, no days off, and only one hour a night to ourselves to write letters. We needed to get permission for the simplest things. Showering or using the bathroom was considered a privilege. Overall it made me more appreciative about life. It opened my eyes and mind and made me see things differently.

They took away your freedom in order for you to serve the free, I think. Boot camp lasted three months even though a single day felt like a year. Training included learning hand to hand combat, martial arts, how to use rifles, and how to repel from a 50-foot tower. It was a time of many firsts. It was also the first time in my entire life that I was exposed to so much cursing, which I thought wasn't necessary. The profanity was so out there. *(Laughs)* The drill instructors cursed constantly, but that was part of the training.

I was learning quickly. I felt that little by little the military was changing me for the better. I went from a person with no ambitions or plans to someone more disciplined, organized, and grateful of the basic necessities of life.

After I finished boot camp, I was sent to Marine Corps Combat Training, where for six weeks I learned small combat tactics. I was put in a fire team of four and learned what to do if I were sent on missions in a four-man team.

Next, I went to Military Occupational Specialty [MOS] school and took an MOS test which determined what job I would specialize in; I was to be a 1391 engineer. I was trained to process fuel for helicopters and jets, which involved using filters, fuel analysis, and scanning oils. Being an engineer also meant that later in Iraq I would be sent on missions to search for and/or destroy Improvised Explosive Devices [IEDs]—an extremely dangerous line of work. My second specialty was as a linguist. I'm fluent in two dialects of Chinese, Cantonese and Mandarin, because my mother taught me Chinese literature when I was growing up. My translation abilities increased my pay by $300 per month. My skills would later come in handy in Djibouti, Africa. Other MOS specialties include supply, infantry, administration, mechanics, and artillery.

After MOS training, I was sent to the Fleet at Camp Pendleton, California, a permanent duty station. I spent 3½ years with the company unit 7th ESB, 1st FSSG. My good performance resulted in my being promoted meritoriously to lance corporal, and I was selected for special assignments and missions. This was where I was stationed when 9/11 happened.

During peacetime, military duty felt like being in the Peace Corps. But 9/11 united the Marines and gave us a feeling of relevance. The tragedy gave everyone a renewed sense of patriotism

After 9/11 I was sent to training operations in Mojave Desert. I did four field operations, each lasting about 1½ months, in the Desert of 29 Palms, a Marine Corps base for Air Ground Task Force in California. While I was there, I personally experienced no less than three sandstorms at 29 Palms. Each sand storm lasted a couple hours. Sand got into your food and canteen cups and you end up eating sand. Sometimes, our tents got blown away due to the strong wind. We couldn't even go to the bathroom because our porta-potties were also getting blown away. During one of the sandstorms, I witnessed another Marine in a porta-potty getting blown away by the strong wind. After the storm subsided a little, he crawled out covered in feces. By the end of the trainings, we felt very confortable for deployment overseas. Everyone in my unit was put on standby status thereafter. We thought we were all going to end up in Afghanistan for sure, but that wasn't the case. It still puzzles me today that the United States sent only 25,000 ground troops in Afghanistan while we have 150,000 in Iraq. I don't know why the government does that. I don't know what the strategic planning behind that is about.

One of the highlights in my military career was when I was sent to join an elite Special Operations unit—the 13th Marine Expeditionary Unit [MEU]. It was in 2002 and I was 19 years old. I learned riot training and went through obstacle courses being shot with pepper spray, which was awfully painful. The pepper spray was ten times stronger than gas chamber training. Gas chamber training is where they send us into a chamber filled with tear gas, and we all have to take off our gas masks. My eyes and skin burned in the gas chamber but it was not as painful as pepper spray.

After all the training and standing by, I finally received my order to Iraq and was deployed to the theater [combat areas]. My first major operation in Iraq was in a little town in the outskirt area of Basra, Iraq. My unit was to guard oil refineries and to stop drug trafficking in border towns. During one of my missions I was specifically assigned to look for IEDs put out by insurgents from Al Qaeda and leftover ammunition of the Republican Guard from Saddam's era, and to destroy these IEDs and ammunition after we found them. Some of these explosives were pressure-activated devices. Others were remote-detonated, which means that a person could be hiding behind a building, waiting to press a button when they saw a target.

We'd travel in a convoy of Humvees or 5-ton trucks. It was really frightening at first. When we were cruising down the road we witnessed a lot of horrific scenes ... like blown up tanks ... and some human remains, which we saw from a distance. We also saw lots of burned up buildings, destroyed vehicles and impoverished villages.

It was my first mission. There was uncertainty in my mind about what to expect. When I was finding IEDs, I saw—you'd see leftover bodies of the Republican Guard, the men from Saddam's army. You could see just what was going on in their minds right before they died. You see how they retreated. You see how they ditched their gear. There weren't tons of bodies, but you'd see one here, two there.

Searching for IEDs and munitions could have easily resulted in death for me at any moment. The explosives have no defined shape and can look like anything, from a rock or a bottle of water to a box. We used metal detectors, and found only a few of them, but I have heard some teams would find 10–15 of them in a day. If these IEDs and leftover munitions weren't found, they might go off and kill Coalition troops, or worse, civilians. When I was in Iraq in 2003, most IEDs were pressure-activated and not remote-controlled because U.S. bombers at the time destroyed a lot of antennas and wireless devices. Wireless connection was out of service. In 2007, IEDs had become more sophisticated, advanced and accurate now that wireless had been brought back.

Besides searching for IEDs, I was assigned on humanitarian missions, where we helped rebuild villages by bringing in electricity and running water.

Some of the locals didn't like us because we were the invaders, of course. Sometimes they cursed at us and threw rocks at us. But we weren't allowed to shoot them because they were civilians. We did a lot of good things for the country. But there was also a lot of destruction; we destroyed buildings. But still, we did some good. I was proud of that. Most of the locals thanked us. This was still early in the war. There wasn't really any resentment against Americans yet. Most of the local people were friendly.

We also constructed tables and chairs for the schools and gave the children school supplies, which was to win the hearts and minds of the locals. When you walked into a school, you didn't see a school. You'd see four walls and no windows, no chairs, tables. You'd see broken doors and broken furniture. But American efforts changed that.

In December 2003, out of nowhere, my unit was ordered to Djibouti for a joint operation with the French army's special forces. The French lieuten-ant and the French soldiers didn't speak English. My lieutenant and colleagues didn't speak French. But there happened to be one French Chinese soldier in the French army. The French Chinese soldier and I ended up translating for our troops in Mandarin Chinese until a French-English linguist was brought in.

In February 2004 we were called to Kenya for a humanitarian mission. We

U.S. Marines with Coalition Forces

landed in the island of Lamu. It's a small island by the east coast of Kenya. I became friends with the Kenyan soldiers. They speak fluent English so we had no problems communicating. Everyone there was really poor. In the first week, we helped them refurbish schools—again an operation to win hearts and minds. Many Kenyan army soldiers assisted us.

I became close to one of the Kenyan soldiers. One day, he asked me if I wanted a gift. Before we landed in Djibouti, we were briefed on their culture and told not to decline any gifts because it's considered disrespectful in Islamic society.

He said, "Hey, Corporal Fang, I have a present to give you." I said, "Great, what is it?" He said, "Okay, I'm going to give you my sister."

He was serious. It was not a joke. I explained to him he can't offer a person as a present because every person has his/her own rights. I tried to talk him out of it, but he kept insisting. I seriously couldn't persuade him, so I talked to my friends. Everyone in my unit tried to talk him out of it. He was advertising his sister saying that he could get her to come down to meet me and that she was really pretty.

At the end of the operation we had a big celebration on the island. We had a lobster feast, but the Kenyans thought it was disgusting. They don't eat much seafood, if any. In Lamu, seafood is really inexpensive, since most locals resent it, but for the seafood lovers, we thought, "Wow, how cheap."

At first sight, what I encountered in Africa was a real culture shock. Whenever we go anywhere new, we experience culture shock. Muslims don't eat pork. And you think shaking hands with your left hand is not a big deal but to them it's really offensive. You realize every culture has their taboos; it's part of their identity. As an American, these taboos don't make sense to me. But people retain them to keep tradition. Sometimes things that are so insignificant to us are a great deal to those guys. The whole stereotyping conflict and all these racial conflicts start because of these little differences in culture.

Are military guys are more open-minded because they see more?

No, not particularly. Most of these guys are educated by Western upbringing and education. When some of them initially encounter something completely different, there's sometimes shock and resentment. They're not exactly understanding at first. But people do come around after a while—at least some people do.

I was the only Asian American in my platoon of 35. I personally knew ten other Chinese Americans from my high school who also signed up for military service. In the military, people did get to know me as a person, but that's everywhere in America. When you talk to a person of another race, the first thing that will come to their mind is what the media has shown then. A lot of times the media portrays Asians as being poor and from third world countries. When they see you, they think, "Oh, you're all that, combined." The first things they see are the bad parts. But I'm sure everyone has encountered some form of stereotyping and racism.

Wherever we went, most of the time we had to carry a 70-pound pack. In Iraq it was hot, and it sucked. There would be sandstorms and you couldn't see anything. We had to wander around blurry-eyed, not being able to see what was in front of us. In Africa, it was not only hot but extremely humid. Besides having combat to deal with, we had the daily struggles with nature. It was a fight within the fight. We had to fight the bad guys and overcome the problems that nature presented.

In Africa, we gave medical aid to locals. Lots of those children I saw suffered malnutrition and were skinny. Most of the parents lacked knowledge of basic hygiene and education—of how to take care of a child or infant.

Most of the kids had never tasted chocolate. When I gave them pieces of chocolate, they'd fight for it because they were curious. They liked it and asked for more. What we think is basic, like the idea of having three meals a day, or candy—is luxury to these guys. They have no healthcare at all there. Being exposed to these things gave me the realization of how fortunate I am in this country, in America. Those little things piled up and gave me aspiration to become something greater. After I went through all those missions I realized I wanted to finish college when I got back home.

Pakee and the French Foreign Legionnaires

I met so many kids who so desperately wanted to go to school. In Lamu, an island off the coast of Kenya, I met a 12-year-old boy who was in fourth grade. He was old for his class. Every morning, the boy ran 15 minutes to get to the other side of the island just to get to class. That was really amazing and you don't see that in America. It made me reflect on how I took school for granted.

Every time I encountered these tragic yet inspirational events, I had this heart-wrenching feeling that made me want to do something to change the way that human beings should live. I saw oppression of females in some Muslim communities, which made me more appreciative of the freedoms in America. My sister can marry who she wants. She can go to the school she chooses to go to, and can follow her heart. A lot of these women can't even go outside their homes without getting permission from the male in charge.

After I completed my assignment with the 13th MEU, I was discharged from active duty and went back to New York on August 4, 2004. I enrolled at City Tech, which was the CUNY school closest to where my family lived. My four years of military experience dramatically changed me. I used to be very belligerent, somewhat naive and ignorant, and now I transformed into someone who cares about everything around me. I became grateful for all that I possessed, for things most people take for granted. My relationships with family improved. In my first year at City Tech, my GPA was 4.0 because I didn't take anything for granted, and appreciated everything offered to me. I was a C-minus average in high school.

My active duty contract terminated on September 17, 2004. But my Reserve contract ended December 22, 2007. When I became a civilian again I noticed a lot of vets are having a hard time trying to relate their emotions and experiences to others. And I know a couple of vets who didn't do go college because they feel like they don't fit in. They started school but didn't finish. Of course, some vets have PTSD; I don't know any personally. I know one guy who committed suicide but I wasn't close to him.

After leaving the military, I found it difficult to adjust to the mediocrity in the performance of daily routines in civilian society. In the military, even when you were just standing by around barracks, you would still feel a sense of purpose and pride—which is something I really don't experience enough in civilian society.

I also have a distaste for the many people who judge—whether they are judging the government, America, or just other people, imposing their own philosophies when they don't really see what's happening, haven't been anywhere, and haven't experienced enough to give them the right to criticize other people.

At City Tech I kept my military experience a secret from my professors and classmates. I knew my professors had their own perspectives about the war, and didn't think it was good to tell them I just came out of the war. I didn't know if they'd have their own agenda, so I chose to keep my service on the down-low. I don't share my military status straight off, unless I meet another veteran or someone asks me about it. It's something only my closest friends know. The general attitude of most students toward education at City Tech is different from mine. My classmates were these teenagers sometimes behaving like kids. They were these 18-year-olds la-de-da-ing.

I studied electrical engineering technology, which is a technical degree and different from an actual electrical engineering degree. After a semester, I transferred to City College of New York, which offers an electrical engineering degree. I plan to get an engineering master's degree as well, even though the GI Bill will not cover that.

* * *

95% of people I know don't want to be there. No one goes in and thinks "I'm going to save the world." It's a job, a sense of duty, like a doctor treating a patient or a lawyer defending a client. That's what you sign up for. 99% of the servicemen and women don't have a political view because they don't want to take part in the political discussions. The reason is to keep your conscience clean from all these political influences.

Some politicians say we're going in for oil, for freedom. You can't really get into the political/intellectual questions because you're going to create this doubt and vacuum in your conscience. If you have to go to the front line, you can't be telling yourself I'm here for the oil, otherwise …

You cannot doubt your mission, otherwise you put yourself in danger and men in danger because of your doubt—your uncertainty about why you're there.

In the military, you don't think about freedom and intangible, abstract things. You think "I'm going to try to keep alive and keep the guy next to me alive and hopefully we can come home safe." When the bullets start flying you can't count on freedom to keep you alive. You count on the M16 and body armor to keep you alive.

Patriotism and freedom—those abstract things—you keep for faith in your prayers at night. But not in combat. You only see those things [the abstract] when you're far away from the theater. "I did this noble service" is something you only say after, not during.

CHAPTER THIRTY

Michael Chan 陳天寶 (1985–　　)
U.S. Marine Corps

Michael Chan grew up in Chinatown, New York, and talks about overcoming a difficult home life and being in street fights. He studied film at the University of Southern California and is making a movie about a troubled youth who, wanting to find a home, decides to join the military after 9/11. He was deployed to Iraq twice.

I was part of India 3rd Battalion 12th Marines. It's an artillery unit based out of Okinawa, but we were attached to 5th Battalion 10th Marines in Camp Lejeune, North Carolina.

On my first tour in September of 2006 I was deployed to Fallujah, Iraq. My first assignment was security for EOD Marines. EOD is the acronym for Explosive Ordinance Disposal. If you have ever watched the film *The Hurt Locker*, we were security for the bomb experts. My second rotation was field artillery in Camp Fallujah. My third rotation was Convoy Security Detachment for the U.S. Army.

What happens in field artillery?

Pretty much, we're on a base. And if someone calls in an artillery mission from within a 20-mile radius, and they need someone to bomb this building, or they have targets they need to wipe out, instead of calling an air strike, they would call for an artillery strike, and that would be us. At night, if Marines are on patrol with low visibility and they need some light in the sky, we'll shoot an illumination round. It's an artillery round that contains a million watts of light that would flare and illuminate the sky for 60 seconds.

And then what was CSD?

I was a CSD, which stands for Convoy Security Detachment. We were attached to the U.S. Army and provided security for them. They would go out with these massive trucks and sweep the streets of Fallujah for Improvised Explosive Devices [IEDs]. These missions would take as long as 30 hours to complete. We would be driving out really slow, like 2 miles an hour, and we stopped almost everywhere to clean out the route of bombs and provide security for the soldiers, making sure they are safe so they can get the job done.

Michael Chan, Parris Island, South Carolina, 2004

What was growing up like?

I was born in New York in 1985, December 27th. I was born in Beth Israel Hospital. I lived in Chinatown and went to P.S. 42, I.S. 131, and then I went to Bayard Rustin High School for the Humanities on West 18th Street. Bayard Rustin High School for the Humanities is gone now. It's broken up into mini schools.

My family was separated, so I never really saw my mother that often. I have a younger sister, but when we were younger I was staying with my maternal grandparents and my sister was staying with my paternal grandparents. She's four years younger than me, and we never really got along. We fought a lot when we were younger. I did my fair share of bullying as a big brother, arguing who's the favorite in the family. We were separated almost my entire life up to the point I left to enlist. We saw each other occasionally but never really talked, and if we did, we spoke about our cousins. I have not talked to her for over 10 years now.

My parents were separated, in a sense. They got back together, and then they finally divorced later. And pretty much at that point when they divorced, I kind of just went and did my own thing. I was maybe like 13 or 14. It was after an incident where my father beat the hell out of me. That incident almost caused me to lose my eye after he threw a glass at my face, shattering into mini razors. My mom tried to hide all of this but my school found out and the police came and went searching for my dad. At that point, I realized I lost trust in my mother. I had to figure out what I wanted to do with my life without them.

And that was when you decided to just go on your own and do your own stuff?

Yeah. I went to school, but I began to cut school a lot. It was not that it was a cool thing to do, but it was the simple fact that I did not value education. And you know, I never did good in school but I managed to graduate from high school with like a 65 average. There was a point when I was 15, and I talked to a recruiter about enlisting. He told me I need a high school diploma or a GED (Good Enough Degree, as they say) to enlist. At that point I straightened up and was motivated to go to school and pass my classes. I skipped lunch to take classes. It was the roughest semester of my life but I did it. I graduated at 17 with a 65 average all around. The next question came.

I wanted to do something else rather than go to college. I had already thought about enlisting when I was 15, when I was a sophomore in high school. But because I was too young at the time, they just didn't really bother with me. A few years passed and I turned 17. I still couldn't enlist because I needed parental consent. I didn't tell my parents anything about enlisting. Summer 2003 I had just graduated from high school and I was thinking about going to college for a semester, but then I ran into financial trouble paying for school. My mother did not want anything to do with me after I turned 18. She threatened to kick me out of the house. I wasn't sure if she was joking or not, but I took it seriously. I went to LaGuardia Community College for a semester, but I felt out of place. I felt like I needed to find some type of spark that would give me the drive to succeed in life. I knew, at that moment, I would rather train to become an applicant of the Marine Corps. So I dropped out of college halfway and decided to train.

At that time, I was trying to get in shape, because I wasn't really in shape to commit to the Marines. The physical demands were a lot more than the Army and the Air Force and the other branches, so I—

When did you first learn about the military, or see it as an option?

You know, 9/11 happened, and I lived on Cherry Street by Pathmark. I was 14 maybe at the time. That's when I thought about it. It was always an idea I considered; to really do something with myself, I guess. It was 2002, I think, when I started thinking about it.

Were they around in your school recruiting, or did you just go to one of the recruitment centers?

No, I approached them. I went to the office over in J&R in City Hall. They're no longer there. They relocated to a new office near BMCC. There were a few people in my high school who were talking about it. One guy who was a year older than me was talking about joining the Marines. I had no idea what the Marines and Army—what the difference was. But he said the Marines trained the hardest. They were considered the most challenging branch of service. Not everyone can be a Marine, or at least that's what I'd been told. And then I did a little research. The Marines train for 13 weeks; the Army trains for 8. It was a cool idea for me [to join the Marines] because, you know, I grew up in New York with this background fighting. And it wasn't the ideal life I wanted; it just happened. I wanted to be the best, and you always want to strive hard to get there.

When you were fighting in the streets, were they fights with kids at school, gangs, or what?

They weren't exactly gang members. They're just a bunch of people with a crew name that represented them. I remember one time after school, in junior high school, I was getting ready to leave the school through the back exit. There was a group of people looking for me, for something stupid I said about one of their friends. I got held up in the back of the school. They were bullies. I didn't think a meaningless comment could get you into so much trouble, you know? Of course I tried to talk them out of it, but that never works. I would go home bleeding and I would try to stay away from the territory where they loiter around. My grandmother lives near the subsidized government housing by Pathmark, and there have been hate crimes since I've lived there for quite some time. I mean you just have to be smart about it and know how to avoid situations like that. I had a fair share of fights with African Americans, Chinese, Hispanics. But most of the time I got in a fight, it was Asian people. They were my own people, or at least I thought they were.

Fast forward, I didn't want to go to college, and I just wanted to leave home. I wanted to do something else. I wanted to go help and fight the war. I just didn't want to stay at home and go to college with everyone else. I wanted meaning in my life. Because everyone else, all my friends, they all went to college.

So that was something that really inspired me to join. I wanted to get away from home. I wanted to get away from the life that I was living. You know, I didn't want anything to do with my family at the time, and things just weren't going so well for me. I wanted to do something different. And that was a perfect opportunity for me. I wanted to try something else.

So when you told your parents—did you tell your parents or did you just tell your grandparents?

No, I didn't tell them. *(Laughs)*

You didn't tell them? (Laughs)

No, I didn't tell them.

So you just went off? And when did they discover you left?

I guess two weeks after I was gone … I was friends with my landlord, Mark. I lived over on Hester Street in front of P.S. 42. I was good friends with Mark, and at boot camp I had written him a letter. Two weeks later, he received the letter. And I guess *he* showed it to my mom. When I left for boot camp, I told only a handful of people. None of my immediate family knew, except for maybe my cousin, but I told him not to say anything.

So did you say anything to your grandparents before you left? What did you tell them? I'm just going somewhere?

I didn't tell them anything.

Final Inspection, Parris Island, South Carolina, 2004

So you just disappeared?

I just disappeared, pretty much. *(Laughs)*

Is that something that you did often, so it didn't surprise them? Had you left home before?

No, I hadn't. I'd never really left home before. But I guess they were assuming that I was staying over at a friend's house or something, maybe. I hated going home and dealing with the drama.

But you weren't scared that if you died in the war, your family might never find out?

No, it's boot camp. Only training goes on in boot camp, although there have been cases where recruits die at boot camp. But when you're enlisting, you're required to include guardian contacts in case something were to happen. On my 18th birthday—it was a Saturday in 2003—two days after Christmas, I went to the recruiter's office. I was sitting in the office all day just filling out paperwork.

They gave me options on duty stations: West Coast, East Coast, or Japan. At the time, I didn't know anything about the West Coast. I'd never flown in a plane before I went to boot camp. I'd never been on a vacation my entire life, so I didn't know anything. I [said], Let me stay on the east coast. They ask you if you have a preference, but you don't really get your preference. You know what I'm saying? If you're a product of the east coast, you're more likely going to get shipped to the east coast.

I got on a plane with a bunch of other people, and we took a plane to South Carolina for boot camp. It was definitely not what I expected as far as what you've seen in the movies, you've heard the stories. But when you're actually there, it's kind of scary, you know?

How many Asians were there? Did you stick out?

There was one Filipino dude, there was one Chinese dude, and then there was one Korean dude. And then the rest of them were either white or Hispanic or black. In my platoon, we had about 40-something people.

Was there hazing?

Not really. When I got in trouble—you get picked on and then after a while it stops, because they start seeing that you don't mess up as much. I was getting into trouble the first month because it was hard for me to adjust. I had no idea what to expect and it was so shocking for me. I think it was for everyone. At one point, I forgot my name; I forgot my past life as a civilian. When I had left boot camp, the world seemed strange and different from what I remembered.

They didn't pick on me specifically, but just … Let's say you got in trouble on Monday. They're going to harass you until Friday.

What do you mean by getting in trouble?

I mean if you're a second late to form the line when reveille is being called, you're in trouble. If you don't run as fast as the group, you're in trouble. For me, I was just being belligerent and didn't really scream as loud—I had lost my voice. I couldn't scream anymore. They wanted me to scream louder, and I'm just like—I'm just tired of it. *(Laughs)* When it came to running, I was the slowest in the platoon. I was this overweight kid who'd never run more than one mile in the last 18 years of my life until enlisting and we were running up to three miles every other day. You do the math.

Well, what are you supposed to do when you lose your voice and they want you to scream and you just don't have a voice?

Yeah, you still scream. *(Laughs)*

Was there anything else shocking about it?

It was more culture shock than anything. I'm from New York and I felt like I was in a different country or something. You meet people from so many cultures, from the south, the north.

We had combat training for a month in North Carolina, and then I was shipped to Oklahoma. They teach you jungle warfare, tactical movements, how to camp out in the woods for two weeks, survival skills, and you learn how to read a map if you're lost. In Fort Sill, Oklahoma, I did artillery training for my main job. You learn how to use the giant 155-millimeter howitzers.

After two months at my duty station in North Carolina, we were deployed to Okinawa for six months. We did training in the cold weather in Mount Fuji. Then I came back to North Carolina to my permanent duty station, which was Camp Lejeune. And then, we were told that we might be going to Iraq, so we went to California for desert training at 29 Palms in California. Six months later, we deployed to Fallujah. We were there seven months, from September '06 to April '07. And then I went back again with a different unit from July or August '07 to late January '08.

How did you feel when you first found out you were going to Iraq?

I was happy because this is what I signed up to do, to hold our enemies accountable for their actions and protect this country. Some people in the military never get an opportunity to deploy. I was ready to get into the good fight.

I was ready to go. When you're based out in the U.S., you're not doing anything—just training, it's like a Monday to Friday job. Some say it's better to get deployed than to stay on U.S. soil. At least in deployment you feel like you're accomplishing goals. But when you're at home, it's like they've always got some bullshit details for you to do. Today you might be picking up trash on the floor for a good hour and then you'll clean the same rifle that you probably cleaned yesterday that may or may not have collected some dust. Yet, the duties of a Marine in garrison require us to remain vigilant.

People have different reasons for joining, but I think one of the reasons that we all had in common was that we wanted to go out there and fight for people who can't fight for themselves.

On my first tour in Fallujah, I did EOD security, field artillery, and convoy security detachment. On my second tour, I did foot patrols. We walked around villages near Fallujah. We pretty much just walked miles every day, and then in the middle [of the deployment], our mission changed. We were still there to look for the bad guys, but at the same time, we were there for the humanitarian mission. Guys would come up to us and complain to us, "Hey, we don't have clean water" and "My daughter is sick" or something. We had a doctor with us, and we would help them out, just kind of building a relationship with the Iraqi people. Our missions completely changed during my second tour. I wasn't sure if we were looking for bad guys or we became the Peace Corps.

The first tour, we got hit so many times, I just don't really—I could have died. I don't know if I can say I liked that tour, but it was a good experience. You kind of absorb the meaning of life when an IED goes off in close proximity.

But the second tour, nothing exciting happened that I can talk about. I can't really compare the two. In the first tour, people got hurt all the time; you didn't know if you were going to live. And you never knew if that meal you were having would be your last. When my second tour was over, I was like "Wow, I didn't even get to fire my gun this time"—you know, you didn't really get to take down any bad guys.

Learning the value of life—I would say I got that in my first tour. Because a lot of vehicles got hit with IEDs. They would go off 30 feet from the vehicle I was sitting in. One of the vehicles would get hit and we would be like "Fuck." I think the scariest part is not knowing if your friends are dead or alive.

And we're in a truck and all you see is dust clouds, and you're checking yourself—okay, you're still alive. Or, at one point, we were dismounted from the vehicle, and we were doing our perimeter search with the EOD Marine, and we got ambushed with pop shots and RPGs. At this point, every little bullshit you

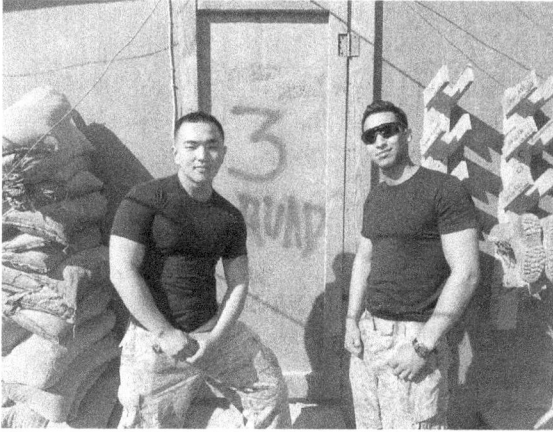

Pumphouse Flanders, Fallujah, Iraq 2007: Michael Chan and David Gil

watch on TV or movies where Rambo picks up a .50-caliber machine gun firing back—that's a joke. The truth of the matter is that the first thing you do is run and take cover. We were all running fast as hell trying to take cover.

They ambushed us. They were shooting at us from where the sun was setting. So they were blinding us from that geometry of fire. It was a really sneaky tactic for them. That was the first time I ever felt my heart beat so fast with flak jacket on. You know, I couldn't even talk that day. I was just speechless. I could have gotten shot in the back or in the head. *(Laughs)*

Where did you get cover? Where did you run to?

I ran to the front of the vehicle, because they were firing from the other direction. I ran in front of the vehicle. And then I thought I could attempt to jump in the vehicle, but that would require my body being exposed for a good five seconds. The vehicle commander who was already inside the vehicle was screaming at me to get in the vehicle—even in a split second if I lifted the door open, I could've gotten hit. My buddy Tony and I decided that this was probably the worst position. We were hoping that our squad would provide fire support to suppress the enemy, but I guess they were frozen, because at the same time, the sun was hitting their faces too, so they couldn't see where they were firing at. That didn't happen, so we ended just taking a leap of faith.

So after all this stuff, you came back intact?

Yeah. I didn't break down. I was just like, "Wow, I could have fucking died out there." And when I got in the vehicle, I kind of just really calmed down, and that's when my heart ... my adrenaline kind of started cooling down, and then you could feel your whole body just—in that shocking moment. My adrenaline started slowing down, and then I started thinking about what could have happened. I tried to think about, was that a good approach? Was that the appropriate action for me to do at that point?

Wow. For people who didn't see Hurt Locker, *can you describe what happens, what this job is?*

The EOD guys, the explosive guys, their job is to disarm bombs. They go out in this truck. Someone says, "There might be a possible bomb on this rice bag. Can you please check it out?" They'll go out there and we'll roll with them as a security team. Our job is to protect them. So we'll roll out with these guys, and sometimes these guys are so crazy, they'll jump out of their vehicle and they don't care.

They'll take a knife and stab the rice bag and see if there's anything in there. And these guys are just mentally not there, but they're definitely great people. They're great people, and they're like just straight-up nuts, you know? And then sometimes they'll take out the robot, which is cool because they have a camera on the robot. The robot blows up. It's like a million-dollar robot, but that's all right. Because at least no one is hurt.

At the end of the day, we'll have a shitload of IEDs—however many we have—we'll take it all to a specific location and we'll dispose of them. Just put it in an open area, put a timer on it, and then we'll go like a mile back and then EOD will detonate them. So that was their job. My job was pretty much to provide security for them.

On holidays—like it was Thanksgiving for us, but I think it was the end of Ramadan—it gets crazy. But on an average, you'll go on four missions, maybe.

Iraq is worse than the ghetto. The houses are just lumber, concrete just falling off, roads all messed up. It looks like ancient times where most houses don't even have power, and the whole thing is just made out of broken down—The whole place is just fucked up. Just think of a ghetto in the United States times ten. The ghettos here, at least we've got project buildings. Over there, there's no windows. I don't know how people survive in the cold. You've got telephone lines or power lines or whatever, they're all tilted or they got run over or something. And the people there, I don't know, it's like they're still living in like the 19th century or something. It just doesn't feel like America, the United States or China, or any other country where technology is more modern.

In my second tour, we were in the village. The guys we were dealing with were mostly farmer guys—although we detained a very important party, which was probably the only thing that happened out there. They called him the four-fingered bandit or something because he had four fingers on one hand.

My active duty ended in 2008. I'm in school now, at USC studying film. I made films when I was in Iraq and Japan. I made little, short, funny films. They were amateurish. Like the stuff you see 10-year-olds make on YouTube nowadays. It was funny, because teenagers couldn't get hold of the footage I got, of the stupid stuff that Marines do—the fighting sometimes, or just being comedians half the time. So I used to make these videos, and I wanted to pursue a career in film. And I ended up coming back home, and with my low grades and my undistinguished academic career, it was really hard for me to go to a good school, even though I had a GI Bill and all that stuff. I went back to LaGuardia Community College for a semester, and then I went back to community college. And it was different, because this time I wanted to learn and stuff.

I graduated from community college in December of 2009, and then I went on to Hunter College for a semester. And when I was attending Hunter College I received my acceptance letter to University of Southern California. And I moved out here for film and now I go to school out here.

Actually, most of my films are more military-oriented stories. The film that I'm about to shoot next month that I've been writing the script for—it's the short film that got me into the USC film school. The film is called *Choice*.

I'm remaking it because I have a lot more experience making films now. It's pretty much a story about this guy who's a troubled youth. And it takes place in 2001, 2002. And he makes a choice in life on whether to go to college or enlist in the military.

Overall, my military experience has been good and bad. It was good because I got to experience what 95% of the people in this world will never experience. And going into the military is such a culture shock, and you learn all this stuff about people. Before, I didn't know half the states' names. I knew there were 50 states in America, but—then you meet someone from Wyoming. You meet different cultures and different people, and you learn a lot about people's histories.

You come out a little more disciplined, being able to think for yourself. I mean, every now and then I would get in trouble, but I would try to correct my mistakes and move on. Learn from my mistakes and just progress as a better person. One day there will be peace and love after the wars are over.

I feel like that's what the military teaches you. Being able to think for yourself and just being able to improve yourself—you know, always improving yourself as a person, individually. I guess I'm trying to say I learned many values.

And I guess the bad part is—I'm going to go back to what I was trying to say about going to war. I felt like, I come home, I'm a different person. I don't want to be that different person. And 9 out of 10 times people come home and they're just not themselves.

At one point, you know, you see that in the movies and stuff, but you never really understand it until years down the line. Then you realize you changed. All of your friends might finally come up and tell you, "You know, you're like a whole different person. I feel like I don't know you anymore," or whatever. I guess what they're trying to say is that I've changed since I was in the military. I've become a different person.

What kind of different person? Did they tell you how you changed?

Yeah, it's good and bad. I guess they were focusing more on the negative parts, where you don't—how should I say it? You're more like an asshole now or something, or you're really just not yourself. Like you're not the person who I remember, like this really nice guy or some stuff like that.

Do you think that's true or do you think they just remember wrong?

I think it's true, and it's false at the same time. I would definitely say I've become more educated after the war. And people's beliefs tend to change over time when they're more knowledgeable in that specific field. So I'm more knowledgeable on the war and terrorism, but at the same time, what do I know? Or what do I believe in? Or do I think the war is right? Do I believe the war is wrong? You know, honestly my answer is I'm just told what to do. I'm just the soldier.

But I also burned friendships when I came home. They didn't really understand what I was going through. Transitioning back home from—like, you're fighting the war last month, and then the next month you're in a classroom with a pen and paper. Things of that nature take time to transition. And I'm still having a hard time transitioning every now and then. They don't understand that aspect—that whatever you did the last four years, you can't just throw it out the window. You can't forget about it. I guess, yeah, that kind of just burned my relationship with most of my friends.

Any thoughts about being Chinese American or the way things are for Chinese Americans?

Yeah. I would say when I first got there in boot camp, I saw three other dudes that were of Asian descent. One Chinese guy, one Filipino and one Korean. And you know, I never saw them afterwards. I guess they all had different jobs. You don't really see a lot of Asians around in the military, at least from what I remembered. Asians made a small population in the Marine Corps.

There was a corporal in charge of me. This dude was from Nebraska—Omaha. This dude, he didn't like me. And he would fuck with me. He would fuck with me and get me to do all these extra details. He was a corporal. I was a PFC, a private first class.

He would mess with me and make me do all the extra shit details. I was getting frustrated. There were times where I wanted to fight him. I just wanted to pick up a hammer and beat him in the head with it. But I guess for me, I told you this—I grew up in a neighborhood where there's no such thing as easy living. It's a dog-eat-dog world. I was good at one thing though: I knew how to fight back. I didn't take shit from people or at least not from people I didn't respect.

And at one point, I just lost it. I started training harder and harder so I could put him in his place. He was still a corporal and I still had to put my hands behind my back and talk to him because of his rank. At one point I spoke my mind, I told him, "The day you get out of the Marine Corps, I'm going to come look for you."

And he asked me if that was a direct threat. And he was like, "Do you want to take this in the room?" And of course I wanted to say yeah, let's get it on.

But I was thinking about the consequences and I knew this dude was a rat; he'd probably dime me out in a heartbeat after I kicked his ass.

I guess I grew up a little different in a sense, but we're all the same. And that's one thing about Asians in the military. I read this one article about how Asians preach on going to school and getting good grades. It really got to me, because I know what they're saying, that you don't really see a lot of Asians in the military. We're a minority, believe it or not. And from my personal experience, I had that situation. But you know, for me, was I really willing to assault somebody and go to jail for him. Knowing my chain of command was all jacked up, I'd probably go to jail for many years for a jab to his face. That dude just really made two years of my life miserable and rough. This guy was not a good person.

* * *

I was part of the American Legion Kimlau Post when I was still in New York. I was working in the recruiter's office downtown with Sergeant Ng who was part of the American Legion. So he connected me. I volunteered at the Chinese New Year's parade and was the color guard.

Do you speak Cantonese or Fujianese?

I speak Cantonese and Fujianese. I'm a firm believer that one day—maybe not in the next 10, 20 years, but one day—Asian Americans are going to have a good, direct representation in the military. There won't be bashing of people of Asian American cultures.

Now that you've come back to civilian society, everyone has a political opinion. Do you have thoughts on the war? Are you against it or for it, or do you have mixed feelings?

I think the war was a waste of money. I think it was really monetary reasons that tied us into this invasion. And the outcome of it really—the question is,

Camp Geiger, North Carolina, 2004

Fallujah, Iraq, 2007

Fallujah, Iraq, 2007: David Gil, Luis Cardena and Michael Chan

where are these weapons of mass destruction?

There was some good stuff that we did out there. We freed the Iraqi people. The ones who wanted to be free of this tyrant, Saddam. That was something good that we did, giving them liberty, and doing this stuff for them. But at the same time, a lot of people lost their lives on their war.

And you know, like the Vietnam War, we lost a lot of people. And we didn't accomplish anything. And I feel like—going back to college and learning about all this history, you really are more educated as far as what's going on with the world.

So in my opinion, I'm not tied with any political party or anything, but to me, I feel like we were told what to do. But do I think the war was right or wrong? That's not for me to judge. I'm not in that position of power to really say whether going to war was the right thing to do or not. I mean—

But as a citizen you do have a right to an opinion.

Well, you know, 9/11 was a horrific tragedy. But I think going to war wasn't absolutely the right answer to that—for the solution. Going to war was not the only solution. When 9/11 happened, even though I didn't have family who lost lives, I was pretty devastated from it, because I lived literally a mile away from there. You know, on Cherry Street. You take the FDR and a mile down, you're at the World Trade. So I was pretty devastated from that, but I feel like war wasn't exactly the solution. Sometimes, the way I look at it, there could have been a different approach.

I think invading a country is definitely not a solution. And trying to change political affairs and trying to—I think the Americans should have really supported apprehending Saddam Hussein, but leaving the innocent people out of the story. A lot of innocent people died in the war. Going to war, you're invading a whole country when you're just looking for one person who's responsible for this.

Graduation, University of Southern California
School of Cinematic Arts, 2012

Like the Taliban—you're looking for a specific group. When you invade a country, you're targeting everybody. And that's just not the right thing to go by. It's not a good solution. It's just poor, poor choices. So I feel like, in regard to going to war, I think we also defended the honor of the victims who died in 9/11.

So when you were in Fallujah, you said you saw some good things, like you helped them get water and stuff. But politically, did nothing really change? Do you think it got better or do you think it's still a big mess?

I think nothing really—I think the whole war, like 10 years we've been over there, nothing has really changed. We invaded a country, pillaged the country and, really, the only good news was we killed Osama bin Laden and captured Saddam. But the Taliban is still there. We spent 10 years trying to find the insurgents, but it looks like they'll never die. And a lot of soldiers, Americans—our brothers and sisters—are dead. You know?

Do you have friends who died or got injured?

My friend, he killed himself. He was on my first tour, and then he went on another tour just like me, but he went to a different unit. And he came home battling PTSD, and he killed himself in 2009.

Did people in your unit get injured?

Yeah, a few people—they got hit with IEDs, but they were very fortunate and lucky to just get a concussion or brain injury rather than losing a limb. So they're alive, but they did get injured in bomb attacks and stuff.

You talked about your friends who said you had a personality change. Did that happen to a lot of your friends in the military, too?

Yeah, yeah. I think a lot of people just really come home different. You change rapidly.

CHAPTER THIRTY-ONE

See-wan Szeto 司徒詩韻 (1978–   )
U.S. Army

See-wan Szeto grew up in the D.C. Metro area very involved in sports, community service, and volunteer work. She joined the ROTC program at Villanova University. While See-wan served as a captain in Afghanistan, her brother Chi was in Iraq. Her military experience involved jumping out of planes, leading a platoon in Afghanistan, and working with village elders to improve their community. She currently lives in Orange County, California, and is Senior Territory Manager and Field Sales Trainer at Johnson & Johnson.

I grew up very fortunate, and by that, I do not mean that I grew up with wealth or many material things. I have been afforded many opportunities in my life, with overwhelming love and support of friends and family. The journey I have been on thus far has been rich with education and a wealth of experiences. It is for this fortune I have always sought to give back.

I grew up the middle child between two boys. My mother quit her job to raise us. I consider this to be one of my fortunes. I first learned about service and giving back from my mother, who volunteered to cart around my brothers and me, our neighbors, and our friends to teeball, ballet and Chinese school. When the PTA needed someone to help out, my mother volunteered. I still remember that every year my elementary school wanted to do a cultural night, and my mother volunteered. Wherever she was needed, she was there. Even now, despite her busy schedule, my mom still volunteers.

When I applied to schools I went to visit Villanova in Pennsylvania. I loved the emphasis on giving back to the community. My parents were very proud of me when I found out that I was accepted but I knew that they could not afford a private school. I decided to look into the Reserve Officer Training Corps [ROTC]. My first exposure to the military was when my brother was accepted into West Point. His friends whose families lived far away always came home with him on breaks. We always drove to every home football game and every Army Navy game. My parents would bring tons of food to tailgate. My parents treated my brother's friends as if they were their own children. To this day, many of my brother's military friends send my parents Christmas cards.

Joining ROTC seemed like an easy choice. I loved the outdoors, I loved volunteering, and I would be getting money for school. I enrolled in ROTC my freshman year and was awarded a 3-year scholarship. It was a relatively

Cpt. Szeto promoted with her NCOs

small program. Because we spent time together in leadership classes and conducted physical training [PT] every morning before classes started, our class became a tight knit group. We did not party every night like most college students. We had to be disciplined enough to get up and exercise. We often spent the weekends at bases conducting field exercises, learning how to shoot an M16, or conducting land navigation. My wealth of experiences in ROTC taught me the importance of leadership, teamwork and service. I knew that I would have a job after graduation. Outside of ROTC, I volunteered for two mission trips and volunteered at the local high school as a track and field coach.

During my sophomore year, I was sent to Airborne School at Ft. Benning, Georgia. This was my first exposure to active duty paratroopers. I would never have thought I would be jumping out of planes, considering I've never been a fan of heights. Attending Airborne School taught me the importance of paying attention to detail, and to face my fears head-on. Jumping out of a plane was frightening and the only time I got a high from it was on the truck headed back to the barracks.

I graduated from Villanova and was commissioned in May of 2000 by my older brother who was already a lieutenant in the Army. By then, my mother had also joined the Public Health Corps and was a lieutenant commander. It was pretty neat having two family members in uniform at my commissioning. I was commissioned as a chemical officer and went to Missouri for a six-month school. After school, I was selected to be stationed at Fort Bragg in North Carolina.

My first year as an officer in the Army was a challenging one. I was a nuclear, biological, chemical [NBC] officer assigned to a UH-60 Blackhawk unit in the 82nd Airborne Division. The mission of the 82nd Airborne Division is to "within 18 hours of notification, strategically deploy, conduct forcible entry parachute assault, and secure key objectives for follow-on military operations in support of U.S. national interests." The 82nd Airborne Division has a long history dating back to World War I. Paratroopers are proud to wear a red beret* and jump boots.

Pilots were not at all interested in training for NBC warfare. If it did not pertain to flying or jumping out of a place, it was not a priority. My duties mostly consisted of doing readiness and forecasting reports. I was the Battalion Air Movement officer and was in charge of air movement operations during operational readiness surveys. I ensured that equipment that was being air dropped for our airborne missions was certified and correctly stowed on pallets. I was also responsible for getting ammunition for aerial door gunneries. I often felt like I had something to prove in this unit, because not only I was not a pilot but also one of a handful of females in a unit that had over 300 paratroopers.

September 11, 2001 occurred when I was still an NBC officer. I remember that infamous day as if it was yesterday. We had a television in our training office and I remember seeing the planes crash into the towers. Immediately Ft. Bragg was on lockdown. The next morning when I carpooled with another lieutenant, we left at 8 a.m. and did not get to our office until 5 p.m. Every gate was manned with a security guard and at each of the gates our car was searched through in and out. Suddenly my job became important because we knew that a deployment was imminent.

Several months later I was assigned to train to become an ordnance officer. I was trained to be in maintenance, ammunition and explosive ordnance disposal. I was assigned back to the 82nd Airborne Division, this time into a unit with fellow logistics officers. I felt comfortable amongst other logistics officers and spent time as a platoon leader for a supply warehouse with items valued over two million dollars. I was responsible for maintaining the health, welfare and morale of 32 paratroopers. I became close with my platoon sergeant and would later deploy with her.

In the summer of 2002, I was selected to deploy as an attachment to another unit. Prior to our deployment, we were sent to the National Training Center [NTC] in Barstow, California. There we simulated training scenarios.

One of the most difficult challenges I had while a platoon leader was out at NTC. I had already counseled one of my sergeants prior to our travels to the training center. He was irresponsible, undisciplined, and if I had one word to describe him, it would be "bonehead." I remember going to a meeting with my sergeant major and telling him that I did not want to deploy with this particular sergeant because I was sure he was going to kill someone. I was told we didn't have enough personnel. During our training at NTC, the same bonehead sergeant was doing donuts with three other soldiers in a Humvee that flipped. One of my soldiers was sitting in the back and was not wearing a seatbelt or helmet. He was killed instantly. During the training rotation we had to go and bury our soldier with his family. His death was so senseless and avoidable. It's one thing

---

* Only airborne units wear red berets.

when a soldier is killed in war, but in peacetime during training? Who knew the trouble would come before we even deployed.

In the winter of 2002, I was deployed to Kandahar, Afghanistan, during Operation Enduring Freedom II. When we first arrived, we were told that it was going to be a peacekeeping mission and that we were only going to be there four months. If you consider the state of war in Afghanistan 10 years later in 2012, clearly, it was never going to be a peacekeeping mission.

I had several jobs while I was in Afghanistan. I originally deployed as a reverse osmosis water purification unit platoon leader. My platoon was responsible for taking non-potable water and running it through a purification process to make the water drinkable. My platoon consisted of mostly 18-year-olds who were not very disciplined. This was one challenging position because these soldiers had no real direction, or motivation for that matter. What I realized was that no one had made the effort to train or take care of these soldiers. My opportunity was to let them know that they did have a leader that cared about them and could be tough on them when necessary. I learned a lot about my soldiers and even more about myself. One of my proudest moments during deployment was when I was able to promote two of the soldiers from this platoon. I watched both soldiers step up and become leaders to their peers.

Shortly after deployment, a reserve unit took over the water purification system. I was then in charge of running the largest supply warehouse in Afghanistan. We processed all types of supplies, from uniforms to flags to infrared lights. Thousands of items were processed and distributed every day. Being on the line and working side by side with my soldiers helped me to understand their everyday struggles, and I got to know them on a whole new level.

I finally was assigned to a maintenance job (and was next assigned as a production control officer in charge of 60 paratroopers). I was in charge of maintenance shops that fixed weapons, night vision goggles, trucks, and generators. Anything that could potentially break, my paratroopers fixed. The job of my soldiers was imperative, because if weapons, trucks were not up and running, the infantry, or any soldiers, could not complete their missions. My years as a lieutenant were the most challenging but also the most rewarding. I couldn't have been prouder to re-enlist, and promote soldiers. As a platoon leader and production control officer I learned how to prioritize.

Due to some unethical actions of my company commander, I was selected to be the take his place for 45 days. The responsibility seemed daunting, but with the unconditional support of my soldiers and my first sergeant, I was able to handle my responsibilities. I remember watching the U.S. attack Iraq on a secured computer. While Operation Iraqi Freedom was kicked off, the war in Afghanistan was put on the back burner. At one point, my older brother was deployed to Iraq while I was in Afghanistan. I can only imagine the anguish my parents felt with both of their children overseas in a war zone. I felt fortunate to have a computer in my office and use of a satellite phone in my boss' office.

On one occasion I had the opportunity to go out on a medical mission into "downtown" Kandahar. We took toothpaste, toothbrushes and items like Pepto-Bismol to help give basic medical care. We would also bring soccer balls and candy for the kids. Something that stood out to me when I was out in the city was that young children, maybe 7- or 10-year-olds, always carried the infants. I came to learn that adults didn't carry infants because they were afraid that the babies wouldn't live long and did not want to build a bond with the infants in case they died. We met with village elders and discussed how to build schools, get fresh water, and what we could do to win the hearts and minds of the people. Things we took for granted back home, like basic plumbing, were non-existent. I remember sitting in the mud hut with the elders, who looked 70 or 80 but were only 40 years old. Their lifestyle definitely aged them.

I spent nine months in Afghanistan. Upon returning from deployment I was in charge of re-integrating the entire task force's equipment. All 3,000 pieces of equipment received first time approvals through inspection. I had 60 paratroopers and 50 civilian contractors working for me. Returning from deployment was an enormous task but as usual my soldiers completed their mission with skill and proficiency.

At this point in my career I was unsure if I wanted to continue to serve or get out of the Army. I attended the Captain's Career Course thinking that I would want to be a company commander. I returned to Ft. Bragg to serve at a division maintenance level job. Shortly after, I decided that I was ready for a different career challenge in my life. I now have been working for Johnson & Johnson in sales for the last nine years.

As an Army officer I built a strong sense of who I was, and I attribute much of my character to my experiences in the Army. My strong work ethic, discipline, and motivation have carried over to corporate America. I have traded in my rucksack and pavement pounding for hiking, beach volleyball and yoga. I learned that nothing is insurmountable and that any challenge can be overcome with the right attitude and with the help of good people.

Currently I spend a lot of my free time volunteering in food distribution and nutrition awareness for kids. I help to recruit veterans at Johnson & Johnson by educating others on the values and experiences veterans bring to a career. I also volunteer for a Disabled Veteran Scuba Project. This program teaches soldiers with Post Traumatic Stress Disorder, paraplegics, and quadriplegics how to scuba dive. This is a form of therapy for many veterans. One of the most important things it teaches vets is that they are still capable of doing normal activities. I am constantly amazed at the determination of these veterans. I am working on my own scuba certification and when I get frustrated I think about the gentleman in our class right now that has no mobility in his legs. If he can overcome his fears, I know I can certainly overcome my own.

I was fortunate to give back to my country and I feel honored to be called a veteran. Being a veteran is understanding that there is a greater good than oneself. It means knowing how to sacrifice for others even at the cost of one's own well-being. When I see an older gentleman with a hat that says World War II, or Korean War or Vietnam, I shake his hand to thank him for his service. The sacrifice of these veterans from these eras often goes untold. When I see active duty service members in uniform, I stop to also thank them for their sacrifice. It is important to not only recognize our service members' sacrifice, but also the sacrifice of their loved ones. These days when I see faces of service members, they seem to get younger and younger. Now I am the one that is fortunate because there are still those who continue to defend my freedoms and way of life.

CHAPTER THIRTY-TWO

Welton Chang 張為棟 (1983–   )
U.S. Army

Welton Chang, from Edison, New Jersey, is a Ph.D. student at the University of Pennsylvania. He worked at the Department of Defense in Washington, D.C. (2010–2014), was a captain while on active duty (2005–2009), and supported the Joint Staff as a Reservist (2010–2012). He shares what it was like growing up in suburban New Jersey and how 9/11 motivated him to join the military. He attended Dartmouth College and Georgetown University.

In total I've served three overseas tours. I served one 15-month tour in Iraq and a 1-year tour in Korea. I was an intelligence officer. I also deployed to Iraq as a civilian after I got off active duty. My job was to assist and advise an Iraqi intelligence agency, leading a team of U.S. military, civilian, and contract personnel. I spent a lot of time thinking about "How do we train these guys" and "How do we get them to be better at what they do?" A big part of the effort was building rapport and ensuring that we were developing strong relationships with our fellow intelligence officers on the Iraqi side.

I just wrote an article about my observation and lessons I learned in the Middle East. Recently I was rereading T.E. Lawrence's [Lawrence of Arabia's] "27 articles" and laughing to myself because years later, so many of the same themes reappear.

I was born in 1983 in Tainan, Taiwan, and I came to the United States in 1986. I grew up in Edison, New Jersey. [My family's story] follows the standard immigrant narrative. My parents wanted to make a better life for us and they didn't see as much opportunity in Taiwan. My dad came over first. He settled in Hoboken with his brother and they went to graduate school together at the Stevens Institute of Technology in New Jersey. And my dad wound up finishing his master's there and my uncle got his Ph.D. My dad is a computer programmer/IT guy but he actually did his master's in electrical engineering. Soon after my father finished his degree and got a job, we followed. I have a younger brother, Woody, who just graduated from Stanford Medical School and is doing his residency in Pittsburgh. The two of us and my mother left Taiwan and joined my father here in the U.S.

My mother was a law school graduate and when she resettled in the States she wound up starting out as a cashier, working at a local Chinese grocery store. I think, for her, the decision to leave was largely based on following my dad.

And with my dad becoming the primary breadwinner after we left Taiwan, my impression is that her goals changed. I am sure she wanted to do a good job raising us.

My dad had a job working at China Steel in Taiwan before he came to the States. And I guess it was probably also fashionable to a certain extent for people from Taiwan to come to the States at that time. There is a large Taiwanese community in New Jersey and all of the parents are about that the same age and immigrated around the same time.

Growing up in Edison, New Jersey, most of my friends were either Chinese or Korean or Jewish. My best friend Peter is Korean and several other friends are Chinese or Taiwanese. It wasn't really a conscious effort on my part to seek out other Asians. It just happened that way, mostly because we ended up taking advanced classes together in school.

I didn't really think about the military growing up. I had friends who did, and they wound up not doing it. I actually had one good friend, who's Taiwanese American, and that's all he talked about—airplanes, tanks, and war. I think he works for a medical device company now. No, it was not something that ever crossed my mind growing up.

I think I wanted to be some kind of dinosaur-hunting astronaut or a baseball player. What every kid wants to be. I don't think I had any kind of realistic idea of what I wanted to be before my senior year of high school. The standard jobs came up. My parents tried to encourage me to be a lawyer or a doctor, kind of the standard professional jobs that are out there. I'm kind of contrarian so I went the opposite direction.

Your parents—what kind of parents were they? Were they the traditional type of Chinese parents or were they pretty open and free and encouraging?

Generally speaking on the Asian parent scale they were probably like a 7. They probably started closer to like a 9. I'm reminded of that viral meme Angry Asian Dad, with the picture of an angry looking Asian man. As I got older, they moved down the scale. I think by the time I graduated high school, they were at like a 5. And it was probably just because I wore them down.

I went to Chinese school every Saturday growing up. I never watched Saturday morning cartoons. I played piano like everybody else. I was involved in Chinese choir and other kinds of Chinese American cultural organizations. I did a lot of volunteer work such as teaching other kids to sing, and singing at nursing homes and all that.

Out of 100,000 people, probably 8,000 people in Edison are either Korean or Chinese. Academic success, it seemed to me, was the result of factors such as economic well-being, culture, and who you have around you. It was a pretty complex experience growing up.

What did you study at Dartmouth and what did you think you would be?

I studied political science and international relations theory, and by that point, I knew I was going to join the military. 9/11 happened when I got back from my freshman outdoors trip. During a pre-freshman orientation, I had met a couple of people who were involved in ROTC and, partly based on their testimony, I was convinced that I wanted to join the military.

There was this Marine Corps recruiter who showed up at my house one day. Out of the blue in my senior year of high school, I answered an online ad that said, "I would like a hat from the military," and a Marine recruiter showed up at my house and said, "Hey, you registered interest in the military? We want to try and recruit you. Take this test." And my parents found out and they freaked. They said, "What are you doing?" But some of the things that the recruiter said to me really resonated.

The idea that I could go off and do something and test myself and it would be serving the country attracted me. It was something that other people I knew, including outside the Asian American community, weren't doing or even thinking about. Service interested me primarily as a way of giving back. This understanding matured as I went further along in my service.

And then, I remember writing my admissions essay for Dartmouth, where I wrote about how I used to never say the Pledge of Allegiance. I thought it was a meaningless bunch of empty words. Then slowly, throughout my time in high school, I came to the realization that no, actually, it means a lot. It was a—that kind of gradual transformative experience going through high school and thinking about the things that I owed back to society for the things that I had. My perspective changed. Add in this Marine guy showing up in full-dress uniform to my house basically trying to harangue me into joining the military, and my parents saying no. That got me thinking more about ROTC. Then 9/11 happened, and that sealed the deal. I knew, at this point, that I was going to join because this was going to be the defining conflict of our lifetime.

Was there any particular event that sparked that feeling that you owe something to society?

No. I think it was just more of a slow, gradual realization that I was different and that I had more opportunities and that there were other Asian kids in our town who didn't. My parents had sacrificed a lot to get me and my brother to where we ended up. A lot of it was the choices that my parents made, the community that they surrounded themselves with, people they associated with. In the larger framework, [it's] living in a country that values merit and ability, and a country that has set up institutions and respect for the rule of law that allows people to excel. And that's not something that every country has, and I probably didn't know that as a freshman in high school. I had no idea. I was much more concerned with what kind of car I was going to drive when I finally got my license.

If you want to look for a proximate cause for the change in perspective, I would say 9/11, and the groundswell of feeling and sympathy throughout the world for what happened, and the fact that there were people out there trying to get us. I grew up in suburban New Jersey where the only danger to you physically is getting hit by a car. So you're pretty sheltered. When I watched the towers falling, I thought, "This is real."

I got back on campus, linked up with the ROTC Program, signed the contracts, got uniforms and I did ROTC for about four years while I was at Dartmouth. I had to rescind my Taiwanese citizenship when I turned 20, which is the official age that you can do that. Taiwan, like South Korea, has universal conscription. So if you're a male and fit the criteria, you have to serve the military.

ROTC was hard to balance with school. Most colleges are pretty liberal and it was hard to fit in and be a part of the campus. For example, you go off for field training on the weekend. When you get back Sunday afternoon it would be Green Key [a party weekend]. All your friends are going out getting drunk and you spent the weekend in Vermont, sleeping on the ground, eating pre-packaged food and going bang, bang, bang in the woods, right? That's a very different experience. So I felt a little bit separate from campus but I was pretty active in a lot of other organizations and I took schoolwork pretty seriously. So I don't feel like it was a totally separate experience. But it was a different experience.

So you graduated, and then did you go right into doing things for the military after that?

Yeah. I graduated and was commissioned in June 2005. I had a month off, and then went on active duty July 2005. I started my training at Fort Benning in Georgia for about six weeks and then I went to Fort Huachuca in Arizona for further training.

After initial officer training I did a year-long tour in South Korea. I was stationed at Camp Red Cloud in Uijeongbu. I was on the division staff for 2nd Infantry Division. I was a part of what we call the G2 Analysis Control Element [ACE]. Basically, it's a 60-person organization that does all the intel analysis for the division if the division ever went to war.

I was stationed in South Korea when North Korea exploded their first nuclear weapon. I was there when they launched a Taepodong missile on July 4, 2006.

Up to that point, I really hadn't spent much time in Asia as an adult. I did do the Beijing Foreign Study Program when I was at Dartmouth. I didn't really go back to Taiwan after I turned 10 because my parents always feared that they would try to retain me to serve in the military. Ironically enough, I joined the American military. And so it was a really, really interesting experience to live in South Korea for over a year. One of the highlights while I was in South Korea was that I got engaged to my wife Meredith. We met at Dartmouth and she stayed with me through my service in the military. When she flew over to South

Welton and his good friend Tom on a patrol in Ba'aj, Iraq

Korea we went down to Jeju, which is a honeymooner's island on the southern end of the peninsula. She was actually still a senior at Dartmouth at that point.

And during your time in the ROTC and also in South Korea, did being Chinese American ever affect anything at your job?

Not at all. I never once experienced any kind of negative sentiment. I never felt in any way that I was being slighted because I was Asian. I know that's probably not the same experience that other people have had. I feel like I was probably shielded from a lot of that because I was an officer and not an enlisted person. But I personally have not faced any kind of discrimination that I know of.

I would say it was rather unusual and when I meet officers now who are Chinese, I usually think "Wow! Another Chinese American officer! I didn't think I'd meet someone like you." So I'm sure they're out there. Three to four percent of the military is Asian American so whatever the statistic is, it's more than just me, but I didn't meet a lot of them.

My duties as a U.S. military intelligence officer in Korea included keeping up with what was going on in North Korea and supporting training exercises. It could be exciting at times. It was boring most of the time. It was a lot of hours of working on documents and PowerPoint and just kind of the standard staff work.

So I got back from Korea and jumped out of some airplanes. I got to Fort Bragg and I was told that I would be deploying within a couple of months to Iraq. So I did initial train up with my unit and we left June 30, 2007. I was the company intelligence officer for a long-range surveillance company [LRS]. My duties were preparing our long-range surveillance teams and platoons for missions. Doctrinal LRS missions included building hide sites to conduct surveillance of a target. They would do this by digging holes—

Digging a hole where?

In the middle of the desert. Let's say your target is in a village and you need to watch that village for several days. Our teams would find a place that they could observe a house from, undetected, and watch the objective from there.

I was never in any holes. My job was to make sure that these guys had all the data that they needed before they went out. The platoon-sized missions included what we call area reconnaissance. And so I got to go out with the guys on those trips sometimes. Two of my best friends to this day, Johnny and Tom, were platoon leaders in the company.

How long was your first deployment?

Fifteen months, as our deployment was a small part of the larger surge effort. I've studied the surge a lot and I'm not really doing it justice here, but at that point in the war there was a realization that "Hey, we really need to get the Iraqis more involved in this because only they can find a political solution to the insurgency." And part of that is getting their security forces to take ownership for the area that they operated in and for them to be effective in patrolling their population and patrolling their borders. And that required more U.S. boots on the ground time.

[After my deployment] I got back to Fort Bragg and I did a very short company command. Imagine, you're in charge of a group of people—and for me it was 280 individuals that were in my command. I was responsible for their training, their welfare, administering the Uniform Code of Military Justice, and supporting whatever events we had going on. I was also responsible for all the millions of dollars of property and equipment that we had. So it's a pretty big responsibility for a junior officer and I was a very junior captain at that point. I had just gotten promoted a month before. The person who had the job before was dismissed because of some misbehavior on her part and so the brigade leadership looked at me and said, "Hey, you're in charge."

Company command was a key experience for me and I learned about parts of the military I didn't even know existed, having spent nearly my entire Army career up to that point either overseas or in training. It really showed me some sides of the military I didn't really ever want to know about, but I wound up having to learn about them anyway. I wound up having to learn about things like family care plans, the Army legal system ... we have a whole system for social work to address problems like violence affecting family members.

It is easy to forget that, as an officer, you made all of your mistakes in your late teen years in the forgiving cocoon of college while many of your soldiers are learning and making those mistakes in the military. This consideration caused me to think hard about punishments versus learning opportunities. I generally

Welton taking notes as the Iraqi general he advised discusses security concerns

erred on the side of leniency but tried to get at the root of the problem and suggest ways that the soldier could change so they didn't wind up in trouble again.

When issues arise, you have to get involved. Many administrative and legal matters fall under your sole purview. I got to get help for soldiers that needed it, whether it was medical help or mental help. It really brought all of those aspects of services provided by the military to my attention: suicides, PTSD and soldier injuries, and how soldiers were being taken care of or not being taken care of. I think a lot of that stuff was invisible to me before command. As a company commander, I had to be the expert on these matters. I tried my best to do the right things for my soldiers and I tried to be an advocate for them, especially when it came to medical care. It was a really enlightening five months.

I did a little bit more time on brigade staff and then I left active duty in December 2009. At that point I transferred into the Reserves, and then I joined the Department of Defense.

I think the deployments were tough on everybody in my family. I didn't call my parents a single time when I was in Iraq for the first time. And I think I talked to them once on the phone on my second tour. My thought process was "out of sight, out of mind". I just didn't want them to worry. I didn't really want them to have to think about what was going on. And I'm sure that didn't stop them from worrying but it's actually something that I really haven't talked to them much about, because I guess I've tried to compartmentalize that part of my life. I've really tried to kind of shield my parents from the military thing.

You were saying, on the Asian parents scale, they went from like a 9 to a 5. And then, at this point when you were in the military, where are they on the scale?

Probably 4 or 3. They're still trying to remind me to do things like brush my teeth and stuff.

It's so interesting because I interviewed someone from World War II and she also said something like, "I was bad. I was on duty and I never called my parents and I never wrote them." It's just kind of funny when I hear similar things in different eras and generations.

Yeah. And I don't know if it is a distinctly Asian thing. I suspect that it might be. I feel like it's your own burden and it's a journey that you're on, and it's not something that you really want your parents involved in.

Being American, or being a Chinese American, do you have any thoughts about your overall experience?

I feel like more Chinese Americans should serve. I don't know. I kind of feel like more Chinese people should take the risk and join the military or join the government or do something that's a little bit unusual like being a writer.

I feel like we can be very conservative as a culture and that's to our detriment. We're not very politically active for the most part. We do ourselves a disservice by not being involved. And you can be very successful as a doctor, as a banker, as a lawyer, that's all great and wonderful. Lots of people do it. It's the path to being [middle class]. It's the path to becoming wealthy, and hopefully money translates into influence, but there are so many other ways to do it. America is built on that kind of bedrock foundation of participation. We take ourselves out of the political process, though. I'm not saying that everyone should go into the military but I feel this idea of service and giving back is lost on a lot of people.

The National Intelligence Cell advisory team taking
a break at Iraq's Tomb of the Unknown Soldier

CHAPTER THIRTY-THREE

Wilem Wong 黃伯聰 (1970–)
U.S. Army

Wilem Wong, a sergeant in the NYPD and a facilitator of the Leadership Training Section of the Police Academy, served as a major with USMC RCT-1/RCT-5 in Helmand, Afghanistan, and as a captain with the XVIII Airborne Corps in Baghdad, Iraq. He was on the Joint Planning Team for Iraq's provincial elections and Iraq's national literacy campaign.

Wilem was a Human Terrain Team (HTT) leader that led a civilian team in central and southern Helmand, conducting socio-cultural research that provided analysis for the U.S. Marine Corps' combatant commanders to make better operational and strategic decisions to stabilize and develop Helmand. He describes conducting socio-cultural research in Afghanistan, interacting with Afghans to understand their perspectives. An avid marathon runner, he initially ran as a form of stress relief in Iraq. Wong was awarded the Bronze Star Medal and NATO Medal. He is a graduate of NYU (BS in Finance), Webster University (MA in Management and Leadership), and U.S. Army Command and General Staff College.

One thing I definitely took away from being in the military so long is a sense of humbleness. When you go to different countries you realize what we have here. I just came back from Afghanistan under a unique program. It's a hybrid team, a military-civilian team, where we had highly educated civilians with master's degrees and Ph.D.s in social sciences like sociology, anthropology, psychology and archeology, who might not necessarily have had previous military background.

So I had to have them understand the military culture. Not just the Army, but the Marine Corps, which we eventually worked for. I was the team leader and I was the military face on the team that interfaced with the staff of the Marine Corps. I worked in Operation Section–Effects cell.

What we did was make sure that when we engaged with the population via civil affairs, agriculture programs, or economic development that we got the intended effects we hoped to achieve. We had to make sure that we could track these effects and hit these metrics if possible. It was a challenge because it wasn't just us in the battlefield. We're working with other inter-agency personnel like the Department of State, the United States Agency for International Develop-

Cpt. Wong breaking bread with Pashto linguists during
engagement with local Afghans (Helmand, Afghanistan, 2011)

ment, the USDA, and also the British.

At that time, I was in Helmand Province, at Camp Dwyer where the area of operation for us was Marjah, which was [the site of] a famous battle in February 2010. [We were also in] Garmsir, Nawa and Khan Neshin. We were building on what the British were doing with economic development, building infrastructure, building the capacity of the government, building the capacity for the Afghan National Army and the Afghan National Police. So we needed to have a secure environment before you can have economic development.

Our job was to go out and find out about the perceptions, motivations, grievances and interests of the local population concerning their government in Kabul, as well as their local and provincial government; about how they feel about us, the coalition forces, the U.S. and U.K., and all the other people that might be in their country—Dutch, Spanish, Norwegians, Swedes, Polish and French. Also we wanted to find out their perceptions about the Taliban. We did a study. It was not a scientific, precise study, because we were in a battlefield, so we always preface with that disclaimer that we were conducting this research in a combat environment. We gathered data and provided analysis to the battlefield commander.

I worked for Regimental Combat Team 1 and eventually Regimental Combat Team 5 before I left, near the end of 2011. One big project we worked on was, "How can we blunt the poppy harvest for the following year?" I came in April of 2011, and it was known that April is usually the beginning of the fighting season because that's when it gets warm and they harvest the poppy. The Taliban and the insurgents use opium to fund their operations, to fight against coalition forces.

When you interviewed people, were they just people you found in the desert? How broad was it? Did you get every single person? How big was the sample size?

A typical district is about 40,000 to 80,000 people, possibly. But there hasn't been a census done in that country for a long time, so that's questionable. But we had to use some figure. We tried to get a minimum of 50 interviewees, but we usually exceeded that by conducting 75–100 interviews. Of course we tried to get a cross-section of the population. The challenge is that you're going to interview [only] males because they're the most readily available individuals in the district out on the street. Women can't be seen outside without being escorted by male kin.

Most of the time, females are prohibited from speaking to coalition forces. They don't represent the interest of the family. The male represents the family. So we had to always speak to the elderly male of that family, because everyone else will fall in line with what he says. Usually, out of respect, when we entered the village, we always tried to speak to the *spingeri*, or whitebeard, the male elder in the village. We tried to get his blessing and say, "We want to interview your villagers and see what they have to say." We tell him what the questions are. Of course it's hard to eliminate certain biases in the questioning because his villagers might repeat whatever he says. So we do ask him his perspective as an elder. Then we ask the perspectives of local villagers.

So what were the findings?

I could tell you some of the projects we worked on, like blunting the poppy harvest to minimize the funding for the Taliban. We tried to look at substitute crops for opium. It's hard to find crops that are as lucrative as opium.

But of course we [coalition forces] would use information operations and psychological operations, then work with them on how to get messages out there to say, "The Qur'an states certain things and opium is not something that you should be growing." But since I'm not Muslim, and I'm not well-versed in the Qur'an, we usually have the Afghan National Army mullahs, religious leaders, that will state that to the local population. So we worked in partnership with the Afghan National Army and Afghan National Police to counteract messages that the Taliban or the insurgents have.

The Taliban might say the Afghan National Army are infidels or the coalition forces are infidels. But we will throw it back at them and say we're children of the Book, meaning: you've got the Torah, then you've got the New Testament, and then you've got the Qur'an. If you look at the Qur'an, that's the third book, so to speak. That's the latest version and in the Qur'an it states that they respect the previous prophets.

We are children of the Book, so we are not considered infidels. We always try to counteract their messaging. Also if they say that the Afghan National Army or Afghan National Police are infidels, [the Army and Police] will actually get the message out there that they have prayers on certain days and invite them to pray with them. To show that they're not infidels and that they're good Muslims just like them. We always tried to counteract any narrative that the Taliban or the insurgents have.

It convinces some people. You can't convince everyone. But you have to try. You can't let the Taliban or the insurgents have their narrative without putting our own out that counteracts theirs. The biggest advantage they have is speed— of putting out what they have, accurate or inaccurate. But we can't put out an inaccurate message. We always have to vet it through. And that takes time.

You talked about how the anthropology team in Afghanistan is similar to what they did in Vietnam.

Yes. I would consider this the current incarnation of what was being achieved in Vietnam, now called the Human Terrain System. I was the team leader on the Human Terrain team. The CORDS, the Civil Operations Revolutionary Development Support, tried to use the Strategic Hamlet [Program] by relocating a population to a secure area [and] filtering out the insurgents within a population. By so-called "draining the swamp" you will find the insurgents that are remaining in the population. It's debatable if it worked or not. I'm not here to debate that.

Did they ever look at you strangely because you're Asian?

Yeah, they did look at me a little differently because I was the only American of Chinese ancestry. There were Filipinos there, but I was the only Chinese. And at my rank as a major, it's unusual. You don't see high-ranking individuals out in the battlefield walking with the junior enlisted Marines a lot of times. I usually take my rank off because you don't want to be a target for snipers.

But if I'm going to tell members of my team to be in the field, I will be in the field with them to share the same risk. I'm the military face of the team. I have to understand what type of data is being gathered in the field and make the data gathering and the eventual analysis relevant to the commanders. I don't want it to be an academic exercise, so to speak, a high concept type of paper where you can't take the analysis and make it operationally relevant to the commander. So one of the biggest things is: how can we use this information to secure the population and eventually stabilize that district? We can do that by fostering economic development and eventually making the narrative of the Taliban or insurgents irrelevant to the population.

Where does Afghanistan stand right now? Do you think America's efforts or the U.S. Military's efforts are getting anywhere?

In counterinsurgency any gains that you have are tenuous. So you have to always keep at it. Sometimes there are not clearly defined metrics of what success looks like. We could go back to what happened in World War II. We're still in Germany, we're still in Japan after 65 years, even though we've won that war. We helped rebuild and stabilize Japan and Germany. Same thing with Afghanistan.

Maj. Wong with his Human Terrain Team and a "Kuchi" or nomad
(Helmand, Afghanistan, 2011)

It's going to be long term to secure the peace, so to speak.

We always want them to be involved in the planning with us, in how to develop their economy and how to better govern their own people. We provide them our own "best practices." We're not going to say, "It's the right way." We'll show you a way, but eventually you find the way that's suitable for you and for your people to feel comfortable with. That's the main thing, it has to be sustainable. The sustainability can only come from them continuing this effort. Not just us, because we can't be there forever and lives and treasure of our country are limited. We don't have unlimited resources.

When you surveyed the people how did most people feel about the coalition forces?

It's getting more positive because they see us out engaging with the population. And we are working in partnership to build the Afghan National Police or the local police, the national army. So they will eventually take the lead on these security efforts. Right now we are in partnership and eventually we're transitioning over to have them take the lead. We're in what they call "overwatch," where we will provide additional resources if need be, but they have to show that they are capable, not just to us, but they also have to convince their local population. The local population has to feel that they have confidence in their own national army and national police or local police. Because those are the people that would eventually secure their country and the borders of their country from outsiders.

Can you tell us one of the most exciting or memorable events in this past tour, or most interesting to you?

I think it was in 2005. The Baghdad Museum was looted, so a lot of artifacts and cultural treasures were gone. The anthropologist on my team, the Ph.D. Marc Abramiuk and I and some other team members went to different cultural heritage sites and Sunni shrines. The Pashtun are predominantly Sunni. We were looking at how to preserve some of these shrines and worked with people in Kabul under the Ministry of Information and Culture, which is like the antiquities department, finding out the process to preserve their cultural heritage sites—so that people feel that their heritage is important.

That's one way of connecting the national government in Kabul to the local population in where we were in Helmand Province. People have to feel that there is a connection to the national government and the provincial government. So we were not just working with MOIC, the Ministry of Information and Culture, but also our Department of State, Cultural Heritage Preservation and hopefully the UN. That effort is still being continued on right now while we're back stateside. So that's one thing we're looking at, but of course we're still in a combat zone, it's still a hostile area. So it's still tough to do something like that, but we're still going to continue the effort as much as we can from here.

The two biggest things in Afghanistan, and even Iraq, are religion [Islam] and agriculture. Understand that Iraq was called the cradle of civilization, Mesopotamia, a fertile area flourishing with agriculture.

Afghanistan as well has a very rich history. Besides Alexander the Great, there was Genghis Khan, and world empires that passed through there; the British, in the last century. So there's a rich world history in Afghanistan. I was just very happy to be serving with the Marines.

But you were part of the Army when you started?

Yeah, even though I'm in the Army, I was serving as a special staff officer to the Marines to at least help the Marines understand how we can better secure the peace in that province. To make the narrative of the Taliban or insurgents irrelevant by engaging the military-age males, which is basically 16 to 45, the guys that are willing to fight the coalition forces. We have to give them an alternative from what the Taliban offers. Most of them are poor farmers. We have to employ them constructively, with other types of jobs or vocational training, literacy, or whatever economic opportunity that we can give them, so they don't just go with the Taliban because they need extra cash because they can't feed their family.

Another big thing we were working on with the Marines was what we call "a voice of religious tolerance," which is to say, there are other countries adjacent to you that have moderate views of Islam. It's not the fanatical version that you need to subscribe to because of what the Taliban or Al Qaeda are saying. What's happening in Jordan, Saudi Arabia, Turkey, is that there are other forms of Islam that are not as fanatical. You can still be a Muslim but it doesn't have to be this interpretation. So the Marines, with the help of the Department of State, were sending mullahs and other religious leaders to these other countries like Jordan, to look at the possibility of a moderate Islamic country.

We can't just tell them that it is out there. They need to see it to believe it. The Pashtuns, most of them didn't believe what happened on 9/11 until we showed them a video. We explained that this is why we are here. We did not get that out correctly to have them understand why we are in Afghanistan, in their country. We did not do that successfully, but we've done that more successfully recently—getting out our message of why we are here as opposed to why the Taliban say we are here.

Because there's nothing besides mud brick houses out in Afghanistan, no higher than three stories, it's hard for someone to believe that there can be a building that's 110 stories tall. So for us to say, "Here the Al Qaeda has crashed two airplanes into our buildings and these buildings were 110 stories tall," it is unbelievable for them. They thought that was exaggerated. They thought it was some Hollywood make-believe stuff till we showed them a video, and then some of them actually cried; they couldn't believe it. They didn't understand why we were there until we actually showed them a video of why we were there.

The code of Pashtunwali is a code that the Pashtun tribe follows. Pashtunwali is a basic common law of the land or "code of life" that predates Islam. Specifically, indigenous Pashtuns in Afghanistan and Pakistan still follow Pashtunwali. The Pashtuns comprise the majority of the Taliban and they believe in justice/revenge or, in Pashto, *badal*. The video we showed the Pashtuns explained that because of what happened on September 11, we were in Afghanistan for justice. The Pashtuns interpret justice and revenge as the same. Once they realized we [coalition forces] were there for justice, they saw us as honorable people seeking justice for the ones killed on September 11. As a result of that understanding, the Pashtuns became aware that we were not there to convert them to Christianity [contrary to the Taliban's narrative of the coalition forces]. And because we were there for justice we actually saw a decrease on attacks and casualties on coalition forces, since they saw our mission as honorable.

Besides other things, we are of course avenging our loss and pursuing Osama Bin Laden. I was there on May 2nd [May 1st EST] in Afghanistan when Osama Bin Laden was killed. It was very emotional for me because, obviously, being born and raised in New York City and being an NYPD police officer, even though I was not a police officer on 9/11/2001, I actually worked at Two World Trade Center back in 1998, 1999, at the New York State [Department of] Tax and Finance. So I lost 40 colleagues there; 10 of them I knew personally. There was one particular person that took my position when I resigned to work for The Gap afterwards. I was working as a criminal investigator for the tax department, and this person was asking me if I was really resigning from this position because he was counting on my vacancy to get married and to start his life with his wife. So I said, sure.

In hindsight, I was very fortunate that I resigned. My mom actually asked me why I resigned from a government job because the Chinese say it's the golden rice bowl; you're not going to go hungry. Eventually we realized, wow it was very fortunate I wasn't working at the World Trade Center. I used to work on the 86th floor with the view of the Statue of Liberty. That tower was hit at the 82nd floor, so it already cut off the rest of the building. So if you were above the 82nd floor it was very hard to get out. I knew a couple of people that got out but a lot of people died.

In June of 2011, I was promoted to major from captain and my immediate supervisor was a lieutenant colonel, John Kit Carson. He's an F-18 pilot. I was very honored to be promoted by a Marine lieutenant colonel and a fighter pilot in a combat zone. It was even sweeter because I was in the top 5% that was promoted early.

I was in Iraq in 2008. I was supposed to be there as a public health officer, but ended up working on the provincial elections, national literacy, and economic development, while also working a little with the health attaché at the U.S. Embassy on public health issues.

The thing is, if you're not literate, you can't read the Qur'an for yourself. So a fanatic could interpret the Qur'an for you. Increasing literacy also leads to better job opportunities. If you can't read, how are you going to have a job in your country?

Also, direct foreign investment was another thing we were looking at. If you don't have a stable country and you don't have a young population that is literate, how are you going to have foreign investments like, let's say McDonalds, or high-tech development firms to come to Iraq and Afghanistan to invest in their country and develop the economy of the country? So we were looking at it for a longer-term point of view.

We wanted the Iraqis to conduct their own elections that are fair and credible in their eyes, even if it's not to our standards, the Western standard. There was a debate about that.

After I finished my time there in 2008, I came back to the civilian world. I had been there for nine months.

You helped build the schools, or did you oversee the curriculum?

We started a pilot program in one school [Hawija]. We were visiting the South Koreans up in Northern Iraq, which is Kurdistan, because their program was acknowledged as one of the best.

The South Koreans were working together with us, with all the coalition forces. The South Koreans funded the literacy programs and all the support and resources. They also went beyond literacy and also had vocational training, which was amazing. They brought their vehicles in, Hyundais, and they were teaching people how to fix vehicles. And other South Korean products, Samsung TVs and LG refrigerators. I thought it was a great thing because if you think about it, down the road when the country gets stabilized, people will have already been introduced to your products. But I don't think they intentionally did it that way.

* * *

I was born on Kenmare Street in 1970, which at that time was more like Little Italy. But Chinatown has expanded, and there are a lot more Chinese people there now. Still some mix of Italians and Hispanics. But in the last five years the neighborhood has changed again to become more gentrified.

My dad was a waiter and my mom was a seamstress in the factories. My dad had a relatively good education when he was growing up. He had a high school diploma equivalent in China. But he didn't speak any English, so obviously it was a challenge for my parents. My parents worked in Chinatown and gave us the best they could. I'm the oldest of four children.

I went to school at P.S. 130 and Junior High School 65, which got converted to I.S. 131. Then I went to Aviation High School in Queens. You learn how to fix airplanes, airframes and power plants. If you attend all the classes, you could actually graduate with a license to fix airframes and power plants and work for the airlines if you wanted to. I was exposed to individuals there that were part of JROTC, but I had no inkling I'd join the military.

The reason I went to Aviation High School was because I didn't want to go to my zoned school, Seward Park, which was a very bad school at that time. It had a lot of Asian gangs—you know, Flying Dragons, Ghost Shadows. But then I realized later when I went to Queens, there were other gangs in Queens too. So I tried to stay out of trouble by staying straight, going to class and everything.

Then I attended Baruch for college, studying business and finance, and somehow it just occurred to me. I said, "You know what, I need a different experience than just a typical college experience." The typical experience that most Chinese students at Baruch have is they usually go play MJ [mahjong], cards, party, or whatever. So I joined the military in 1988. I did one year of college and the summer of '89, I went to basic training at Fort Dix, New Jersey. Then I went to my Advanced Individual Training [AIT] class down in Fort Sam Houston. My military job was hospital food service specialist. In the civilian world that would be a dietician's aide. We learned about nutrition and how you feed patients in the hospital. Eventually, I was trained as a combat medic and concluded my enlisted service as a practical nurse. I was a commissioned officer after 12 years as an enlisted soldier.

Were your parents okay with you going into this line of work?

Definitely not. My dad was pissed off. Actually I didn't tell my parents that I joined the service until six months after. First thing he asked was, "Did you join the Marines?" I said, no. Because he was like, "Oh, I'll disown you if you joined the Marines." I didn't understand that.

What did they want you to be?

I don't think my parents ever had a clear-cut goal [for me] except go to college and get a professional job. I really did not get that type of guidance

Specialist Wong next to Black Hawk helicopter of the South Carolina
Air National Guard (La Union, El Salvador, 1996)

that I think most people in the U.S. might receive from their parents. It wasn't anything specific except to do well in school and get a professional job.

After I came back from basic training and AIT around November of '89, I found out I had access to the GI Bill. So I ended up applying and transferring to NYU.

In my Army Reserve career, I proceeded to pick up some other military occupational specialties. I became a combat medic, at that time it was called 91 Bravo. Then I became 91 Charlie which is the LPN, practical nurse. Eventually I got my license as a practical nurse in New York State. When I passed the licensure for LPN I already had my degree from NYU in finance. But I continued on because I like the military, because it was a different experience.

Eventually I started working for the city at different departments—the Parks Department, the Buildings Department, the City Comptroller's Office. And eventually I started working at New York State Tax and Finance using my finance degree. I did 12 years as an enlisted soldier and then I was thinking about leaving.

The best experience I had that kept me interested in staying in the military was going to Germany twice. I went to El Salvador in 1996 and Panama in 1997 on Humanitarian and Civic Assistance [HCA] missions. I was there to provide medical support to any of our soldiers in the Army Corps of Engineers if they were injured, while they rebuilt roads, bridges, built schools and health clinics. But we would also give assistance as needed to local nationals; do check-ups and vaccinations as a goodwill gesture from our country to their country. We also provided drinking water. As medical guys, we assessed the drinkability of the water out there when the Army Corps of Engineers drilled for wells. We were working with the Department of State to help other countries strengthen their infrastructures.

So in your civilian life you were doing finance, but then in the military as a reservist you were doing nutrition and medicine?

Yes. It's much more stimulating because it breaks the monotony from your regular job. So the big plus for me staying in the military, even though at that time I was a junior-ranking enlisted person, was the opportunity to travel to different countries, to get training opportunities.

Eventually I was offered to be a commissioned officer. I was commissioned as a second lieutenant in 2000. Because I had three medical military occupational specialties, with a business degree, I eventually became a health services planning and operations officer.

I became a company commander, executive officer on active duty and in the reserves. I was also called for active duty in 2005 to train truck drivers in Fort Leonard Wood in Missouri even though I was in medical service.

When I first got there around May, the company commander—which was a captain and I was a first lieutenant at that time—they thought it was a joke that a medical service guy was going to train truck drivers. Eventually I became their executive officer and trained truck drivers even though that was not my specialty. The executive officers basically are the second-in-command to the company commander when he's away, to make sure that training or whatever needs to be done to accomplish the mission of that unit. So I did that from 2005 to 2006.

So after the 2008 tour, you came back?

I came back. I joined the Police Department in 2004, eventually got called for Iraq in November 2007 and came back end of 2008. Then I went back to the Police Department, the NYPD, in 2009. Eventually I got called back up for Afghanistan in 2011. So it seems to be a cycle, every two to three years I get called back up for a combat tour.

I want to talk about your family and your parents. How do they feel about your promotion?

My dad might be emotional; my mom is stoic. But I don't think they understand the military. And they don't understand the promotion process. They don't understand in general a lot of things about Western life, being in the military, being in the police department. Obviously my parents were not big on me being in the military or the police department because those are the types of professions with highest risk. And at that time I was their only son before my brother was born. So joining the military as the only son was a big no-no for them because they expected me to be around—which I am, but to be more available, I should say, because I'm always being called off for the military duty I have to perform.

Being Chinese American, there's the obligation to take care of the parents.

Yeah. My parents immigrated here. My dad is from Toisan and my mom's from Sahjang just outside of Hong Kong. My dad was relatively well-educated for his era, having a high school diploma back in China. My grandfather, I found out from my father, was a school teacher, so he was also relatively highly educated back then in that era. Our family eventually got into peanut farming, and my mom's family, they were oyster breeders in Hong Kong. My dad immigrated here in the mid-'60s, and then went back and was introduced to my mom and married her. They met through a mutual friend and they were together here in '69. I was born in '70. They started their life with dad in the restaurant business as a waiter, and my mom was a seamstress in a garment factory. Eventually I had two sisters. Then my baby brother eventually came, 20 years after us, unplanned of course. But I found that he was a blessing to us to keep us together. Because it was weird [for a family to stay together as adults] in the Western culture. We value individuality, so it was easy for us to split after we graduated. But I think what held us together more was my brother being born, and I wouldn't say I had the obligation, but the sense of responsibility to make sure that we could give him what we didn't receive from our parents ... better guidance and insights to make better decisions.

Just before the World Trade Center attacks of 9/11 I was working as a compliance officer for corporate social responsibility for Gap [Inc]. My job was to make sure that minimum wage, overtime, and child labor laws were not being violated to make products for these brands. Next, I worked for the San Francisco Police Department. I did that for a year. Fred Lau, the chief of police in San Francisco, was my role model. I believe he was the first major municipal police chief of Chinese American descent. He was my Asian American role model.

Eventually I came back to New York, realizing that there's a lot I could be doing in New York after 9/11. I felt that if I'm going to be a police officer, why not be a police officer in New York City? And my brother was still young at that time, so I felt a sense of responsibility to make sure that he had an older brother available for guidance. So I could help him and give some guidance to him, which I never had the opportunity to get growing up. That was one of the main reasons I came back to New York at the end of 2002.

You've been traveling so much, so do your family and your wife get worried? Every time you go to a high combat area, are they okay with it?

When I met my wife I already had 15 years in the Army Reserves so I think she was already aware [of what it would be like] when she married me. We got married when I was still in the NYPD Police Academy. At that time we realized that I was getting notified and that I might be called for Afghanistan. Yes, it's tough on the relationship, because we had been married about eight years. At that time I'd been on active duty overseas or at least Stateside for military training, 18 months in a combat zone, a year stateside in Missouri, and another six months in Kansas on training mission to train to go to Afghanistan. So it's a little tough. I know I give credit to my wife that she could tolerate this. It's very hard for someone to be subjected to this. But I always try to tell her there's a bigger picture to this. On top of serving our country, a pension. Hopefully we can realize and enjoy the benefit of the pension down the road.

Being of Asian descent, I was subjected to racist slurs and blatant discrimination that I know other legionnaires here [at the Kimlau Post] had also probably experienced in boot camp. But it also opened up my eyes to other people from other parts of the country, from the West Coast, the Midwest, and the South. Many of them had never seen an Asian person and I had never interacted so closely with individuals of those backgrounds. So we got to understand each other. You could see different viewpoints out there and try to understand. You might not have to necessarily agree with them, but you can at least try to understand different viewpoints from different parts of the country.

You talked about how the military opened things up for you and gave you a lot. Do you have any thoughts about being Chinese American in the higher levels?

There was a captain of Filipino ancestry when I was in Afghanistan. He asked me how I got promoted below the zone [early]. I felt I had an obligation to mentor him, because I never had that kind of mentorship from another higher-ranking person.

Initially I just said, "Oh, it's effort, man. Hard work, being persistent, and taking the hard jobs that no one wants." A lot of times people are ungrateful for your efforts. But that's part of being in leadership. You got to do it because you want to do it, not because of any extrinsic rewards. Intrinsically you want to do it because you want to make the organization the best you can. So I told him, "Hey, don't take the easy job." It's easy to take the path of least resistance. That's not how you're going to get promoted in the future.

I overheard this general officer telling some battalion commanders who were complaining about having the roughest battalions, "You're not in a leadership position because it's easy. You're in a leadership position specifically because it's not easy. That's why you're in the leadership. If it was that easy, why would you be placed in a leadership position to begin with?" When I heard that I said, "You're right."

You said that the days in Iraq were so stressful that at night you ran so much that it was pretty much indirectly training you for marathon running.

That's true. In Iraq my day starts about 6 a.m. I go to the chow hall, I get to the office by 7 a.m. or quarter after and watch a 100- to 150-slide PowerPoint presentation General Petraeus is leading. Then we might take a mid-afternoon break and then we're back in the office until about 6 p.m., listen to another briefing till about 7 p.m. or 8 p.m., and then I'm not usually out of there, depending on the so-called homework we have to do the night before for our presentation the next day. I'm there usually about 7 p.m. at least—7 p.m. or 8 p.m. But then I can't go to sleep.

So eventually I started doing long distance running on the treadmill. I can't go outside because we are on a secure base, so we can't really run anywhere. So I run on the treadmill at 9 p.m. or 10 p.m. and I run for two hours at a time sometimes. To the point where by the end of the tour I could run a half marathon without a problem.

Eventually I just said, "Let me just run a marathon," and I ran three marathons after I got back from Iraq. I was still on active duty, on leave, when I ran the Honolulu Marathon in 2008. I did the same thing this time around. After I came back from Afghanistan, I ran the LA Marathon before I got off active duty. So I guess it's my own little tradition of ending my combat tour. I finish it off with a marathon as a tribute to the troops, the Marines, Army soldiers that were killed.

How did you get involved with this post, the Kimlau Post?

I have been a legionnaire for 12 years already. But I had been more involved just recently after coming back from Iraq. The Kimlau Post actually was instrumental in sponsoring an event that I helped coordinate in Iraq at Camp Victory. They sent over 800 T-shirts. I coordinated a 5K run to commemorate the anniversary of 9/11 in 2008, the 7th year anniversary. They screen-printed 800 shirts and I was able to distribute them to the soldiers, sailors and Marines.

Gabe Mui was the Post commander at that time and Fang Wong helped, and it was great. I felt, as a police officer, it was an appreciation to people serving, because of 9/11. This was coming directly from the American Legion Post closest to the World Trade Center.

There was another chilling moment last year. Last year Osama Bin Laden was killed on May 2nd [May 1st EST] while I was in Afghanistan, and the 10-year anniversary of 9/11 was last year. And I just happened to be serving in Afghanistan with the Marines. So it was a very meaningful experience to be out there at that time. All in all, even though I already have 20 years in the service and my wife probably wants me to retire at this point, I'll see how much more I can serve. It's very meaningful to be serving at this time. That's how I feel.

For Further Reading:

Wong, W. (2013, Summer) "Securing the Peace on the Global War on Terrorism." *Inside Homeland Security*, volume 11, issue 2, pp. 49–51.

Gunn, B. (2011, Oct-Dec) "Building Credibility: Engaging Local Religious Leaders in Central Helmand Valley." *Military Intelligence Professional Bulletin*, volume 37, number 4, pp. 77–83.

CHAPTER THIRTY-FOUR

Cindy Wu 吳照欣 (1986–   )
U.S. Navy

Cindy Wu grew up in Flushing, New York, attended Stuyvesant High School, and now works at Samsung as a technician while attending college part-time in Austin, Texas. She talks about defying her parents to join the Navy, being female in the military, and dealing with hazing.

I was part of the Navy as a Nuclear Electronics technician. Basically, I sit in front of a panel and operate nuclear reactors, kind of like Homer Simpson's job on *The Simpsons*. I did maintenance and everything else that went along with keeping an aircraft carrier afloat on the reactor side.

Nuclear reactors provide electrical power and steam to the ship. To become a reactor operator, there's a lot of training that goes along with it. It takes almost two years of training and school before you actually show up to your ship, and then it takes about another year and a half to get fully qualified to sit in front of the panel by yourself. Your final board is with the commanding officer of the ship (which is the highest ranking officer on an aircraft carrier of 5,000 people). To finally get to him, you have to pass six other boards. I've seen people get all the way to the commanding officer and get sent all the way back to the first board because he felt like they did not know enough to operate a nuclear reactor by themselves.

We have two reactors and we were in the Middle East doing flight ops (when they fly the planes off and drop bombs) and they accidentally brought down one of the plants while they were doing maintenance. We had a tactical situation and I was the next person who was going to be reactor operator: I had to start up the reactor. I went down to the engineering space to relieve the off-going watch stander. He was sitting there in shock with an operating manual in his lap, with his hands grabbing so tightly on the armrest that his knuckles were white. We always train for situations like this with drills at least three to four times a week, but it's rare that we have an actual emergency situation. It was pretty intense. There was a lot of pressure there; everyone was relying on me to do this. All the important people including the commanding officer of the ship were there watching me. I was so nervous, but I just zoned everyone out and pretended it was just a drill, and the only person watching me was my drill observer.

At RIMPAC, the world's largest international maritime warfare exercise,
hosted by the U.S. Navy's Pacific Fleet. Canada, 2010

In the worst case scenario, what can actually happen?

Japan [Fukushima]. Or Chernobyl. But we have a lot of safety checks. We
have auto-locks that prevent that. It will never happen in the U.S. because there's
so much training. Whenever we do anything, we have to have to do it according
to a book in front of us, and there's always a second person watching us to make
sure we're doing things correctly.

*Maybe you can talk about when and where you were born and how you got on this
path.*

I was born in Nanjing, China. I came to America when I was four with my
mom. My dad was already here for two years. He was working here and getting
established here before he brought us over. So I grew up in Flushing, New York,
and then when I was 13 I moved to Fresh Meadows and I got into Stuyvesant
High School.

I never liked school. I was never a good student. I didn't like doing homework, didn't like studying. So when I was 18, recruiters showed up at my door
and I joined the Navy. My parents already had a semester paid for at Buffalo
State [College]. So I went there that semester to keep them happy so they didn't

feel like they were wasting their money.

As soon as I got home, I got shipped out to boot camp. I was 18. Before they came to my house, I had signed up for a thing online asking [for information about the military]. It was one of those things that said, "Do you want to see the world? Do you want to do this?" And I didn't know what it was for.

The recruiter who showed up at my door was actually Chinese. I felt safer joining because he was Chinese and because he was successful in the military. He was either a storekeeper or a postal clerk. There are storekeepers in the military. Basically they're in charge of all the shipments that come on the ship and they run the ship's store.

He talked to me first before talking to my parents. After that, I told my parents I was going to join and they didn't believe me. My mom said, "You're not going to join. There's no way." And I showed them the contracts and my dad went to my recruiter and asked, "Can you undo this?" And the recruiter said, "There's nothing I can do. She's 18; she can do whatever she wants." It was pretty intense. It was the first time I'd ever seen my dad cry.

They were upset since I didn't follow their set plan. Their friends' kids were going to colleges and everyone else around them had kids going to these Ivy League schools. I was never a good student and I just didn't really want to go to college that much. They were disappointed that I didn't go to college. Older Asians are very judgmental. I think a lot of their "friends" looked down on my parents because I didn't finish college.

Did your parents come around with you being in the military, or are they still a little bit in shock?

My parents are okay with whatever I do now as long as I am healthy and happy. I was an only child. My dad works for a lighting company and my mom is a human resources administrator at the Jewish Museum. They came to the U.S. to have a better future. There are more opportunities in America than in China.

Did you get to choose your military job, or was it decided for you?

You take a test. I wanted to be a 'nuke' because my recruiters told me it was really hard to get into. He told me I had to be the best of the best. So I was thought, "Okay, I'll do this." And I knew I'd be able to get in.

I got a 99 on my ASVAB, so I thought I was too good for some of the menial jobs like being a cook or in infantry or undesignated. Because I was born in China, they didn't think I would be able to get my security clearance. So I had to take another test. I think the cut-off is—I don't remember what it was. You need to get 10 points above the cut-off or you're not going to get clearance. So I took it and made the cut.

I went into boot camp knowing that I was going to do something with nukes. I thought I was going to operate nuclear weapons. I didn't think I was go-ing to be operating nuclear reactors. When I got out of boot camp, they shipped me to South Carolina. The first part of school is called A-school. They teach you basic electronic theory and everything you need to know about electronics. It's a lot crammed into six months. They made the school a lot easier than it used to be. Our instructors who went through the same process many years ago used to tell us that the attrition rate was about 33%. I feel like if you count everyone signed in to be a nuke and fast forwarded six years later to those who ended their contract as a nuke, it is probably about the same attrition rate, if not higher.

The second part of the six months is called Nuclear Power School. They teach you how a basic nuclear reactor operates and the basic principles that go into it. The third part of school is prototype, where they actually let you operate a nuclear reactor on land. There are two prototypes, one in Saratoga Springs, New York and one in Charleston, South Carolina. They teach you how to operate a nuclear reactor so you actually get the feel of it before you operate the nuclear reactor on your ship. I've heard stories about people killing themselves during prototype because they couldn't handle the stress, although none of that happened in the year that I was there. The instructors in school were way nicer than anyone I ever met on my ship. I'm guessing it's because they didn't want you to hate the Navy before you even got to your first duty command.

I did this for six years. I got to travel the world. I went on two and a half deployments. I was stationed out of San Diego. I went to Dubai because it was a pit spot and then I went to Korea, Singapore, Japan, Hong Kong, Malaysia, and Thailand. And I've been to Victoria, British Columbia in Canada, and I've been through Hawaii and Guam.

In the civilian world, there's being politically correct, and everyone has to be nice to each other. But once you're in the military, they can treat you however they want to treat you. And you're stuck with these people day in and day out. If you want to complain, it's best not to complain, because that just gets your peers against you. It's nothing like the civilian world is like. It's just one of those things where they can do whatever they want. I learned how to block things out because there's a lot of harassment, a lot of hazing in any branch of the military. In my branch, in the Navy where I worked, it was pretty ridiculous, the amount of hazing and harassment that goes on. I've seen a guy get duct taped to a chair at the arms and legs and his eyes taped open because he was falling asleep. I've been held down in a chair in uniform and had "Dust Off" sprayed on me upside down. To this day I still have a freeze-burn scar on my stomach from it. I've seen a guy get picked up solely by his nipples. I've seen a girl get prank-called over and over again in berthing. No one in my division liked her because she was always finding ways to get out of doing work, so one of the guys decided to prank her and pretend to be a guy interested in her. It was pretty juvenile and cruel but I can't say I didn't find it hilarious at the time.

Everyone gets hazed. They find any reason to make fun of you and they see how well you take it. If you take it well, they leave you alone and find their next victim. The thing that they want is to get a reaction out of you.

Are "they" peers, or superiors, or is it everyone?

It's peers, it's superiors, it's everyone. But not the captains or officers or the really high superiors; it's the enlisted. They harass people all the same. I was the only Asian female in my group for the longest time. Another one showed up right when I was about to get out. There were a couple of Asian guys—a Korean guy, a half-Filipino/half-Chinese guy, and then there was a full-Chinese guy in my group, and we had about 60 people. Once, I left my e-mail open and someone sent an email to the entire division from me saying how the "Asian Mafia is going to take over Reactor Controls division and how I was going to force-feed everyone rice," or something like that. In the real world, there would have been an HR investigation and someone would have gotten fired, but everyone just laughed.

As a female, there was a lot of harassment, but it wasn't because of anything I did. It was because of things that girls before me had done. I noticed a lot of times girls join the military and then they realize how hard it is, so they don't want to get deployed. So they just pretend they're crazy or maybe they are actually crazy. Or sometimes you get girls who would just get pregnant so they don't have to go on deployment, since they don't want to deal with how hard it is.

So when I showed up to my ship, guys were making bets on whether I was going to get pregnant or psych out. In our class, people usually show up every two months. Up until I showed up, all the girls that came in in the last three years all had either gotten pregnant or psyched out. So the guys were just kind of sick of dealing with that. You're supposed to be there to do your job and, instead of doing their job, the girls would just decide, "Oh, this is so hard," and go complain to the ship's psych or get knocked up. Deployments are always hard. It's always right before deployment where girls start getting pregnant or going crazy so they don't have to go. It's the freaking military. Of course you're going to get deployed and people are going to tell you what to do whether you like it or not. I don't know what they were expecting. It's not just girls, although there are so few of us, the percentage of girls dropping like flies compared to guys is significantly higher.

When I read the article about Danny Chen, I just shook my head. Everyone is so quick to play the race card. I don't believe he was specifically picked on because he was Asian. Blacks and Whites get picked on just as much as Asians. If we have a guy from West Virginia, we always make fun of him for sleeping with his cousins. There was a black girl in my division and we used to joke that when the lights are out, all we can see are her eyes and teeth. If there was a Mexican in our division, we'd joke that they should be mowing the lawn or washing dishes. There was a guy who was overweight and we used to say that he was the goldfish because like a goldfish, he'd grow into his uniforms no matter what size they were. Danny Chen just had wrong expectations about the military. People in the military are not nice and forgiving. It is a stressful environment, especially

Cindy Wu with best friend
on deployment in 2008

since we are at war right now. He was a guard in Afghanistan. He was supposed to keep the bad people off the base so his comrades could be safe. How is he supposed to do that if he's asleep at his watch station? I am not condoning the actions of his fellow soldiers but I do believe that if Danny wasn't so sheltered and had thicker skin, he would not have committed suicide.

Navy boot camp is not hard. It's pretty easy for girls. There are different standards for girls and guys. Guys have to run a mile and a half in 12 minutes or something, if you're an 18-year-old guy. For a girl, you have 14 minutes and 45 seconds, which is almost a 10-minute mile, which is plenty of time. For push-ups, I think guys have to do 50 and girls have to do only about 20. So it's not that hard to pass boot camp. What gets most people is the stress level when there's someone in your face yelling at you all the time. That's when most people crack.

I'm going to the Veterans Association right now because they're treating me for post-traumatic stress disorder from what I went through on my ship. I didn't really think I was going to get anything out of it, because usually people who get disability are people that go to medical all the time and complain about every little problem that they have. I hated going to medical because some of the people in ship's medical are incompetent and they just give you an 800 milligram ibuprofen for just about everything. So when I went to my first doctor's appointment for the Veteran's Association because I was trying to get some dental work done, they saw scratch marks on my arms and asked, "Are you depressed?" I said no. And they said, "Well, what's that on your arms?" And I had scars from mosquito bites. I got a lot of mosquito bites when I was little and from wherever there's a lot of mosquitoes, and I pick at them. They itch and they scar up. They said, "A lot of Asian women pick at their scars because they can't really talk about their emotions." So they recommended I get treated for post-traumatic stress disorder.

So now I get care on a regular basis. I started telling about the harassment about the guys making bets on me, if I was going to get pregnant or psych out. The nurse practitioner actually gave me a hug because she was horrified at some of the things that I was telling her. Being in the navy for six years, I've gotten numb to it, but to someone who has never been exposed to that kind of environment, it just seemed unbearable. The guys were pretty mean to me, actually. But I think they were just trying to make sure I was actually going to stick around. Toward the end they were nicer, they accepted me, but in the beginning they would make me clean the male bathroom. The senior guys would call the new guys NUBs, which stands for "non-useful bodies." It was basically a boys club. There would be a bunch of guys playing cards at a table and they'd say, "Oh hey, you're a girl, we need paint. Go get this 5-gallon bucket of paint." I can't carry that. "Oh, but you're in the military. You get paid just as much as we do."

Five-gallon paint cans are no joke, but guys that weren't in my division would see me struggling across the hangar bay and they would help me. In the civilian world, you have janitors that clean and take care of your office space. In the military, you do your job and you have to clean, and you have to take care of the painting and the housekeeping for your workspace and living space.

There were times on deployment where I hadn't slept for three days because I was doing maintenance or standing watch. Those were times that I freaked out. But the thing that kept me going was the fact that I left home telling my parents that I was going to do six years and if I came back before six years, they would have known I'd given up. I didn't want to have that for them to hold against me. I didn't want my parents to say, "Oh, I told you so." Leaving was never an option even though times were really hard sometimes.

But you would have stayed even if you knew it wasn't you, but that the system was wrong?

The system is always wrong. There's nothing you can do about it.

So it wouldn't really reflect badly on you per se, right?

Well, my contract was six years, so if I got an early out it would be for something like a medical discharge, which will show up when I apply for jobs. If I get anything other than an honorable discharge, I can't get my GI benefits and healthcare benefits. There are some ways to get out before your time is up, but none of them are good.

So how would you describe your overarching feelings about your experience in the military?

It's an experience. It helped me grow up a lot. When I graduated boot camp, they gave us our freedoms in intervals. For example, the first 4 weeks, you were only allowed to wear your uniform everywhere and you were not allowed to drink alcohol or drive a car, and you had a curfew every day. From 4 to 8 weeks, you can wear civilian clothes only on weekends and you were allowed to drink alcohol on weekends but you still couldn't drive, and you had a curfew every day. After 8 weeks, you were allowed to wear civilian clothes after 4 p.m. and on weekends, and you can drive, but you still had a curfew on weekdays. There were people that had poor hygiene and they would get assigned mandatory showers, where someone would stand outside of their shower at a certain time and made sure they bathed. If you don't pay your bills and they end up going to collections, your command will find out and take it out of your paycheck. A lot of the things that the military did were ridiculous but I do believe it helped me become a responsible adult.

I learned not to rely on other people. A lot of things were promised to us, like days off, and then they would just get taken away. You would be promised rewards for doing well, but then the rewards would never happen, so it kind of also made me cynical. It taught me to hope for the best but expect the worst. I'm never disappointed anymore because my expectations for everything are so low.

What are you doing now?

I finished my contract about a year ago. I'm going to school part-time right now in Austin, Texas at a community college, and I'm working full-time at Samsung as a technician. I was studying business administration but then I took an Intro to Psychology class and fell in love with it. I had no idea what I was going to do with my psychology degree at first, but recently a very good friend of mine passed away from a prescription drug overdose. He was 25 and in the Navy with me. He had a lot of issues going on in his life that he needed help for, but instead of helping him through counseling, military doctors just kept on writing him prescriptions for anti-depressants, sleeping pills, and anti-anxiety medication, which eventually killed him. I want to use my psychology degree to help people through therapy.

Did you ever have moral or philosophical qualms about being part of the war?

Whether you believe in war or not, it is going to happen. Our country's founding fathers started war with the British and that's how America was established. I never saw direct combat and I didn't have to take innocent lives, so it really doesn't bother me. I am reaping the benefits of being a war veteran. I have my GI Bill and I was able to get a good job without having a college degree and being tens of thousands of dollars in debt.

Do you have any thoughts about being Chinese American in the military? Or do you have advice for other Chinese Americans who want to go into the military?

Well, this is advice for just anyone, not only for other Chinese Americans: You have to be really hardheaded to make it through. You have to not let other people get to you, otherwise you are not going to make it through. You just have to take it day by day. It's not easy and people are stressed when they're away from their families. And when you're stuck with the same people day in and day out, you'll run out of stuff to talk about and you'll just start making fun of them or harassing them. It's not rainbows and butterflies that people in the real world are used to.

So if you have kids, if you had a daughter who pretty much wants to take the path that you took, would you advise her against it, or just let her do what she wants?

I would tell her like it is, that it's not easy and people are going to treat you like shit. I would advise her against joining a field that does not have any application in the civilian world. And if she wants to make a career out of it, more power to her. The military definitely needs more strong female leaders to look up to. I definitely did not have any while I was going through school or on my ship. I would also tell her not to get pregnant or pull any of the dumb stuff that people do to get out early. It's definitely not worth it to have a dishonorable discharge follow you for the rest of your life.

CHAPTER THIRTY-FIVE

Howard Chin 陳煥寧 (1959–   )
U.S. Army

Howard Chin is a police officer in the Port Authority Police Department. He was in the Army (Reserves) for 29 years, achieving the rank of lieutenant colonel. In Iraq, he served as Military Police and participated in board hearings to determine the release of Iraqis. With the Asian Jade Society, he won a lawsuit against the Port Authority for denying promotions to qualified Asian American officers.

I was in Iraq from July 2005 to August 2006 in Operation Iraqi Freedom. The Army sends soldiers to the combat zone in one of two ways: as an individual, or as a unit. I was mobilized as an individual augmentee, or IA as it is called. The Army does not care if the soldier selected is Active Duty, Reserve, or National Guard. You are selected based on your rank and MOS. It just so happened I was promoted to lieutenant colonel in 2005, and my name popped up. Within a month, I was on my way to Iraq. The Army sent me to Camp Victory, one of many bases that were on the outskirts of Baghdad.

It was a frightening experience. In 2004–2005, the insurgents were maiming or killing us with IEDs [Improvised Explosive Devices], or roadside bombs. Part of my mission, at that time, was to go on convoys between bases to conduct business. It was pretty scary—I was always thinking, "Let today not be my day."

I was born in December 1959 here in New York, New York. Chinatown. My mother was a seamstress and my father was a manager of a Chinese restaurant in uptown Manhattan. My father was the first person in my family to come to America. He came in 1952, from Canton, and when he made enough money, my mother came in 1956.

I went to P.S. 23, on Mulberry Street. It was mostly Chinese and Italians. I then went to Junior High School 65 for two years, and then Brooklyn Technical High School for four years. While in high school, I started thinking about the military. I saw recruitment commercials on TV. It looked interesting and adventuresome, but in my heart, I knew my parents would disapprove. They would rather see me go to a 4-year school and graduate than to join the military. My parents wanted me to pursue a traditional career like law or medicine, or any professional fields, where the prestige and income are good. But neither of those professions interested me.

In 1977 I graduated high school and went to SUNY at Buffalo. After one

Lt. Col. Howard Chin, Army photograph

year there, I found I did not really like the school or the city. I came back to New York City and obtained an associate's degree at Queensborough Community College. I then transferred to a four-year school at City College. At this time, I thought about the military again.

I started thinking about all the services: Army, Navy, Air Force, Marines, Coast Guard—which one should I join? The Army offered me the best opportunity, just three years active duty or eight years in the Reserves. I said, "Hmmm, part-time soldier, part-time fun? That sounds good." The commitment was one weekend a month, and two weeks during the summer. I said to myself, "I can handle that." So I took the second option: the Reserve.

I remember when I joined the Army in 1982, there were very few Asians. In those days, friends and family would say, "Why do you want to be a police officer? Police officers are lazy. Why do you want to be a soldier? They are lazy, they have low intellect, and can't hold a meaningful job. Is that what you want to do?" They'll tell you, "Get a life." The Chinese community did not want to see their sons and daughters in non-traditional fields. The Chinese favor professional occupations like lawyers, doctors, engineers, scientists, accountants, etc.

I enrolled in the college ROTC program and a local Army Reserve unit simultaneously. At the end of two years, I was commissioned a second lieutenant in the Army Reserve. My MOS was communications-electronics officer.

At the same time, I was working for the Board of Education at night. I was a para-professional and helped teachers tutor high school GED students—older adults in their 20s, 30s, and 40s who for some reason were not able to graduate from high school.

This combination of working at night and a part-time income from the Army Reserve helped defray the cost of my college education. (I was glad I attended a city university rather than a private college!). Because of this, it took me more than four years to get my bachelor's degree.

You went to school, you worked for the Board of Education and you were in the military, all at the same time?

Yes. Three things at once. It wasn't easy juggling three balls, but somehow, I got it done.

After working for the Board of Education, I went to work for the Federal Bureau of Investigation full-time. I worked there as an electronics technician. While the work was interesting and the pay decent, the novelty wore off after a few years. I could not see myself making a career of it. The law enforcement field seemed more enticing, and had the potential of earning more. I then thought of becoming an FBI special agent.

However, as a special agent, you were subject to relocation every few years. That did not appeal to me. I then decided to join the Port Authority Police, a police department that has jurisdiction in both New York and New Jersey, where I remain to this day.

I was the only oddball in the family. At that time, it was unusual for Asians to join the military or become a police officer. These occupations are generally not held in high esteem by the Asian community. My friends say I am cuckoo for being different, but I took the plunge nonetheless. Both my brothers pursued career fields that were more typical of Asians. My older brother worked in the education field and my younger brother went into accounting. So much for being mainstream, USA!

My career in the Army is coming to an end. In six weeks, I have to retire. Army regulations dictate how long you can stay as a commissioned officer. In total, I will have 29 years and 10 months of service.

Today, you are still with the Port Authority?

Yes, for about 25 years now.

* * *

When I went to Iraq, my son was 15 and my daughter 11. As with any family, they were unhappy because they wanted me home. They did not want to see me go to war. The hard part was going to be the long family separation.

I was there [in Iraq] for 13 months and it was a pretty scary experience. Unless you have official business, you're not allowed to leave the base. I left the base because I had to travel to the Green Zone. That's where they had the parole board hearings. It's called the CRRB [Combined Review and Release

Board]. We had three or four high-ranking U.S. soldiers on one side and four or five high-ranking Iraqi officials on the other side. We'd sit at this big long table and review the folder of the detainees. We would then individually record our vote (in secrecy) [on whether they should remain detained] and turn it in to the court clerk.

At that time, we were rounding up, picking up, thousands of Iraqis because— I'll give you a good example. Let's say, an American unit is out on patrol. All of a sudden, they receive gunfire from a house. The patrol unit thinks the gunfire is coming from that house, so they rush to that house and investigate if anyone in that house is involved in the shooting. They would look for weapons and bomb-making materials, and any MAM—MAM is an acronym for "Military Age Male" or any male between the ages of 16 to 50—just because we think they may have shot at us. The patrol unit would round them up, bring them back, and put them in holding cells, to be transferred later on to larger brigade or division internment facilities.

Anyone who they think might possibly have shot at you, you'd pick up?

We would round them up, sometimes with bad evidence and sometimes with good evidence. We would review these folders, thousands of folders, and say, "Do we have sufficient evidence to hold this person?" If the majority said, "Yes, there is sufficient evidence to hold him," we keep him. If we say, "There's scant evidence. We don't think this guy's the one," we vote to release. So that's it. We basically gathered thousands of Iraqis, some innocent, some guilty. We don't know yet, and hold them for days, until their folders are reviewed.

As U.S. soldiers, we follow U.S. law. If we think there is credible evidence to hold him, we hold him. The Iraqis would say, "What do you Americans know about our people? I'm from this country. I know who the insurgents are. That person is guilty. That person is innocent." It was a fine balancing act. Since it's their country and their prisoners, we want them to have a say in their legal process. There were three different ethnic groups: Shiites, Sunnis, and Kurds. The Sunnis were supposed to be the bad guys. The Shiites were somewhat supportive of us. And the Kurds were generally friendly to us. We did not have much interaction with the Kurds because they were up north.

For example, if the voting members of the board are Shiites and the detainee is a Sunni, they'll say, "He's guilty." Whereas if the board member is a Sunni and the detainee is a Sunni, he'll say, "He's a good guy. Let him go." That's where the conflict is.

Do you think, overall, that the system is fair or just still completely random?

Neither fair nor completely random, but more toward the random side. I found that on the U.S. side we tend to say, "Keep him," whereas on the Iraqi side, they tend to say, "Release."

What happens when the votes are deadlocked and there isn't a majority decision?

Usually, because this is their country, and ultimately they'll be handling them as their prisoners, we let them have the final say. However, if the detainee is a "high value threat," the American general has veto authority. If he doesn't like the vote, he can say, "No, keep him," even though the Iraqis vote to release him. That's above my level. They don't really tell us what happens if we can't reach an agreement. We were told that if there's a tie on both sides, we tend to go with the Iraqi vote. In America, the presiding judge can throw out a jury verdict, but that is very rare.

My earlier assignment was to travel around the country inspecting prisons to make sure the prisoners or detainees were not being abused. As you recall from the Abu Ghraib incident, American soldiers were teasing and humiliating Iraqi prisoners. The picture of naked Iraqi prisoners being forced to perform indecent acts caused an international outcry and gave the United States a black eye. During my inspections, I saw no evidence of abuse. Our soldiers [guards] were pretty much gun-shy.

Gun-shy?

Gun-shy means the reluctance to using force. If anything, it's really the Iraqis—Iraqi on Iraqi. In the United States, a guard is not allowed to beat prisoners. In Iraq, they do that. We try to tell them, "No, no, you can't do that. You can't mistreat the prisoners. It's against the Geneva Convention laws."

Abu Ghraib was not normal and it should not have happened. My personal feeling was that it was just a couple of Military Police. They were bored and improperly supervised. Working in a jail environment is not pleasing. All day long, all you see is prisoners. Sometimes, the prisoners say things to insult you or throw things at you. You don't like that. You think, "Oh, you're insulting me? Well, screw you! Here's one for you!" The guards would whack them, or shoot them with a water hose, or deprive them of privileges. I don't know, I wasn't there. It was their outlet for relieving stress and boredom. Their actions were not the norm.

In a war zone, there is not much of anything [activities] you can do outside your normal work hours. We had to stay focused on the mission. We worked 12–14 hours a day, 7 days a week. When off duty, we had nowhere to go. Leaving the base was strictly forbidden. It was very dangerous "outside the wire" because you are an easy target. The insurgents know and can blend in with the neighborhood. What may seem like a friendly shop owner may actually be a perpetrator setting you up to be killed. You have to be on guard at all times.

When I first went there, we had no trailers. Everybody lived in tents; you could fit 16 to 20 people in a tent. We called the area we were in "Tent City North," or "Tent City South." Then, two or three months later, we were able to move into trailers. The Army decided to build more trailers when it became apparent we were not going to leave Iraq any time soon. The trailers were divided

A recruitment poster of veteran Port Authority police officers from various military branches to encourage more veterans to join the department.

into three sections, with two soldiers per section, or a total of six soldiers per trailer. As you move up the ranks, you get a little more space with less soldiers per trailer. The trailer has air conditioning, so it's a little bit more comfortable. Instead of sleeping on a cot, you now have a bed and a mattress. Instead of living out of your duffel bag, you now have a small closet. The one bad thing is the long walk to the nearest porta-john. We had to drink lots of water during the day just to stay hydrated. At night, all that water you just drank had to come out! There were hundreds of porta-johns scattered throughout the base. Needless to say, in the 120° heat, it can smell pretty bad. For showers, it was a community shower. However, after showering and walking back to your tent, you had dust all over you again. Iraq had frequent sandstorms. The sand got into everything; your clothing, your equipment, everything.

* * *

What was it like when you came back home to your family? That was after 13 months?

They were very, very happy to see me. I came home intact, in one piece. No bullet holes, no missing arms or missing legs. They were relieved. My wife said I look a little malnourished, but I felt great. I had lost 7 pounds in the sand box! There was a short readjustment period. I spent the next few weeks relaxing, purchased a new vehicle, and went back to work.

While in Iraq, I tried to call home at least once a week just to let them know I was still alive. There's an 8-hour difference between Baghdad time and New York time, with Baghdad time being 8 hours ahead. Soldiers were encouraged to call home every so often to keep the communications channel open with the family. Talking to family and friends was a good way to keep your sanity in check. Concurrently, the Army does not want soldiers getting too wrapped up with home life issues or problems. It detracts from your ability to stay focused on the mission.

Where were you on 9/11?

On 9/11 I was at Fort Lee, Virginia for a two-week Army Logistics course. When the news media reported that a plane had crashed into the Twin Towers, students were saying, "What kind of dipshit was piloting that plane? It was a perfectly clear day." However, when a second plane crashed into the other Tower we said, "What is going on? Something is not right." Within an hour, the school commandant ordered all classes cancelled and all students return to quarters for further instructions. The Department of Defense was expecting more attacks and ordered all military bases on high alert. They stopped classes for a day and a half while the intelligence community tried to put the pieces together.

At that time, my family was living in Chinatown, one mile from Ground Zero. The awful thing was the phones did not work. I called maybe 15 or 20 times. I just could not get through to my wife. At the same time, she was trying to contact me to say that everyone is fine.

We completed the course at the school (Army Logistics Management College), told to go home, and be prepared for mobilization. So it was kind of "Uh-oh," you know. We were all looking each other. Who are they going to call? Is it going to be a New York unit? Is it going to be a Pennsylvanian unit? After 9/11, the Asian community also got caught up with the patriotic fervor that was sweeping the country. Many of them started joining the military.

* * *

There are pros and cons to being a police officer. Now, as I look back, I ask myself, "Would I do it again? Did I regret anything? How would my life be different if I stayed in the technical field [electronics]?"

After 23½ years of being a police officer, I was finally promoted to sergeant. What I don't like about [the Port Authority] is that they are discriminatory. Blacks and Hispanics have sued the department in the past; and Asians are now suing due to the lack of representation in the supervisory ranks. We have a glass ceiling and can't go up above a certain level. I made sergeant based on a lawsuit.

Was this a class action suit?

I belong to a group called the Asian Jade Society. It is like a fraternal organization. The Hispanics have the Hispanics Society. for the Italians, it is the Columbia Association. for the Irish, it is the Emerald Society. for the Blacks, it is called the Bi-State Shields, for the Germans, it is the Steuben Association, etc. For us, it is the Asian Jade Society. We have perhaps 40 members. A group of us decided to take action after seeing many officers get promoted, many of whom we think are less qualified. In all quantifiable areas, Asians in general score higher on written tests, have better sick and discipline records, more education, and more seniority than other candidates that were promoted ahead of us. For example, I have two master's degrees. One from John Jay College of Criminal Justice (Public Administration), and one from Seton Hall University (Education). These degrees helped me in my promotion to Lieutenant Colonel in the Army, but it didn't help me at all with the police department

In our department, taking a written test is the first step in the promotion process. However, achieving a higher test score does not make you more qualified. They look at other criteria, such as academic qualifications, attendance records, discipline records, etc. Candidates are then placed on a horizontal list, not a vertical list. There is no ranked order, and seniority does not count. Essentially, the department can promote whoever they want. When we presented our case in court, the court found we were under-represented in the supervisory ranks and awarded us damages.

Would you let your children join the military if they wanted to?

I have no problem with my son or daughter wanting to join the military, but my wife said no way. She said one in the family is enough. It was very scary to her when the Army sent me to Iraq. Right now, I'm very happy in the sense that the year 2012 will be a very significant year for our family. It is when I get to retire from the Army. My son will graduate from college with a degree in Computer Science, and my daughter will graduate from high school and pursue accounting as a major. The Post-9/11 GI Bill that was signed into law gave veterans the choice of transferring their educational benefits to their spouse or children if they don't use it. I transferred half to my son and half to my daughter.

CHAPTER THIRTY-SIX

Cliff Chen 陳定宇 (1968–　　)
U.S. Marine Corps

Cliff Chen was a colonel in the United States Marines, where he served for 23 years. He graduated from UC Berkeley and the Naval Postgraduate School. He currently resides in Honolulu, Hawaii, and recently published a series of children's books called *My Dad Is a Marine*.

My father, an American-born Chinese from New York City, attended Perkiomen Prep School and Brooklyn Friends School, and was drafted into the U.S. Army in World War II. He served in Italy near the end of the war.

There is a story that my grandmother went to the draft board and said, "It's okay to take my son, but please don't send him to the Pacific." I assume she was worried about him being mistaken as Japanese.

He had some interesting experiences, being the only Chinese American in his unit. At Fort Sill, Oklahoma, he found out the Post snack bars were run by Chinese. Apparently they might have been related to the Pershing Chinese—Chinese from Mexico that had helped the Americans against Pancho Villa during Pershing's Punitive Expedition, and who in thanks Pershing had brought back to Texas as an exception to the Chinese Exclusion Act.

My dad also recalls a time in Durham, North Carolina, when he was at Fort Bragg getting ready to go overseas. Apparently, he had a cousin who ran a popular Chinese restaurant in town. There was a long line waiting to get seated but my dad and his friends got seated right away, ahead of officers and everybody else, because of the Chinese connection. The funny thing he mentions is that in those days the front staff and waitresses in Chinese restaurants were all white. Apparently back then most white people didn't want to deal with Chinese-speaking wait staff.

My dad made it to Italy before the end of the war and was part of the Po Valley campaign. He was assigned to the 617th Field Artillery Observation Battalion attached to IV Corps and specialized in counter battery detection through sound and flash. He had some contact with the 442nd Infantry Regiment and remembers them being friendly to him in recognizing another Asian. He came home a private first class, got out like thousands of other veterans, and went to college at Rensselaer Polytechnic Institute in Troy, NY, on the GI Bill. He became a mechanical engineer, married my mom, and we lived first in West

Hempstead, Long Island, and later in Irvine, California.

I got good grades in high school, went to UC Berkeley, and studied to be a mechanical engineer like my older brother and my dad before me. But a funny thing happened while I was at school. I had always had an interest in serving in the military and had received Army and Navy ROTC scholarships until I was disqualified because I was colorblind.

And it dawned on me—here I was, an Asian American studying to be an engineer, in a literal sea of Asian Americans studying to be engineers, doctors, or lawyers. All Asian people cared about when they talked to me was, "What are you going to do? How much money will you make?"

To join the Marine Corps would be just about the most un-Asian thing I could do. And better yet, the Marine Corps didn't care if I was colorblind. This Platoon Leaders Class program was great. I could go to two six-week summer sessions and could quit any time before I swore the oath.

My parents were somewhat upset when I told them about wanting to go to Officer Candidates School—my dad less so, but my mom is first-generation, and she was in full Chinese Mom mode.

"Why you want go army? No good go army!" There is a Chinese saying that I think goes through the mind of every Chinese mom when you mention the military. I don't know it in Chinese, but in English it's "One does not make nails from the best iron, nor soldiers from the best men."

My recruiter told me before he put me on a plane to Washington National, "You're great on the mental side of the house, but you need a little work on your physical side." He had set me up with a Chinese American second lieutenant from Hayward State and he ran me up and down the fire trails of the Berkeley Hills until I could get a barely decent run time.

My recruiter was a black officer who happened to be married to a Korean woman. One day we were talking and he mentioned that, being black, he was hoping to recruit more black officers, but in the Bay Area he found that the only

Cliff and Al Chen at Marine Corps Air Station, Miramar

minority he seemed to be able to get were Asians! I distinctly remember once being on a break before a combat obstacle course. As I peeled off my socks, it seemed like half the skin on my foot came off with my sock. The Corpsman bandaged me up and told me to sit it out but when my sergeant instructor saw me, he yelled at me and told me to get in line with everyone else. So I got up and limped over in line with everyone else, and as I crawled through the mud under strands of barbed wire he said something to the effect of, "Good job Chen. Ain't no pussies in my platoon."

I say this because I know most Asian Americans are more familiar with Bruce Yamashita's story and how he sued the Marine Corps because he felt he had been dropped from OCS because of a racist staff. My drill instructors were mostly black or Hispanic and, if anything, I felt they encouraged and motivated me more than the other white candidates.

There was a 4th-generation Japanese and a Vietnamese guy in my platoon, and I think there was a Korean kid somewhere, but we were few in number. What the layperson doesn't understand about OCS is that it is not a training camp—the staff is not there to train you to be an officer. They are there to screen out those who will not make good officers.

It doesn't matter if you can pass every test, because if you don't have the character, they don't want you. They are interested in whether you have what it takes to be an officer—if you have the heart and the ability to undergo everything they can throw at you and still keep charging ahead. If what they threw at me materialized in the form of statements about my race, then so be it. My race never seemed to be an issue with my staff. The staff was black and Hispanic and during the second summer there were a couple of incidents involving my race, but they were not malicious, and only meant to get my attention.

The first was when I was daydreaming, looking at the presidential helicopters flying from their Quantico Base, and missed a command during close order drill. Marching may seem mindless but really does require you to pay attention and concentrate. In any case, I failed to move when commanded, and my platoon sergeant shouted, "Wake up Chen! There are people being run over by tanks in China!" He was of course referring to Tiananmen Square. I didn't know anything about it since we were isolated in training—no TV news at the time. Many people find the image of a lone student standing in front of a tank as inspirational, but my sergeant knew a tank would sustain absolutely no damage running over a student, and therefore commented, "What an idiot."

The second time my race was a topic was when a drill instructor called me and a Vietnamese candidate up and started asking us how many languages we spoke. I had to admit I only spoke English. The Vietnamese kid could speak Vietnamese, English, and French, so I looked pretty bad. When I said I could only speak English, my Hispanic drill instructor shouted, "What's the matter? Don't you have any pride in your racial heritage? My kids speak Spanish!" A couple of times I remember them specifically saying something to me as an aside that they weren't making fun of my race—just trying to sling stress.

After I graduated from my Senior Session of OCS, I think my parents hoped I would come to my senses and give up this hair-brained scheme of joining the Marines. I made a half-hearted attempt at interviewing for a couple of engineering jobs, but when I finished senior year at school and graduation came, I decided if I didn't join then I would regret it for the rest of my life.

In June of 1990, I raised my right hand and accepted a commission as a second lieutenant in the Marine Corps. Every Marine Officer attends a six-month school called The Basic School or TBS and it is there that they really train you to be an officer and basic leader. Like in OCS, there were very few Asian Americans. In fact, I think we were outnumbered by exchange officers from South Korea and Taiwan.

Here, I found, as I have throughout my life, that I was never the subject of institutionalized prejudice, but occasionally found good-hearted attempts at humor which more sensitive people find offensive. Over 85% of the officers in the Marine Corps are white. Some have probably never even met an Asian before, let alone worked with one, and I've found that as an Asian American, your nickname invariably ends up being something related to Charlie Chan, Bruce Lee, ninja, samurai, or something like that. If you take it and yourself too seriously, you just confuse them.

I've found that the best way to overcome prejudice or ignorance is to show you can perform, and the Marine Corps has been good at recognizing and promoting people based on their performance and not on their race. The Marines have a very strong Equal Opportunity Program and I was inculcated from my earliest days at OCS that Marines only come in one color: green.

After TBS, I was assigned the job of aircraft maintenance officer and was stationed in Tustin, California, where my parents were very happy because I could live at home with them. I deployed aboard a helicopter carrier for six months, and we cruised through South East Asia and the Persian Gulf with stops in Kenya and Australia.

When we stopped in Hong Kong, I did not feel at home like some people thought I would. It became all the more obvious that I was an American at heart. People in Hong Kong thought I was Filipino because I had a tan! So I experienced the same confusion I suppose all Asian Americans feel at one time or another. I look like all these people, but I can't speak their language, they don't act the same or think the same, yet when I go home to America, people think I'm a foreigner. You just can't win!

Later, I would also participate in Operation Restore Hope, unloading equipment from ships in Mogadishu, Somalia. Having seen the abject poverty that a great portion this world lives in, I can only reemphasize how fortunate I feel to be an American, despite the flaws that we as a society still have.

Asian Americans continue to grow as a demographic, but their representation in the Armed Forces is a little low. Is it really a cultural bias against the

Colonel Clifford Chen, USMC

military, or is it that Asians are more interested in financial gain rather than service to country?

My second tour would take me to Marine Corps Recruit Depot San Diego, where I served as a series commander and company commander. There, I was responsible for the supervision of drill instructors and the training of thousands of Marine recruits. San Diego basically handles all males recruited from west of the Mississippi, so we always had a pretty diverse bunch of kids to work with. But here again, I found Asians to be underrepresented. There were a handful of either new Chinese or Vietnamese immigrants in each class, and it is interesting that they were almost always first-generation. I think that they are the ones who appreciate what this country has to offer more and are more interested in serving it.

I always took great pains to talk to Asian recruits that were being sent home for failing. Some just could not adapt to the Marine culture. Sometimes it was the language barrier. Sometimes it was lack of heart. I suppose it can be strange, an Asian American belonging to a military unit whose greatest battles have been fought in succession against Japs, Chinks, and Gooks. I have often talked to veterans who, without thinking, use these expressions to my face. But as time has gone on, I think people have become more aware, and I think because they see that I too now wear the same uniform they did, they know that I am the same as them because I've shown I am willing to make the same sacrifices and endure the same hardships they did for this country.

A funny story about my time at boot camp: My first sergeant said he was talking to his dad in Michigan, and they were talking about things and some-how his father happened to ask, "How are those Chinamen doing out there?" this being the appropriate term for someone of his generation. My first sergeant had to say, "They're doing pretty good. One of them is my boss."

The Marine Corps is doing its best, not only to make Marines, but also to make better Americans, and a great part of the training we conducted involved values. We were required to talk about racism and how it was prohibited in the Marines. Those with racist tattoos were sent home or required to have them removed.

I remember one time a recruit muttered something about a Hispanic DI calling him a "taco-eating bastard." He was reported by other recruits. So I made an example of him in front of a whole company of some 500 recruits and punished him administratively, and explained to them all that racism or anything relating to it would not be tolerated. It didn't matter where they came from or what their parents had taught them; the Marines did not discriminate, period. Well, I didn't have anything put in his record, and the young lad went on to do fine. Close to graduation there is a dinner to allow parents to meet their sons' DIs. I happened to be there and this man comes up to me and introduces himself as this kid's dad, shakes my hand, and thanks me for what I'd done for him. I was at a loss. What had his son told him about me? In the end, all I can say is I'm glad I had the opportunity to affect these kids' lives in a positive way.

With the political tension with China, there are sometimes jokes about where my loyalty lies. I knew they were kidding but I had to say, "Hey, that's the kind of crap that got people put in relocation camps!" I had a boss who would joke about taking care of my car when I was put in a concentration camp. It's that kind of banter that could easily be totally taken in wrong directions if you always want to file a hurt feelings report.

When the question of loyalty comes up, I always think of the 442nd Regimental Combat Team. I suppose, as Asian Americans in the military, we all like to recognize the Japanese Americans who served with the 442nd RCT, because they set the precedent that Asians, despite the blatant racism present in America, were still loyal citizens. People easily forget the sacrifices of those men and the hardships they endured in the name of loyalty. They forget that people like my dad served quietly and without any fanfare. As a whole, it seems Asian Americans have done well in this country despite the prejudices of others, and I think we owe our country our service.

I have had an interesting career overall. I did grad school in Monterey and further posts in Quantico, Virginia; Beaufort, South Carolina; Hawaii and Okinawa. I was selected to command one of the largest squadrons in the Marine Corps, approximately 1,000 Marines and sailors in Marine Aviation Logistics Squadron 11 in Miramar, California, and from there was selected for promotion to colonel. There are only a handful of APAs [Asian Pacific Americans] in the rank of colonel on active duty—probably fewer than five.

Brigadier General Daniel Yoo is one of the first APAs to ever get selected for General in the USMC. That was just 2011. So it goes to show there's still room for APAs to get more involved and keep pushing the bamboo ceiling. The more APAs join the military, the more APAs will be accepted as truly a part of this great nation. Only 1% of officers in the Marine Corps claimed to be APAs, truly an elite club. Only 1.93% of enlisted Marines were APAs. There are and will continue to be great opportunities for Asian Americans in the Marines. I won't kid you though—the military, and the Marine Corps in particular, are not for everybody. But if you are up to the challenge, serving in the military is a rewarding experience that you just can't get anywhere else. Some would like to draw broad, sweeping conclusions about the existence of racism in the military. I would just say that experiences vary, and how people deal with situations varies, but I think the military as an institution strives very hard to be a meritocracy and has a strong equal opportunity policy.

CHAPTER THIRTY-SEVEN

Juliet Shum 岑美莉 (1986–　　)
U.S. Marine Corps

After being immersed in a male-dominated sphere during her service as a Marine, Juliet went the other extreme, attending floral school and participating in beauty pageants to explore her femininity. She talks about community life in New York's Chinatown, and sexual harassment in her military experience. She presently studies air traffic control in college.

When did you start to decide to go into the military?

I had a really strong passion for independence. I was very unhappy growing up, being an only child, and I wanted to travel—pretty much just escape my life here and learn new things.

My mom was very strict. I remember when I was in high school I told her that I wanted to take a driving course and I was going to pay for it myself. All I needed was her parental consent to sign the form, and she wouldn't let me go do the course even though I told her I was going to pay for it myself. She said, "You will learn how to drive in the military."

So she already had ideas of you to going into the military?

She did not have ideas of me joining the military. That was my own doing. I really just wanted to go someplace where I could be challenged and be part of a group, and have pride, and make my family proud. I chose the Marines because I wanted the challenge.

What was it like growing up in [New York's] Chinatown?

I was a tomboy growing up and I hung out with all of my cousins, who were boys. I had a pretty sheltered life because I was an only child. My parents, like most Chinese parents, were very strict and I wasn't allowed to have too many friends or go out. My parents are divorced now. They divorced when I was in Okinawa with the military. I went to elementary school at P.S. 124, Yung Wing Public School.

I did Chinese folk dance and kung fu with the Southern Praying Mantis group; I did lion dance. So I was very involved with the Chinese community and activities. I also played the flute. I thought maybe I'd be a professional musician or a martial arts instructor because I was very drawn to the discipline and the values of my kung fu family.

All my values centered around my kung fu family because I spent more time with them than my own family. Like many other Chinese families, my family's idea of a family gathering was to go to Atlantic City and gamble. When I got older I told my mom that I didn't want to go anymore and I'd stay home and hang out with friends.

I was an obeident daughter pushed to the edge. My parents controlled every aspect of my life—I cooked, cleaned, bought groceries, etc. I was very responsible at a young age. I even took myself to and from school. My parents were always working and I was home alone most of the time, so I had to take care of myself and do whatever my parents asked of me because we were poor.

So I did something crazy and I shaved off my hair. I was going into my sophomore year. I told my mom before I did it, "You guys try and control everything about me. You can't control my hair. *(Laughs)* I'm going to shave it off because I want to." She was like, "You better not." I did it anyway just to prove a point to her.

But when it came time for me to actually enlist, I was underage. I was 17 and I had to get an age waiver.

When did you first find out about the military?

I think I was always drawn to the military, just because of my kung fu background, its discipline, and being a tomboy growing up. Growing up, I played with POGs, basketball cards, comic books, guns, and planes. Whatever my cousins did, I followed suit.

I have an aggressive personality. It just seemed right and fitting for me to join the military. I was probably in junior high or high school when I came to that realization that I had a strong passion for wanting to join the military. You know what? I have to say, I was always interested in watching war movies, especially *G.I. Jane.* I thought that was pretty cool. She was my idol at the time. I had a strong desire to be the best that I could be.

So when did you enlist?

I was 17 and I walked into the recruiter's office. It was in City Hall next to J&R, I remember. I walked up there after school one day and I talked to the recruiter, and I was hooked. At first I was planning on going for Officer Candidate School, the ROTC route. But they were telling me that you have to do four years of school first and then you go to boot camp. I wanted to go to boot camp as soon as possible.

My dad basically was like, "Well, it's four years of your life!" My mom, I don't think she was happy about my decision but they both wanted to support me on my decision. Their attitude was: it's your life, so be it. Unlike most traditional Chinese parents, they never forced me to go for a professional job. They never told me, I want you to be a doctor, a lawyer. I know most Chinese families put a lot of pressure on their children, but I guess I'm an exception.

You weren't scared?

I was more excited than scared. Like I said, I couldn't wait to escape my life at the time. My parents were always fighting and I didn't feel like there was really anything for me to leave behind. It wasn't a very hard decision for me to leave everything behind and start a new life. On my first day of boot camp, I was in a zombie-like state. All you did was follow orders, get screamed at, and sign papers. They purposely kept you up over 24 hours to get you registered with all your documentation and to issue your gear to get you ready for boot camp. It was hectic and chaotic.

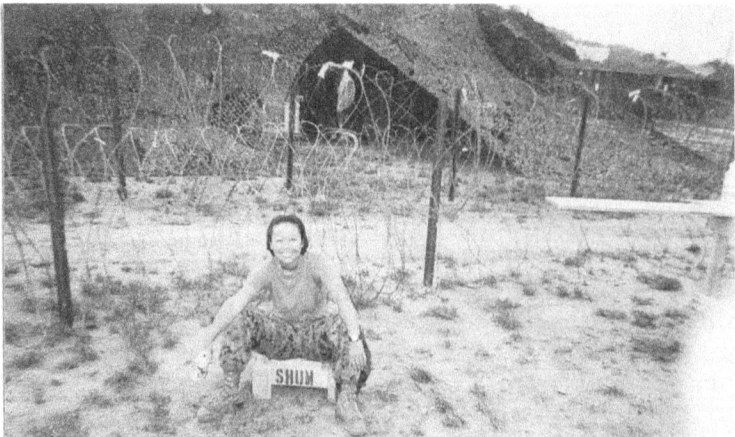

VFL exercise, South Korea, 2004

I will never forget it. I can close my eyes and remember the yellow footprints, getting off the bus, having to sit in the classroom, and after signing the papers they gave us permission to put our head down for two minutes. Good memories.

Can you talk a little bit about your military life? What position did you have and what were your duties?

My MOS was 1341 Heavy Equipment Mechanic. I know I don't look like it. The school was very difficult for me. When I went into the Marines I didn't think about what job I was going to end up doing. I just wanted to be a Marine, and I wish that I had chosen a different occupational specialty.

Regardless, I still made the best out of it. My first post assignment was in Okinawa, Japan. It was a very small shop. I was attached to the Engineer Section. We had generators, forklifts, electricians, water dogs [water technicians], and combat engineers. So it was good to be around different trades, because after I was done with my job I had to help my coworkers with theirs. I would learn from them. I went to Korea and Thailand with them and that was a good learning experience. I just wish I had absorbed more knowledge from them because if I really did take all the information that they knew, I could probably build my own house by now.

What were your duties in Korea and Okinawa?

Well, basically I was fixing forklifts, but because we had an abundance of mechanics, and I guess because my superiors didn't really have any experience with women in the military. They isolated me and assigned me a different billet. I had to do paperwork called MIMMS—Marine Corps Integrated Maintenance Management Systems. I would liaison with the supply and motor transport sections to get repair parts for my section.

So I did that job, and even though the Marines usually switch out and do different billets, I was stuck in that billet for the longest time. Even though it was actually a Non-Commissioned Officer position, like a middle management type job, they assigned it to me anyway and I did it for the whole time that I was in Okinawa, even though I was only a lance corporal. Eventually I requested to go to school, and they sent me to school so I could have some credibility behind my work.

I'm getting that you didn't like that job.

I liked it because after I was done I was able to just walk around freely and do whatever else I wanted in the shop. After a while I didn't have any supervision because I knew what I was doing. My bosses trusted me because they never had any problems with me.

Aside from that, I actually didn't like it, which is why I changed and requested to do Marine Security Guard Duty, which is a different job. I got approved for it and that's when I went to Venezuela, Hong Kong, and Belgium for the rest of my career.

As security?

Yes, in the Embassies.

Did anything frightening ever happen in those situations as a security guard?

Well, Venezuela was a somewhat dangerous country. Hong Kong was very easygoing. So was Belgium. The only real incident we had to respond to was a house robbery in Venezuela. They had a lot of protests. I remember one time our neighbor was getting robbed and we had to respond to that.

Basically what happened was our neighbor had his own AK-47 so he took the situation into his own hands. I guess that's how they handle their problems. They don't call authorities. That was a little frightening, but nothing too serious.

So that aspect of doing security was something you enjoyed?

At the time I was pretty much planning out my military career. The way it works is that only a certain number of Marines within an MOS can get promoted. I just wanted to make a route to try and pick up rank as soon as I could so that I could pursue drill instructor duty. That was really my dream. Unfortunately, I had medical issues and that fell through. I had foot problems. I was basically a very fit Marine. Aside from the requirements of a minimum of running three times a week for three miles, I would also PT on my own all the time.

What's PT?

Physical Training. I was in very good shape except for my foot problems. And by the time I was in Belgium, I failed a run, meaning I did not complete the three-mile run in under 31 minutes. That was when I did a medical evaluation board. At that time I was already in my second enlistment and I got separated from the Marines early.

So you enlisted for a second time.

Yes. I reenlisted when I was in Venezuela. I was having a blast. Being a Marine was fun and by the time I reenlisted, that was when it went downhill. I had my foot problem and I guess the morale of the troops at the Embassies was different. It was a different ball game. Basically the people who traveled around pitching us the Marine Security Guard program made it sound like it was a really good deal.

But in reality, you're given a chef, you have drivers, you have a maid for a reason. And the reason is because they work you until you drop. We would do response drills three times a month; there was no defined line between when you are on duty and when you are not. So I could come home from work and then they'll activate the response drill and next thing I know I'm back at the embassy. You just had to be ready to go back to the embassy any time of the day. If a visiting official wanted dinner and pictures with the Marines, we'd accommodate their request to preserve good relations with the embassy community.

The only time that you had to yourself was when you were standing post alone. That's the reason why you had to have a maid and a chef to do those things for you, so you could do your job. So I think the morale was really low, because another issue was that we had very few Marines on hand. We would always be low on manpower and I think that was one aspect about the Marines in general, just never having enough people to get the job done. But we always made do with what we had.

How many years did you end up spending in the military?

Five years, from September 2003 until December of 2008.

Are there any most memorable moments that you'd like to share?

There's one thing I want to share. The craziest time I had was in Okinawa. My sergeant was very adventurous and he took me and three other Marines out to an unmarked cave one time. I mean, I'm down for adventure anytime. So we were just kind of getting all dirty and falling in the cave, we would lay down little lights and make a path. But as soon as we were deep inside the cave, my sergeant told me, "Oh, by the way, I just want to mention to you guys that there are a lot of cockroaches in here." It was so disgusting. I've never seen so many cockroaches in my entire life. The whole ground was covered with cockroaches, big ones. I probably squashed like ten of them by accident. I mean they were crawling everywhere. And it reeked. It was dank and dark in there, but it was the most fun I've ever had. That was a really fun, exciting, and scary moment for me. Just being with the guys and having fun outside of work.

So overall you're happy with your experience in the military?

Overall, I don't regret signing up. I had a very fun time. Nonetheless it was, I guess, more or less bittersweet for me because I'm a woman in the Marines and it's different for women because you have to remember that you're a woman in a men's club. The Marines are a brotherhood.

In the pictures there are only two women including you.

Yeah.

What was that like?

When I first got there I was the only female and it was kind of scary because I felt really isolated sometimes, and not having another female leader to look up to was difficult. Even then, there were other female officers or superior command, but they weren't very readily accessible. So mentoring-wise I think I did not receive any benefit because we had very strict rules on fraternization, conduct and etiquette, and I think my superiors were not very comfortable working with females in the first place.

So it was a tough time for me, especially with other females who came later on. My roommate got pregnant, and another female who came later also got pregnant. People like that just kind of make a bad name for the rest of us. I remember my co-workers were joking around. They were like, "Shum, now it's your turn to get pregnant." So it was kind of tough. You have to have tough skin. Being a woman, you always have to try harder to prove yourself to the male Marines.

Did the guys who impregnated the girls get in any trouble?

No. I don't even know who impregnated the other girl. She claimed she was pregnant. Some people do things to themselves to get out easy. It draws bad attention on them. She was one of them. When you get pregnant, you get on light duty, they call it. And you're not required to do all the rigorous training.

Did they see you as a woman first and foremost, before they saw you as an Asian or a Chinese person? As part of your identity, did being a woman come first?

Yeah. I know Asians were probably looked down on in the military as a whole and had to face racial slurs or whatever. But I think in my case since I'm an Asian woman, I'm a double minority. I feel like sometimes they just saw me as that. I remember the first time I walked into the chow hall because my corporal was giving me a tour. I walked in there and literally I felt like time stood still, because everybody, every male in uniform just stopped what they were doing and they looked at me.

In what way? Like surprised, or with disdain or—

Just in awe, I guess, because they have never seen what appears to be an Okinawan girl in their uniform. Because I was in Okinawa and they were like, Wait a second—because all the servers in the chow hall were Okinawan, but here they see me in their uniform. So I think I caught them by surprise maybe.

How many Asian or Chinese people were there when you worked?

I saw very few. I think my whole time in Okinawa I probably bumped into two.

Two Asians?

Yeah, or maybe three. I think two guys and one girl. But I don't know if she was. It was hard because, in the Marines' eyes, women are classified as either sluts, lesbians or bitches. That's just how they viewed us, unfortunately. Just like you're a PT stud or a religious freak or an alcoholic, you get classified. You fall into one of these categories. That's how the perception is. They sum you up right away. And I've been called all three.

Maybe more than one at a time, I don't know. It's the interpersonal relationships that you have with your co-workers—that's how they perceive you. Unfortunately, if they don't like me, then that's what they're going to call me. It's not my job to make them like me either. I'm just doing my job. I don't have to be nice to you. That's why when I picked up rank it was a lot easier as a female, because then I could talk to them and they couldn't talk back to me.

How true are the types, at least for the guys? You said that there are archetypes, the PT stud or the alcoholic or the religious freak going to the church every week. Can you pretty much sum up most people like that?

Yeah, pretty much. I'd say the majority are just alcoholics. If they're not drinking then they're smoking. You have some health freaks, the PT studs, but for the most part, everybody either drinks or smokes on their free time because there really wasn't anything to do.

We were in Okinawa; we were on a rock. Besides just partying and drinking, your life is so regimented. When you wake up every day, you don't have to think about what you have to do. You just know that you have to do whatever you have to do because you're told to. You put on this uniform because this is all you wear. The only time you have to think about what you want to wear today is when you have your own free time. Everything is taken care of for us, our meals and our housing. So what else could the Marines do with their money and their free time besides waste it? There were some productive Marines. I got my scuba diving license in Okinawa. So that was fun. There are Marines that try to better themselves and there are ones that unfortunately take the wrong route and hurt themselves by abusing drugs.

What are the rules? Are the Marines not allowed to touch alcohol and drugs at all, or are they allowed to drink on their free time and stuff? I think someone told me that if you're found with any of these things you can be kicked out.

Oh, we had urinalysis tests very frequently. I was always tested, but I know that there's a way around it. I know there's corruption and people just paying people off. They have their means.

But what's the rule? The rule is that you cannot drink?

If you're under 21, basically, you're not supposed to be drinking. A lot of the Marines' attitudes and mentality was, "I don't understand why I can die for my country, but you're not going to let me enjoy a beer." There was a lot of underage drinking, but that was just part of the culture, part of the Marine culture.

What was the rank that you left with?

Sergeant. That's like a middle-management position. Since I was in a Marine security guard job, I didn't really have much of a chance to exercise the authority, versus if I was to be a sergeant in my Marine Headquarters Group Section in the fleet, because when you're out there, then you have more Marines under you. But when I was in the Marine Security Guard Program, everybody around me was the same rank. Even if you're a sergeant you're still taking out the trash.

And you said that men under you had to respect you with your rank.

Respect is not automatic. I feel like it has to be earned. I don't expect people to respect me. If I treat people with respect, then they should treat me the same way. Like I said, the morale was so low. People just didn't want to follow the rules out there. You had to be very careful and watch your back. Silly things—if somebody doesn't like you they can find a way to burn you. That's what I saw in my experience.

When I was in Belgium I think a few Marines got in trouble for doing some silly things and that was the reason why our detachment had so few Marines. The leadership wanted to get rid of these Marines for whatever wrongdoing they were involved with, and they didn't have any plan for replacing them.

That was why we had so few Marines. Our embassy was required to have a certain number, but we were way below that. So we were overworked a lot of the time. Especially when I was in Hong Kong, my detachment commander, our boss, had some issues and he had to leave. And I also had to leave early. So by the time I left, there were just three Marines left. And the way the duty schedule works is that you have the day shift, the eves shift and the mids shift. So between the three of them, they didn't have any time off. One person was assigned the days, one person for eves, and one person for mids. So it was nonstop working for them. I felt really bad. But that's how the manpower was.

I guess we can move on to what happened after the military or since the military. Unless there are other things you want to share.

Like I said earlier, it was bittersweet experience for me because of the fact that I was a woman in the Marines. Unfortunately, I don't have very good memories from some of my experiences. One reason why I got kicked out of Hong Kong early was because I had a sexual harassment issue with my detachment commander.

Is this a huge issue in the military? We hear about sexual harassment and harassment in the news all the time. Do you want to talk about it a little bit?

First of all, this was not the first instance. I have had quite a few instances of sexual harassment and sexual assault. But in this case, he was my boss. What happened was I went to post to change duty with another Marine. My boss was in the embassy drunk. We were alone and in the changing room, I changed over, and before I was going to load up my weapon, he kissed me. After that happened, I took a step back.

I actually told my fellow Marines about it and their response was, "Gunny has been in for over 20 years, he's a veteran. He's never done anything like this to the other females." And they said, "If something like this happens again, you make sure that you tell us about it." At the time I was very conflicted on what kind of action to take. I confided in my fellow Marines but they really weren't of much help. I told my boyfriend at the time. He was in another post. We had written emails with each other and that was how he knew about it.

My sergeant told us one time that our gunny was having domestic issues at home. He said to be on the lookout for his behavior. The regional security officer who was the civilian Department of State officer in charge of the Marines was the highest ranking security officer there. He asked me what happened.

One day he came in to the post and chatted with me like, "Hey, how's everything?" and "Is there's anything going on with Gunny?" He just kept mentioning Gunny, and I was like, Oh maybe he knows something. I was scared and I told him about what happened. He said, "Oh okay. All right." Then he kind of walked out and the next thing I knew, the next day, the regional officer from Thailand flew in to conduct an investigation. All the Marines had to write a statement including myself and it didn't work out in my favor.

What was the statement supposed to be about? What they know happened?

Yeah. I didn't read their statements. I mean they didn't know. Basically what happened was they covered for the boss and I had to leave Hong Kong early.

To cover for him did they just said you were lying?

I can't say because I really don't know what they said. We weren't allowed to talk to each other about it. Unfortunately because of that incident, I had to leave Hong Kong early.

Did they demote you in any way?

No.

So they just left it, they didn't address it, and they just shipped you to a different place?

Basically they just swept it under the carpet, which is what they do for everything else. I'll give you another incident. When I was in Okinawa, not to be prejudiced or whatever, but everybody had a feeling that one of our corporals was gay.

One day he went out with a Motor-T Marine to go drinking. The next morning the Marine woke up, they were in a room together and his pants were half down. He just put two and two together because he was so messed up and was wasted because they went out on liberty together to go drinking. He just started beating up the corporal. What had happened was my corporal had raped the male Marine.

The way the leadership handled that situation was, I guess, he was just going to get non-judicial punishment. I don't really know what happened to him. He didn't get demoted, my corporal. But I know the Marine and he got sent to another section. That's pretty much how they handle problems like that.

They just try and keep it hush. I mean luckily I was not raped. But there are many instances of male Marines getting raped by their co-workers. I've had several issues with my co-workers, and it really sucks because you feel like you're brothers and you can trust them. But unfortunately that's just what happened.

Do you have thoughts on DADT, Don't Ask Don't Tell?

I just think it's better to be open about the topic if you're gay. Your sexuality has nothing to do with your performance as a Marine. That's just your lifestyle, your preference, and I don't think it should affect your commitment to your job.

In that case I would have preferred that he was open about it instead of staying in the dark. If they can openly date other Marines, then maybe something like that wouldn't happen if it was accepted. If gays were accepted, and they would have to adhere to the same fraternization rules, then I don't think the issue of sexual harassment or sexual assault would be that rampant.

So, having seen all this really tough stuff, does it change your view of whether you should have been in the military or not? Do you feel like maybe you've seen too much and that you shouldn't have seen those things, or are you still glad that you had this experience?

I would have preferred not to have been betrayed by my co-workers. I'm not going to say that I would want to change anything. I learned after drinking with my co-workers that I can't do that with the male Marines. I can't just go out and party with them. I can't just let loose. It was different for me but at the same time it made me who I am today, even though I do suffer from military sexual trauma.

Right now I go to counseling every week for therapy because I never actually talked about it in the Marines. I never told anybody this is what happened to me. So I had to deal with a lot of these issues on my own, and I guess it has affected me. The way I am around men and having trust issues and all that. But nonetheless, it made me the person that I am today.

And who is that person today?

A feminist. Very hard-headed. I don't let people push me around and I'm still the same aggressive person, but at the same time I'm fragile. Yeah, I wouldn't take it back.

I just wish that more women would join the military to even out the playing field. They always preach about covering sexual harassment in training seminars but it's just a facade. They do it as a check in the box to say we have covered this policy. Everybody knows sexual harassment, but do they do anything to change it? No. So I think the only way to really address that is if there's an equal ratio of male and female Marines so that they really have to turn their attention toward how to better handle the situation.

Because right now it's still just being swept under the carpet. If you have more females then they will be forced to address the work dynamic. The one thing I constantly had to face was sexual tension between myself and my co-workers or my bosses. It was difficult.

When I was in Venezuela, I rejected a Marine because he basically asked me if I wanted to have sex with him, and I said no. Since I rejected him, he gave me a hard time the whole time throughout my time in Venezuela. I was the only woman there and it was very, very difficult for me because my leadership [depended on] the camaraderie. My boss even took me aside one time and said,

"Shum, I don't understand why you're not getting along with the Marines. Why can't you try harder?" And I was like, "Sorry, Gunny." I mean, I didn't tell him. Eventually I told my sergeant about it and said, "You know, male Marines just don't look up to female leadership the way they look up to you."

You went through so much.

Going back to the way I separated from the military—Basically I had a condition called Os Naviculare in my left foot. That's what it says on my DD214. I have a little bone growth in my foot and I have a whole bunch of things wrong with my feet. It makes it very painful to run. I could walk very far distances, but for some reason when I'm just standing stationary, it's very painful for me. That could probably be because of my work. I mean, we had to stand 8 hours a day with our duty belt, and it had our pistol, handcuffs, baton, and two magazines. So that was a little bit of weight.

Then when we had to do the response drills, we would have more weight on. I had the flak jacket and helmet, backpack, the shotgun, extra stuff. On top of that, I wasn't wearing a female size. I was wearing a men's large because they didn't have my size. I think all that weight and all that stress just compounded my foot problems.

So I had to take care of my health issues first, and I got enrolled with the VA and all that. After I got my surgery, I really wanted to do floral school. I was thinking about doing it before I got out, and they only had one 1-month class offered throughout the year. So when I wasn't even healed yet, I went to Boston to attend floral school. I was on my crutches, but I don't regret doing it. It was painful going there, but I wanted to do floral school before I started going to college. So after I attended floral school, then I started at Vaughn College of Aeronautics.

Wow, floral school! That's the complete opposite of the military. What were you thinking then?

That was the rebel side of me coming out. The thing about the Marines is I was so taken by the uniformity. Every day we all wear the same thing. Everybody has to do the same thing. I guess that was what bred the desire for me to be different, because until then I never really liked doing girly things. The Marine Corps orders just regulated every aspect of our lives, which is kind of similar to how my parents were always controlling me.

So one way for me to get around these rules was to read all the orders and know what I was allowed to do and what I wasn't allowed to do. For instance, on liberty, when we had free time to go off-base and dress in civilian attire, that was when I was able to be more girly.

For me, being in the Marines made me girly. I was like, well it doesn't say anything about wearing high heels. So I started wearing high heels in the Marines. But we weren't allowed to wear spaghetti strap shirts, mid-riff shirts. We had to adhere to very strict rules.

Actually, my personality is just extremes. Joining the Marine Corps is one extreme and I guess the only way I could balance that is to fall to the other extreme. Joining floral school and doing something so totally different just helped me to counteract all the male testosterone, I guess, to get away from all that.

Being in the Marines, having that financial independence, gave me the ability to pursue my dreams, because I grew up poor and I never had any nice clothes or whatever. Now, I was saving up my money ever since I first started and I'm very thankful to one of my gunnys. He was trying to encourage us to start our thrift savings plan when it was first offered. And I remember I maxed it out at the highest percentage that I was allowed to at the time. I didn't have any debt or bills. I would just put half my paycheck into my retirement.

If there's anything that I learned from my parents, it was to save my money. So I saved up my money and I was like, "You know what, I'm going to do this. I'm going to floral school." I have the will power and now I have the financial backing. There's nothing stopping me. I've already gone all over the world. There isn't really anything that I can't do. I just thought it was fun then. I wanted to learn and play with flowers so I did it.

Was that a great experience for you, floral school?

Yeah. Because at that time when you first separate, you're closing a chapter to your life and you're thinking, "What am I going to do with myself now that I'm losing that part of my identity?"

I'm not saying that I'm not a Marine anymore. I am a Marine. I'm always going to be a Marine. But that's not my lifestyle anymore and I have to figure out what I want to do for the rest of my life or what I want to do next. What's my next move? And I just feel like everything that I do is just adding tools to my toolbox.

When I went to floral school, I attended a floral business skills seminar, and that basically taught me that I didn't want to own my own business. At least the only way you're going to figure out what you want to do is by figuring out what you don't want to do first. I learned that I really love and enjoy designing flowers, making floral arrangements, but the other side of the business is running your own business. My family has had businesses before, and I know after attending that, it's a lot of work, and that's not what I want. I know what I'm capable of. I know my weaknesses; I know my strengths.

So this is why I'm taking the traditional route, going to school and taking full advantage of my government benefits. I actually was taking some classes during my time in the military because when you're on active duty [versus Reserve status] you can take college classes for free also. At the time, I took classes in Japan, actually, and I took several online classes whenever I was able to manage the workload.

I was taking sociology as a major. And when I got out, my friends and fam-

Ms. Chinatown USA, 2012, San Francisco

ily convinced me to change my major, because they were saying, It's honorable that you want to help people, but becoming a social worker is not going to help yourself financially. I knew they were right, so that's when I went back to the drawing board and decided. I saw an ad: Make a lot of money as an air traffic controller. And I was like, I'm going to go for it.

At that time I didn't think about joining another male dominated industry. I didn't think about that. But obviously when I show up in my aviation school, it's just engineers, pilots, mechanics, and I've immersed myself in the same environment. Air traffic controllers are all type-A personalities, very aggressive, and I think I would probably fit in perfectly. I feel like everything has prepared me for this path.

So you're an air traffic controller now?

No. I'm studying to be an air traffic controller. My dual major is in airport and airline management. Hopefully in two years I'll have my bachelor's degree.

Where are you attending now?

It's called Vaughn College of Aeronautics in Flushing, Queens, next to La Guardia airport.

Okay, so there's another part of your life that we haven't covered yet, which is being a contestant in beauty pageants. Can you talk about that and how you got into that?

After I got out of the military, I told you I just started embracing my feminine side more. My friend, a female Marine who I was hanging out with in Hong Kong, she was the one who introduced me to going to spas and relaxation, pampering yourself, because I never did that before. So she helped bring that out of me. Since I got out, I started getting facials and I'm a patron of this one lady called Katy. She owns a spa in Chinatown called Katy's Face and that's where I go get all my facials. She was the one who recommended I try and become a contestant for this competition.

She said, "Oh, it's a very good opportunity." At first, I really didn't want to do it because I'm a feminist. My idea of taking my clothes off to get some recognition, that's not how I want to get acknowledgement. I'd rather get acknowledgement for my work instead of my image and my beauty. I don't think that should be rewarded. But to appease her I said, "Okay, I'll interview for it." And the next thing you know, I shelled out $400 to do a photo shoot and I found myself just kind of caught up in this fantasy, I guess.

What pageant were you in?

The Miss Chinatown USA. Three girls—myself, Ashley and Rosanna—we went to San Francisco to represent New York Chinatown. There were girls from the Chinatowns of Hawaii, Texas, and San Francisco. All the girls there had pageant experience. I was the only one without.

I mean I was a Little Miss New Jersey when I was young, but that's really nothing. I never knew how to do the catwalk or know how to be graceful. That was also another reason why I took this on. Because I told you, growing up I never really played with Barbie dolls or did anything girlie. I was very tomboyish, hanging out with my male cousins. So this was kind of an opportunity for me to dress up and be a girl and enjoy it and meet other girls that are like me, because all my life I'd been surrounded by guys. It's just change of scenery.

Aside from the photos [the pageant] wanted, I had to submit a talent video. So I had to figure out what I wanted to do. When I was in Venezuela, I had my own room, which was separate from the Marine house. I was kind of like a loner, just because of the environment. I didn't really get along with any of the Marines. I just kept to myself, but I spent my free time doing belly dance. I had my own DVD and I taught myself how to do a belly dance routine. I decided to use that for the competition.

That's great. So you represented New York and you are Miss Chinatown New York?

Well, on our sashes, it just said our names. I never actually won a title from the local beauty pageant; I know they had a local one here. I really don't know how that works out. Somehow I just got the hook-up and got sent to San Francisco [for the San Francisco pageant]. I really just went there with the mentality that I'm just going to go there and have fun.

I got along with all the girls and we had escorts. We had 23 male escorts. It was fun because I was never spoiled growing up, and I did security. I really don't need my own security. But they had to do everything for us. We were treated like princesses. They would hold our jackets, our coats, and they would get us food at the table. I couldn't even go to the bathroom by myself. They had to escort me to the bathroom for security and safety reasons, because the Miss Chinatown event was very highly publicized. I think there were instances of sexual harassment from the public toward the contestants a few years back maybe. After the pageant, we would travel around with our own security.

The San Francisco P.D. would walk around with us to make sure that we were safe. It was a very fun and enjoyable time. Like Katy said, it's a once-in-a-lifetime opportunity, and I'm very grateful that I had a chance to go there and just be a girl, have fun, and compete. So I'm glad that I had fun and also made some friends.

Actually, at the pageant, I had the opportunity to go visit a senior citizen home and a hospital. It felt really good to bring some joy to their lives even though we just showed up in our dresses and handed out fruit to them.

It's very important for the older generation to see that we're continuing these traditions and carrying on the heritage. It brings me back to the values of Chinese tradition and culture. Even though my family is not very traditional, it gives me a sense of belonging to my community. Even though I didn't feel like I was accomplishing anything, I know that just by being there and warming their hearts—it was just good spending time with them.

Everywhere we went, we were told to say, "Gung hey fat choy," "Sun tai geen hong." And I'm very Americanized. I don't usually say that kind of stuff, but it helps me connect with my roots again. When I have time I'm going to seek out my Shum family association. Because in San Francisco I visited some family associations and they were very generous. They presented us with gifts. They gave me a gum pai, which is a gold necklace with my family name on it. So I want to try and seek them out and see what it's all about.

2012 Ms. Chinatown USA Beauty Pageant,
San Francisco, California

Belly dance performance for
talent competition

CHAPTER THIRTY-EIGHT

Mo Pan 潘言 (1969–   )
U.S. Army

Mo Pan was born in Taipei, Taiwan, and talks about how being Taiwanese American feels like being a minority within a minority within the Chinese community. He was deployed to Germany and Iraq. Currently, he is an OCT for the 75th Training Division in the U.S. Army Reserves, training and evaluating soldiers during field exercises. Pan has been in the Army since 1993 and lives in Staten Island, New York.

My dad was an artist and he came to the States to study to become an art professor. And then, I guess, he had me and plans changed. He had to somehow support a family. A friend gave him an idea to start a restaurant. My parents owned a Chinese take-out restaurant, like the typical immigrant family.

From 3 to 5 I pretty much grew up in a restaurant, in a bad neighborhood in Philadelphia, because my parents worked long hours. There were always people trying to rob my dad. But he just dealt with it and tried to make a living. You had no other choice. That was the only place to open a restaurant that he could afford. We moved to New York, in Westchester for a year or two. We opened a restaurant in the Lower East Side, First Avenue and 10th. It was a really rough neighborhood then—drug addicts, gangs, all sorts of urban plights.

In elementary school, there was one Asian girl in my class. Her parents owned a dry cleaning place on First Avenue and 14th Street. We weren't that many.

[When I was] in sixth grade, my family bought a house and moved to East Elmhurst, Queens. I guess things were going better at the restaurant. I went to a private Catholic school in Manhattan for a few years. Then I went to the Bronx High School of Science.

Then I wound up going to Polytechnic University in Brooklyn, now known as Polytechnic Institute of New York City, where I studied mechanical engineering. A classmate told me, "Oh, you can go to this ROTC thing where you can shoot rifles and throw hand grenades and do all this exciting stuff for gym credits. You don't even have to join the Army afterwards. You can just do this for two years with no commitment." I said, "Oh, that's great."

At this point, what did you want to be when you grew up?

At that point, I didn't really know. My parents wanted me to graduate and

Mo Pan in Baghdad, Iraq

to be something. So I just said, "Oh, maybe engineering sounds good." At that age, who knows? I was just going to college for the sake of it, because my parents said I needed to go to college.

So I joined ROTC without the intent of actually signing up. There were classes in military leadership, drill and ceremony. We'd go out to do field training exercises, where we'd run around the woods and play soldier. After a while, I started enjoying it. And I enjoyed the group of people I was with. I had never experienced that level of camaraderie, where people actually looked out for you, and you're doing fun and challenging stuff.

In my third year, I had to make a choice about whether to continue with the ROTC. I didn't like the idea of committing so many years to something I didn't know much about. I didn't come from a military family. I had no clue about the military other than what I was exposed to in movies. But I knew that I enjoyed the camaraderie. I liked the excitement of the challenges we faced. It was this thing I couldn't find anywhere else. And even when I was a young boy, I liked playing soldier. I always had interest in rifles and stuff.

I said, "All right, what the hell? Let me sign up." So far I was having a good time, and the camaraderie was what really sealed the deal for me. This was around '88, '89, '90. There was no war. I think it was the last year of my ROTC where I had already signed a contract when Desert Storm was happening. But since I was still training, I wasn't shipped out.

My initial contract with the Army Reserve was eight years. I didn't think I was going to go beyond that. Right after my training, I went straight to the reserve unit where you do one weekend a month and two weeks in the summer, which was good for me, because it wasn't a major commitment and I was able to live a civilian life.

And what was the racial make-up then in the reserves?

Within my reserve unit, the New York City unit, all the members came from local New York areas—we had a mix of all sorts of people. There weren't a lot of

Asians in my unit, but offhand, I would say maybe 5%.

So I'm in the reserves now, and I'm thinking, I'm just going to do my 8 years and be done with it. Basically, every month, you'd put on your uniform, go to the unit and play soldier. You hang with out with your friends and get paid.

And then 9/11 happened, which changed the whole scenario. Before 9/11, I never thought we would get called up. First of all, it happened in New York, so it hit very close to home. I was working a few blocks away from the towers. I saw the whole thing go down. One of my friends, a fireman, died in the Towers. There's not one person in New York that didn't know somebody that was affected by it on a personal basis. It was huge in magnitude. Now you knew that the reserves were going to get called up. We geared up and got ready. Instead of using the reserves as a last resort, they were using the reserves in conjunction with the active duty troops now.

So I got activated. But they sent me to Germany instead of Afghanistan for a year under OEF, Operation Enduring Freedom. I did anti-terrorism analysis, analyzing information and assisting the U.S. Army Europe with counterterrorism and identifying threats. The threats were worldwide. Some of the 9/11 terrorists came from Germany. Some studied at universities there. We tried to identify the bad guys by doing a lot of information analysis.

I was right at the 8-year mark of my contract when 9/11 happened and I got activated. By the time it was all over, I was at my 10-year mark. That's where you have to decide whether to stick it out for the 20 to get your full retirement benefits. When you've stayed that long, you might as well do your whole 20 years.

After a 1-year tour in Germany, I came back home. Four months later, I got called up to go to Iraq. I was in Iraq—boots on the ground—for ten months. I was an intelligence officer and again it was running military intelligence operations—gathering information, analysis, identifying threats. It was a lot of just monotony and boredom. Then moments of terror. In such an environment, emotions—joy, fear, boredom, and sadness, are magnified exponentially. Any day

At the firing range

could be your last day. They were shelling us on a daily basis. There were snipers. Everything was intense.

In such an environment, you make really close friends. You learn how to have a really good time. Casualties happened. More often than you want. I mean, once is too much. If you ever experienced a military memorial service, it's a very powerful ceremony where you really feel the loss of the person.

For the memorial service in the Army—the body is not there, because it's being processed to go back home. The whole unit comes together, and they would say a few words in remembrance. They would display the boots and the rifle stuck in the ground upside down with the helmet on top and dog tags. It reminds you that these are the belongings of the soldier that passed. Then the First Sergeant would call everybody to attention and do a roll call. The last name to be called is the soldier that passed. This is met with silence, which is broken with Taps, a short and sorrowful bugle call. And then they have the 21-gun salute, where the soldiers stand in line and shoot off 21 rounds. Seven soldiers will shoot off a round from the rifle three times in honor of the passed soldier. It is a sobering reminder that war is not a game or something to be romanticized.

* * *

What have you been doing in your civilian life?

I currently manage an IT department for the Department of Treasury in New York. Prior to that, I had various jobs in the computer IT field.

When you went to Iraq, how did your family react?

Well, my parents never liked the idea of me being in the military in the first place, because in Taiwan, there's a mandatory draft. People would avoid it at all costs, so my parents had a different attitude toward military service unlike in the States, where people see it as an honor. At least some people do. They didn't really like it, but again, what could they do about it?

Mo Pan and Kathrin Pan

Do you have any overall thoughts or general thoughts about being Chinese American, or being Chinese American in the military?

Yeah. I guess you join the military and you actually feel that no one can ever question your loyalty to America. I feel that it adds legitimacy to Asian Americans when you see them in uniform.

When people see me in a uniform, I feel they don't see me as a Chinese guy. They see me as a soldier first and don't question me about being American. [Before I signed up] I saw myself as American but I started to realize other people saw me differently. Some kids teased me with slanty-eye comments. Or you would hear well-meaning but ignorant remarks from adults like, "Oh, you speak English so well." Well, why shouldn't I? Why would you even say that? I've been speaking English since I was a little kid. They just never see you as truly belonging in this country. You're always some sort of outsider because of the color of your skin. But I didn't join the military to add legitimacy. I joined because I just wanted action and adventure. It just turned out that you have the added benefit of legitimizing yourself.

In the military, they didn't really care what race you were. We were all dedicated to getting the job done. That's one thing I liked. Being from New York, my ROTC group was racially diverse, with Whites, Blacks, Latinos, Asians, etc., all in the same unit. One saying stuck with me: "There is no such thing as black, white, brown, or yellow in the Army. We are all green!"

Now that's not to say that there's no racism in the military, in the Army. It's a force of 500,000 soldiers. There's bound to be a few knuckleheads. But in general, it's an organization that tries to be fair. If anything, it should be a model of how the rest of society should work toward racial harmony, which is that people of different races and backgrounds can work together if there's a common goal.

So it sounds like, in your experience, it was pretty much teamwork and it worked well.

Yeah, overall. I can't say that there weren't little incidents here and there. But it was more ignorance, and not overt, blatant racism. I might be lucky in that respect. It's possible I didn't see as much racism because I am an officer. If I was a lower rank, I might have seen more abuse.

I never thought I would say this about the military, but everything about me is military. I try not to be the hard core military type, but I owe everything I have to the military at this point. I have a pretty decent job because of it. I even met my girlfriend while I was stationed in Germany. She's a German girl.

There were a few instances [of racism], but they're kind of minor in the bigger picture of things. Once we got into Baghdad, they set up a mobile field kitchen to feed the troops in the field. They tried to make it somewhat homely, they set up tables and seats outside, and they had a chalkboard listing the menu and the special of the day. I guess one cook thought it was funny—they were serving rice that day. He painted a caricature of this buck-toothed Asian guy with the conical hat. On the bottom, he wrote, "Got Rice?" Basically, I chewed the soldier out saying, "That's not funny. You need to take that down right now." He looked pretty scared, and he took it down. Again, I think I had the benefit of rank. But again, it's ignorance. I don't know if he understood it was offensive, but I believe that when you see things like that you need to say something, especially if you have the rank to influence change.

When I meet strangers who happen to be veterans, it's as if you've known them for many years, because we share that common bond. Maybe it's because I'm an only child, but being in the military provided me that brotherhood or sisterhood I didn't have when I was growing up.

I enjoy military life. It's the best decision I ever made. Maybe I'm just lucky that it turned out good for me. It's interesting, after you come back from war, all of a sudden, everybody wants to talk to you. I had reporters come to my house, from Channel 7. This is right after I came back in 2004. I got all these phone calls and e-mails from friends who saw me on TV. I didn't realize how many people watch Channel 7 news.

I've been in the reserves since 1993. I plan to finish at 20 years and go for retirement, and focus on other things.

I am part of the American Legion Kimlau Post. A friend of mine is a member. I went to one meeting, and what I liked about it is that all the members are Chinese Americans. I said, I don't really have much time. And then one of the officers, an older gentleman, said, "That's fine. I don't really care. We just want your money." And I thought that was funny and honest. I said, "All right, fine. You've got it." And it's only $20 a year. It's nothing. For the cause, why not?

I hope for the day that the term "Asian American" will be obsolete and we would all just be seen as Americans regardless of the color of our skin. That day is still a ways away but we're one step closer since a member of our post,

Fang Wong, became the first Asian American to be American Legion National Commander. He heads the largest veterans' organization in America. When I first met him a few years ago he told me that he was going to run for national commander. At that time, I thought he was full of shit. I said, "Yeah, okay, whatever. Good luck buddy. That will never happen. They're going to vote an Asian American?" I guess I'm a little bit cynical that way. But hey, it happened and that's great. I went to his victory banquet.

CHAPTER THIRTY-NINE

Astrid Szeto 司徒陸錦霞 (1950–　　)
U.S. Public Health Service

Astrid Luk Szeto is a captain (06) in the United States Public Health Service (USPHS). Astrid shares the experiences that shaped her unique views, philosophies, and openness to her children joining the armed services. She was inspired to serve in the USPHS because of her son Chi-hung who attended West Point and who later served in Iraq and her daughter See-wan who served in Afghanistan.

What made you decide to serve your country in uniform?

Most people have not heard of the U.S. Public Health Service Commissioned Corps because we only have about 6,000 officers and no enlisted personnel. It is one of the seven branches of Uniformed Services of the United States. Since we do not bear arms, we are not considered armed forces or military. We started out providing medical care to seamen along the Atlantic coast over 200 years ago. Because we were sea service related, we wear uniforms similar to the Navy and use Navy ranks. I was impressed by my older son Chi-hung when he came home from West Point talking about country, duty, and honor. I liked the idea but I was too old and physically unable to be a military officer until I accidentally learned of USPHS, totally believed in its mission, loved the idea of wearing uniforms, and joined at a ripe "mature" age of 45. So I took after my children, not the other way around.

Your daughter See-wan explained you were always very nurturing as a mother, and always involved in community-oriented activities. What is your philosophy about living life or raising children?

I have had my share of misfortunes but I am a very positive person and try to accept people the way they are. I strongly believe in doing what is right without worrying about skeptics and rewards; about sharing one's good fortunes and blessings; and about making the world a better place just because I am in it. If I achieve this, I won't have wasted the time God allowed me here. I tried to encourage my children to take responsibilities and opportunities to become what they are capable of and believe they can achieve more than they think.

Three patriotic commissioned officers in one proud family! Taken at daughter See-wan's commissioning ceremony. With family of five; present are four of Astrid's five siblings.

What events in your life led you to have this philosophy that is so different and so much more open than most other Chinese and Chinese American families?

I am not sure but I credit my mother in being the "radical" that she was at her time, her amazing strength, strong value, and ability to see the big picture. She supported me coming to the U.S. for college when my father was totally against it because the oldest son (my older brother) didn't go to college. My father thought I should just stay at my nice bank teller job in Hong Kong, get married and have babies.

Also, it could be that I am a very independent person. I do what I think is right and could not care less what others think. If my children want to be soldiers, and they can be good ones, I will support them.

I believe that whatever is meant to be is meant to be. I sure worried about my two children in Iraq and Afghanistan, as I worried about my younger son who was a civilian. But I carried on with my work and life because I knew they were trained to do their job, they were good at it, and if the good Lord wanted them home, that would happen. I should let them go and treasure all the wonderful time we've had. I prepare for misfortune but I don't get heartbroken over the possibilities of it. I have the fortunate experience that every time things appeared to come to a dead end or became hopeless, a door mysteriously opened for me. In addition, all the nice people of different races and backgrounds I met reaffirmed my faith and positivity.

What were your aspirations as a child and as a young woman and/or as a mother?

I really had no aspirations as a child, as I was pretty protected growing up, not knowing what was out there. As a young woman in junior and high school, I met many foreigners when I helped at my mom's gift store, and I was fascinated by their languages, interests, customs—and dreamed of seeing the world. When I came to the United States for college at 19, I wanted to get my degree and go home to a good-paying job that was challenging. As a mother, I wanted to give my children opportunities to excel and do the things I never got to learn or do. I want them to be responsible, productive, healthy, happy and proud citizens who make a positive difference to those around them.

When did you come to the U.S. and why did you choose to come when you did?

I came to U.S. in January 1970 as a foreign student, attending California State University, Fresno. After high school graduation, I got a job at a prestigious foreign bank in Hong Kong as a bank teller, which was then a very desirable job for a young lady. However, I didn't like the people I worked with, as we didn't share the same value or interests, and was bored to tears counting money and filing papers every day. I decided that I needed higher education if I wanted a more challenging job. Back then, it was relatively easy to be accepted to an American college and more affordable, as most foreign students could find work to put themselves through college.

Did you ever think that you couldn't reach your dream (whatever it may be) because you are a woman or because you are Asian?

I didn't even have dreams, as I was raised a very logical and practical person. However, I learned from my mother that gender should not be an issue in achieving one's goal. If you want something bad enough, you will work hard and persevere.

Did you always feel like a "real American" and if so, is there a moment that epitomizes it?

No, not until I started wearing my uniform 13 years ago and sang the National Anthem in front of the Colors.

I also felt like "a real American" at my children's commissioning ceremony and my promotion to captain. In my ceremony with my family and fellow officers cheering me on, I knew that only in America can I have the opportunity to get where I am today.

I enjoy the challenge of being an officer even though I regularly do jobs similar to my civilian counterparts. I have opportunities for special training for emergency preparedness; to go on deployment where I can really make a difference in people's lives; to recruit and mentor new officers and see them grow and excel; and to challenge myself to keep fit and healthy for readiness. Hey, a lot of people are impressed by my uniform and rank.

What obstacles (if any) did you face as a Chinese American, either from the Chinese or the American communities, for the choices you made?

Sometimes I don't feel I fit in the Chinese/Asian community because of my values and thought process. It's rare, but sometimes I do feel that maybe I failed as a mom because my children are not as "proper" or as "successful" as my Asian friends' children.

When I first came to the States, I did experience mostly subtle discrimination in American communities because I spoke with an accent and sometimes was not sure of myself. I will not call this discrimination or profiling. But this experience brought me to realize that I may believe and act like an American, but others still see my black hair, brown eyes, skin, and hear my accent and consider me a "foreigner." Three years ago, when I was the commander of a group of about 100 officers deployed to Mississippi to provide emergency assistance [after hurricane] Katrina, I was a commander in rank then, and there were several captains under my command who questioned my ability and decisions, and tried to intimidate me. I had four strikes against me then—I was low in rank, small in stature, Asian, and female. I tried to be fair and diplomatic, hold my ground, and I believed I gained quite some respect when I left.

I have to admit, though, as a minority twice over, I have to work extra hard to prove myself. My cultural baggage from the way I was brought up does not help either. I do resent it when people question my patriotism, as I believe I am more American and a proud one because I chose to be one, not because I was born one.

Were there specific moments in your childhood or adult life that affected you and made you who you are today?

My two Army captain children taught me what real officers are: they lead and care for all those under them. They serve with dignity and honor. I am obviously very proud of them and deeply appreciate their fellow heroes who put themselves in harm's way to allow us to enjoy freedom and democracy at home. I have tremendous respect for the military family members who endure pain, separation and worry while their loved ones are far away serving our great nation.

What was it like growing up, and what was your family like?

I was born in Kowloon, Hong Kong in the '50s. Life was pretty hard when I was young. We had a wet kitchen with a mud hole where we burned wood or paper to cook. We had an outhouse for a bathroom where one had to squat.

My family was poor, but we never felt it because mom worked very hard and pinched pennies to meet our needs and to put us through private schools. Our main responsibility was to learn and do well in school. We were raised to be honest, responsible, hard-working, appreciative, helpful, and have great respect for our elders and family and obey the laws.

My family has always been very close and we were taught to be considerate of others. We tip-toed around the house if anyone was still sleeping, and we were taught not to hog food at meals. My mom was very strict but trusting of us. We never dreamed of disappointing our parents.

We walked miles to go to school. From grade school on, we helped mom with her store after school. We stocked supplies, cleaned, and manned the store. Behind the storefront, we rented out rooms to another family and a small business. The open hanging attic in the back was our living area where eight of us slept, ate, did our homework, and entertained ourselves. All the children slept on one wide-open bed made of a spread of wood planks. There was a narrow plank of wood that stood up to divide the "bed" between the parents and children. The baby slept in a wood box on top of the big cedar wood chest.

My family was very traditional in some ways and radical in others. Radical in that it was my mom who disciplined us, was the breadwinner, and was in charge of finances and all. It was traditional in that the six of us children were drummed with traditional Chinese values.

My dad was not religious and my mom was a Taoist with very strong values. My mom treated her sons and daughters equally and supported us at whatever we wanted to do. We never said, "I love you" to each other, but we sensed it through each other's actions. In other words, we are doers, not talkers.

What did your parents and siblings do and how did that affect what you wanted for your future and your family?

My father owned and ran a Chinese restaurant with partners, and because of his schedule, we hardly ever saw him. He was an easy-going man, proud to be a businessman, and never disciplined us. He had a few years of education, but did not finish grade school.

My mother was an orphan who never went to school but managed to read Chinese newspapers and speak fluent Japanese and broken English. Growing up, she lived with a distant uncle to help raise their children. At 15, she went out on her own to be a nanny for foreigners [British and Japanese during World War II]. She was an exceptionally intelligent and sharp woman with goals in mind that she always achieved. She saved money wisely and invested it in real estate and made herself a multi-millionaire.

Both my parents were very hardworking; they emphasized education, saw the big picture, planned ahead, set goals, and persevered. They believed in giving back to the community and helping the less fortunate. It carried through to every one of us in my family. My siblings and I all started as foreign students and are now physicians, Ph.D., CPA, realtor, and public health official.

I learned from my mom that when the situation gets tough, the tough keep going. No complaints. No excuses. We keep our destiny in our own hands.

CHAPTER FORTY

William Chan 陳永強 (1976–　　)
U.S. Army

William Chan was in the U.S. Army Reserve from 1999 to 2011. His unit participated in the invasion of Iraq. He is a photographer with a degree from the Fashion Institute of Technology and is currently pursuing a MFA at the School of Visual Arts. He talks about his thoughts on Jackie Chan and Jeremy Lin, and how he became a drill instructor to counteract stereotypes. He lives in New York City with his wife and 5-year-old son.

Are there interesting or memorable moments from your military experience you can share?

The whole experience of boot camp was really shocking. I went to basic training in Fort Benning in Georgia. I grew up in New York City, so there was definitely culture shock, but I was able to handle it. I was 24 by then. Had I gone when I was 17, I'd have reacted differently. But I remember the first or the second day of basic training. We lived in an open bay, meaning it was basically one big room with 30 bunk beds for 60 recruits.

Our first shower was what we call a 30-second shower, which is actually less than 30 seconds, with all 60 of us. It's an open shower. You have about 10 shower heads and then guys would just file in. So we were lined up, 60 people in front of this group shower. And we all had to soap up dry outside. So we were naked. We all had to pass a bar of soap down the row. We had to soap ourselves up and then we would be led into this shower bay one by one in groups of six. So you go in. As soon as you go in, they will give you about five seconds and the drill sergeant will say, "Get out! Get out!" They will do a countdown, 10 seconds. So you have five seconds to wash yourself, thinking that you have 55 seconds more to finish it up, but you don't. So after five seconds, they start counting down from 10 to 1. Basically now you're going crazy because you got soap all over the place and then by the time they count down to zero, you have to run out.

So basically you have 15 seconds to shower in the nude in this open bay. And for me that was such a weird, weird thing. Talk about privacy, it's just crazy. Talk about the difference in anatomy between different races, that's a whole different thing too. That's a whole different subject. Boot camp did a lot for me. The cliché is what doesn't break you makes you stronger. So I definitely felt that way. I felt empowered, I felt like I became a man, so to speak, and went through a rite of passage. I did a lot of things I didn't think I was going to do.

After about 10 weeks of boot camp, I went to MOS School, which is where they train you to do your job, which for me was a mechanic. I did another 10 weeks there. As reservists at the time, we didn't expect to do too much. Things were fairly standard. We train two weeks a year and we meet one week in a month. And at the time, with no conflict, it was just kind of a ho-hum thing, until 9/11 happened.

I actually happened to work in Building Four of the World Trade Center early in 2001, although by September 11th I was in the midtown office of the same project. Basically the same people were split between midtown and the World Trade Center. That was a really significant moment in my lifetime, in most people's lifetime who were there.

Subsequently, in the fall of 2002, my unit was activated. Presumably for Afghanistan, because this was way before Iraq was even potentially a spot to go into. So I got deployed. We landed in Kuwait on Thanksgiving 2002. So by then we knew we were going to Iraq versus Afghanistan, because just logistically, we were south of Iraq. We were so far away from Afghanistan. So we trained in Kuwait and we listened to the news as much as we could. And we could hear the build-up, the pitch, you know, to the public and the international community about the case to go into Iraq. Eventually, I think it was middle of March— I don't remember the actual date—my unit, along with all the other units from Kuwait, started the invasion into Iraq.

I was part of that invasion support at the 3rd infantry division. It was like a 20-hour convoy going from the north of Kuwait into the south of Iraq. That was an experience. My unit did not take in any casualties during that period. Actually, during the whole deployment my unit did not take in any casualties. We were attacked and many of us were subsequently awarded the Combat Action Badge, whatever that means. So it turned out really good in the sense that I can reflect now on—I feel very fortunate that, with what we witnessed, nobody got hurt, for the most part. And I feel very fortunate that I could sit here 10 years later and just talk about it without a lost limb or lost friends and so on. It makes me think I don't want to waste any day of my life, in that cliché sense. I'm always trying to do something because there are people who don't have this opportunity to go on with their lives. So I feel they're kind of living vicariously through me as well. I think that was my biggest thing about coming back from Iraq.

I was a mechanic with the transportation company and we provided support. We were there about 9 months, maybe; 80% of the time, we were doing missions of some sort. When a convoy rolls out, we as mechanics trail them. It's kind of like AAA with a tow truck. We trail them, and when one truck gets stuck for whatever reason, they get left behind. The mission continues, and one or two trucks stay behind. Then the maintenance crew will go and pick them up and try to either fix the trucks so they go back on the road, or we'll just tow the truck away. In that sense it's a little bit more dangerous because you're by yourself.

William Chan during Operation Iraqi Freedom, 2003

You're your own security. But thank goodness nothing happened.

Our interactions with the locals were always, for the most part, pleasant. Regardless of what agenda they may or may not have, nobody came up and tried to stab me or anything like that. We got to meet the locals and it was really good in the sense that I learned a lot. It's one thing to read about the experience through the *New York Times* or the *Washington Post*, but to see it first hand, to deal with the kids and some of the issues, I think it was a really good experience.

You talked about being a DI, a drill instructor.

Yeah. I came back from Iraq in 2003. I found a new unit and I became a drill sergeant. It was something I always wanted to do. At that point, I was really cognizant of being an Asian American, and I wanted to raise the ceiling. By that time I actually reenlisted again, because I had to reenlist as part of my promotion. I had six more years to my contract and I really wanted to kind of stretch the possibilities.

I'm the least likely candidate to be a drill sergeant. Generally, when people look at me they don't see that. I don't even see it for myself, but I think that was the part that really excites me. That I was trying to do something that was not imaginable for myself.

We all have this box we put ourselves in. So for me to go and break out of that box, that kind of internal boundary, I thought was really exciting. So I pursued that. I went to a Drill Sergeant Unit and I paid my dues. I went to Drill Sergeant School, and I became a drill sergeant in either '07 or '08.

How old were you then?

30 years old maybe.

In your first deployment, how many Asians and Chinese Americans were there?

There were probably about 4 out of maybe 150.

So you wanted people in the military to see an Asian American leader?

Well, the funny thing is I wanted to be a drill sergeant because I'd never seen an Asian American drill sergeant, and in particular, any Chinese American drill sergeant. But as soon as I went to the unit, I met a drill sergeant who was born in Taiwan. He's my best friend now. I said, "Oh, wow there's another Chinese guy who's a drill sergeant." Then when I went to Drill Sergeant School, one of the instructors was also Chinese. So now all of a sudden I'm like, "Wow, I didn't know that there's already these people doing these things." But that didn't stop me, I just added to it. Generally speaking there are not that many Asians or Chinese Americans in the military, let alone drill sergeants. I think a lot of my thought process was that we need to see Asian Americans in general in different positions.

It was funny—I remember watching Jackie Chan movies in college. He came to America and tried to become a movie star in America. One of the first movies was *Rumble in the Bronx*, and it was such a stupid movie. I hope Jackie Chan never hears this. But it was so out of place, it was so dumb. They were trying to make this thing in the Bronx but it doesn't look like the Bronx. And it just really irritated me that local Asian American actors could not find opportunity and the opportunities are given to people who are imported from Asia. Like Chow Yun-fat, Jackie Chan, Rain from South Korea. So they're given all these opportunities in America while local Americans are not. And the worse thing about it is that, because they're here to just become international stars, they're willing to accept roles that are very pigeonholed.

So the thing is, most Americans look at Jackie Chan and they think that he represents Asian Americans, but he doesn't. You know Jackie Chan is this kung fu guy. No matter how much we Americans admire Jackie Chan, we don't see him as anything aside from being a kung fu guy. So you would never necessarily want to date Jackie Chan. You might want to have him fight with you in a bar maybe, but you will never expect Jackie Chan to speak proper English. You will never expect Jackie Chan to be a boyfriend, let's say. So it's a kind of propaganda with how they project the image of Asian Americans.

I really didn't like it, even if they don't do it on purpose. Same thing with Jet Li. He does not speak English the same way an Asian American would, through no fault of his own. But people who rarely see Asian Americans will look at Jackie Chan and Jet Li as representations of Asian Americans, and that just got me so upset.

Part of me wanting to be a drill sergeant was that I want to see more Asian Americans doing different jobs. Because growing up, I didn't see it. When I was in the military, I did not see an Asian American in a leadership position. So I wanted to be one. First I had to earn it. Once I earned it, I wanted to be in that position so that people coming up, Asian or not, could see it. So my recruits could see that the Asian American is not just this one-dimensional person.

Think about Jeremy Lin right now, how incredible that is. I mean Yao Ming is a great basketball player, and he's Chinese, but he's not Asian American. He's literally a Chinese import. But Jeremy Lin is somebody that I can relate to because he went through pretty much what we are going through now. He studies hard and he basically kind of broke the ceiling on basketball. And it's funny. It's so simple, but when you see somebody do it, for some reason it makes you understand the possibility.

You know, we're such a visual society. We see Michael Jordan dunk from the foul line, and all of a sudden we say, "Oh wow, maybe we could do it." Yet if I just told you that that's possible, you might not believe it. Like last year, if I told you that I could be a basketball player, everybody would be like, "Eh, maybe." But today, there's a lot more believability because of somebody like Jeremy Lin, who's not the biggest guy, who's not your typical pro-basketball player. So I really appreciate what he does for himself, but also what he does for the Asian American community. He broke a ceiling that was there before.

And now you attend art school and do fashion photography. So how do you juggle family, work, the military, and fashion?

I'm not that much into fashion. In 2011 I wanted to reenlist again. I was at the end of my 12 years. I think part of me wanted to reenlist and keep going with this and go up the ladder, and maybe become an officer. But by then I had a kid and I think my wife was not really happy about it. At the end of the day, she'd made a lot of sacrifices for me, for my pursuits, and then she basically said this was a deal breaker. She would not want me to potentially go back to Iraq. If I were to reenlist there'd be a good chance I'd have at least one more deployment left before I retired. So she said, No more deployments, and then that was it.

But now there's a void. I kind of lost a lot of purpose in my life once I left the reserves. So I work like everybody else, but then recently, about two years ago, I pursued being an artist, a photographer in particular. This also came from the same tangent as wanting to do something I didn't think I could do.

I think being an artist is a really daunting thing. It's very competitive. Most people can't make a living. But that to me was another challenge. So with the Post-9/11 GI Bill, I was able to go to FIT for free pretty much, with stipends to take home. I'm currently at the end of my second year at FIT. I'll be done with FIT this semester and then I'm looking to do my MFA and it's going to be paid for by the Post-9/11 GI Bill down the road.

For me, it's all about continuing this aspect of building [myself] for my kid. So that when my kid grows up, he doesn't feel like there are any glass ceilings. He could be an artist, a basketball player, a doctor, a soldier, whatever he wants; whereas when I was growing up, there were not always that many role models. I didn't see a lot of basketball players who were Asian Americans, and so on. I think that's my life's goal—that my kid will have greater opportunities. Which is no different than what my parents did for me.

My parents came here and, like a lot of immigrant parents, they didn't speak the language. And, like most immigrant parents, they probably would have had an easier time just staying in their own country. You know, it's easier to just live in an environment where you speak the language, where you're able to walk around. But my parents sacrificed that for me and my sister. Basically they came here and they were confined in Chinatown. The life of an immigrant Chinese American usually means working in the factory or a restaurant and then gambling or going home and watching imported drama from Hong Kong or China. I mean, that's pretty much it, whereas, when my parents were in Hong Kong, they had an unlimited lifestyle. They could go and hangout with their friends. They really don't have that here. And I think their sacrifice was all about me and my sister.

My family came to the U.S. in '84, when I was 9 years old. My grandfather already lived here. For a long time, my grandfather tried to get us to come to the U.S. So we were approved in the early '80s. We were basically approved two times and the embassy was saying that this was our final chance. If you don't come and take advantage of this, you would no longer be allowed to come. You will have to get back in line, and by that time, to come to the States, there was a much longer wait.

In 1984, it was the third and final time that my family could come to the States. So it was either that, or they were going to forfeit the opportunity. In 1997, which was the turnover of Hong Kong back to China from the British control, there was a lot of anxiety for people who lived in Hong Kong. They were worried about Communism and so on. So my parents said, "Let's just leave," even though economically there was no reason to leave. Economically we were fine. We just decided, "Let's take advantage of this opportunity."

Your parents are such a huge part of Chinatown and Chinese American culture.

Basically both my parents worked for a big bakery chain in Hong Kong before they came here. So they knew a lot of people. They worked in this bakery chain called Maria's Bakery.

—Which everyone knows about.

At that time, it was big in Hong Kong. It was probably equivalent to what Burger King is, in the American consciousness. It's not necessarily McDonald's. The funny thing is, my mom's side of the family, which is still in Hong Kong, opened up Taipan Bakery in Hong Kong. So we have a very large history of retail bakery. My parents are actually in Hong Kong right now. They work there.

Wow. Well, aren't Taipan and Maria's considered rivals?

I know, I shouldn't get into that. I think, like a lot of immigrant small business owners, my parents lacked education about their local environment, so they really needed help. My parents really relied on me and my older sister to help out. I think this is the story of the immigrant American: that those who are lucky to have a business and make money still need a lot of help. And you expect that from your kids. My sister and I helped out for a long time, and that's part of the reason why I had to leave.

I got so tired of it. I did it for about two years. I was running the bakery on Walker Street and Canal Street. After two years, I said, "I've had enough man. I just want to get out of here." So I decided to join the military. At that time I was, like, 24. I just didn't want to do this for the rest of my life. I didn't come to America to run a bakery for 30 years. So that's that.

What projects are you working on now?

I'm 36 now and I think I'm just looking at how to live the rest of my life. What's my life going to mean at the end of the day? You might have seen in *The Hurt Locker*, for those who have seen it, this man in Iraq does all kinds of crazy stuff, deactivates explosives on the ground like mines and so on. In the end, he comes back from Iraq unscathed and he's shopping with his wife at the supermarket and he's bored out of his mind. It's hard to go from that experience and come back and do the day-to-day grind.

I feel that way in a sense; I'm kind of bored. Not a lot of things excite me in the civilian life. So I'm always looking for something to do, whether it is to excite me or to have a purpose. I think that's something that the military gave me, purpose and excitement.

So helping with this Chinese American veterans project gives me a lot of purpose. We feel that the people who've blazed this trail for us, whether they did it on purpose or not—the first American Legion National Commander, the first officers, the first fire fighters, those who served in World War II when people hated Asian Americans or Japanese Americans in particular—those people they should not go undocumented. To me it's not even about the heroics or single events. It's about this life. I think there's something heroic about living this life. And there's something that we all could learn as future generations. We could always take away something from other people's experiences.

I think we could learn to be more empathetic toward others when we see what everyone has to go through. Once again it goes back to my kids and everybody else's kids. It's important for my kids to love what I did, and what my dad did. When I come to the American Legion, maybe because my parents are not living with me in the States anymore, I see my grandparents. I see my parents when I see a lot of these veterans. Because they did for me what my parents did for me, which is, they set a foundation for me to rise on. I can't complain. I've had a good life. A lot of it is due to those who came before me, who did it. I think that's why I wanted to do this project.

ENDNOTES

1   Fong, Jim and Marjorie Lee, "The Unsung 390." Marjorie Lee, ed. *Duty & Honor: A Tribute to Chinese American World War II Veterans of Southern California*. Los Angeles: CHSSC, 1998: p. 81.

2   Kwong, Peter and Dušanka Miščević, *Chinese America: The Untold Story of America's Oldest New Community*. New York: The New Press, 2005: pp. 207–208.

3   Yee, Lili Y., "Appendix 3b: What they were: Women's Branches of Service of the U.S. Armed Forces in WWII." Marjorie Lee, ed. *Duty & Honor: A Tribute to Chinese American World War II Veterans of Southern California*. Los Angeles: CHSSC, 1998: p. 238.

4   Wong, K. Scott, *Americans First: Chinese Americans and the Second World War*. Cambridge, Massachusetts: Harvard University Press, 2005: pp. 162, 164.

5   Ibid.

6   Lim, Christina M. and Sheldon H. Lim, "In the Shadow of the Tiger: The 407th Air Service Squadron, Fourteenth Air Force, CBI, World War II." San Mateo, JACP, 1993: p. v.

7   Wong, K. Scott, *Americans First: Chinese Americans and the Second World War*. Cambridge, Massachusetts: Harvard University Press, 2005: p. 162.

8   Lim, Christina M. and Sheldon H. Lim, "In the Shadow of the Tiger: The 407th Air Service Squadron, Fourteenth Air Force, CBI, World War II." San Mateo, JACP, 1993: pp. 15–16.

9   Ngai, Mae M, *Impossible Subjects: Illegal Aliens and the Making of Modern America*. Princeton, NJ: Princeton University Press, 2004: p. 205.

10 Fong, Jim and Marjorie Lee, "The Unsung 390." *Duty & Honor: A Tribute to Chinese American World War II Veterans of Southern California*. Los Angeles: CHSSC, 1998: pp. 82–83

11 Ngai, Mae M, *Impossible Subjects: Illegal Aliens and the Making of Modern America*. Princeton, NJ: Princeton University Press, 2004: p. 203.

12 Kwong, Peter and Dušanka Miščević, *Chinese America: The Untold Story of America's Oldest New Community*. New York: The New Press, 2005: p. 207.

13 Ibid., p. 210

14 Ibid.

15 Chang, Iris, *The Chinese in America: A Narrative History*. New York: Penguin Books, 2003: p. 251.

16 Ngai, Mae M, *Impossible Subjects: Illegal Aliens and the Making of Modern America*. Princeton, NJ: Princeton University Press, 2004: p. 209.

17 Kwong, Peter and Dušanka Miščević, *Chinese America: The Untold Story of America's Oldest New Community*. New York: The New Press, 2005: p. 220.

18 Ibid.

19 Chang, Iris, *The Chinese in America: A Narrative History*. New York: Penguin Books, 2003: pp. 253–256.

20 Ibid., pp. 248, 250, 251.

21 Lau, Estelle T., *Paper Families: Identity, Immigration Administration, and Chinese Exclusion*. Durham: Duke University Press, 2006: p. 116.

22 Kwong, Peter and Dušanka Miščević, *Chinese America: The Untold Story of America's Oldest New Community*. New York: The New Press, 2005: p. 225.

23 Huen, Floyd. "The Advent and Origins of the Asian American Movement in the San Francisco Bay Area: A Personal Perspective." *Asian Americans: The Movement and the Moment. Ed. Steve Louie and Glenn Omatsu*. Los Angeles, CA: UCLA Asian American Studies Center, 2001: p. 279.

24 Kwong, Peter and Dušanka Miščević, *Chinese America: The Untold Story of America's Oldest New Community*. New York: The New Press, 2005: p. 269–270.

25 Ibid., pp. 270, 272

26 http://apimovement.com/red-guard/history-red-guard-party

27 Hersh, Seymour M. *Against All Enemies: Gulf War Syndrome: The War between America's Ailing Veterans and Their Government*. New York: Ballantine, 1998: p. 1

28 Kendrick, Michelle. "Kicking the Vietnam Syndrome: CNN's and CBS's Video Narratives of the Persian Gulf War." *Seeing through the Media: The Persian Gulf War*. Ed. Susan Jeffords and Lauren Rabinovitz. New Brunswick, NJ: Rutgers UP, 1994: p. 60.

29 Ibid., p. 59.

30 Hersh, Seymour M. *Against All Enemies: Gulf War Syndrome: The War between America's Ailing Veterans and Their Government*. New York: Ballantine, 1998: p. 2.

31 Institute of Medicine. *Gulf War Medicine: Treating Symptoms and Syndromes*. Washington, D.C.: The Academies Press, 2001: p. 13.

32 Hersh, Seymour M. *Against All Enemies: Gulf War Syndrome: The War between America's Ailing Veterans and Their Government*. New York: Ballantine, 1998: p. 5.

33 Ibid., p. 6.

34 Ibid.

35 Ibid. pp. 7–8.

36 Maass, Peter. "The Toppling." *The New Yorker*. Condé Nast, 10 Jan. 2011. Web. 27 Jan. 2014. <http://www.newyorker.com/reporting/2011/01/10/110110fa_fact_maass#ixzz1rlDz9s9t>.

37 Ibid.

38 McAvoy, Audrey. "Marine Found Not Guilty in Hazing Suicide Case." MSNBC.com. Associated Press, 24 Feb. 2012. Web. 5 Mar. 2013. <http://www.nbcnews.com/id/46520079/ns/us_news-life/t/marine-found-not-guilty-hazing-suicide-case/#. UcSKPULhBG4>

39 Chu, Judy. "Military Hazing Has to Stop." *The New York Times*, 3 Aug. 2012. Web. 12 Mar. 2013. <http://www.nytimes.com/2012/08/04/opinion/military-hazing-has-to-stop.html>

40 Oh, Inae. "Danny Chen Hazing Trial: Mother, Suzhen Chen, Says No Justice Was Served In Soldiers' Punishments." *The Huffington Post*, 18 Dec. 2012. Web. 12 Mar. 2013. <http://www.huffingtonpost.com/2012/12/18/danny-chen-hazing-trial-mother_n_2324247.html >

41 Semple, Kirk. "Soldier's Death Raises Suspicions in Chinatown." *The New York Times*, 11 Oct. 2011. Web. 12 Mar. 2013.http://www.nytimes.com/2011/10/31/nyregion/after-soldiers-death-a-chinatown-family-seeks-answers.html

42 Oh, Inae. "Danny Chen Hazing Trial: Mother, Suzhen Chen, Says No Justice Was Served In Soldiers' Punishments." *The Huffington Post*, 18 Dec. 2012. Web. 12 Mar. 2013. <http://www.huffingtonpost.com/2012/12/18/danny-chen-hazing-trial-mother_n_2324247.html >

43 Ibid.

44 Semple, Kirk. "Soldier talked of Suicide Over Hazing, Friend Says" *The New York Times*, 26 Jul. 2012. Web. 13 Mar. 2013. <http://www.nytimes.com/2012/07/27/nyregion/pvt-danny-chen-talked-of-suicide-over-hazing-friend-testifies.html>

45 Perry, Tony. "Marine Recruitment Effort Targets Asian Americans, Pacific Islanders." *Los Angeles Times*, 08 May 2013. Web. 12 Mar. 2013. <http://www.latimes.com/news/nation/nationnow/la-na-nn-marines-advertising-campaign-20130508,0,5724448.story>

BIBLIOGRAPHY

http://apimovement.com/red-guard/history-red-guard-party

Chang, Iris. *The Chinese in America: A Narrative History*. New York: Penguin Books, 2003.

Christina M. Lim and Sheldon H. Lim, "In the Shadow of the Tiger: The 407th Air Service Squadron, Fourteenth Air Force, CBI, World War II." San Mateo, JACP, 1993.

Chu, Judy. "Military Hazing Has to Stop." *The New York Times*, 3 Aug. 2012. Web. 12 Mar. 2013. <http://www.nytimes.com/2012/08/04/opinion/military-hazing-has-to-stop.html>

Huen, Floyd. "The Advent and Origins of the Asian American Movement in the San Francisco Bay Area: A Personal Perspective." *Asian Americans: The Movement and the Moment. Ed. Steve Louie and Glenn Omatsu*. Los Angeles, CA: UCLA Asian American Studies Center, 2001.

Fong, Jim and Marjorie Lee, "The Unsung 390." Marjorie Lee. Ed. *Duty & Honor: A Tribute to Chinese American World War II Veterans of Southern California*. Los Angeles: CHSSC, 1998.

Hersh, Seymour M. *Against All Enemies: Gulf War Syndrome: The War between America's Ailing Veterans and Their Government*. New York: Ballantine, 1998: p. 1

Huen, Floyd. "The Advent and Origins of the Asian American Movement in the San Francisco Bay Area: A Personal Perspective." *Asian Americans: The Movement and the Moment. Ed. Steve Louie and Glenn Omatsu*. Los Angeles, CA: UCLA Asian American Studies Center, 2001.

Institute of Medicine. Gulf War Medicine: *Treating Symptoms and Syndromes*. Washington, D.C.: The Academies Press, 2001.

Kendrick, Michelle. "Kicking the Vietnam Syndrome: CNN's and CBS's Video Narratives of the Persian Gulf War." *Seeing through the Media: The Persian Gulf War*. Ed. Susan Jeffords and Lauren Rabinovitz. New Brunswick, NJ: Rutgers UP, 1994.

Wong, K. Scott, *Americans First: Chinese Americans and the Second World War*. Cambridge, Massachusetts: Harvard University Press, 2005.

Lau, Estelle T., *Paper Families: Identity, Immigration Administration, and Chinese Exclusion*. Durham: Duke University Press, 2006.

Maass, Peter. "The Toppling." *The New Yorker*. Condé Nast, 10 Jan. 2011. Web. 27 Jan. 2014. <http://www.newyorker.com/reporting/2011/01/10/110110fa_fact_maass#ixzz1rlDz9s9t>.

McAvoy, Audrey. "Marine Found Not Guilty in Hazing Suicide Case." MSNBC. *Associated Press*, 24 Feb. 2012. Web. 5 Mar. 2013. <http://www.nbcnews.com/id/46520079/ns/us_news-life/t/marine-found-not-guilty-hazing-suicide-case/#.UcSKPULhBG4>

Ngai, Mae M, *Impossible Subjects: Illegal Aliens and the Making of Modern America*. Princeton, NJ: Princeton University Press, 2004.

Oh, Inae. "Danny Chen Hazing Trial: Mother, Suzhen Chen, Says No Justice Was Served In Soldiers' Punishments." *The Huffington Post*, 18 Dec. 2012. Web. 12 Mar. 2013. <http://www.huffingtonpost.com/2012/12/18/danny-chen-hazing-trial-mother_n_2324247.html>

Perry, Tony. "Marine Recruitment Effort Targets Asian Americans, Pacific Islanders." *Los Angeles Times*, 08 May 2013. Web. 12 Mar. 2013. <http://www.latimes.com/news/nation/nationnow/la-na-nn-marines-advertising-campaign-20130508,0,5724448.story>

Kwong, Peter and Dušanka Miščević, *Chinese America: The Untold Story of America's Oldest New Community*. New York: The New Press, 2005.

Semple, Kirk. "Soldier's Death Raises Suspicions in Chinatown." *The New York Times*, 11 Oct. 2011. Web. 12 Mar. 2013. <http://www.nytimes.com/2011/10/31/nyregion/after-soldiers-death-a-chinatown-family-seeks-answers.html>

Yee, Lili Y., "Appendix 3b: What they were: Women's Branches of Service of the U.S. Armed Forces in WWII." Marjorie Lee. Ed. Duty & Honor: *A Tribute to Chinese American World War II Veterans of Southern California*. Los Angeles: CHSSC, 1998.

ABOUT THE AUTHOR

Victoria Moy was born and raised in New York's Chinatown and currently lives in Los Angeles, where she is pursuing a MFA in Playwriting, Screenwriting, and TV writing at the University of Southern California. She has written for *Brooklyn Rail, Huffington Post, New York Press* and other publications. She is a graduate of Yung Wing Public School 124, The Dalton School, and Dartmouth College.